Honda
Fit
Automotive
Repair
Manual

by Jeff Killingsworth
and John H Haynes

Member of the Guild of Motoring Writers

Models covered:

Honda Fit - 2007 through 2013

Does not include information specific to Fit EV models

ABCDE
FGHIJ
KLMNO
PQRST

Haynes Publishing Group

Sparkford Nr Yeovil
Somerset BA22 7JJ England

Haynes North America, Inc

861 Lawrence Drive
Newbury Park
California 91320 USA

Acknowledgements

Technical writers who contributed to this project include Demian Hurst, Dennis Gibb, Jay Hayes, John Wegmann, Tracy Martin and Scott "Gonzo" Weaver.

© **Haynes North America, Inc. 2015**

With permission from J.H. Haynes & Co. Ltd.

A book in the Haynes Automotive Repair Manual Series

Printed in the U.S.A.

ISBN-13: 978-1-62092-142-5
ISBN-10: 1-62092-142-1

Library of Congress Control Number: 2015949755

Contents

Haynes photographer and mechanic with a Honda Fit

About this manual

Its purpose

The purpose of this manual is to help you get the best value from your vehicle. It can do so in several ways. It can help you decide what work must be done, even if you choose to have it done by a dealer service department or a repair shop; it provides information and procedures for routine maintenance and servicing; and it offers diagnostic and repair procedures to follow when trouble occurs.

We hope you use the manual to tackle the work yourself. For many simpler jobs, doing it yourself may be quicker than arranging an appointment to get the vehicle into a shop and making the trips to leave it and pick it up. More importantly, a lot of money can be saved by avoiding the expense the shop must pass on to you to cover its labor and overhead costs. An added benefit is the sense of satisfaction and accomplishment that you feel after doing the job yourself.

Using the manual

The manual is divided into Chapters. Each Chapter is divided into numbered Sections, which are headed in bold type between horizontal lines. Each Section consists of consecutively numbered paragraphs.

The reference numbers used in illustration captions pinpoint the pertinent Section and the Step within that Section. That is, illustration 3.2 means the illustration refers to Section 3 and Step (or paragraph) 2 within that Section.

Procedures, once described in the text, are not normally repeated. When it's necessary to refer to another Chapter, the reference will be given as Chapter and Section number. Cross references given without use of the word "Chapter" apply to Sections and/or paragraphs in the same Chapter. For example, "see Section 8" means in the same Chapter.

References to the left or right side of the vehicle assume you are sitting in the driver's seat, facing forward.

Even though we have prepared this manual with extreme care, neither the publisher nor the author can accept responsibility for any errors in, or omissions from, the information given.

NOTE

A **Note** provides information necessary to properly complete a procedure or information which will make the procedure easier to understand.

CAUTION

A **Caution** provides a special procedure or special steps which must be taken while completing the procedure where the Caution is found. Not heeding a Caution can result in damage to the assembly being worked on.

WARNING

A **Warning** provides a special procedure or special steps which must be taken while completing the procedure where the Warning is found. Not heeding a Warning can result in personal injury.

Introduction

This manual covers 2007 through 2013 Honda Fit models.

The transversely mounted 1.5L SOHC four-cylinder engine used on these models are equipped with a sequential multi-port electronic fuel injection system.

The engine transmits power to the front wheels through either a five-speed manual transaxle or a five-speed automatic transaxle via independent driveaxles.

The Fit has a steel uni-body structure, with independent suspension on the front end and a semi-independent beam-type axle at the rear end. The rack-and-pinion steering unit is mounted behind the engine. An Electrical Power Steering (EPS) system is used, in which an electric motor is mounted to the steering gear to provide the power assist.

All models are equipped with power-assisted front disc brakes and rear drum brakes. An anti-lock braking system is standard equipment on all models.

Vehicle identification numbers

Modifications are a continuing and unpublicized process in vehicle manufacturing. Since spare parts manuals and lists are compiled on a numerical basis, the individual vehicle numbers are essential to correctly identify the component required.

Vehicle Identification Number (VIN)

This very important identification number is located on a plate attached to the dashboard inside the windshield on the driver's side of the vehicle (see illustration). The VIN also appears on the Vehicle Certificate of Title and Registration. It contains information such as where and when the vehicle was manufactured, the model year and the body style.

VIN engine and model year codes

Two particularly important pieces of information found in the VIN are the engine code and the model year code. Counting from the left, the engine code letter designation are the 4th through 6th characters and the model year code designation is the 10th character.

On the models covered by this manual the engine codes are:

GD3 (2007 and 2008 models)
1.5L SOHC (L15A1)
GE8 (2009 and later models)
1.5L SOHC (L15A7)

On the models covered by this manual the model year codes are:

7 2007
8 2008
9 2009
A 2010
B 2011
C 2012
D 2013

Manufacturer's Certification Regulation label

The Manufacturer's Certification Regulation label is attached to the driver's side door post (see illustration). The label contains the name of the manufacturer, the month and year of production, the Gross Vehicle Weight Rating (GVWR), the Gross Axle Weight Rating (GAWR) and the certification statement.

Engine identification number

On 2008 and earlier models, the engine identification number can be found on a pad on the front (radiator) side of the cylinder block, behind the starter. On 2009 and later models it's also on the front side of the engine block, on a machined pad near the transaxle (see illustration).

Transaxle identification numbers

The transaxle identification number is located on a label affixed to the front (radiator) side of the bellhousing (see illustration).

The Vehicle Identification Number (VIN) is visible through the driver's side of the windshield

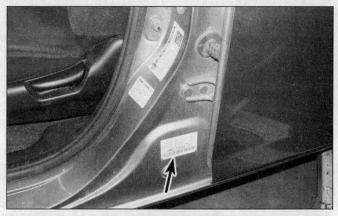

The Manufacturer's Certification Regulation label is affixed to the driver's side door post

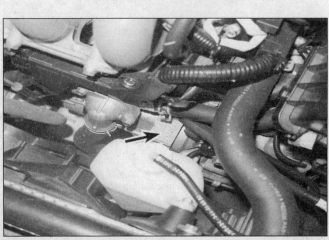

Engine identification number location - 2009 and later models

The transaxle ID number is located on the front side of the bellhousing (manual transaxle shown, automatic transaxles similar)

Vehicle Emissions Control Information (VECI) label

The emissions control information label is found on the underside of the hood. This label contains information on the emissions control equipment installed on the vehicle, and, in some cases, a vacuum diagram (see illustration).

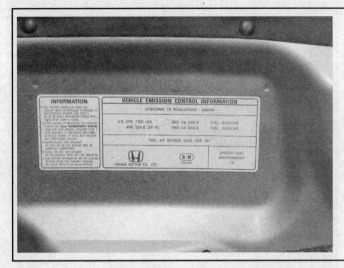

3.9 The Vehicle Emissions Control Information (VECI) label is located on the underside of the hood

Recall information

Vehicle recalls are carried out by the manufacturer in the rare event of a possible safety-related defect. The vehicle's registered owner is contacted at the address on file at the Department of Motor Vehicles and given the details of the recall. Remedial work is carried out free of charge at a dealer service department.

If you are the new owner of a used vehicle which was subject to a recall and you want to be sure that the work has been carried out, it's best to contact a dealer service department and ask about your individual vehicle - you'll need to furnish them your Vehicle Identification Number (VIN).

The table below is based on information provided by the National Highway Traffic Safety Administration (NHTSA), the body which oversees vehicle recalls in the United States. The recall database is updated constantly. For the latest information on vehicle recalls, check the NHTSA website at www.nhtsa.gov, www.safercar.gov, or call the NHTSA hotline at 1-888-327-4236.

Recall date	Recall campaign number	Model(s) affected	Concern
JUL 06, 2006	06V270000	2007 Fit	The owner's manual may contain incorrect contact information for the National Highway Traffic Safety Administration's (NHTSA) vehicle safety hotline. The language in the owner's manuals is not in accordance with the current mandatory requirements.
DEC 03, 2007	07V549000	2007 Fit	The wire harness for the Occupant Detection System (ODS) and the Occupant Position Detection System (OPDS) on some models may break from exposure to road salt and snow from driver's shoes that melts, and may penetrate the carpet and leak into the wire harness, causing the SRS indicator light to illuminate. A failure of the ODS and OPDS may not detect the presence of a child seat or an out-of-position passenger, and deployment of both the front seat passenger's frontal and side airbags will not be suppressed. In the event of a crash, a deploying front passenger airbag or front passenger's side airbag will increase the risk of injury to small or out-of-position occupants.

Recall date	Recall campaign number	Model(s) affected	Concern
FEB 02, 2010	10V033000	2007, 2008 Fit	Under severe conditions, water may enter the driver's window and reach the master power window switch; overheating and failure of the switch may result, which can cause smoke, melting and fire.
DEC 15, 2010	10V624000	2007, 2008 Fit	On some models, due to an error during installation of the wiring harness for the combination switch that controls low headlight beam function, the wires for the lower beam circuit were pulled tighter than intended. After repeated use of the headlight switch, the electrical connector terminal for the low beam headlight circuit can become worn as a result of this tension, which can result in low conductivity and cause an accumulation of copper oxide in the area of the contacts. The low beam headlights can become inoperative decreasing the driver's visibility as well as the vehicle's visibility to other drivers, increasing the risk of a crash.
FEB 17, 2011	11V101000	2009, 2010 Fit	On some models there is a potential for one or more of the four spring assemblies on the engine's variable valve timing and lift electronic control (VTEC) system to fail. A failure of the spring assemblies may cause the vehicle to stall during operation increasing the risk of a crash.
APR 24, 2013	13V157000	2012, 2013 Fit	On some models the Electronic Stability Control (ESC) system may allow excessive yaw rates at high steering angles with certain tires, increasing the risk of a crash.
JUN 24, 2013	13V260000	2007, 2008 Fit	On some models, over time, the plastic cover may separate from the master power window switch allowing water to enter the driver's window and reach the master power window switch. If the master power window switch is damaged as a result of the water intrusion, overheating and failure of the switch may result. An overheated switch can cause smoke, melting and fire.

Notes

Buying parts

Replacement parts are available from many sources, which generally fall into one of two categories - authorized dealer parts departments and independent retail auto parts stores. Our advice concerning these parts is as follows:

Retail auto parts stores: Good auto parts stores will stock frequently needed components which wear out relatively fast, such as clutch components, exhaust systems, brake parts, tune-up parts, etc. These stores often supply new or reconditioned parts on an exchange basis, which can save a considerable amount of money. Discount auto parts stores are often very good places to buy materials and parts needed for general vehicle maintenance such as oil, grease, filters, spark plugs, belts, touch-up paint, bulbs, etc. They also usually sell tools and general accessories, have convenient hours, charge lower prices and can often be found not far from home.

Authorized dealer parts department: This is the best source for parts which are unique to the vehicle and not generally available elsewhere (such as major engine parts, transmission parts, trim pieces, etc.).

Warranty information: If the vehicle is still covered under warranty, be sure that any replacement parts purchased - regardless of the source - do not invalidate the warranty!

To be sure of obtaining the correct parts, have engine and chassis numbers available and, if possible, take the old parts along for positive identification.

Maintenance techniques, tools and working facilities

Maintenance techniques

There are a number of techniques involved in maintenance and repair that will be referred to throughout this manual. Application of these techniques will enable the home mechanic to be more efficient, better organized and capable of performing the various tasks properly, which will ensure that the repair job is thorough and complete.

Fasteners

Fasteners are nuts, bolts, studs and screws used to hold two or more parts together. There are a few things to keep in mind when working with fasteners. Almost all of them use a locking device of some type, either a lockwasher, locknut, locking tab or thread adhesive. All threaded fasteners should be clean and straight, with undamaged threads and undamaged corners on the hex head where the wrench fits. Develop the habit of replacing all damaged nuts and bolts with new ones. Special locknuts with nylon or fiber inserts can only be used once. If they are removed, they lose their locking ability and must be replaced with new ones.

Rusted nuts and bolts should be treated with a penetrating fluid to ease removal and prevent breakage. Some mechanics use turpentine in a spout-type oil can, which works quite well. After applying the rust penetrant, let it work for a few minutes before trying to loosen the nut or bolt. Badly rusted fasteners may have to be chiseled or sawed off or removed with a special nut breaker, available at tool stores.

If a bolt or stud breaks off in an assembly, it can be drilled and removed with a special tool commonly available for this purpose. Most automotive machine shops can perform this task, as well as other repair procedures, such as the repair of threaded holes that have been stripped out.

Flat washers and lockwashers, when removed from an assembly, should always be replaced exactly as removed. Replace any damaged washers with new ones. Never use a lockwasher on any soft metal surface (such as aluminum), thin sheet metal or plastic.

Fastener sizes

For a number of reasons, automobile manufacturers are making wider and wider use of metric fasteners. Therefore, it is important to be able to tell the difference between standard (sometimes called U.S. or SAE) and metric hardware, since they cannot be interchanged.

All bolts, whether standard or metric, are sized according to diameter, thread pitch and length. For example, a standard 1/2 - 13 x 1 bolt is 1/2 inch in diameter, has 13 threads per inch and is 1 inch long. An M12 - 1.75 x 25 metric bolt is 12 mm in diameter, has a thread pitch of 1.75 mm (the distance between threads) and is 25 mm long. The two bolts are nearly identical, and easily confused, but they are not interchangeable.

In addition to the differences in diameter, thread pitch and length, metric and standard bolts can also be distinguished by examining the bolt heads. To begin with, the distance across the flats on a standard bolt head is measured in inches, while the same dimension on a metric bolt is sized in millimeters (the same is true for nuts). As a result, a standard wrench should not be used on a metric bolt and a metric wrench should not be used on a standard bolt. Also, most standard bolts have slashes radiating out from the center of the head to denote the grade or strength of the bolt, which is an indication of the amount of torque that can be applied to it. The greater the number of slashes, the greater the strength of the bolt. Grades 0 through 5 are commonly used on automobiles. Metric bolts have a property class (grade) number, rather than a slash, molded into their heads to indicate bolt strength. In this case, the higher the number, the stronger the bolt. Property class numbers 8.8, 9.8 and 10.9 are commonly used on automobiles.

Strength markings can also be used to distinguish standard hex nuts from metric hex nuts. Many standard nuts have dots stamped into one side, while metric nuts are marked with a number. The greater the number of

dots, or the higher the number, the greater the strength of the nut.

Metric studs are also marked on their ends according to property class (grade). Larger studs are numbered (the same as metric bolts), while smaller studs carry a geometric code to denote grade.

It should be noted that many fasteners, especially Grades 0 through 2, have no distinguishing marks on them. When such is the case, the only way to determine whether it is standard or metric is to measure the thread pitch or compare it to a known fastener of the same size.

Standard fasteners are often referred to as SAE, as opposed to metric. However, it should be noted that SAE technically refers to a non-metric fine thread fastener only. Coarse thread non-metric fasteners are referred to as USS sizes.

Since fasteners of the same size (both standard and metric) may have different

strength ratings, be sure to reinstall any bolts, studs or nuts removed from your vehicle in their original locations. Also, when replacing a fastener with a new one, make sure that the new one has a strength rating equal to or greater than the original.

Tightening sequences and procedures

Most threaded fasteners should be tightened to a specific torque value (torque is the twisting force applied to a threaded component such as a nut or bolt). Overtightening the fastener can weaken it and cause it to break, while undertightening can cause it to eventually come loose. Bolts, screws and studs, depending on the material they are made of and their thread diameters, have specific torque values, many of which are noted in the Specifications at the beginning of each Chapter. Be sure to follow the torque recommen-

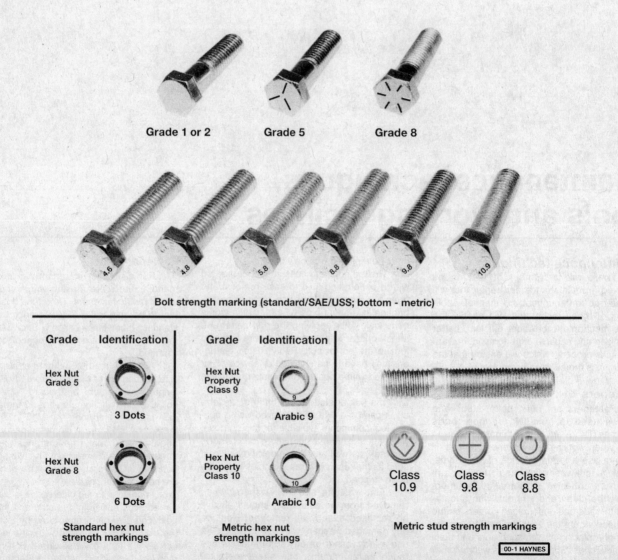

Grade 1 or 2   Grade 5   Grade 8

Bolt strength marking (standard/SAE/USS; bottom - metric)

Grade	Identification
Hex Nut Grade 5	3 Dots
Hex Nut Grade 8	6 Dots

Standard hex nut strength markings

Grade	Identification
Hex Nut Property Class 9	Arabic 9
Hex Nut Property Class 10	Arabic 10

Metric hex nut strength markings

Class 10.9   Class 9.8   Class 8.8

Metric stud strength markings

dations closely. For fasteners not assigned a specific torque, a general torque value chart is presented here as a guide. These torque values are for dry (unlubricated) fasteners threaded into steel or cast iron (not aluminum). As was previously mentioned, the size and grade of a fastener determine the amount of torque that can safely be applied to it. The figures listed here are approximate for Grade 2 and Grade 3 fasteners. Higher grades can tolerate higher torque values.

Fasteners laid out in a pattern, such as cylinder head bolts, oil pan bolts, differential cover bolts, etc., must be loosened or tightened in sequence to avoid warping the component. This sequence will normally be shown in the appropriate Chapter. If a specific pattern is not given, the following procedures can be used to prevent warping.

Initially, the bolts or nuts should be assembled finger-tight only. Next, they should be tightened one full turn each, in a criss-cross or diagonal pattern. After each one has been tightened one full turn, return to the first one and tighten them all one-half turn, following the same pattern. Finally, tighten each of them one-quarter turn at a time until each fastener has been tightened to the proper torque. To loosen and remove the fasteners, the procedure would be reversed.

Metric thread sizes	Ft-lbs	Nm
M-6	6 to 9	9 to 12
M-8	14 to 21	19 to 28
M-10	28 to 40	38 to 54
M-12	50 to 71	68 to 96
M-14	80 to 140	109 to 154

Pipe thread sizes		
1/8	5 to 8	7 to 10
1/4	12 to 18	17 to 24
3/8	22 to 33	30 to 44
1/2	25 to 35	34 to 47

U.S. thread sizes		
1/4 - 20	6 to 9	9 to 12
5/16 - 18	12 to 18	17 to 24
5/16 - 24	14 to 20	19 to 27
3/8 - 16	22 to 32	30 to 43
3/8 - 24	27 to 38	37 to 51
7/16 - 14	40 to 55	55 to 74
7/16 - 20	40 to 60	55 to 81
1/2 - 13	55 to 80	75 to 108

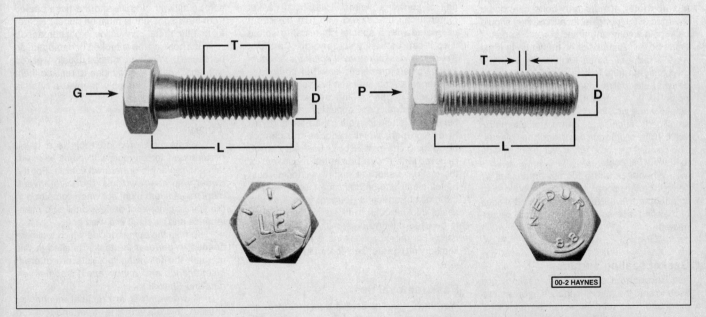

Standard (SAE and USS) bolt dimensions/grade marks

G   Grade marks (bolt strength)
L   Length (in inches)
T   Thread pitch (number of threads per inch)
D   Nominal diameter (in inches)

Metric bolt dimensions/grade marks

P   Property class (bolt strength)
L   Length (in millimeters)
T   Thread pitch (distance between threads in millimeters)
D   Diameter

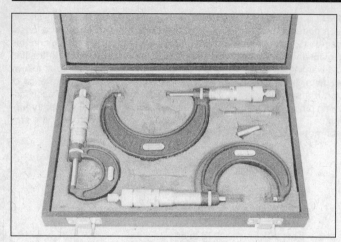

Micrometer set

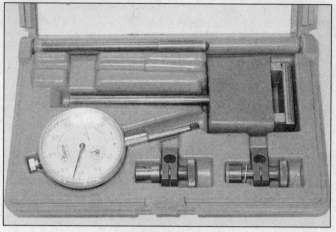

Dial indicator set

Component disassembly

Component disassembly should be done with care and purpose to help ensure that the parts go back together properly. Always keep track of the sequence in which parts are removed. Make note of special characteristics or marks on parts that can be installed more than one way, such as a grooved thrust washer on a shaft. It is a good idea to lay the disassembled parts out on a clean surface in the order that they were removed. It may also be helpful to make sketches or take instant photos of components before removal.

When removing fasteners from a component, keep track of their locations. Sometimes threading a bolt back in a part, or putting the washers and nut back on a stud, can prevent mix-ups later. If nuts and bolts cannot be returned to their original locations, they should be kept in a compartmented box or a series of small boxes. A cupcake or muffin tin is ideal for this purpose, since each cavity can hold the bolts and nuts from a particular area (i.e. oil pan bolts, valve cover bolts, engine mount bolts, etc.). A pan of this type is especially helpful when working on assemblies with very small parts, such as the carburetor, alternator, valve train or interior dash and trim pieces. The cavities can be marked with paint or tape to identify the contents.

Whenever wiring looms, harnesses or connectors are separated, it is a good idea to identify the two halves with numbered pieces of masking tape so they can be easily reconnected.

Gasket sealing surfaces

Throughout any vehicle, gaskets are used to seal the mating surfaces between two parts and keep lubricants, fluids, vacuum or pressure contained in an assembly.

Many times these gaskets are coated with a liquid or paste-type gasket sealing compound before assembly. Age, heat and pressure can sometimes cause the two parts to stick together so tightly that they are very difficult to separate. Often, the assembly can

be loosened by striking it with a soft-face hammer near the mating surfaces. A regular hammer can be used if a block of wood is placed between the hammer and the part. Do not hammer on cast parts or parts that could be easily damaged. With any particularly stubborn part, always recheck to make sure that every fastener has been removed.

Avoid using a screwdriver or bar to pry apart an assembly, as they can easily mar the gasket sealing surfaces of the parts, which must remain smooth. If prying is absolutely necessary, use an old broom handle, but keep in mind that extra clean up will be necessary if the wood splinters.

After the parts are separated, the old gasket must be carefully scraped off and the gasket surfaces cleaned. Stubborn gasket material can be soaked with rust penetrant or treated with a special chemical to soften it so it can be easily scraped off. **Caution:** *Never use gasket removal solutions or caustic chemicals on plastic or other composite components.* A scraper can be fashioned from a piece of copper tubing by flattening and sharpening one end. Copper is recommended because it is usually softer than the surfaces to be scraped, which reduces the chance of gouging the part. Some gaskets can be removed with a wire brush, but regardless of the method used, the mating surfaces must be left clean and smooth. If for some reason the gasket surface is gouged, then a gasket sealer thick enough to fill scratches will have to be used during reassembly of the components. For most applications, a non-drying (or semi-drying) gasket sealer should be used.

Hose removal tips

Warning: *If the vehicle is equipped with air conditioning, do not disconnect any of the A/C hoses without first having the system depressurized by a dealer service department or a service station.*

Hose removal precautions closely parallel gasket removal precautions. Avoid scratching or gouging the surface that the

hose mates against or the connection may leak. This is especially true for radiator hoses. Because of various chemical reactions, the rubber in hoses can bond itself to the metal spigot that the hose fits over. To remove a hose, first loosen the hose clamps that secure it to the spigot. Then, with slip-joint pliers, grab the hose at the clamp and rotate it around the spigot. Work it back and forth until it is completely free, then pull it off. Silicone or other lubricants will ease removal if they can be applied between the hose and the outside of the spigot. Apply the same lubricant to the inside of the hose and the outside of the spigot to simplify installation.

As a last resort (and if the hose is to be replaced with a new one anyway), the rubber can be slit with a knife and the hose peeled from the spigot. If this must be done, be careful that the metal connection is not damaged.

If a hose clamp is broken or damaged, do not reuse it. Wire-type clamps usually weaken with age, so it is a good idea to replace them with screw-type clamps whenever a hose is removed.

Tools

A selection of good tools is a basic requirement for anyone who plans to maintain and repair his or her own vehicle. For the owner who has few tools, the initial investment might seem high, but when compared to the spiraling costs of professional auto maintenance and repair, it is a wise one.

To help the owner decide which tools are needed to perform the tasks detailed in this manual, the following tool lists are offered: *Maintenance and minor repair, Repair/overhaul* and *Special.*

The newcomer to practical mechanics should start off with the *maintenance and minor repair* tool kit, which is adequate for the simpler jobs performed on a vehicle. Then, as confidence and experience grow, the owner can tackle more difficult tasks, buying additional tools as they are needed. Eventually the basic kit will be expanded into the *repair and overhaul* tool set. Over a period of time, the

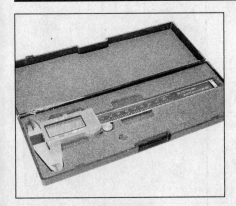

Dial caliper

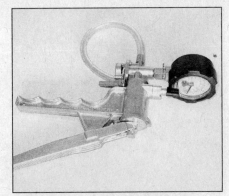

Hand-operated vacuum pump

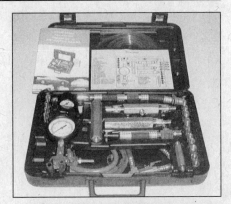

Fuel pressure gauge set

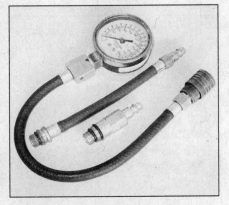

Compression gauge with spark plug hole adapter

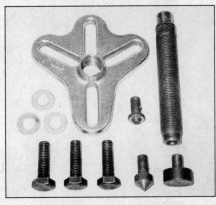

Damper/steering wheel puller

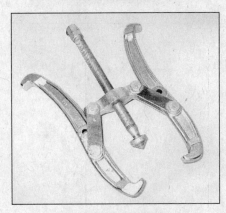

General purpose puller

Hydraulic lifter removal tool

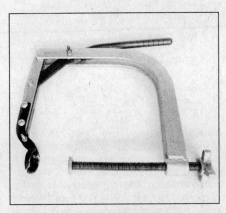

Valve spring compressor

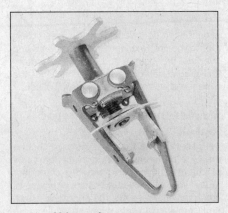

Valve spring compressor

Ridge reamer

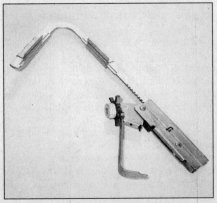

Piston ring groove cleaning tool

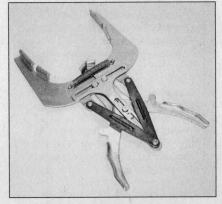

Ring removal/installation tool

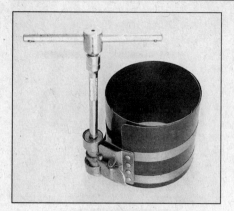

Ring compressor

Cylinder hone

Brake hold-down spring tool

Torque angle gauge

Clutch plate alignment tool

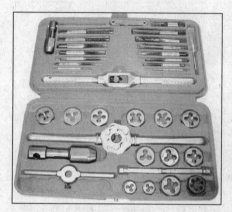

Tap and die set

experienced do-it-yourselfer will assemble a tool set complete enough for most repair and overhaul procedures and will add tools from the special category when it is felt that the expense is justified by the frequency of use.

Maintenance and minor repair tool kit

The tools in this list should be considered the minimum required for performance of routine maintenance, servicing and minor repair work. We recommend the purchase of combination wrenches (box-end and open-end combined in one wrench). While more expensive than open end wrenches, they offer the advantages of both types of wrench.

> *Combination wrench set (1/4-inch to*
> *   1 inch or 6 mm to 19 mm)*
> *Adjustable wrench, 8 inch*
> *Spark plug wrench with rubber insert*
> *Spark plug gap adjusting tool*
> *Feeler gauge set*
> *Brake bleeder wrench*
> *Standard screwdriver (5/16-inch x*
> *   6 inch)*
> *Phillips screwdriver (No. 2 x 6 inch)*
> *Combination pliers - 6 inch*
> *Hacksaw and assortment of blades*
> *Tire pressure gauge*
> *Grease gun*
> *Oil can*
> *Fine emery cloth*

> *Wire brush*
> *Battery post and cable cleaning tool*
> *Oil filter wrench*
> *Funnel (medium size)*
> *Safety goggles*
> *Jackstands (2)*
> *Drain pan*

Note: *If basic tune-ups are going to be part of routine maintenance, it will be necessary to purchase a good quality stroboscopic timing light and combination tachometer/dwell meter. Although they are included in the list of special tools, it is mentioned here because they are absolutely necessary for tuning most vehicles properly.*

Repair and overhaul tool set

These tools are essential for anyone who plans to perform major repairs and are in addition to those in the maintenance and minor repair tool kit. Included is a comprehensive set of sockets which, though expensive, are invaluable because of their versatility, especially when various extensions and drives are available. We recommend the 1/2-inch drive over the 3/8-inch drive. Although the larger drive is bulky and more expensive, it has the capacity of accepting a very wide range of large sockets. Ideally, however, the mechanic should have a 3/8-inch drive set and a 1/2-inch drive set.

> *Socket set(s)*
> *Reversible ratchet*

> *Extension - 10 inch*
> *Universal joint*
> *Torque wrench (same size drive as*
> *   sockets)*
> *Ball peen hammer - 8 ounce*
> *Soft-face hammer (plastic/rubber)*
> *Standard screwdriver (1/4-inch x 6 inch)*
> *Standard screwdriver (stubby -*
> *   5/16-inch)*
> *Phillips screwdriver (No. 3 x 8 inch)*
> *Phillips screwdriver (stubby - No. 2)*
> *Pliers - vise grip*
> *Pliers - lineman's*
> *Pliers - needle nose*
> *Pliers - snap-ring (internal and external)*
> *Cold chisel - 1/2-inch*
> *Scribe*
> *Scraper (made from flattened copper*
> *   tubing)*
> *Centerpunch*
> *Pin punches (1/16, 1/8, 3/16-inch)*
> *Steel rule/straightedge - 12 inch*
> *Allen wrench set (1/8 to 3/8-inch or*
> *   4 mm to 10 mm)*
> *A selection of files*
> *Wire brush (large)*
> *Jackstands (second set)*
> *Jack (scissor or hydraulic type)*

Note: *Another tool which is often useful is an electric drill with a chuck capacity of 3/8-inch and a set of good quality drill bits.*

Special tools

The tools in this list include those which are not used regularly, are expensive to buy, or which need to be used in accordance with their manufacturer's instructions. Unless these tools will be used frequently, it is not very economical to purchase many of them. A consideration would be to split the cost and use between yourself and a friend or friends. In addition, most of these tools can be obtained from a tool rental shop on a temporary basis.

This list primarily contains only those tools and instruments widely available to the public, and not those special tools produced by the vehicle manufacturer for distribution to dealer service departments. Occasionally, references to the manufacturer's special tools are included in the text of this manual. Generally, an alternative method of doing the job without the special tool is offered. However, sometimes there is no alternative to their use. Where this is the case, and the tool cannot be purchased or borrowed, the work should be turned over to the dealer service department or an automotive repair shop.

> *Valve spring compressor*
> *Piston ring groove cleaning tool*
> *Piston ring compressor*
> *Piston ring installation tool*
> *Cylinder compression gauge*
> *Cylinder ridge reamer*
> *Cylinder surfacing hone*
> *Cylinder bore gauge*
> *Micrometers and/or dial calipers*
> *Hydraulic lifter removal tool*
> *Balljoint separator*
> *Universal-type puller*
> *Impact screwdriver*
> *Dial indicator set*
> *Stroboscopic timing light (inductive pick-up)*
> *Hand operated vacuum/pressure pump*
> *Tachometer/dwell meter*
> *Universal electrical multimeter*
> *Cable hoist*
> *Brake spring removal and installation tools*
> *Floor jack*

Buying tools

For the do-it-yourselfer who is just starting to get involved in vehicle maintenance and repair, there are a number of options available when purchasing tools. If maintenance and minor repair is the extent of the work to be done, the purchase of individual tools is satisfactory. If, on the other hand, extensive work is planned, it would be a good idea to purchase a modest tool set from one of the large retail chain stores. A set can usually be bought at a substantial savings over the individual tool prices, and they often come with a tool box. As additional tools are needed, add-on sets, individual tools and a larger tool box can be purchased to expand the tool selection. Building a tool set gradually allows the cost of the tools to be spread over a longer period of time and gives the mechanic the freedom to choose only those tools that will actually be used.

Tool stores will often be the only source of some of the special tools that are needed, but regardless of where tools are bought, try to avoid cheap ones, especially when buying screwdrivers and sockets, because they won't last very long. The expense involved in replacing cheap tools will eventually be greater than the initial cost of quality tools.

Care and maintenance of tools

Good tools are expensive, so it makes sense to treat them with respect. Keep them clean and in usable condition and store them properly when not in use. Always wipe off any dirt, grease or metal chips before putting them away. Never leave tools lying around in the work area. Upon completion of a job, always check closely under the hood for tools that may have been left there so they won't get lost during a test drive.

Some tools, such as screwdrivers, pliers, wrenches and sockets, can be hung on a panel mounted on the garage or workshop wall, while others should be kept in a tool box or tray. Measuring instruments, gauges, meters, etc. must be carefully stored where they cannot be damaged by weather or impact from other tools.

When tools are used with care and stored properly, they will last a very long time. Even with the best of care, though, tools will wear out if used frequently. When a tool is damaged or worn out, replace it. Subsequent jobs will be safer and more enjoyable if you do.

How to repair damaged threads

Sometimes, the internal threads of a nut or bolt hole can become stripped, usually from overtightening. Stripping threads is an all-too-common occurrence, especially when working with aluminum parts, because aluminum is so soft that it easily strips out.

Usually, external or internal threads are only partially stripped. After they've been cleaned up with a tap or die, they'll still work. Sometimes, however, threads are badly damaged. When this happens, you've got three choices:

1) *Drill and tap the hole to the next suitable oversize and install a larger diameter bolt, screw or stud.*
2) *Drill and tap the hole to accept a threaded plug, then drill and tap the plug to the original screw size. You can also buy a plug already threaded to the original size. Then you simply drill a hole to the specified size, then run the threaded plug into the hole with a bolt and jam nut. Once the plug is fully seated, remove the jam nut and bolt.*
3) *The third method uses a patented thread repair kit like Heli-Coil or Slimsert. These easy-to-use kits are designed to repair damaged threads in straight-through holes and blind holes. Both are available as kits which can handle a variety of sizes and thread patterns. Drill the hole, then tap it with the special included tap. Install the Heli-Coil and the hole is back to its original diameter and thread pitch.*

Regardless of which method you use, be sure to proceed calmly and carefully. A little impatience or carelessness during one of these relatively simple procedures can ruin your whole day's work and cost you a bundle if you wreck an expensive part.

Working facilities

Not to be overlooked when discussing tools is the workshop. If anything more than routine maintenance is to be carried out, some sort of suitable work area is essential.

It is understood, and appreciated, that many home mechanics do not have a good workshop or garage available, and end up removing an engine or doing major repairs outside. It is recommended, however, that the overhaul or repair be completed under the cover of a roof.

A clean, flat workbench or table of comfortable working height is an absolute necessity. The workbench should be equipped with a vise that has a jaw opening of at least four inches.

As mentioned previously, some clean, dry storage space is also required for tools, as well as the lubricants, fluids, cleaning solvents, etc. which soon become necessary.

Sometimes waste oil and fluids, drained from the engine or cooling system during normal maintenance or repairs, present a disposal problem. To avoid pouring them on the ground or into a sewage system, pour the used fluids into large containers, seal them with caps and take them to an authorized disposal site or recycling center. Plastic jugs, such as old antifreeze containers, are ideal for this purpose.

Always keep a supply of old newspapers and clean rags available. Old towels are excellent for mopping up spills. Many mechanics use rolls of paper towels for most work because they are readily available and disposable. To help keep the area under the vehicle clean, a large cardboard box can be cut open and flattened to protect the garage or shop floor.

Whenever working over a painted surface, such as when leaning over a fender to service something under the hood, always cover it with an old blanket or bedspread to protect the finish. Vinyl covered pads, made especially for this purpose, are available at auto parts stores.

Jacking and towing

Jacking

Warning:The *jack supplied with the vehicle should only be used for changing a tire or placing jackstands under the frame. Never work under the vehicle or start the engine while this jack is being used as the only means of support.*

1   The vehicle should be on level ground. Place the shift lever in Park, if you have an automatic, or Reverse if you have a manual transaxle. Block the wheel diagonally opposite the wheel being changed. Set the parking brake.

2   Remove the spare tire and jack from stowage. Remove the wheel cover and trim ring (if so equipped) with the tapered end of the lug nut wrench by inserting and twisting the handle and then prying against the back of the wheel cover. Loosen the wheel lug nuts about 1/4 to 1/2 turn each.

3   Place the scissors-type jack under the side of the vehicle and adjust the jack height until it engages with the elongated tab that protrudes from the vertical rocker panel flange nearest the wheel to be changed. There is a front and rear jacking point on each side of the vehicle (see illustration).

4   Turn the jack handle clockwise until the tire clears the ground. Remove the lug nuts and pull the wheel off, then install the spare.

5   Install the lug nuts with the beveled edges facing in. Tighten them snugly. Don't attempt to tighten them completely until the vehicle is lowered or it could slip off the jack. Turn the jack handle counterclockwise to lower the vehicle. Remove the jack and tighten the lug nuts in a diagonal pattern to the torque listed in the 1 Chapter 1 Specifications 0.

6   Install the cover (and trim ring, if used) and be sure it's snapped into place all the way around.

7   Stow the tire, jack and wrench. Unblock the wheels.

Towing

8   These vehicles can be towed with the front (drive) wheels off the ground. If they can't be raised, place them on a dolly. The ignition key must be in the ACC position to unlock the steering column lock. A sling-type tow truck cannot be used, as body damage will occur. The best way to tow the vehicle is with a flat-bed car carrier.

9   The vehicle can be towed with all four wheels on the ground, but not more than 50 miles or over 35 mph. To do this:

Manual transaxle models:

Place the shifter in Neutral and release the parking brake.
Turn the ignition key to the ACC position.

Automatic transaxle models:

Start the engine, shift into Drive and leave it there for five seconds. Shift to Neutral and allow the engine to idle for three minutes, then turn the engine off.
Place the ignition key in the ACC position and release the parking brake.

10   Equipment specifically designed for towing should be used. It should be attached to the main structural members of the vehicle, not the bumpers or brackets.

Note: *These vehicles are equipped with an emergency tow hook (stored with the spare tire tool kit) that threads into a hole behind a small plug in the bumper cover. This method is only intended to free the vehicle if it is stuck in snow, mud or sand.*

11   Safety is a major consideration when towing and all applicable state and local laws must be obeyed. A safety chain system must be used at all times.

The jack fits over the elongated tab that protrudes from the rocker panel flange (there are two jacking points on each side of the vehicle)

Booster battery (jump) starting

1   Observe the following precautions when using a booster battery to start a vehicle:
Before connecting the booster battery, make sure the ignition switch is in the Off position.
Turn off the lights, heater and other electrical loads.
Your eyes should be shielded. Safety goggles are a good idea.
Make sure the booster battery is the same voltage as the dead one in the vehicle.
The two vehicles MUST NOT TOUCH each other.
Make sure the transmission is in Park (automatic).
2   Connect the red jumper cable to the positive (+) terminals of each battery.
3   Connect one end of the black cable to the negative (-) terminal of the booster battery. The other end of this cable should be connected to a good ground on the engine block (see illustration). Make sure the cable will not come into contact with the fan, drivebelts or other moving parts of the engine.
4   Start the engine using the booster battery, then, with the engine running at idle speed, disconnect the jumper cables in the reverse order of connection.

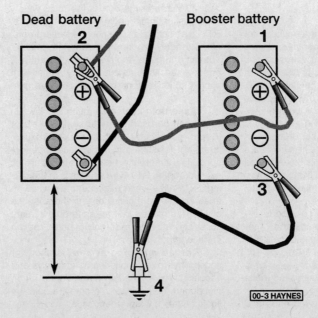

Dead battery   Booster battery

Make the booster battery cable connections in the numerical order shown (note that the negative cable of the booster battery is NOT attached to the negative terminal of the dead battery)

00-3 HAYNES

Automotive chemicals and lubricants

A number of automotive chemicals and lubricants are available for use during vehicle maintenance and repair. They include a wide variety of products ranging from cleaning solvents and degreasers to lubricants and protective sprays for rubber, plastic and vinyl.

Cleaners

Carburetor cleaner and choke cleaner is a strong solvent for gum, varnish and carbon. Most carburetor cleaners leave a dry-type lubricant film which will not harden or gum up. Because of this film it is not recommended for use on electrical components.

Brake system cleaner is used to remove brake dust, grease and brake fluid from the brake system, where clean surfaces are absolutely necessary. It leaves no residue and often eliminates brake squeal caused by contaminants.

Electrical cleaner removes oxidation, corrosion and carbon deposits from electrical contacts, restoring full current flow. It can also be used to clean spark plugs, carburetor jets, voltage regulators and other parts where an oil-free surface is desired.

Demoisturants remove water and moisture from electrical components such as alternators, voltage regulators, electrical connectors and fuse blocks. They are non-conductive and non-corrosive.

Degreasers are heavy-duty solvents used to remove grease from the outside of the engine and from chassis components. They can be sprayed or brushed on and, depending on the type, are rinsed off either with water or solvent.

Lubricants

Motor oil is the lubricant formulated for use in engines. It normally contains a wide variety of additives to prevent corrosion and reduce foaming and wear. Motor oil comes in various weights (viscosity ratings) from 0 to 50. The recommended weight of the oil depends on the season, temperature and the demands on the engine. Light oil is used in cold climates and under light load conditions. Heavy oil is used in hot climates and where high loads are encountered. Multi-viscosity oils are designed to have characteristics of both light and heavy oils and are available in a number of weights from 0W-20 to 20W-50.

Gear oil is designed to be used in differentials, manual transmissions and other areas where high-temperature lubrication is required.

Chassis and wheel bearing grease is a heavy grease used where increased loads and friction are encountered, such as for wheel bearings, balljoints, tie-rod ends and universal joints.

High-temperature wheel bearing grease is designed to withstand the extreme temperatures encountered by wheel bearings in disc brake equipped vehicles. It usually contains molybdenum disulfide (moly), which is a dry-type lubricant.

White grease is a heavy grease for metal-to-metal applications where water is a problem. White grease stays soft under both low and high temperatures (usually from -100 to +190-degrees F), and will not wash off or dilute in the presence of water.

Assembly lube is a special extreme pressure lubricant, usually containing moly, used to lubricate high-load parts (such as main and rod bearings and cam lobes) for initial start-up of a new engine. The assembly lube lubricates the parts without being squeezed out or washed away until the engine oiling system begins to function.

Silicone lubricants are used to protect rubber, plastic, vinyl and nylon parts.

Graphite lubricants are used where oils cannot be used due to contamination problems, such as in locks. The dry graphite will lubricate metal parts while remaining uncontaminated by dirt, water, oil or acids. It is electrically conductive and will not foul electrical contacts in locks such as the ignition switch.

Moly penetrants loosen and lubricate frozen, rusted and corroded fasteners and prevent future rusting or freezing.

Heat-sink grease is a special electrically non-conductive grease that is used for mounting electronic ignition modules where it is essential that heat is transferred away from the module.

Sealants

RTV sealant is one of the most widely used gasket compounds. Made from silicone, RTV is air curing, it seals, bonds, waterproofs, fills surface irregularities, remains flexible, doesn't shrink, is relatively easy to remove, and is used as a supplementary sealer with almost all low and medium temperature gaskets.

Anaerobic sealant is much like RTV in that it can be used either to seal gaskets or to form gaskets by itself. It remains flexible, is solvent resistant and fills surface imperfections. The difference between an anaerobic sealant and an RTV-type sealant is in the curing. RTV cures when exposed to air, while an anaerobic sealant cures only in the absence of air. This means that an anaerobic sealant cures only after the assembly of parts, sealing them together.

Thread and pipe sealant is used for sealing hydraulic and pneumatic fittings and vacuum lines. It is usually made from a Teflon compound, and comes in a spray, a paint-on liquid and as a wrap-around tape.

Chemicals

Anti-seize compound prevents seizing, galling, cold welding, rust and corrosion in fasteners. High-temperature anti-seize, usually made with copper and graphite lubricants, is used for exhaust system and exhaust manifold bolts.

Anaerobic locking compounds are used to keep fasteners from vibrating or working loose and cure only after installation, in the absence of air. Medium strength locking compound is used for small nuts, bolts and screws that may be removed later. High-strength locking compound is for large nuts, bolts and studs which aren't removed on a regular basis.

Oil additives range from viscosity index improvers to chemical treatments that claim to reduce internal engine friction. It should be noted that most oil manufacturers caution against using additives with their oils.

Gas additives perform several functions, depending on their chemical makeup. They usually contain solvents that help dissolve gum and varnish that build up on carburetor, fuel injection and intake parts. They also serve to break down carbon deposits that form on the inside surfaces of the combustion chambers. Some additives contain upper cylinder lubricants for valves and piston rings, and others contain chemicals to remove condensation from the gas tank.

Miscellaneous

Brake fluid is specially formulated hydraulic fluid that can withstand the heat and pressure encountered in brake systems. Care must be taken so this fluid does not come in contact with painted surfaces or plastics. An opened container should always be resealed to prevent contamination by water or dirt.

Weatherstrip adhesive is used to bond weatherstripping around doors, windows and trunk lids. It is sometimes used to attach trim pieces.

Undercoating is a petroleum-based, tar-like substance that is designed to protect metal surfaces on the underside of the vehicle from corrosion. It also acts as a sound-deadening agent by insulating the bottom of the vehicle.

Waxes and polishes are used to help protect painted and plated surfaces from the weather. Different types of paint may require the use of different types of wax and polish. Some polishes utilize a chemical or abrasive cleaner to help remove the top layer of oxidized (dull) paint on older vehicles. In recent years many non-wax polishes that contain a wide variety of chemicals such as polymers and silicones have been introduced. These non-wax polishes are usually easier to apply and last longer than conventional waxes and polishes.

Conversion factors

Length (distance)

Inches (in)	X 25.4	= Millimeters (mm)	X 0.0394	= Inches (in)
Feet (ft)	X 0.305	= Meters (m)	X 3.281	= Feet (ft)
Miles	X 1.609	= Kilometers (km)	X 0.621	= Miles

Volume (capacity)

Cubic inches (cu in; in^3)	X 16.387	= Cubic centimeters (cc; cm^3)	X 0.061	= Cubic inches (cu in; in^3)
Imperial pints (Imp pt)	X 0.568	= Liters (l)	X 1.76	= Imperial pints (Imp pt)
Imperial quarts (Imp qt)	X 1.137	= Liters (l)	X 0.88	= Imperial quarts (Imp qt)
Imperial quarts (Imp qt)	X 1.201	= US quarts (US qt)	X 0.833	= Imperial quarts (Imp qt)
US quarts (US qt)	X 0.946	= Liters (l)	X 1.057	= US quarts (US qt)
Imperial gallons (Imp gal)	X 4.546	= Liters (l)	X 0.22	= Imperial gallons (Imp gal)
Imperial gallons (Imp gal)	X 1.201	= US gallons (US gal)	X 0.833	= Imperial gallons (Imp gal)
US gallons (US gal)	X 3.785	= Liters (l)	X 0.264	= US gallons (US gal)

Mass (weight)

Ounces (oz)	X 28.35	= Grams (g)	X 0.035	= Ounces (oz)
Pounds (lb)	X 0.454	= Kilograms (kg)	X 2.205	= Pounds (lb)

Force

Ounces-force (ozf; oz)	X 0.278	= Newtons (N)	X 3.6	= Ounces-force (ozf; oz)
Pounds-force (lbf; lb)	X 4.448	= Newtons (N)	X 0.225	= Pounds-force (lbf; lb)
Newtons (N)	X 0.1	= Kilograms-force (kgf; kg)	X 9.81	= Newtons (N)

Pressure

Pounds-force per square inch (psi; lbf/in^2; lb/in^2)	X 0.070	= Kilograms-force per square centimeter (kgf/cm^2; kg/cm^2)	X 14.223	= Pounds-force per square inch (psi; lbf/in^2; lb/in^2)
Pounds-force per square inch (psi; lbf/in^2; lb/in^2)	X 0.068	= Atmospheres (atm)	X 14.696	= Pounds-force per square inch (psi; lbf/in^2; lb/in^2)
Pounds-force per square inch (psi; lbf/in^2; lb/in^2)	X 0.069	= Bars	X 14.5	= Pounds-force per square inch (psi; lbf/in^2; lb/in^2)
Pounds-force per square inch (psi; lbf/in^2; lb/in^2)	X 6.895	= Kilopascals (kPa)	X 0.145	= Pounds-force per square inch (psi; lbf/in^2; lb/in^2)
Kilopascals (kPa)	X 0.01	= Kilograms-force per square centimeter (kgf/cm^2; kg/cm^2)	X 98.1	= Kilopascals (kPa)

Torque (moment of force)

Pounds-force inches (lbf in; lb in)	X 1.152	= Kilograms-force centimeter (kgf cm; kg cm)	X 0.868	= Pounds-force inches (lbf in; lb in)
Pounds-force inches (lbf in; lb in)	X 0.113	= Newton meters (Nm)	X 8.85	= Pounds-force inches (lbf in; lb in)
Pounds-force inches (lbf in; lb in)	X 0.083	= Pounds-force feet (lbf ft; lb ft)	X 12	= Pounds-force inches (lbf in; lb in)
Pounds-force feet (lbf ft; lb ft)	X 0.138	= Kilograms-force meters (kgf m; kg m)	X 7.233	= Pounds-force feet (lbf ft; lb ft)
Pounds-force feet (lbf ft; lb ft)	X 1.356	= Newton meters (Nm)	X 0.738	= Pounds-force feet (lbf ft; lb ft)
Newton meters (Nm)	X 0.102	= Kilograms-force meters (kgf m; kg m)	X 9.804	= Newton meters (Nm)

Vacuum

Inches mercury (in. Hg)	X 3.377	= Kilopascals (kPa)	X 0.2961	= Inches mercury
Inches mercury (in. Hg)	X 25.4	= Millimeters mercury (mm Hg)	X 0.0394	= Inches mercury

Power

Horsepower (hp)	X 745.7	= Watts (W)	X 0.0013	= Horsepower (hp)

Velocity (speed)

Miles per hour (miles/hr; mph)	X 1.609	= Kilometers per hour (km/hr; kph)	X 0.621	= Miles per hour (miles/hr; mph)

Fuel consumption*

Miles per gallon, Imperial (mpg)	X 0.354	= Kilometers per liter (km/l)	X 2.825	= Miles per gallon, Imperial (mpg)
Miles per gallon, US (mpg)	X 0.425	= Kilometers per liter (km/l)	X 2.352	= Miles per gallon, US (mpg)

Temperature

Degrees Fahrenheit = (°C x 1.8) + 32

Degrees Celsius (Degrees Centigrade; °C) = (°F - 32) x 0.56

*It is common practice to convert from miles per gallon (mpg) to liters/100 kilometers (l/100km), where mpg (Imperial) x l/100 km = 282 and mpg (US) x l/100 km = 235

DECIMALS to MILLIMETERS

Decimal	mm	Decimal	mm
0.001	0.0254	0.500	12.7000
0.002	0.0508	0.510	12.9540
0.003	0.0762	0.520	13.2080
0.004	0.1016	0.530	13.4620
0.005	0.1270	0.540	13.7160
0.006	0.1524	0.550	13.9700
0.007	0.1778	0.560	14.2240
0.008	0.2032	0.570	14.4780
0.009	0.2286	0.580	14.7320
		0.590	14.9860
0.010	0.2540		
0.020	0.5080		
0.030	0.7620		
0.040	1.0160	0.600	15.2400
0.050	1.2700	0.610	15.4940
0.060	1.5240	0.620	15.7480
0.070	1.7780	0.630	16.0020
0.080	2.0320	0.640	16.2560
0.090	2.2860	0.650	16.5100
		0.660	16.7640
0.100	2.5400	0.670	17.0180
0.110	2.7940	0.680	17.2720
0.120	3.0480	0.690	17.5260
0.130	3.3020		
0.140	3.5560		
0.150	3.8100		
0.160	4.0640	0.700	17.7800
0.170	4.3180	0.710	18.0340
0.180	4.5720	0.720	18.2880
0.190	4.8260	0.730	18.5420
		0.740	18.7960
0.200	5.0800	0.750	19.0500
0.210	5.3340	0.760	19.3040
0.220	5.5880	0.770	19.5580
0.230	5.8420	0.780	19.8120
0.240	6.0960	0.790	20.0660
0.250	6.3500		
0.260	6.6040		
0.270	6.8580	0.800	20.3200
0.280	7.1120	0.810	20.5740
0.290	7.3660	0.820	21.8280
		0.830	21.0820
0.300	7.6200	0.840	21.3360
0.310	7.8740	0.850	21.5900
0.320	8.1280	0.860	21.8440
0.330	8.3820	0.870	22.0980
0.340	8.6360	0.880	22.3520
0.350	8.8900	0.890	22.6060
0.360	9.1440		
0.370	9.3980		
0.380	9.6520		
0.390	9.9060		
		0.900	22.8600
0.400	10.1600	0.910	23.1140
0.410	10.4140	0.920	23.3680
0.420	10.6680	0.930	23.6220
0.430	10.9220	0.940	23.8760
0.440	11.1760	0.950	24.1300
0.450	11.4300	0.960	24.3840
0.460	11.6840	0.970	24.6380
0.470	11.9380	0.980	24.8920
0.480	12.1920	0.990	25.1460
0.490	12.4460	1.000	25.4000

FRACTIONS to DECIMALS to MILLIMETERS

Fraction	Decimal	mm	Fraction	Decimal	mm
1/64	0.0156	0.3969	33/64	0.5156	13.0969
1/32	0.0312	0.7938	17/32	0.5312	13.4938
3/64	0.0469	1.1906	35/64	0.5469	13.8906
1/16	0.0625	1.5875	9/16	0.5625	14.2875
5/64	0.0781	1.9844	37/64	0.5781	14.6844
3/32	0.0938	2.3812	19/32	0.5938	15.0812
7/64	0.1094	2.7781	39/64	0.6094	15.4781
1/8	0.1250	3.1750	5/8	0.6250	15.8750
9/64	0.1406	3.5719	41/64	0.6406	16.2719
5/32	0.1562	3.9688	21/32	0.6562	16.6688
11/64	0.1719	4.3656	43/64	0.6719	17.0656
3/16	0.1875	4.7625	11/16	0.6875	17.4625
13/64	0.2031	5.1594	45/64	0.7031	17.8594
7/32	0.2188	5.5562	23/32	0.7188	18.2562
15/64	0.2344	5.9531	47/64	0.7344	18.6531
1/4	0.2500	6.3500	3/4	0.7500	19.0500
17/64	0.2656	6.7469	49/64	0.7656	19.4469
9/32	0.2812	7.1438	25/32	0.7812	19.8438
19/64	0.2969	7.5406	51/64	0.7969	20.2406
5/16	0.3125	7.9375	13/16	0.8125	20.6375
21/64	0.3281	8.3344	53/64	0.8281	21.0344
11/32	0.3438	8.7312	27/32	0.8438	21.4312
23/64	0.3594	9.1281	55/64	0.8594	21.8281
3/8	0.3750	9.5250	7/8	0.8750	22.2250
25/64	0.3906	9.9219	57/64	0.8906	22.6219
13/32	0.4062	10.3188	29/32	0.9062	23.0188
27/64	0.4219	10.7156	59/64	0.9219	23.4156
7/16	0.4375	11.1125	15/16	0.9375	23.8125
29/64	0.4531	11.5094	61/64	0.9531	24.2094
15/32	0.4688	11.9062	31/32	0.9688	24.6062
31/64	0.4844	12.3031	63/64	0.9844	25.0031
1/2	0.5000	12.7000	1	1.0000	25.4000

Safety first!

Regardless of how enthusiastic you may be about getting on with the job at hand, take the time to ensure that your safety is not jeopardized. A moment's lack of attention can result in an accident, as can failure to observe certain simple safety precautions. The possibility of an accident will always exist, and the following points should not be considered a comprehensive list of all dangers. Rather, they are intended to make you aware of the risks and to encourage a safety conscious approach to all work you carry out on your vehicle.

Essential DOs and DON'Ts

DON'T rely on a jack when working under the vehicle. Always use approved jackstands to support the weight of the vehicle and place them under the recommended lift or support points.

DON'T attempt to loosen extremely tight fasteners (i.e. wheel lug nuts) while the vehicle is on a jack - it may fall.

DON'T start the engine without first making sure that the transmission is in Neutral (or Park where applicable) and the parking brake is set.

DON'T remove the radiator cap from a hot cooling system - let it cool or cover it with a cloth and release the pressure gradually.

DON'T attempt to drain the engine oil until you are sure it has cooled to the point that it will not burn you.

DON'T touch any part of the engine or exhaust system until it has cooled sufficiently to avoid burns.

DON'T siphon toxic liquids such as gasoline, antifreeze and brake fluid by mouth, or allow them to remain on your skin.

DON'T inhale brake lining dust - it is potentially hazardous (see *Asbestos* below).

DON'T allow spilled oil or grease to remain on the floor - wipe it up before someone slips on it.

DON'T use loose fitting wrenches or other tools which may slip and cause injury.

DON'T push on wrenches when loosening or tightening nuts or bolts. Always try to pull the wrench toward you. If the situation calls for pushing the wrench away, push with an open hand to avoid scraped knuckles if the wrench should slip.

DON'T attempt to lift a heavy component alone - get someone to help you.

DON'T rush or take unsafe shortcuts to finish a job.

DON'T allow children or animals in or around the vehicle while you are working on it.

DO wear eye protection when using power tools such as a drill, sander, bench grinder, etc. and when working under a vehicle.

DO keep loose clothing and long hair well out of the way of moving parts.

DO make sure that any hoist used has a safe working load rating adequate for the job.

DO get someone to check on you periodically when working alone on a vehicle.

DO carry out work in a logical sequence and make sure that everything is correctly assembled and tightened.

DO keep chemicals and fluids tightly capped and out of the reach of children and pets.

DO remember that your vehicle's safety affects that of yourself and others. If in doubt on any point, get professional advice.

Steering, suspension and brakes

These systems are essential to driving safety, so make sure you have a qualified shop or individual check your work. Also, compressed suspension springs can cause injury if released suddenly - be sure to use a spring compressor.

Airbags

Airbags are explosive devices that can **CAUSE** injury if they deploy while you're working on the vehicle. Follow the manufacturer's instructions to disable the airbag whenever you're working in the vicinity of airbag components.

Asbestos

Certain friction, insulating, sealing, and other products - such as brake linings, brake bands, clutch linings, torque converters, gaskets, etc. - may contain asbestos or other hazardous friction material. Extreme care must be taken to avoid inhalation of dust from such products, since it is hazardous to health. If in doubt, assume that they do contain asbestos.

Fire

Remember at all times that gasoline is highly flammable. Never smoke or have any kind of open flame around when working on a vehicle. But the risk does not end there. A spark caused by an electrical short circuit, by two metal surfaces contacting each other, or even by static electricity built up in your body under certain conditions, can ignite gasoline vapors, which in a confined space are highly explosive. Do not, under any circumstances, use gasoline for cleaning parts. Use an approved safety solvent.

Always disconnect the battery ground (-) cable at the battery before working on any part of the fuel system or electrical system. Never risk spilling fuel on a hot engine or exhaust component. It is strongly recommended that a fire extinguisher suitable for use on fuel and electrical fires be kept handy in the garage or workshop at all times. Never try to extinguish a fuel or electrical fire with water.

Fumes

Certain fumes are highly toxic and can quickly cause unconsciousness and even death if inhaled to any extent. Gasoline vapor falls into this category, as do the vapors from some cleaning solvents. Any draining or pouring of such volatile fluids should be done in a well ventilated area.

When using cleaning fluids and solvents, read the instructions on the container carefully. Never use materials from unmarked containers.

Never run the engine in an enclosed space, such as a garage. Exhaust fumes contain carbon monoxide, which is extremely poisonous. If you need to run the engine, always do so in the open air, or at least have the rear of the vehicle outside the work area.

The battery

Never create a spark or allow a bare light bulb near a battery. They normally give off a certain amount of hydrogen gas, which is highly explosive.

Always disconnect the battery ground (-) cable at the battery before working on the fuel or electrical systems.

If possible, loosen the filler caps or cover when charging the battery from an external source (this does not apply to sealed or maintenance-free batteries). Do not charge at an excessive rate or the battery may burst.

Take care when adding water to a non maintenance-free battery and when carrying a battery. The electrolyte, even when diluted, is very corrosive and should not be allowed to contact clothing or skin.

Always wear eye protection when cleaning the battery to prevent the caustic deposits from entering your eyes.

Household current

When using an electric power tool, inspection light, etc., which operates on household current, always make sure that the tool is correctly connected to its plug and that, where necessary, it is properly grounded. Do not use such items in damp conditions and, again, do not create a spark or apply excessive heat in the vicinity of fuel or fuel vapor.

Secondary ignition system voltage

A severe electric shock can result from touching certain parts of the ignition system (such as the spark plug wires) when the engine is running or being cranked, particularly if components are damp or the insulation is defective. In the case of an electronic ignition system, the secondary system voltage is much higher and could prove fatal.

Hydrofluoric acid

This extremely corrosive acid is formed when certain types of synthetic rubber, found in some O-rings, oil seals, fuel hoses, etc. are exposed to temperatures above 750-degrees F (400-degrees C). The rubber changes into a charred or sticky substance containing the acid. *Once formed, the acid remains dangerous for years. If it gets onto the skin, it may be necessary to amputate the limb concerned.*

When dealing with a vehicle which has suffered a fire, or with components salvaged from such a vehicle, wear protective gloves and discard them after use.

Troubleshooting

Contents

Engine

1 Engine will not rotate when attempting to start

1   Battery terminal connections loose or corroded (Chapter 1).
2   Battery discharged or faulty (Chapter 1).
3   Automatic transaxle not completely engaged in Park (Chapter 7A) or clutch pedal not completely depressed (Chapter 8).
4   Broken, loose or disconnected wiring in the starting circuit (Chapters 5 and 12).
5   Starter motor pinion jammed in flywheel ring gear (Chapter 5).
6   Starter solenoid faulty (Chapter 5).
7   Starter motor faulty (Chapter 5).
8   Ignition switch faulty (Chapter 12).
9   Starter pinion or flywheel teeth worn or broken (Chapter 5).
10   Faulty Body Control Module (BCM) or Intelligent Power Distribution Module (IPDM) (see Chapter 12).

2 Engine rotates but will not start

1   Fuel tank empty.
2   Battery discharged (engine rotates slowly) (Chapter 5).
3   Battery terminal connections loose or corroded (Chapter 1).
4   Leaking fuel injector(s), faulty fuel pump, pressure regulator, etc. (Chapter 4).
5   Broken timing chain (Chapter 2A).
6   Ignition system problem (Chapter 5).
7   Worn, faulty or incorrectly gapped spark plugs (Chapter 1).
8   Broken, loose or disconnected wiring in the starting circuit (Chapter 5).
9   Loose distributor is changing ignition timing (Chapter 5).
10   Defective MAF/IAT sensor (see Chapter 6).

3 Engine hard to start when cold

1   Battery discharged or low (Chapter 1).
2   Malfunctioning fuel system (Chapter 4).
3   Faulty coolant temperature sensor or intake air temperature sensor (Chapter 6).
4   Injector(s) leaking (Chapter 4).
5   Faulty ignition system (Chapter 5).
6   Defective MAF/IAT sensor (see Chapter 6).

4 Engine hard to start when hot

1   Air filter clogged (Chapter 1).
2   Fuel not reaching the fuel injection system (Chapter 4).
3   Corroded battery connections, especially ground (Chapter 1).
4   Faulty coolant temperature sensor or intake air temperature sensor (Chapter 6).

5 Starter motor noisy or excessively rough in engagement

1   Pinion or flywheel gear teeth worn or broken (Chapter 5).
2   Starter motor mounting bolts loose or missing (Chapter 5).

6 Engine starts but stops immediately

1   Insufficient fuel reaching the fuel injector(s) (Chapters 1 and 4).
2   Vacuum leak at the gasket between the intake manifold/plenum and throttle body (Chapters 1 and 4).

7 Oil puddle under engine

1   Oil pan gasket and/or oil pan drain bolt washer leaking (Chapter 2A).
2   Oil pressure sending unit leaking (Chapter 2B).
3   Valve cover leaking (Chapter 2A).
4   Engine oil seals leaking (Chapter 2A).
5   Timing chain cover leaking (Chapter 2A).

8 Engine lopes while idling or idles erratically

1   Vacuum leakage (Chapters and 4).
2   Air filter clogged (Chapter 1).
3   Fuel pump not delivering sufficient fuel to the fuel injection system (Chapter 4).
4   Leaking head gasket (Chapter 2A).
5   Timing chain and/or sprockets worn (Chapter 2A).
6   Camshaft lobes worn (Chapter 2A).

9 Engine misses at idle speed

1   Spark plugs worn or not gapped properly (Chapter 1).
2   Vacuum leaks (Chapters 2B, 2A and 4).
3   Uneven or low compression (Chapter 2B).
4   Problem with the fuel injection system (Chapter 4).
5   Faulty ignition coils (Chapter 5).

10 Engine misses throughout driving speed range

1   Fuel filter clogged and/or impurities in the fuel system (Chapter 1).
2   Low fuel output at the fuel injector(s) (Chapter 4).
3   Faulty or incorrectly gapped spark plugs (Chapter 1).
4   Faulty ignition coils (Chapter 5).
5   Faulty emission system components (Chapter 6).

6   Low or uneven cylinder compression pressures (Chapter 2B).
7   Vacuum leak in fuel injection system, throttle body, intake manifold, or vacuum hoses (Chapter 4).

11 Engine stumbles on acceleration

1   Spark plugs fouled (Chapter 1).
2   Problem with fuel injection system (Chapter 4).
3   Fuel filter clogged. The filter isn't replaceable; the fuel pump module must be replaced (Chapter 4).
4   Intake manifold air leak (Chapters 2A and 4).
5   EGR system malfunction (Chapter 6).

12 Engine surges while holding accelerator steady

1   Intake air leak (Chapter 4).
2   Fuel pump or fuel pressure regulator faulty (Chapter 4).
3   Problem with fuel injection system (Chapter 4).
4   Problem with the emissions control system (Chapter 6).

13 Engine stalls

1   Fuel filter clogged and/or water and impurities in the fuel system (Chapters 1 and 4).
2   Faulty emissions system components (Chapter 6).
3   Faulty or incorrectly gapped spark plugs (Chapter 1).
4   Vacuum leak in the fuel injection system, intake manifold or vacuum hoses (Chapters 2A and 4).
5   Valve clearances incorrectly set (Chapter 1).

14 Engine lacks power

1   Faulty or incorrectly gapped spark plugs (Chapter 1).
2   Problem with the fuel injection system (Chapter 4).
3   Plugged air filter (Chapter 1).
4   Brakes binding (Chapters 1 and 9).
5   Automatic transaxle fluid level incorrect (Chapter 1).
6   Clutch slipping (Chapter 8).
7   Fuel filter clogged. The filter isn't replaceable; the fuel pump module must be replaced (Chapter 4).
8   Emission control system not functioning properly (Chapter 6).
9   Low or uneven cylinder compression pressures (Chapter 2B).
10   Obstructed exhaust system.

15 Engine backfires

1   Emission control system not functioning properly (Chapter 6).
2   Problem with the fuel injection system (Chapter 4).
3   Vacuum leak at fuel injector(s), intake manifold or vacuum hoses (Chapters 2A and 4).
4   Valve clearances incorrectly set and/or valves sticking (Chapter 1).

16 Pinging or knocking engine sounds during acceleration or uphill

1   Incorrect grade of fuel.
2   Fuel injection system faulty (Chapter 4).
3   Improper or damaged spark plugs (Chapter 1).
4   Malfunctioning knock sensor (Chapter 6).
5   Vacuum leak (Chapters 2A and 4).

17 Engine runs with oil pressure light on

1   Low oil level (Chapter 1).
2   Idle rpm below specification (Chapter 1).
3   Short in wiring circuit (Chapter 12).
4   Faulty oil pressure sender (Chapter 2B).
5   Worn engine bearings and/or oil pump (Chapters 2A and 2B).

18 Engine continues to run after switching off

Faulty ignition switch (Chapter 12), Powertrain Control Module (PCM) (Chapter 6), or Body Control Module (BCM).

Engine electrical system

19 Battery will not hold a charge

1   Alternator drivebelt worn or not adjusted properly (Chapter 1).
2   Battery electrolyte level low (Chapter 1).
3   Battery terminals loose or corroded (Chapter 1).
4   Alternator not charging properly (Chapter 5).
5   Loose, broken or faulty wiring in the charging circuit (Chapter 5).
6   Internally defective battery (Chapters 1 and 5).

20 Alternator light fails to go out

1   Faulty alternator or charging circuit (Chapter 5).
2   Alternator drivebelt defective or out of adjustment (Chapter 1).
3   Alternator voltage regulator inoperative (Chapter 5).

21 Alternator light fails to come on when key is turned on

1   Warning light bulb defective (Chapter 12).
2   Fault in the instrument cluster, dash wiring or bulb holder (Chapter 12).

Fuel system

22 Excessive fuel consumption

1   Dirty or clogged air filter element (Chapter 1).
2   Emissions/engine control system not functioning properly (Chapter 6).
3   Fuel injection system not functioning properly (Chapter 4).
4   Low tire pressure or incorrect tire size (Chapter 1).

23 Fuel leakage and/or fuel odor

1   Leaking fuel line (Chapters 1 and 4).
2   Tank overfilled.
3   Problem with fuel injection system (Chapter 4).

Cooling system

24 Overheating

1   Insufficient coolant in system (Chapter 1).
2   Drivebelt defective or out of adjustment (Chapter 1).
3   Radiator core blocked or grille restricted (Chapter 3).
4   Thermostat faulty (Chapter 3).
5   Electric coolant fan inoperative or blades broken (Chapter 3).
6   Radiator cap not maintaining proper pressure (Chapter 3).

25 Overcooling

Faulty thermostat (Chapter 3).

26 External coolant leakage

1   Deteriorated/damaged hoses; loose clamps (Chapters 1 and 3).
2   Water pump defective (Chapter 3).
3   Leakage from radiator core or coolant reservoir bottle (Chapter 3).
4   Engine drain or water jacket core plugs leaking.

27 Internal coolant leakage

1   Leaking cylinder head gasket (Chapter 2A).
2   Cracked cylinder bore or cylinder head (Chapters 2B or 2A).

28 Coolant loss

1   Too much coolant in system (Chapter 1).
2   Coolant boiling away because of overheating (Chapter 3).
3   Internal or external coolant leakage (Chapter 3).
4   Faulty radiator cap (Chapter 3).

29 Poor coolant circulation

1   Inoperative water pump (Chapter 3).
2   Restriction in cooling system (Chapters 1 and 3).
3   Water pump drivebelt defective/out of adjustment (Chapter 1).
4   Thermostat sticking (Chapter 3).

Clutch

30 Pedal travels to floor - no pressure or very little resistance

1   Hydraulic release system leaking or air in the system (Chapter 8).
2   Broken release bearing or fork (Chapter 8).

31 Unable to select gears

1   Faulty transaxle (Chapter 7A).
2   Faulty clutch disc or pressure plate (Chapter 8).
3   Faulty release lever or release bearing (Chapter 8).
4   Faulty shift lever assembly or cable(s) (Chapter 8).

32 Clutch slips (engine speed increases with no increase in vehicle speed)

1 Clutch plate worn (Chapter 8).
2 Clutch plate is oil soaked by leaking rear main seal (Chapter 8).
3 Warped pressure plate or flywheel (Chapter 8).
4 Weak diaphragm spring in pressure plate (Chapter 8).
5 Piston stuck in bore of clutch release cylinder, preventing clutch from fully engaging (Chapter 8).

33 Grabbing (chattering) as clutch is engaged

1 Oil on clutch plate lining, burned or glazed facings (Chapter 8).
2 Worn or loose engine or transaxle mounts (Chapter 2A).
3 Worn splines on clutch plate hub (Chapter 8).
4 Warped pressure plate or flywheel (Chapter 8).
5 Burned or smeared resin on flywheel or pressure plate (Chapter 8).

34 Transaxle rattling (clicking)

1 Release bearing defective (Chapter 8).
2 Internal transaxle problem.

35 Noise in clutch area

Faulty bearing (Chapter 8).

36 Clutch pedal stays on floor

1 Defective release cylinder (Chapter 8).
2 Hydraulic release system leaking or air in the system (Chapter 8).

37 High pedal effort

1 Piston binding in bore of release cylinder (Chapter 8).
2 Pressure plate faulty (Chapter 8).

Manual transaxle

38 Knocking noise at low speeds

1 Worn driveaxle constant velocity (CV) joints (Chapter 8).
2 Worn side gear shaft counterbore in differential case (Chapter 7A).*

39 Noise most pronounced when turning

Differential gear noise (Chapter 7A).*

40 Clunk on acceleration or deceleration

1 Loose engine or transaxle mounts (Chapter 2A).
2 Worn differential pinion shaft in case.*
3 Worn side gear shaft counterbore in differential case (Chapter 7A).*
4 Worn or damaged driveaxle inboard CV joints (Chapter 8).

41 Clicking noise in turns

Worn or damaged outboard CV joint (Chapter 8).

42 Vibration

1 Rough wheel bearing (Chapter 10).
2 Damaged driveaxle (Chapter 8).
3 Out-of-round tires.
4 Tire out of balance.
5 Worn CV joint (Chapter 8).

43 Noisy in neutral with engine running

1 Damaged input gear bearing (Chapter 7A).*
2 Damaged clutch release bearing (Chapter 8).

44 Noisy in one particular gear

1 Damaged or worn constant mesh gears (Chapter 7A).*
2 Damaged or worn synchronizers (Chapter 7A).*
3 Bent reverse fork (Chapter 7A).*
4 Damaged fourth speed gear or output gear (Chapter 7A).*
5 Worn or damaged reverse idler gear or idler bushing (Chapter 7A).*

45 Noisy in all gears

1 Insufficient lubricant (Chapter 7A).
2 Damaged or worn bearings (Chapter 7A).*
3 Worn or damaged input gear shaft and/or output gear shaft (Chapter 7A).*

46 Slips out of gear

1 Worn or improperly adjusted linkage (Chapter 7A).
2 Shift linkage does not work freely, binds (Chapter 7A).
3 Input gear bearing retainer broken or loose (Chapter 7A).*
4 Worn shift fork (Chapter 7A).*

47 Leaks lubricant

1 Side gear shaft seals worn (Chapter 7A).
2 Excessive amount of lubricant in transaxle (Chapter 1).
3 Loose or broken input gear shaft bearing retainer (Chapter 7A).*
4 Input gear bearing retainer O-ring and/or lip seal damaged (Chapter 7A).*
5 Shifter shaft seal leaking (Chapter 7A).

48 Hard to shift

1 Shift cable(s) worn (Chapter 7A).

Note: *Although the corrective action necessary to remedy the symptoms described is beyond the scope of this manual, the above information should be helpful in isolating the cause of the condition so that the owner can communicate clearly with a professional mechanic.*

Automatic transaxle

49 Fluid leakage

1 On most models, automatic transaxle fluid is a deep red color. Fluid leaks should not be confused with engine oil, which can easily be blown onto the transaxle by air flow.
2 To pinpoint a leak, first remove all built-up dirt and grime from the transaxle housing with degreasing agents and/or steam cleaning. Then drive the vehicle at low speeds so air flow will not blow the leak far from its source. Raise the vehicle and determine where the leak is coming from. Common areas of leakage are:

a) PanDipstick tube
b) Transaxle oil lines
c) Speed sensor (Chapter 7A)
d) Driveaxle oil seals (Chapter 7A)

50 Transaxle fluid brown or has a burned smell

Transaxle fluid overheated (Chapter 1).

51 General shift mechanism problems

1   Chapter 7B deals with checking and adjusting the shift cable on automatic transaxles. Common problems which may be attributed to a poorly adjusted cable are:

a) *Engine starting in gears other than Park or Neutral*

b) *Indicator on shifter pointing to a gear other than the one actually being used*

c) *Vehicle moves when in Park*

2   Refer to Chapter 7B for the shift cable adjustment procedure.

52 Transaxle will not downshift with accelerator pedal pressed to the floor

The transaxle is electronically controlled. This type of problem - which is caused by a malfunction in the control unit, a sensor or solenoid, or the circuit itself - is beyond the scope of this book. Take the vehicle to a dealer service department or a competent automatic transmission shop.

53 Engine will start in gears other than Park or Neutral

Neutral start switch out of adjustment or malfunctioning (Chapter 7B).

54 Transaxle slips, is noisy or has no drive in forward or reverse gears

There are many probable causes for the above problems, but the home mechanic should be concerned with only one possibility - fluid level. Before taking the vehicle to a repair shop, check the level and condition of the fluid as described in Chapter 1. Correct the fluid level as necessary or change the fluid if needed. If the problem persists, have a professional diagnose the cause.

Driveaxles

55 Clicking noise in turns

Worn or damaged outboard CV joint (Chapter 8).

56 Shudder or vibration during acceleration

1   Excessive toe-in (Chapter 10).

2   Worn or damaged inboard or outboard CV joints (Chapter 8).

3   Sticking inboard CV joint assembly (Chapter 8).

57 Vibration at highway speeds

1   Out of balance front wheels and/or tires.

2   Out of round front tires.

3   Worn CV joint(s) (Chapter 8).

Brakes

58 Vehicle pulls to one side during braking

1   Incorrect tire pressures (Chapter 1).

2   Front end out of alignment (have the front end aligned).

3   Front, or rear, tire sizes not matched to one another.

4   Restricted brake lines or hoses (Chapter 9).

5   Malfunctioning caliper assembly (Chapter 9).

6   Loose suspension parts (Chapter 10).

7   Excessive wear of brake pad material or disc on one side.

59 Noise (high-pitched squeal when the brakes are applied)

Front and/or rear disc brake pads/rear shoes worn out. Replace pads or shoes with new ones immediately (Chapter 9).

60 Brake roughness or chatter (pedal pulsates)

1   Excessive lateral runout (Chapter 9).

2   Uneven pad wear (Chapter 9).

3   Defective disc or drum (Chapter 9).

61 Excessive brake pedal effort required to stop vehicle

1   Malfunctioning power brake booster (Chapter 9).

2   Partial system failure (Chapter 9).

3   Excessively worn pads (Chapter 9).

4   Piston in caliper stuck or sluggish (Chapter 9).

5   Brake pads contaminated with brake fluid, oil or grease (Chapter 9).

6   Brake disc or drum grooved and/or glazed (Chapter 1).

7   New pads installed and not yet seated. It will take a while for the new material to seat against the disc.

62 Excessive brake pedal travel

1   Partial brake system failure (Chapter 9).

2   Insufficient fluid in master cylinder (Chapters 1 and 9).

3   Air trapped in system. Bleed the brakes (Chapter 9).

63 Dragging brakes

1   Master cylinder pistons not returning correctly (Chapter 9).

2   Restricted brakes lines or hoses (Chapter 9).

3   Incorrect parking brake adjustment (Chapter 9).

64 Grabbing or uneven braking action

Contaminated brake linings (Chapter 9).

65 Brake pedal feels spongy when depressed

1   Air in hydraulic lines. Bleed the system (Chapter 9).

2   Master cylinder defective (Chapter 9).

66 Brake pedal travels to the floor with little resistance

1   Leak in the brake system (Chapters 1 and 9).

2   Loose or damaged brake lines (Chapter 9).

67 Parking brake does not hold

Parking brake improperly adjusted (Chapter 9).

Suspension and steering systems

68 Vehicle pulls to one side

1   Mismatched or uneven tires.

2   Broken or sagging springs (Chapter 10).

3   Wheel alignment out of specifications.

4   Front brake dragging (Chapter 9).

69 Abnormal or excessive tire wear

1   Wheel alignment out of specifications (Chapter 10).

2   Sagging or broken springs (Chapter 10).
3   Tire out-of-balance.
4   Worn strut damper (Chapter 10).
5   Overloaded vehicle.
6   Tires not rotated regularly.

70   Wheel makes a thumping noise

1   Blister or bump on tire.
2   Improper strut damper action (Chapter 10).

71   Shimmy, shake or vibration

1   Tire or wheel out-of-balance or out-of-round.
2   Worn wheel bearings (Chapters 1, 8 and 10).
3   Worn tie-rod ends (Chapter 10).
4   Worn balljoints (Chapters 1 and 10).
5   Excessive wheel runout.
6   Blister or bump on tire.

72   Hard steering

1   Lack of lubrication at balljoints or tie-rod ends (Chapter 10).
2   Front wheel alignment out of specifications.
3   Low tire pressure(s) (Chapter 1).

73   Poor returnability of steering to center

1   Worn balljoints or tie-rod ends (Chapter 10).
2   Binding in balljoints (Chapter 10).
3   Binding in steering column (Chapter 10).
4   Worn steering gear assembly (Chapter 10).
5   Front wheel alignment out of specifications.

74   Abnormal noise at the front end

1   Worn balljoints or tie-rod ends (Chapter 10).

2   Damaged strut mounting (Chapter 10).
3   Worn control arm bushings or tie-rod ends (Chapter 10).
4   Loose stabilizer bar (Chapter 10).
5   Loose wheel nuts.
6   Loose suspension bolts (Chapter 10)

75   Wander or poor steering stability

1   Mismatched or uneven tires.
2   Worn balljoints or tie-rod ends (Chapter 10).
3   Worn strut assemblies (Chapter 10).
4   Loose stabilizer bar (Chapter 10).
5   Broken or sagging springs (Chapter 10).
6   Wheels out of alignment.

76   Erratic steering when braking

1   Wheel bearings worn (Chapter 10).
2   Broken or sagging springs (Chapter 10).
3   Leaking caliper (Chapter 9).
4   Warped brake discs (Chapter 9).

77   Excessive pitching and/or rolling around corners or during braking

1   Loose stabilizer bar (Chapter 10).
2   Worn strut dampers or mountings (Chapter 10).
3   Broken or sagging springs (Chapter 10).
4   Overloaded vehicle.

78   Suspension bottoms

1   Overloaded vehicle.
2   Worn strut dampers or springs (Chapter 10).

79   Cupped tires

1   Front wheel or rear wheel alignment out of specifications.
2   Worn strut dampers (Chapter 10).
3   Wheel bearings worn (Chapter 10).
4   Excessive tire or wheel runout.
5   Worn balljoints (Chapter 10).

80   Excessive tire wear on outside edge

1   Inflation pressures incorrect (Chapter 1).
2   Excessive speed in turns.
3   Front end alignment incorrect (excessive toe-in). Have professionally aligned.
4   Suspension arm bent (Chapter 10).

81   Excessive tire wear on inside edge

1   Inflation pressures incorrect (Chapter 1).
2   Front end alignment incorrect (toe-out). Have professionally aligned.
3   Loose or damaged steering components (Chapter 10).

82   Tire tread worn in one place

1   Tires out-of-balance.
2   Damaged wheel. Inspect and replace if necessary.
3   Defective tire (Chapter 1).

83   Excessive play or looseness in steering system

1   Wheel bearing(s) worn (Chapter 10).
2   Tie-rod end loose (Chapter 10).
3   Steering gear loose (Chapter 10).
4   Worn or loose steering intermediate shaft (Chapter 10).

84   Rattling or clicking noise in steering gear

1   Steering gear loose (Chapter 10).
2   Steering gear defective.

Notes

Chapter 1
Tune-up and routine maintenance

Contents

Specifications

Recommended lubricants and fluids

Note: *Listed here are manufacturer recommendations at the time this manual was written. Manufacturers occasionally upgrade their fluid and lubricant specifications, so check with your local auto parts store for current recommendations.*

Engine oil	
Type	API "certified for gasoline engines"
Viscosity	
2010 and earlier models	SAE 5W-20
2011 and later models	SAE 0W-20
Fuel	Unleaded gasoline, 87 octane or higher
Manual transaxle lubricant	Honda Manual transmission fluid (MTF)
Automatic transmission fluid	Honda ATF DW-1 transmission fluid
Brake and clutch fluid	DOT 3 brake fluid or equivalent
Engine coolant	Honda long life antifreeze/coolant Type 2 (this coolant is pre-mixed; do not add water)

Capacities*

Engine oil (including filter)	3.8 quarts (3.6 liters)
Coolant (including reservoir tank)	
With automatic transaxle	3.98 quarts (3.7 liters)
With manual transaxle	4 quarts (3.8 liters)
Automatic transaxle	
Fluid change	2.5 quarts (2.4 liters)
Dry fill	6.3 quarts (6.0 liters)
Manual transaxle	1.6 quarts (1.5 liters)

Note: **All capacities approximate. Add as necessary to bring up to appropriate level.*
Note: ***The best way to determine the amount of fluid to add during a routine fluid change is to measure the amount drained.*

Ignition system

Spark plugs
    Type
        NGK.. IZFR6K13 or equivalent
        DENSO... SKJ20DR-M13 or equivalent
    Gap .... 0.042 to 0.051 inch (1.2 to 1.3 mm)
Firing order 1-3-4-2

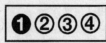

FRONT OF
VEHICLE

Cylinder locations

Valve clearance (engine cold)

Intake valves... 0.006 to 0.007 inch (0.15 to 0.19 mm)
Exhaust valves .... 0.010 to 0.012 inch (0.26 to 0.30 mm)

Cooling system

Thermostat starts to open.. 176 to 183-degrees F (80 to 84-degrees C)
Thermostat fully open .... 203-degrees F (95-degrees C)

Brakes

Brake lining thickness (minimum)
    Front pad... 1/16 inch (1.6 mm)
    Rear shoe... 5/64 inch (2.0 mm)
Brake pedal .... See Chapter 9
Parking brake adjustment
    2007 and 2010 and later models.. 5 to 7 clicks
    2008 and 2009 models.. 6 to 8 clicks

Suspension and steering

Steering wheel freeplay limit... 1-3/8 inches
Balljoint allowable movement .... 0 inch

Torque Specifications

	Ft-lbs (unless otherwise indicated)	Nm
Note: *One foot-pound (ft-lb) of torque is equivalent to 12 inch-pounds (in-lbs) of torque. Torque values below approximately 15 foot-pounds are expressed in inch-pounds, because most foot-pound torque wrenches are not accurate at these smaller values.*		
Engine oil drain plug	29	39
Drivebelt tensioner mounting bolts (2009 and later models)	17	24
Drivebelt tensioner pulley bolt (2009 and later models)	33	44
Automatic transaxle drain plug	36	49
Manual transaxle fill and drain plugs		
Drain plug	29	39
Check/fill plug	33	44
Spark plugs	20	27
Wheel lug nuts	80	108

Typical engine compartment components (2007/2008 model)

1	Clutch fluid reservoir	6	Radiator cap	11	Engine oil filler cap
2	Brake fluid reservoir	7	Air filter housing	12	Ignition coils/spark plugs
3	Battery	8	Engine oil dipstick		(back of valve cover)
4	Fuse/relay box	9	Windshield washer fluid reservoir	13	PCV valve (not visible)
5	Coolant reservoir (not visible)	10	Drivebelt		

Typical engine compartment underside components (2007/2008 manual transaxle model)

1	Engine oil filter	4	Manual transaxle drain plug	7	Radiator drain fitting
2	Engine oil drain plug	5	Brake caliper	8	Drivebelt
3	Driveaxle boot	6	Brake caliper		

Typical rear underside components

1	Exhaust system hanger	3	Coil spring	5	Fuel tank
2	Shock absorber	4	Axle beam		

1 Maintenance schedule

The maintenance intervals in this manual are provided with the assumption that you, not the dealer, will be doing the work. These are the minimum maintenance intervals recommended by the factory for vehicles that are driven daily. If you wish to keep your vehicle in peak condition at all times, you may wish to perform some of these procedures even more often. Because frequent maintenance enhances the efficiency, performance and resale value of your car, we encourage you to do so. If you drive in dusty areas, tow a trailer, idle or drive at low speeds for extended periods or drive for short distances (less than four miles) in below freezing temperatures, shorter intervals are also recommended.

When your vehicle is new, it should be serviced by a factory authorized dealer service department to protect the factory warranty. In many cases, the initial maintenance check is done at no cost to the owner.

Every 250 miles or weekly, whichever comes first

Check the engine oil level (Section 4)
Check the engine coolant level (Section 4)
Check the windshield washer fluid level (Section 4)
Check the battery electrolyte (Section 4)
Check the brake fluid level (Section 4)
Check the clutch fluid level (Section 4)
Check the tires and tire pressures (Section 5)

Every 3000 miles or 3 months, whichever comes first

Check the automatic transaxle fluid level (Section 6)
Change the engine oil and filter (Section 7)

Every 7500 miles or 6 months, whichever comes first

Note: Or as indicated by the Maintenance Reminder on the instrument panel.
Inspect and replace if necessary the wiper blades (Section 8)
Check and service the battery (Section 9)
Check the engine drivebelt (Section 10)
Inspect and replace if necessary all underhood hoses (Section 11)
Check the cooling system (Section 12)
Rotate the tires (Section 13)

Every 15,000 miles or 12 months, whichever comes first

Note: All items listed above plus:
Inspect the brake system (Section 14)*
Replace the cabin air filter (Section 15)
Inspect the fuel system (Section 17)
Check the manual transaxle lubricant level (Section 18)
Inspect the suspension and steering components (Section 19)
Inspect the exhaust system (Section 20)
Check the driveaxle boots (Section 21)

Every 30,000 miles or 24 months, whichever comes first

Note: All items listed above plus:
Replace the air filter (Section 16)*
Service the cooling system (drain, flush and refill) (Section 23)
Inspect the evaporative emissions control system (Section 24)
Check and replace if necessary the PCV valve (Section 27)

Every 36 months

Replace the brake fluid (Section)

Every 60,000 miles or 48 months, whichever comes first

Change the automatic transaxle fluid (Section 25)**
Change the manual transaxle lubricant (Section 26)**
If noisy, check and adjust the valve clearances (Section 28)

Every 105,000 miles or 72 months, whichever comes first

Replace the spark plugs (Section 25)

* This item is affected by "severe" operating conditions as described below. If your vehicle is operated under "severe" conditions, perform all maintenance indicated with an asterisk (*) at half the indicated intervals. Severe conditions are indicated if you mainly operate your vehicle under one or more of the following conditions:
  a) Operating in dusty areas
  b) Towing a trailer
  c) Idling for extended periods and/or low speed operation
  d) Operating when outside temperatures remain below freezing and when most trips are less than 4 miles

** If operated under one or more of the following conditions, change the automatic transmission fluid and differential lubricant every 30,000 miles:
  a) In heavy city traffic where outside temperature regularly reaches 90-degrees F (32-degrees C) or higher
  b) In hilly or mountainous terrain
  c) Frequent trailer pulling

2 Introduction

1   This Chapter is designed to help the home mechanic maintain the Honda Fit for peak performance, economy, safety and long life.
2   Included in this Chapter is a master maintenance schedule, followed by Sections dealing specifically with each item on the schedule. Visual checks, adjustments, component replacement and other helpful items are included. Refer to the accompanying illustrations of the engine compartment and the underside of the vehicle for the location of various components.
3   Servicing your Fit in accordance with the mileage/time maintenance schedule and the following Sections will provide it with a planned maintenance program that should result in a long and reliable service life. This is a comprehensive plan, so maintaining some items but not others at the specified service intervals will not produce the same results.
4   As you service your vehicle, you will discover that many of the procedures can, and should, be grouped together because of the nature of the particular procedure you're performing or because of the close proximity of two otherwise unrelated components to one another.
5   For example, if the vehicle is raised for any reason, you should inspect the exhaust, suspension, steering and fuel systems while you're under the vehicle. When you're rotating the tires, it makes good sense to check the brakes and wheel bearings since the wheels are already removed.
6   Finally, let's suppose you have to borrow or rent a torque wrench. Even if you only need to tighten the spark plugs, you might as well check the torque of as many critical fasteners as time allows.
7   The first step of this maintenance program is to prepare yourself before the actual work begins. Read through all Sections pertinent to the procedures you're planning to do, then make a list of and gather together all the parts and tools you will need to do the job. If it looks as if you might run into problems during a particular segment of some procedure, seek advice from your local auto parts stores or dealer service department.

3 Tune-up general information

1   The term tune-up is used in this manual to represent a combination of individual operations rather than one specific procedure.
2   If, from the time the vehicle is new, the routine maintenance schedule is followed closely and frequent checks are made of fluid levels and high wear items, as suggested throughout this manual, the engine will be kept in relatively good running condition and the need for additional work will be minimized.
3   More likely than not, however, there will be times when the engine is running poorly due to lack of regular maintenance. This is even more likely if a used vehicle, which has not received regular and frequent maintenance checks, is purchased. In such cases, an engine tune-up will be needed outside of the regular routine maintenance intervals.
4   The first step in any tune-up or engine diagnosis to help correct a poor running engine would be a cylinder compression check. A check of the engine compression (see Chapter 2B) will give valuable information regarding the overall performance of many internal components and should be used as a basis for tune-up and repair procedures. If, for instance, a compression check indicates serious internal engine wear, a conventional tune-up will not help the running condition of the engine and would be a waste of time and money.
5   The following series of operations are those most often needed to bring a generally poor running engine back into a proper state of tune.

Minor tune-up
Check all engine related fluids (Section 4)
Clean, inspect and test the battery (Section 9)
Check the drivebelts (Section 10)
Check all underhood hoses (Section 11)
Check the cooling system (Section 12)
Check the air filter (Section 16)

Major tune-up
All items listed under Minor tune-up, plus. . .
Replace the air filter (Section 16)
Check the fuel system (Section 17)
Replace the spark plugs (Section 22)
Check the charging system (Chapter 5)
Check for the presence of any stored trouble codes (Chapter 6)

4 Fluid level checks (every 250 miles or weekly)

1   Fluids are an essential part of the lubrication, cooling, brake, clutch and other systems. Because these fluids gradually become depleted and/or contaminated during normal operation of the vehicle, they must be periodically replenished. See Recommended lubricants and fluids and Capacities in this Chapter's Specifications0 before adding fluid to any of the following components.
Note: *The vehicle must be on level ground before fluid levels can be checked.*

Engine oil
2   The engine oil level is checked with a dipstick located at the front of the engine (see illustration).
3   The oil level should be checked before the vehicle has been driven, or about 5 minutes after the engine has been shut off. If the oil is checked immediately after driving the vehicle, some of the oil will remain in the upper engine components, producing an inaccurate reading on the dipstick.
4   Pull the dipstick out and wipe all the oil from the end with a clean rag or paper towel. Insert the clean dipstick all the way back in and pull it out again. Observe the oil at the end of the dipstick; the level should be between the L and H marks (see illustration).
5   It takes about one quart of oil to raise the level from the L mark to the H mark on the

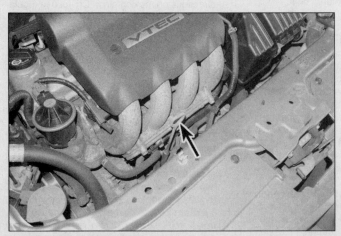

4.2 Engine oil dipstick location

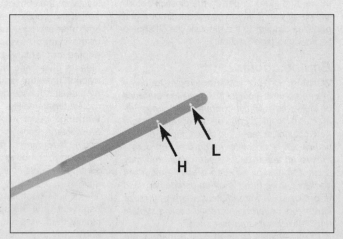

4.4 The oil level should be at or near the H mark - if it isn't, add enough oil to bring the level to near the H mark

4.6 Oil filler cap location

4.8a Coolant reservoir MIN and MAX marks; add coolant to bring the level half-way between the marks - 2007/2008 models

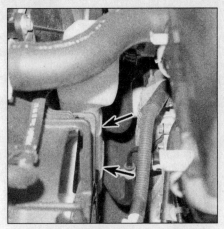

4.8b Coolant reservoir MIN and MAX marks - 2009 and later models

dipstick. Do not allow the level to drop below the L mark or oil starvation may cause engine damage. Conversely, overfilling the engine (adding oil above the H mark) may cause oil fouled spark plugs, oil leaks or oil seal failures.

6   Wipe the area around the filler cap, then remove the cap from the valve cover to add oil (see illustration). Use a funnel to prevent spills. After adding the oil, install the filler cap hand tight. Start the engine and look carefully for any small leaks around the oil filter or drain plug. Stop the engine and check the oil level again after it has had sufficient time to drain from the upper block and cylinder head galleys.

7   Checking the oil level is an important preventive maintenance step. A continually dropping oil level indicates oil leakage through damaged seals, from loose connections, or past worn rings or valve guides. If the oil looks milky in color or has water droplets in it, a cylinder head gasket may be leaking. The cylinder head should be checked immediately. The condition of the oil should also be checked. Each time you check the oil level, slide your thumb and index finger up the dipstick before wiping off the oil. If you see small dirt or metal particles clinging to the dipstick, the oil should be changed (see Section 7).

Engine coolant

Warning: *Do not allow antifreeze to come in contact with your skin or painted surfaces of the vehicle. Flush contaminated areas immediately with plenty of water. Don't store new coolant or leave old coolant lying around where it's accessible to children or pets - they're attracted by its sweet smell and may drink it. Ingestion of even a small amount of coolant can be fatal! Wipe up garage floor and drip pan spills immediately. Keep antifreeze containers covered and repair cooling system leaks as soon as they're noticed.*

8   All vehicles covered by this manual are equipped with a pressurized coolant recovery system. A white coolant reservoir located in the front of the engine compartment is connected by a hose to the base of the radiator cap (see illustrations). If the coolant gets too hot during engine operation, coolant can escape through the relief valve in the cap, then through a connecting hose into the reservoir. As the engine cools, the coolant is automatically drawn back into the cooling system to maintain the correct level.

9   The coolant level should be checked regularly. It must be between the MAX and MIN lines on the tank. If it isn't, allow the fluid in the tank to cool, then remove the cap from the reservoir and add coolant to bring the level mid-way between the marks. Use only the specified type of coolant recommended by your owner's manual or in this Chapter's Specifications. Do not use supplemental inhibitor additives. If only a small amount of coolant is required to bring the system up to the proper level, water can be used. However, repeated additions of water will dilute the recommended antifreeze and water solution. In order to maintain the proper ratio of antifreeze and water, it is advisable to top up the coolant level with the correct coolant.

10   If the coolant level drops within a short time after replenishment, there may be a leak in the system. Inspect the radiator, hoses, engine coolant filler cap, drain plugs, air bleeder plugs and water pump. If no leak is evident, have the radiator cap pressure tested by a dealer service department or other automotive repair facility.

Warning: *Never remove the radiator cap or the coolant recovery reservoir cap when the engine is running or has just been shut down, because the cooling system is hot. Escaping steam and scalding liquid could cause serious injury.*

11   If it is necessary to open the radiator cap, wait until the system has cooled completely, then wrap a thick cloth around the cap and slowly unscrew it. If you hear hissing or if any steam escapes, wait until the system has cooled further, then remove the cap.

12   When checking the coolant level, always note its condition. It should be relatively clear. If it is brown or rust colored, the system should be drained, flushed and refilled. Even if the coolant appears to be normal, the corrosion inhibitors wear out with use, so it must be replaced at the specified intervals.

13   Do not allow antifreeze to come in contact with your skin or painted surfaces of the vehicle. Flush contacted areas immediately with plenty of water.

Windshield washer fluid

14   Fluid for the windshield washer system is stored in a plastic reservoir which is located on the right side of the engine compartment, just behind the headlight (see illustrations). In milder climates, plain water can be used to top up the reservoir, but the reservoir should be kept no more than two-thirds full to allow for expansion should the water freeze. In colder climates, the use of a specially designed windshield washer fluid, available at your dealer and any auto parts store, will help lower the freezing point of the fluid. Mix the solution with water in accordance with the manufacturer's directions on the container. Do not use regular antifreeze. It will damage the vehicle's paint.

Battery electrolyte

15   On models not equipped with a sealed battery, check the electrolyte level of all six battery cells. On models with a translucent battery case, minimum and maximum level marks are present on the side of the case; keep the electrolyte level at the MAX mark. On models with an opaque case, carefully remove the cell caps to check the level or add water. Some batteries have six individual cell plugs that can be unscrewed, but others have two cell caps that must be carefully pried off (see illustration).

Caution: *Overfilling the cells may cause electrolyte to spill over during periods of heavy charging, causing corrosion or damage.*

4.14a Windshield washer fluid reservoir location (2007/2008 models shown)

4.14b On 2007 and 2008 models, remove the cap and pull out the dipstick to check the windshield washer fluid level

4.14c Windshield washer fluid reservoir (2009 and later models)

4.15 Some maintenance-type batteries have individual cell plugs that can be unscrewed, while others have caps which must be pried off

4.17a Brake fluid reservoir (A) and clutch fluid reservoir (B) MIN and MAX marks (2007/2008 models)

4.17b Brake fluid reservoir MAX and MIN marks (2009 and later models)

Brake and clutch fluids

16   The brake master cylinder is mounted on the front of the power booster unit in the engine compartment. The hydraulic clutch master cylinder used on manual transaxle vehicles is located next to the brake master cylinder.

17   To check the fluid level of the brake and clutch master cylinders, simply look at the MAX and MIN marks on the reservoir (see illustrations). The level should be between the marks.

18   If the level is low, wipe the top of the reservoir cover with a clean rag to prevent contamination of the brake system before lifting the cover.

19   Add only the specified brake fluid to the brake and clutch reservoirs (see this Chapter's Specifications or your owner's manual). Mixing different types of brake fluid can damage the system. Fill the brake master cylinder reservoir only to the MAX line.

Warning: *Use caution when filling the reser-*

voir - brake fluid can harm your eyes and damage painted surfaces. Do not use brake fluid that is more than one year old or has been left open. Brake fluid absorbs moisture from the air. Excess moisture can cause a dangerous loss of braking.

20   While the reservoir cap is removed, inspect the master cylinder reservoir for contamination. If deposits, dirt particles or water droplets are present, the system should be drained and refilled.

21   After filling the reservoir to the proper level, make sure the lid is properly seated to prevent fluid leakage and/or system pressure loss.

22   The fluid in the brake master cylinder will drop slightly as the brake pads at each wheel wear down during normal operation. If either master cylinder requires repeated replenishing to keep it at the proper level, this is an indication of leakage in the brake or clutch system, which should be corrected immediately. If the brake system shows an

indication of leakage, check all brake lines and connections, along with the calipers, wheel cylinders and booster (see Section 14). If the hydraulic clutch system shows an indication of leakage, check all clutch lines and connections, along with the clutch release cylinder (see Chapter 8).

23   If, upon checking the brake or clutch master cylinder fluid level, you discover one or both reservoirs empty or nearly empty, the systems should be bled (see Chapters 8 and 9).

5   Tire and tire pressure checks (every 250 miles or weekly)

1   Periodic inspection of the tires may spare you from the inconvenience of being stranded with a flat tire. It can also provide you with vital information regarding possible problems in the steering and suspension systems before major damage occurs.

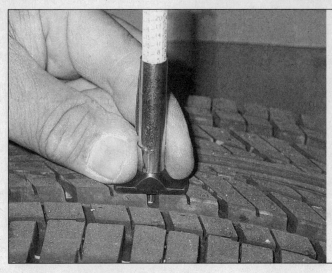

5.2 A tire tread depth indicator should be used to monitor tire wear - they are available at auto parts stores and service stations and cost very little

2   Normal tread wear can be monitored with a simple, inexpensive device known as a tread depth indicator (see illustration). When the tread depth reaches the specified minimum, replace the tire(s).

3   Note any abnormal tread wear (see illustration). Tread pattern irregularities such as cupping, flat spots and more wear on one side than the other are indications of front end alignment and/or balance problems. If any of these conditions are noted, take the vehicle to a tire shop or service station to correct the problem.

4   Look closely for cuts, punctures and embedded nails or tacks. Sometimes a tire will hold its air pressure for a short time or leak down very slowly even after a nail has embedded itself into the tread. If a slow leak persists, check the valve stem core to make sure it is tight (see illustration). Examine the tread for an object that may have embedded itself into the tire or for a plug that may have begun to leak (radial tire punctures are repaired with a plug that is installed in a puncture). If a puncture is suspected, it can be easily verified by spraying a solution of soapy water onto the puncture area (see illustration). The soapy solution will bubble if there is a leak. Unless the puncture is inordinately large, a tire shop or gas station can usually repair the punctured tire.

5   Carefully inspect the inner sidewall of each tire for evidence of brake fluid leakage. If you see any, inspect the brakes immediately.

6   Correct tire air pressure adds miles to the lifespan of the tires, improves mileage and enhances overall ride quality. Tire pressure cannot be accurately estimated by looking at a tire, particularly if it is a radial. A tire pressure gauge is therefore essential. Keep an accurate gauge in the glove box. The pressure gauges fitted to the nozzles of air hoses at gas stations are often inaccurate.

7   Always check tire pressure when the tires are cold. "Cold" in this case, means the

UNDERINFLATION

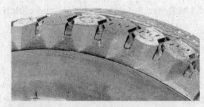

CUPPING

Cupping may be caused by:
- Underinflation and/or mechanical irregularities such as out-of-balance condition of wheel and/or tire, and bent or damaged wheel.
- Loose or worn steering tie-rod or steering idler arm.
- Loose, damaged or worn front suspension parts.

OVERINFLATION

INCORRECT TOE-IN OR EXTREME CAMBER

FEATHERING DUE TO MISALIGNMENT

5.3 This chart will help you determine the condition of your tires, the probable cause(s) of abnormal wear and the corrective action necessary

vehicle has not been driven over a mile in the three hours preceding a tire pressure check. A pressure rise of four to eight pounds is not uncommon once the tires are warm.

8   Unscrew the valve cap protruding from the wheel or hubcap and push the gauge firmly onto the valve (see illustration). Note the reading on the gauge and compare this figure to the recommended tire pressure shown on the tire placard on the left door. Be sure to reinstall the valve cap to keep dirt and moisture out of the valve stem mechanism. Check all four tires and, if necessary, add enough air to bring them up to the recommended pressure levels.

9   Don't forget to keep the spare tire inflated to the specified pressure (consult your owner's manual). Note that the air pressure specified for the compact spare is significantly higher than the pressure of the regular tires.

6   Automatic transaxle fluid level check (every 3000 miles or 3 months)

1   The level of the automatic transaxle fluid should be carefully maintained. Low fluid level can lead to slipping or loss of drive, while overfilling can cause foaming, loss of fluid and transaxle damage.

2   The transaxle fluid level should only be checked when the transaxle is hot (at its normal operating temperature). If the vehicle has just been driven over 10 miles (15 miles in a frigid climate), and the fluid temperature is 160 to 175-degrees F, the transaxle is hot. **Caution:** *If the vehicle has just been driven for a long time at high speed or in city traffic in hot weather, or if it has been pulling a trailer, an accurate fluid level reading cannot be obtained. Allow the fluid to cool down for about 30 minutes.*

3   If the vehicle has not been driven, park the vehicle on level ground, set the parking brake, then start the engine and bring it to operating temperature. While the engine is idling, depress the brake pedal and move the selector lever through all the gear ranges, beginning and ending in Park.

4   Turn off the engine. Remove the dipstick from its bore (see illustrations) and check the level of the fluid on the dipstick.

5   Wipe the fluid from the dipstick with a clean rag and reinsert it back into the transaxle completely.

6   Pull the dipstick out again and note the fluid level. If the level is at the low side of the range, add the specified automatic transaxle fluid into the dipstick hole using a funnel.

7   Add just enough of the recommended

5.4a If a tire loses air on a steady basis, check the valve core first to make sure it's snug (special inexpensive wrenches are commonly available at auto parts stores)

5.4b If the valve core is tight, raise the corner of the vehicle with the low tire and spray a soapy water solution onto the tread as the tire is turned slowly - slow leaks will cause small bubbles to appear

5.8 To extend the life of your tires, check the air pressure at least once a week with an accurate gauge (don't forget the spare!)

6.4a Transaxle dipstick location

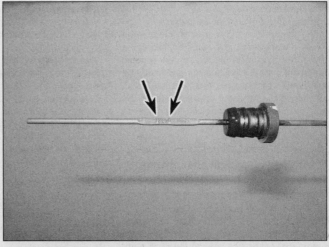

6.4b The fluid level should be within the crosshatched range

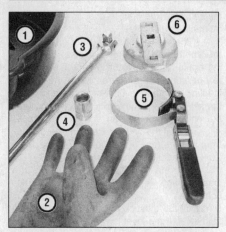

7.2 These tools are required when changing the engine oil and filter

1   **Drain pan** - *It should be fairly shallow in depth, but wide in order to prevent spills*
2   **Rubber gloves** - *When removing the drain plug and filter, it is inevitable that you will get oil on your hands (the gloves will prevent burns)*
3   **Breaker bar** - *Sometimes the oil drain plug is pretty tight and a long breaker bar is needed to loosen it*
4   **Socket** - *To be used with the breaker bar or a ratchet (must be the correct size to fit the drain plug)*
5   **Filter wrench** - *This is a metal band-type wrench, which requires clearance around the filter to be effective*
6   **Filter wrench** - *This type fits on the bottom of the filter and can be turned with a ratchet or breaker bar (different size wrenches are available for different types of filters)*

7.5 Use a proper size box-end wrench or socket to remove the oil drain plug and avoid rounding it off

7.10 The oil filter is located on the front side of the oil pan. Use an oil filter wrench for removal; DO NOT use the wrench to tighten the new filter

fluid to fill the transaxle to the proper level. Add the fluid a little at a time and keep checking the level until it is correct. Once the fluid level is correct, reinstall the dipstick, making sure it seats completely.
Caution: *Don't overfill the transaxle.*
8   The condition of the fluid should also be checked along with the level. If the fluid at the end of the dipstick is black or a dark reddish brown color, or if it emits a burned smell, the fluid should be changed (see Section 25). If you are in doubt about the condition of the fluid, purchase some new fluid and compare the two for color and smell.

---

7   Engine oil and oil filter change (every 7500 miles or 6 months)

Note: *These vehicles are equipped with a Maintenance Minder system on the instrument panel that notifies the driver when the system deems it necessary to change the oil. A number of factors are taken into consideration to determine when the oil should be considered*

worn out. Generally, this system will allow the vehicle to accumulate more miles between oil changes than traditional intervals, but we believe that frequent oil changes are cheap insurance and will prolong engine life. If you do decide not to change your oil every 7500 miles and rely on the oil life indicator instead, make sure you don't exceed 10,000 miles before the oil is changed, regardless of what the oil life indicator shows.
1   Frequent oil changes are the best preventive maintenance the home mechanic can give the engine, because aging oil becomes diluted and contaminated, which leads to premature engine wear.
2   Make sure that you have all the necessary tools before you begin this procedure (see illustration). You should also have plenty of rags or newspapers handy for mopping up any spills.
3   Park the vehicle on a level spot. Start the engine and allow it to reach its normal operating temperature (the needle on the temperature gauge should be at least above the bottom mark). Warm oil and contaminates will flow out more easily. Turn off the engine when it's warmed up. Remove the filler cap from the valve cover.
4   Raise the vehicle and support it securely on jackstands.
Warning: *To avoid personal injury, never get beneath the vehicle when it is supported only by a jack. The jack provided with your vehicle is designed solely for raising the vehicle to remove and replace the wheels. Always use jackstands to support the vehicle when it becomes necessary to place your body underneath the vehicle.*
5   Being careful not to touch the hot exhaust components, place the drain pan under the drain plug in the bottom of the pan and remove the plug (see illustration). You may want to wear gloves while unscrewing the plug the final few turns if the engine is really hot.
6   Allow the old oil to drain into the pan. It may be necessary to move the pan farther

under the engine as the oil flow slows to a trickle.
7   After all the oil has drained, wipe off the drain plug with a clean rag. Even minute metal particles clinging to the plug would immediately contaminate the new oil. Inspect the old oil for the presence of metal shavings and chips.
8   Clean the area around the drain plug opening, reinstall the plug and tighten it to the torque listed in this Chapter's Specifications.
9   Move the drain pan into position under the oil filter.
10   Loosen the oil filter by turning it counterclockwise with the filter wrench (see illustration). Once the filter is loose, use your hands to unscrew it. Just as the filter is detached from the block, immediately tilt the open end up to prevent the oil inside the filter from spilling out.
11   With a clean rag, wipe off the oil filter mounting surface. Make sure that none of the old gasket remains stuck to the mounting surface. It can be removed with a scraper if necessary.
12   Compare the old filter with the new one to make sure they are the same type. Smear some engine oil on the rubber gasket of the new filter and screw it into place (see illustration). Because over-tightening the filter will damage the gasket, do not use a filter wrench to tighten the filter. Tighten it by hand until the gasket contacts the seating surface. Then seat the filter by giving it an additional 3/4-turn.
13   Remove all tools, rags, etc. from under the vehicle, being careful not to spill the oil in the drain pan, then lower the vehicle.
14   Add new oil to the engine. Use a spout or funnel to prevent oil from spilling onto the top of the engine. Pour 3.8 quarts of fresh oil into the engine. Wait a few minutes to allow the oil to drain into the pan, then check the level on the oil dipstick (see Section 4 if necessary). If the oil level is at or near the H mark, install the filler cap hand tight, start the engine and allow the new oil to circulate.

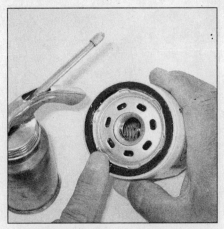

7.12 Lubricate the oil filter gasket with clean engine oil before installing the filter on the engine

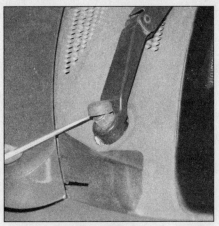

8.3 Gently pry off the trim cap and check the tightness of the wiper arm retaining nut

8.5a Some wiper blades are equipped with a lock piece that must be pried up first

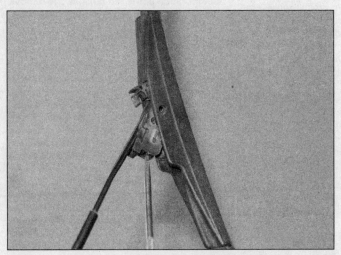

8.5b Press on the release tab and push the blade assembly down out of the hook in the arm

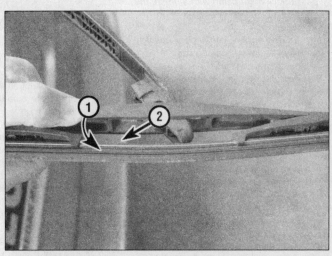

8.8 Rotate the rear wiper blade perpendicular to the arm (1), then pull the blade out of the slot in the arm (2)

15   Allow the engine to run for about a minute. While the engine is running, look under the vehicle and check for leaks at the oil pan drain plug and around the oil filter. If either is leaking, stop the engine and tighten the plug or filter slightly.

16   Wait a few minutes to allow the oil to trickle down into the pan, then recheck the level on the dipstick and, if necessary, add enough oil to bring the level to the H mark.

17   During the first few trips after an oil change, make it a point to check frequently for leaks and proper oil level.

18   The old oil drained from the engine cannot be reused in its present state and should be disposed of. Check with your local auto parts store, disposal facility or environmental agency to see if they will accept the oil for recycling. After the oil has cooled it can be drained into a container (capped plastic jugs, topped bottles, milk cartons, etc.) for transport to one of these disposal sites. Don't dispose

of the oil by pouring it on the ground or down a drain!

19   Reset the Maintenance Minder (see Section 30).

8   Wiper blade inspection and replacement (every 7500 miles or 6 months)

1   The windshield wiper and blade assembly should be inspected periodically for damage, loose components and cracked or worn blade elements.

2   Road film can build up on the wiper blades and affect their efficiency, so they should be washed regularly with a mild detergent solution.

3   The action of the wiping mechanism can loosen bolts, nuts and fasteners, so they should be checked and tightened, as neces-

sary (see illustration), at the same time the wiper blades are checked.

4   If the wiper blade elements are cracked, worn or warped, or no longer clean adequately, they should be replaced with new ones.

Windshield wiper blades

5   Lift the arm assembly away from the glass for clearance, press on the release lever, then slide the wiper blade assembly out of the hook in the end of the arm (see illustrations).

6   Installation is the reverse of removal.

Rear wiper blade

7   Raise the wiper arm and blade away from the glass.

8   Rotate the blade perpendicular to the arm, then detach the blade from the slot in the arm (see illustration).

9   Installation is the reverse of removal.

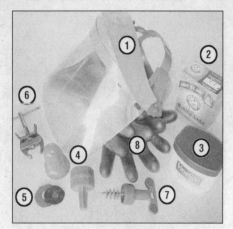

9.1 Tools and materials required for battery maintenance

1   *Face shield/safety goggles - When removing corrosion with a brush, the acidic particles can easily fly up into your eyes*

2   *Baking soda - A solution of baking soda and water can be used to neutralize corrosion*

3   *Petroleum jelly - A layer of this on the battery posts will help prevent corrosion*

4   *Battery post/cable cleaner - This wire brush cleaning tool will remove all traces of corrosion from the battery posts and cable clamps*

5   *Treated felt washers - Placing one of these on each post, directly under the cable clamps, will help prevent corrosion*

6   *Puller - Sometimes the cable clamps are very difficult to pull off the posts, even after the nut/bolt has been completely loosened. This tool pulls the clamp straight up and off the post without damage*

7   *Battery post/cable cleaner - Here is another cleaning tool that is a slightly different version of Number 4 above, but it does the same thing*

8   *Rubber gloves - Another safety item to consider when servicing the battery; remember that's acid inside the battery!*

---

9   Battery check, maintenance and charging (every 7500 miles or 6 months)

Warning: *Certain precautions must be followed when checking and servicing the battery. Hydrogen gas, which is highly flammable, is always present in the battery cells, so keep lighted tobacco and all other open flames and sparks away from the battery. The electrolyte inside the battery is actually dilute sulfuric acid, which will cause injury if splashed on your skin or in your eyes. It will also ruin clothes and painted surfaces. When removing the battery cables, always detach the negative cable first and hook it up last!*

9.6a Battery terminal corrosion usually appears as light, fluffy powder

1   A routine preventive maintenance program for the battery in your vehicle is the only way to ensure quick and reliable starts. But before performing any battery maintenance, make sure that you have the proper equipment necessary to work safely around the battery (see illustration).

2   There are also several precautions that should be taken whenever battery maintenance is performed. Before servicing the battery, always turn the engine and all accessories off and disconnect the cable from the negative terminal of the battery.

3   The battery produces hydrogen gas, which is both flammable and explosive. Never create a spark, smoke or light a match around the battery. Always charge the battery in a ventilated area.

4   Electrolyte contains poisonous and corrosive sulfuric acid. Do not allow it to get in your eyes, on your skin or on your clothes. Never ingest it. Wear protective safety glasses when working near the battery. Keep children away from the battery.

5   Note the external condition of the battery. If the positive terminal and cable clamp on your vehicle's battery is equipped with a rubber protector, make sure it isn't torn or damaged. It should completely cover the terminal. Look for any corroded or loose connections, cracks in the case or cover or loose hold-down clamps. Also check the entire length of each cable for cracks and frayed conductors.

6   If corrosion, which looks like white, fluffy deposits (see illustration) is evident, particularly around the terminals, the battery should be removed for cleaning. Loosen the cable clamp bolts with a wrench, being careful to remove the ground cable first, and slide them off the terminals (see illustration). Then disconnect the hold-down clamp bolt and nut, remove the clamp and lift the battery from the engine compartment.

7   Clean the cable clamps thoroughly with a battery brush or a terminal cleaner and a solution of warm water and baking soda (see illustration). Wash the terminals and the top of the battery case with the same solution but

9.6b Removing a cable from the battery post with a wrench - sometimes special battery pliers are required for this procedure if corrosion has caused deterioration of the nut hex (always remove the ground cable first and hook it up last!)

make sure that the solution doesn't get into the battery. When cleaning the cables, terminals and battery top, wear safety goggles and rubber gloves to prevent any solution from coming in contact with your eyes or hands. Wear old clothes too - even diluted, sulfuric acid splashed onto clothes will burn holes in them. If the terminals have been extensively corroded, clean them up with a terminal cleaner (see illustration). Thoroughly wash all cleaned areas with plain water.

8   Make sure the battery tray is in good condition and the hold-down clamp bolt or nut is tight. If the battery is removed from the tray, make sure no parts remain in the bottom of the tray when the battery is reinstalled. When reinstalling the hold-down clamp bolt or nut, do not over-tighten it.

9   Information on removing and installing the battery can be found in Chapter 5. Information on jump starting can be found at the front of this manual. For more detailed battery checking procedures, refer to the Haynes Automotive Electrical Manual.

Cleaning

10   Corrosion on the hold-down components, battery case and surrounding areas can be removed with a solution of water and baking soda. Thoroughly rinse all cleaned areas with plain water.

11   Any metal parts of the vehicle damaged by corrosion should be covered with a zinc-based primer, then painted.

Charging

Warning: *When batteries are being charged, hydrogen gas, which is very explosive and flammable, is produced. Do not smoke or allow open flames near a charging or a recently charged battery. Wear eye protection when near the battery during charging. Also, make sure the charger is unplugged before connecting or disconnecting the battery from the charger.*

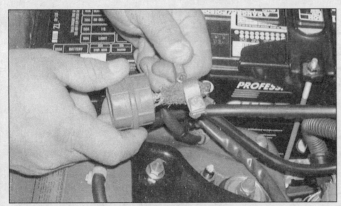

9.7a When cleaning the cable clamps, all corrosion must be removed (the inside of the clamp is tapered to match the taper on the post, so don't remove too much material!)

9.7b Regardless of the type of tool used to clean the battery posts, a clean, shiny surface should be the result

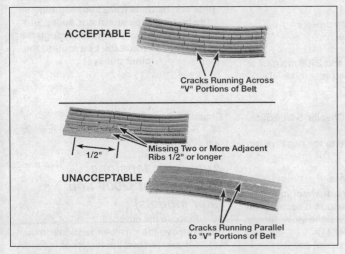

10.3 Here are some of the more common problems associated with drivebelts (check the belts very carefully to prevent an untimely breakdown)

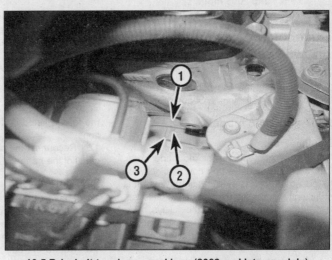

10.5 Drivebelt tensioner markings (2009 and later models)

| 1 | Stationary mark | 3 | Wear limit |
| 2 | New belt range | | |

12   Slow-rate charging is the best way to restore a battery that's discharged to the point where it will not start the engine. It's also a good way to maintain the battery charge in a vehicle that's only driven a few miles between starts. Maintaining the battery charge is particularly important in the winter when the battery must work harder to start the engine and electrical accessories that drain the battery are in greater use.

13   It's best to use a one or two-amp battery charger (sometimes called a "trickle" charger). They are the safest and put the least strain on the battery. They are also the least expensive. For a faster charge, you can use a higher amperage charger, but don't use one rated more than 1/10th the amp/hour rating of the battery. Rapid boost charges that claim to restore the power of the battery in one to two hours are hardest on the battery and can damage batteries not in good condition. This type of charging should only be used in emergency situations.

14   The average time necessary to charge a battery should be listed in the instructions that come with the charger. As a general rule, a trickle charger will charge a battery in 12 to 16 hours.

10   Drivebelt check (every 7500 miles or 6 months) and replacement

Check

1   The good condition and proper tension of the drivebelt is critical to the operation of the engine. Because of their composition and the high stresses to which they are subjected, drivebelts stretch and deteriorate as they get older. They must therefore be periodically inspected.

2   The serpentine drivebelt transmits power to all the accessories. On 2007 and 2008 models, the drivebelt tension is adjusted by the alternator's position in its mounting bracket. On 2009 and later models, an automatic tensioner is used.

3   With the engine off, open the hood and locate the drivebelt. With a flashlight, check the belt for separation of the adhesive rubber on both sides of the core, core separation from the belt side, a severed core, separation of the ribs from the adhesive rubber, cracking or separation of the ribs, and torn or worn ribs or cracks in the inner ridges of the ribs (see illustration). Also check for fraying and glazing, which gives the belt a shiny appearance. Both sides of the belt should be inspected, which means you will have to twist the belt to check the underside. Use your fingers to feel the belt where you can't see it. If any of the above conditions are evident, replace the belt.

2007 and 2008 models

4   Apply about 20 pounds of force to the belt along the longest belt run and see how much the belt deflects. The belt should deflect no more than 1/4-inch. If it deflects more than that, it's in need of adjustment.

2009 and later models

5   Check the drivebelt wear indicator for excessive stretch (see illustration). If the drivebelt indicator is out of limit, replace the drivebelt.

10.7 Drivebelt tension adjuster bolt (2007 and 2008 models)

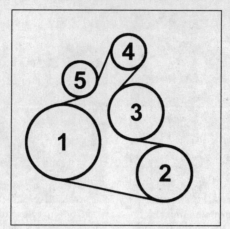

10.8 Drivebelt routing diagram

1   *Crankshaft pulley*
2   *Air conditioning compressor*
3   *Water pump pulley*
4   *Alternator*
5   *Idler pulley (2007 and 2008 models) or tensioner (2009 and later models)*

10.14 Release the tension using a wrench, rotating the tensioner counterclockwise (this can be done from above to remove the belt from the alternator pulley, but it will be necessary to work through the wheelwell to route the belt around the other pulleys)

Drivebelt replacement (and, on 2007 and 2008 models, adjustment)

6   Disconnect the cable from the negative terminal of the battery (see Chapter 5).

2007 and 2008 models

Replacement

7   Loosen the alternator mounting bolts, then turn the adjuster bolt counterclockwise to loosen the belt (see illustration). When it is sufficiently loose, slip the belt off the pulleys.
8   Install the new belt over the pulleys, making sure it's routed correctly (see illustration). Also make sure the belt is properly seated on all of the pulleys.
9   Reset the Maintenance Minder (see Section 30).

Adjustment

10   Loosen the alternator mounting bolts (if not already done). Turn the adjuster bolt (see illustration 10.7) clockwise to apply tension to the belt until it deflects no more than 1/4-inch when about 20 pounds of force is applied to the longest belt run.
Caution: *Don't overtighten the belt.*
11   Tighten the alternator mounting bolts to

the torque listed in the Chapter 5 Specifications.
12   Reconnect the cable to the negative terminal of the battery.

2009 and later models

13   Loosen the right front wheel lug nuts. Raise the vehicle and support it securely on jackstands. Remove the right inner fender splash shield (see Chapter 11).
14   Rotate the belt tensioner counterclockwise using a wrench on the hex casting of the tensioner arm to release tension on the drivebelt, then remove the drivebelt from the pulleys (see illustration).
15   Install the new drivebelt, making sure that it's properly routed (see illustration 10.8).
16   Reconnect the battery (see Chapter 5). Install the inner fender splash shield and the wheel and lug nuts, tightening the lug nuts finger tight. Lower the vehicle and then tighten the lug nuts to the torque listed in this

Chapter's Specifications.
17   Reset the Maintenance Minder (see Section 30).

Automatic tensioner replacement (2009 and later models)

18   Remove the drivebelt.
19   Remove the drivebelt tensioner mounting bolts and remove the tensioner (see illustration).
20   Installation is the reverse of removal. Tighten the tensioner mounting bolts to the torque listed in this Chapter's Specifications.

Tensioner pulley replacement (2009 and later models)

21   Remove the tensioner.
22   Remove the tensioner pulley bolt, washer and pulley.
23   Install the new pulley and washer. Tighten the pulley bolt to the torque listed in this Chapter's Specifications.

---

11   Underhood hose check and replacement (every 7500 miles or 6 months)

Caution: *Replacement of air conditioning hoses must be left to a dealer service department or air conditioning shop that has the equipment to depressurize the system safely. Never remove air conditioning components or hoses until the system has been depressurized.*

10.19 Drivebelt tensioner lower mounting bolt; upper bolt is accessed from above (2009 and later models)

General

1   High temperatures in the engine compartment can cause the deterioration of the rubber and plastic hoses used for engine, accessory and emission systems operation. Periodic inspection should be made for cracks, loose clamps, material hardening and leaks.

2   Information specific to the cooling system hoses can be found in Section 12.

3   Some, but not all, hoses are secured to the fittings with clamps. Where clamps are used, check to be sure they haven't lost their tension, allowing the hose to leak. If clamps aren't used, make sure the hose has not expanded and/or hardened where it slips over the fitting, allowing it to leak.

Vacuum hoses

4   It's quite common for vacuum hoses, especially those in the emissions system, to be color coded or identified by colored stripes molded into them. Various systems require hoses with different wall thickness, collapse resistance and temperature resistance. When replacing hoses, be sure the new ones are made of the same material.

5   Often the only effective way to check a hose is to remove it completely from the vehicle. If more than one hose is removed, be sure to label the hoses and fittings to ensure correct installation.

6   When checking vacuum hoses, be sure to include any plastic T-fittings in the check. Inspect the fittings for cracks and the hose where it fits over the fitting for distortion, which could cause leakage.

7   A small piece of vacuum hose (1/4-inch inside diameter) can be used as a stethoscope to detect vacuum leaks. Hold one end of the hose to your ear and probe around vacuum hoses and fittings, listening for the hissing sound characteristic of a vacuum leak. **Warning:** *When probing with the vacuum hose stethoscope, be very careful not to come into contact with moving engine components such as the drivebelts, cooling fan, etc.*

Fuel hose

Warning: *There are certain precautions which must be taken when inspecting or servicing fuel system components. Work in a well ventilated area and do not allow open flames (cigarettes, appliance pilot lights, etc.) or bare light bulbs near the work area. Mop up any spills immediately and do not store fuel-soaked rags where they could ignite.*

8   Check all rubber fuel lines for deterioration and chafing. Check especially for cracks in areas where the hose bends and just before fittings, such as where a hose attaches to the fuel filter.

9   High quality fuel line, meeting the manufacturer's original specifications, should be used for fuel line replacement. Never, under any circumstances, use unreinforced vacuum line, clear plastic tubing or water hose for fuel lines.

10   Spring-type clamps are commonly used on fuel lines. These clamps often lose their tension over a period of time, and can be sprung during removal. Replace all spring-type clamps with screw clamps whenever a hose is replaced.

Metal lines

11   Sections of metal line are often used for fuel line between the fuel pump and fuel injection unit. Check carefully to be sure the line has not been bent or crimped and that cracks have not started in the line.

12   If a section of metal fuel line must be replaced, only seamless steel tubing should be used, since copper and aluminum tubing don't have the strength necessary to withstand normal engine vibration.

13   Check the metal brake lines where they enter the master cylinder and brake proportioning unit (if used) for cracks in the lines or loose fittings. Any sign of brake fluid leakage calls for an immediate thorough inspection of the brake system.

12   Cooling system check (every 7500 miles or 6 months)

1   Many major engine failures can be attributed to a faulty cooling system. If the vehicle is equipped with an automatic transaxle, the cooling system also cools the transaxle fluid and thus plays an important role in prolonging transaxle life.

2   The cooling system should be checked with the engine cold. Do this before the vehicle is driven for the day or after the engine has been shut off for at least three hours.

3   Slowly unscrew the radiator cap. If you hear a hissing sound (indicating there is still pressure in the system), wait until it stops. Continue turning until the cap can be removed. Thoroughly clean the cap, inside and out, with clean water. Also clean the filler neck on the radiator. All traces of corrosion should be removed. The coolant inside the radiator should be relatively transparent. If it's rust colored, the system should be drained and refilled (see Section 23). If the coolant level isn't up to the top, add additional antifreeze/coolant mixture (see Section 4).

4   Carefully check the large upper and lower radiator hoses along with the smaller diameter heater hoses which run from the engine to the firewall. Inspect each hose along its entire length, replacing any hose which is cracked, swollen or shows signs of deterioration. Cracks may become more apparent if the hose is squeezed (see illustration). Regardless of condition, it's a good idea to replace hoses with new ones every two years.

5   Make sure that all hose connections are tight. A leak in the cooling system will usually show up as white or rust colored deposits on the areas adjoining the leak. If wire-type clamps are used at the ends of the hoses, it may be a good idea to replace them with

Check for a chafed area that could fail prematurely.

Check for a soft area indicating the hose has deteriorated inside.

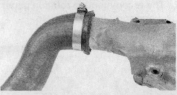

Overtightening the clamp on a hardened hose will damage the hose and cause a leak.

Check each hose for swelling and oil-soaked ends. Cracks and breaks can be located by squeezing the hose.

12.4 Hoses, like drivebelts, have a habit of failing at the worst possible time - to prevent the inconvenience of a blown radiator or heater hose, inspect them carefully as shown here

more secure screw-type clamps.

6   Use compressed air or a soft brush to remove bugs, leaves, etc. from the front of the radiator or air conditioning condenser. Be careful not to damage the delicate cooling fins or cut yourself on them.

7   Every other inspection, or at the first indication of cooling system problems, have the cap and system pressure tested. If you don't have a pressure tester, most repair shops will do this for a minimal charge.

13   Tire rotation (every 7500 miles or 6 months)

1   The tires should be rotated at the specified intervals and whenever uneven wear is noticed. Since the vehicle will be raised and the tires removed anyway, check the brakes (see Section 14) at this time.

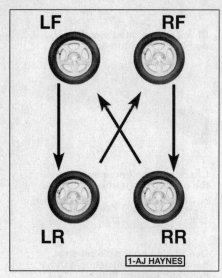

13.2a The recommended rotation pattern for non-directional tires

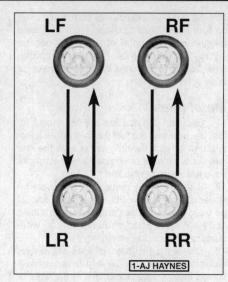

13.2b The recommended tire rotation pattern for directional tires

14.6 You will find an inspection hole like this in each caliper - placing a ruler across the hole should enable you to determine the thickness of remaining pad material

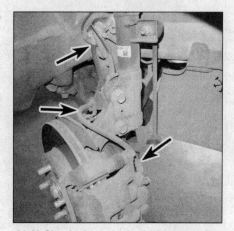

14.11 Check along the brake hoses and at each fitting for deterioration and cracks

2   Tires must be rotated in a specific pattern (see illustrations).
3   Refer to *Jacking and towing* at the front of this manual for the proper procedures to follow when jacking the vehicle and changing a tire. If the brakes are to be checked, do not apply the parking brake as stated. Make sure the tires are blocked to prevent the vehicle from rolling.
4   Preferably, the entire vehicle should be raised at the same time. This can be done on a hoist or by jacking up each corner and then lowering the vehicle onto jackstands placed under the frame rails. Always use four jackstands and make sure the vehicle is firmly supported.
5   After rotation, check and adjust the tire pressures as necessary and tighten the wheel lug nuts to the torque listed in this Chapter's Specifications.
6   Reset the Maintenance Minder (see Section 30).
7   For further information on the wheels and tires, refer to Chapter 10.

14   Brake check (every 15,000 miles or 12 months)

Warning: *The dust created by the brake system is harmful to your health. Never blow it out with compressed air and don't inhale any of it. An approved filtering mask should be worn when working on the brakes. Do not, under any circumstances, use petroleum-based solvents to clean brake parts. Use brake system cleaner only! Try to use non-asbestos replacement parts whenever possible.*
Note: *For detailed photographs of the brake system, refer to Chapter 9.*
1   In addition to the specified intervals, the brakes should be inspected every time the wheels are removed or whenever a defect is suspected. Any of the following symptoms could indicate a potential brake system defect: The vehicle pulls to one side when the brake pedal is depressed; the brakes make squealing or dragging noises when applied; brake pedal travel is excessive; the pedal pulsates; brake fluid leaks, usually onto the inside of the tire or wheel.
2   The disc brake pads have built-in wear indicators which should make a high-pitched squealing or scraping noise when they are worn to the replacement point. When you hear this noise, replace the pads immediately or expensive damage to the discs can result.
3   Loosen the wheel lug nuts.
4   Raise the vehicle and support it securely on jackstands.
5   Remove the wheels (see Chapter 10, Section 8, or your owner's manual, if necessary).

Front disc brakes

6   There are two pads (an outer and an inner) in each caliper. The pads are visible through inspection holes in each caliper (see illustration), as well as from the top and bot-

tom of each pad.
7   Check the pad thickness by looking at each end of the caliper and through the inspection hole in the caliper body. If the lining material is less than the thickness listed in this Chapter's Specifications, replace the pads.
Note: *Keep in mind that the lining material is riveted or bonded to a metal backing plate and the metal portion is not included in this measurement.*
8   If it is difficult to determine the exact thickness of the remaining pad material by the above method, or if you are at all concerned about the condition of the pads, remove the caliper(s), then remove the pads from the calipers for further inspection (see Chapter 9).
9   Once the pads are removed from the calipers, clean them with brake cleaner and re-measure them with a ruler or a vernier caliper.
10   Measure the disc thickness with a micrometer to make sure that it still has service life remaining. If any disc is thinner than the specified minimum thickness, replace it (see Chapter 9). Even if the disc has service life remaining, check its condition. Look for scoring, gouging and burned spots. If these conditions exist, remove the disc and have it resurfaced (see Chapter 9).
11   Before installing the wheels, check all brake lines and hoses for damage, wear, deformation, cracks, corrosion, leakage, bends and twists, particularly in the vicinity of the rubber hoses at the calipers (see illustration). Check the clamps for tightness and the connections for leakage. Make sure that all hoses and lines are clear of sharp edges, moving parts and the exhaust system. If any of the above conditions are noted, repair, re-route or replace the lines and/or hoses as necessary (see Chapter 9). Install the wheel and install the lug nuts finger tight. Remove the jackstands and lower the vehicle, then tighten the wheel lug nuts to the torque listed in this Chapter's Specifications.

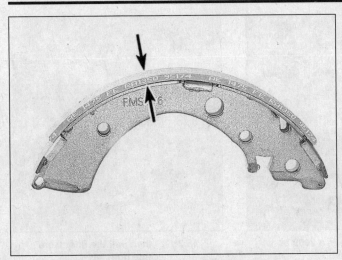

14.13 If the lining is bonded to the brake shoe,measure the lining thickness from the outer surface to the metal shoe, as shownhere; if the lining is riveted to the shoe, measure from the lining outersurface to the rivet head

15.3a Unclip the front of the filter tray/cover. . .

Rear drum brakes

12   Remove the brake drums (see Chapter 9).

13   Note the thickness of the lining material on the brake shoes (see illustration) and look for signs of contamination by brake fluid and grease. If the lining material is within 1/16-inch of the recessed rivets or metal shoes, replace the brake shoes with new ones. The shoes should also be replaced if they are cracked, glazed (shiny lining surfaces) or contaminated with brake fluid or grease (see Chapter 9).

14   Check the shoe return and hold-down springs and the adjusting mechanism to make sure they're installed correctly and in good condition (see Chapter 9). Deteriorated or distorted springs, if not replaced, could allow the linings to drag and wear prematurely.

15   Check the wheel cylinders for leakage by carefully peeling back the rubber boots. If brake fluid is noted behind the boots, the wheel cylinders must be replaced (see Chapter 9).

16   Check the drums for cracks, score marks, deep scratches and hard spots, which will appear as small discolored areas. If imperfections cannot be removed with emery cloth, the drums must be resurfaced by an automotive machine shop (see Chapter 9).

17   Install the brake drums (see Chapter 9). Install the wheels and install the wheel lug nuts finger tight. Remove the jackstands and lower the vehicle, then tighten the wheel lug nuts to the torque listed in this Chapter's Specifications.

Brake booster check

18   Sit in the driver's seat and perform the following sequence of tests.

19   With the brake fully depressed, start the engine - the pedal should move down a little when the engine starts.

20   With the engine running, depress the brake pedal several times - the travel distance should not change.

21   Depress the brake, stop the engine and hold the pedal in for about 30 seconds - the pedal should neither sink nor rise.

22   Restart the engine, run it for about a minute and turn it off. Then firmly depress the brake several times - the pedal travel should decrease with each application.

23   If your brakes do not operate as described above when the preceding tests are performed, the brake booster is either in need of repair or has failed. Refer to Chapter 9 for the removal procedure.

Parking brake

24   Actuate the parking brake with a normal amount of force and count the number of clicks. The adjustment should be within the range listed in the Chapter 9 Specifications. If you hear more or fewer clicks, adjust the parking brake (see Chapter 9).

25   An alternative method of checking the parking brake is to park the vehicle on a steep hill with the parking brake set and the transaxle in Neutral (be sure to stay in the vehicle during this check!). If the parking brake cannot prevent the vehicle from rolling, it is in need of adjustment (see Chapter 9).

15   Cabin air filter replacement (every 15,000 miles or 12 months)

1   The cabin air filter is behind the glove box, in blower motor housing.

2   Open the glove box, push in the sides to disengage the stop on each side of the box, then lower the glove box completely.

3   Remove the filter tray from the blower motor housing (see illustrations).

4   Pull the cabin air filter out of the tray (see illustration).

5   Installation is the reverse of removal.

Note: *Make sure the arrow on the filter is pointing DOWN when installed.*

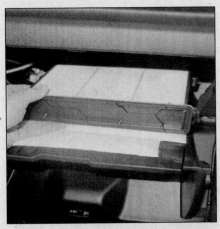

15.3b . . . then slide the assembly out of the housing

15.4 Separate the filter from the tray

16.2a Release the locking clips; this is a 2007/2008 model . . .

16.2b . . . and this is a 2009 or later model. . .

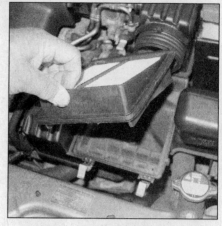

16.2c . . . then pull the filter from the housing

16   Air filter check and replacement (every 30,000 miles or 12 months)

1   The air filter is located inside the air filter housing at the left (driver's) side of the engine compartment.
2   Release the four spring clips that secure the two halves of the housing together, then separate the upper half from the lower half (see illustrations).
3   Pull the filter out of the housing.
4   Inspect the outer surface of the filter element. If it is dirty, replace it. If it is only moderately dusty, it can be reused by blowing it clean from the back to the front surface with compressed air. Because it is a pleated paper type filter, it cannot be washed or oiled. If it cannot be cleaned satisfactorily with compressed air, discard and replace it. While the cover is off, be careful not to drop anything down into the housing.
Caution: *Never drive the vehicle with the air filter removed. Excessive engine wear could result and backfiring could even cause a fire*

under the hood.
5   Wipe out the inside of the air filter housing.
6   Place the new filter into the housing, making sure it seats properly.
7   Reassemble the housing halves and snap the clips into place.
8   Reset the Maintenance Minder (see Section 30).

17   Fuel system check (every 15,000 miles or 12 months)

Warning: *Gasoline is extremely flammable, so take extra precautions when you work on any part of the fuel system. Don't smoke or allow open flames or bare light bulbs near the work area, and don't work in a garage where a gas-type appliance (such as a water heater or clothes dryer) is present. Since gasoline is carcinogenic, wear fuel-resistant gloves when there's a possibility of being exposed to fuel, and, if you spill any fuel on your skin, rinse it off immediately with soap and water. Mop*

up any spills immediately and do not store fuel-soaked rags where they could ignite. The fuel system is under constant pressure, so, if any fuel lines are to be disconnected, the fuel pressure in the system must be relieved first (see Chapter 4). When you perform any kind of work on the fuel system, wear safety glasses and have a Class B type fire extinguisher on hand.

1   If you smell gasoline while driving or after the vehicle has been sitting in the sun, inspect the fuel system immediately.
2   Remove the gas cap and inspect it for damage and corrosion. The gasket should have an unbroken sealing imprint. If the gasket is damaged or corroded, remove it and install a new one.
3   Inspect the fuel feed and return lines for cracks. Make sure the threaded flare nut type connectors (which secure the metal fuel lines to the fuel injection system) and the clamps (which secure the hoses to the in-line fuel filter) are tight.
4   Since some components of the fuel system - the fuel tank and part of the fuel feed and return lines, for example - are underneath the vehicle, they can be inspected more easily with the vehicle raised on a hoist. If that's not possible, raise the vehicle and support it securely on jackstands.
5   With the vehicle raised and safely supported, inspect the gas tank and filler neck for punctures, cracks and other damage. The connection between the filler neck and the tank is particularly critical. Sometimes a rubber filler neck will leak because of loose clamps or deteriorated rubber (see illustration). These are problems a home mechanic can usually rectify.
6   Carefully check all rubber hoses and metal lines leading away from the fuel tank (see illustration). Check for loose connections, deteriorated hoses, crimped lines and other damage. Carefully inspect the lines from the tank to the fuel rail. Repair or replace damaged sections as necessary (see Chapter 4).

17.5 Inspect the fuel filler hoses for cracks and make sure the clamps are tight

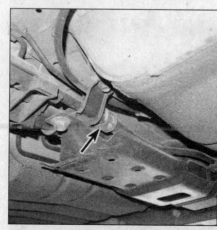

17.6 Carefully inspect the fuel line quick-connect fittings

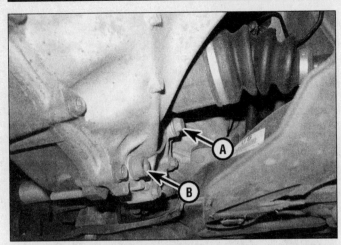

18.1 Manual transaxle check/fill plug (A) and drain plug (B)

19.1 Steering wheel freeplay is the amount of travel between an initial steering input and the point at which the front wheels begin to turn (indicated by a slight resistance)

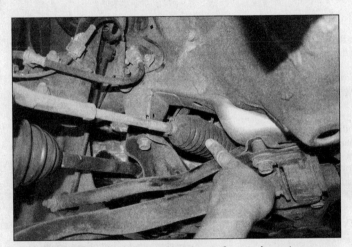

19.6a Check the steering gear boots for cracks or tears

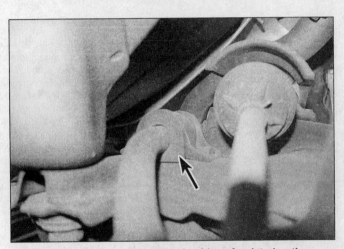

19.6b Check the stabilizer bar bushings for deterioration

18 Manual transaxle lubricant level check (every 15,000 miles or 12 months)

1   The manual transaxle does not have a dipstick. To check the fluid level, raise the vehicle and support it securely on jackstands. Remove the check/fill plug, located just behind the driver's side driveaxle (see illustration). The fluid level should be even with the bottom of the filler plug hole.

2   If the transaxle needs more lubricant, use a gear oil pump to add lubricant until it is up to the filler plug hole. Use the lubricant type listed in this Chapter's Specifications.

3   Install the fill plug and tighten it to the torque listed in this Chapter's Specifications.

19 Steering and suspension check (every 15,000 miles or 12 months)

Note: *For detailed illustrations of the steering and suspension components, refer to Chapter 10.*

With the wheels on the ground

1   With the vehicle stopped and the front wheels pointed straight ahead, rock the steering wheel gently back and forth. If freeplay (see illustration) is excessive, a front wheel bearing, intermediate shaft U-joint, control arm balljoint, tie-rod end or steering gear is worn. Refer to Chapter 10 for the appropriate repair procedure.

2   Other symptoms, such as excessive vehicle body movement over rough roads, swaying (leaning) around corners and binding as the steering wheel is turned, may indicate faulty steering and/or suspension components.

3   Check the shock absorbers by pushing down and releasing the vehicle several times at each corner. If the vehicle does not come back to a level position within one or two bounces, the shocks/struts are worn and must be replaced. When bouncing the vehicle up and down, listen for squeaks and noises from the suspension components.

Under the vehicle

4   Raise the vehicle with a floor jack and support it securely on jackstands.

5   Check the tires for irregular wear patterns and proper inflation (see Section 5).

6   Inspect the universal joint between the steering shaft and the steering gear housing. Check the steering gear housing for grease leakage. Make sure that the boots are not damaged and that the boot clamps are not loose (see illustration).Check the tie-rod ends for excessive play. Look for loose bolts, broken or disconnected parts and deteriorated rubber bushings on all suspension and steering components (see illustration). While an assistant turns the steering wheel from side-to-side, check the steering components for free movement, chafing and binding. If the steering components do not seem to be reacting with the movement of the steering wheel, try to determine where the slack is located.

7   Check the balljoints by moving each control arm up-and-down with a prybar to ensure that the balljoint has no play. If any balljoint does have play, replace it. See Chapter 10 for

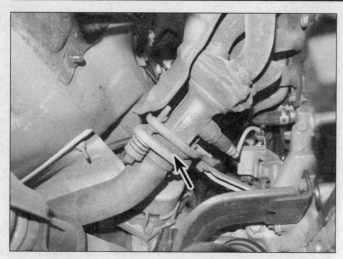

20.2 Check the flange connections for exhaust leaks - also check that the retaining bolts or nuts are securely tightened

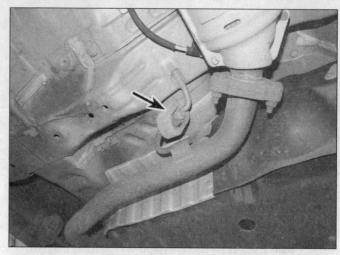

20.4 Check the exhaust system hangers for damage and cracks

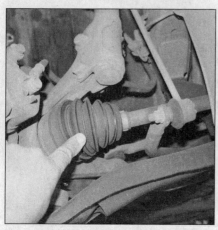

21.2 Check the driveaxle boot for cracks or leaking grease

the front balljoint replacement procedure.

8   Inspect the balljoint boots for damage and leaking grease. Replace the balljoints with new ones if they are damaged (see Chapter 10).

20 Exhaust system check (every 15,000 miles or 12 months)

1   With the engine cold (at least three hours after the vehicle has been driven), check the complete exhaust system from its starting point at the engine to the end of the tailpipe. This should be done on a hoist where unrestricted access is available.

2   Check the pipes and connections for evidence of leaks (see illustration), severe corrosion or damage. Make sure that all brackets and hangers are in good condition and tight.

3   At the same time, inspect the underside of the body for holes, corrosion, open seams,

etc. which may allow exhaust gases to enter the passenger compartment. Seal all body openings with silicone or body putty.

4   Rattles and other noises can often be traced to the exhaust system, especially the mounts and hangers (see illustration). Try to move the pipes, muffler and catalytic converter. If the components can come in contact with the body or suspension parts, secure the exhaust system with new mounts.

5   Check the running condition of the engine by inspecting inside the end of the tailpipe. The exhaust deposits here are an indication of engine state-of-tune. If the pipe is black and sooty or coated with white deposits, check for the presence of any stored trouble codes (see Chapter 6).

21 Driveaxle boot check (every 15,000 miles or 12 months)

1   The driveaxle boots are very important because they prevent dirt, water and foreign material from entering and damaging the constant velocity (CV) joints.

2   Inspect the boots for tears and cracks as well as loose clamps (see illustration). If there is any evidence of cracks or leaking lubricant, they must be replaced (see Chapter 8).

22 Spark plug check and replacement (every 105,000 miles or 72 months)

1   Spark plug replacement requires a spark plug socket and extension which fits onto a ratchet. This socket is lined with a rubber grommet to protect the porcelain insulator of the spark plug and to hold the plug while you remove it. You will also need a wire-type feeler gauge to check and adjust the spark plug gap

and a torque wrench to tighten the new plugs to the specified torque (see illustration).

2   Inspect each of the new plugs for defects. If there are any signs of cracks in the porcelain insulator of a plug, don't use it.

3   Check the electrode gaps of the new plugs. Check the gap by inserting the wire gauge of the proper thickness between the electrodes at the tip of the plug (see illustration). The gap between the electrodes should be identical to that listed in this Chapter's Specifications. If the gap is incorrect, the spark plug must be replaced.

Caution: *The gap can only be checked. Do not adjust the gap, the spark plug must be replaced if the gap is incorrect.*

4   If the side electrode is not exactly over the center electrode, the spark plug should be replaced.

Caution: *These spark plug tips are covered in iridium or platinum; do not use a wire wheel or brush to clean them.*

Removal

5   If you're working on a 2008 or earlier model, disconnect the MAP sensor electrical connector and detach the MAP sensor harness from the bracket.

6   If you're working on a 2009 or later model, remove the cowl panel and the lower cowl (see Chapter 11).

7   These models are equipped with individual ignition coils which must be removed first to access the spark plugs (see Chapter 5).

8   If compressed air is available, blow any dirt or foreign material away from the spark plug area before proceeding.

9   Remove the spark plugs from the cylinder head.

10   Compare the spark plug with the chart located on the inside back cover of this book to get an indication of the general running condition of the engine (see illustration).

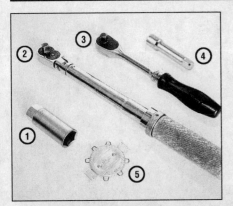

22.1 Tools required for changing spark plugs

1   **Spark plug socket** - This will have special padding inside to protect the spark plug porcelain insulator
2   **Torque wrench** - Although not mandatory, use of this tool is the best way to ensure that the plugs are tightened properly
3   **Ratchet** - Standard hand tool to fit the plug socket
4   **Extension** - Depending on model and accessories, you may need special extensions and universal joints to reach one or more of the plugs
5   **Spark plug gap gauge** - This gauge for checking the gap comes in a variety of styles. Make sure the gap for your engine is included

Installation

11   Prior to installation, apply a coat of anti-seize compound to the plug threads (see illustration). It's often difficult to insert spark plugs into their holes without cross-threading them. To avoid this possibility, fit a short piece of snug-fitting rubber hose over the end of the spark plug (see illustration). The flexible hose acts as a universal joint to help align the plug with the plug hole. Should the plug begin to cross-thread, the hose will slip on the spark plug, preventing thread damage. Tighten

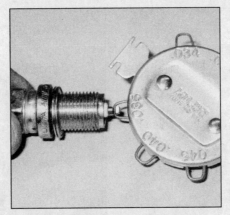

22.3 Spark plug manufacturers recommend using a wire-type gauge when checking the gap - if the wire does not slide between the electrodes with a slight drag, the spark plug will have to be replaced

the plug to the torque listed in this Chapter's Specifications.
12   Follow the above procedure for the remaining spark plugs.
13   After replacing all the plugs, install the ignition coils (see Chapter 5).
14   Reset the Maintenance Minder (see Section 30).

23   Cooling system servicing (draining, flushing and refilling) (every 30,000 miles or 24 months)

Warning: *Wait until the engine is completely cool before beginning this procedure.*
Warning: *Do not allow engine coolant (antifreeze) to come in contact with your skin or painted surfaces of the vehicle. Rinse off spills immediately with plenty of water. Antifreeze is highly toxic if ingested. Never leave antifreeze laying around in an open container or in puddles on the floor; children and pets are attracted by it's sweet smell and may drink it. Check with local authorities about disposing of used antifreeze. Many communities have col-*

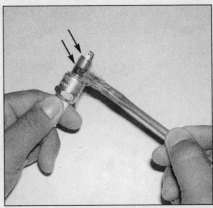

22.11a Apply a coat of anti-seize compound to the spark plug threads, being careful not to get any near the lower threads

lection centers which will see that antifreeze is disposed of safely.
1   Periodically, the cooling system should be drained, flushed and refilled to replenish the antifreeze mixture and prevent formation of rust and corrosion, which can impair the performance of the cooling system and cause engine damage. When the cooling system is serviced, all hoses and the radiator cap should be checked and replaced if necessary.

Draining

2   Apply the parking brake and block the wheels. If the vehicle has just been driven, wait several hours to allow the engine to cool down before beginning this procedure.
3   Slowly unscrew the radiator cap. If you hear a hissing sound (indicating there is still pressure in the system), wait until it stops, then remove it.
4   Move a large container under the radiator drain to catch the coolant. Using a large screwdriver, open the radiator drain plug and direct the coolant into the container (see illustration).
5   After the coolant stops flowing out of the

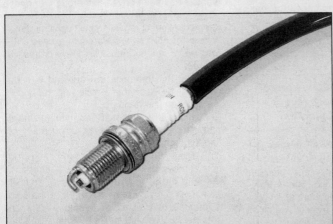

22.11b A length of snug-fitting rubber hose will save time and prevent damaged threads when installing the spark plugs

23.4 The radiator drain fitting is located at the bottom of the radiator

23.5 After draining the radiator, fully drain the cooling system by removing the engine block drain plug (2007/2008 model shown, intake manifold removed for clarity. On 2009 and later models, the drain plug is located on the back of the engine block)

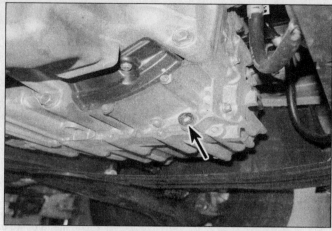

25.7 Automatic transaxle fluid drain plug

radiator, move the container under the engine block drain plug (see illustration). Remove the plug and allow the coolant in the block to drain.

Note: *On 2008 and earlier models, the drain plug is located on the front side of the engine block, just above the oil filter. On 2009 and later models, it's located on the back of the engine block, at the right end, just above the right driveaxle.*

6   While the coolant is draining, check the condition of the radiator hoses, heater hoses and clamps (see Section 11).

7   Replace any damaged clamps or hoses (see Chapter 3).

8   Tighten the radiator drain fitting and install the engine block drain plug.

Flushing

9   Fill the cooling system with clean water, following the Refilling procedure (see Steps 16 through 22).

10   Start the engine and allow it to reach normal operating temperature, then rev up the engine a few times.

11   Turn the engine off and allow it to cool completely, then drain the system as described earlier.

12   Repeat Steps 9 through 11 until the water being drained is free of contaminants.

13   Remove the coolant reservoir (see Chapter 3). Drain the reservoir and flush it with clean water, then reconnect the hose.

14   In severe cases of contamination or clogging of the radiator, remove the radiator (see Chapter 3) and have a radiator repair facility clean and repair it if necessary.

15   Many deposits can be removed by the chemical action of a cleaner available at auto parts stores. Follow the procedure outlined in the manufacturer's instructions.

Note: *When the coolant is regularly drained and the system refilled with the correct anti-freeze/water mixture, there should be no need to use chemical cleaners or descalers.*

Refilling

16   Close and tighten the radiator drain. Install and tighten the engine block drain plug.

17   Make sure the heater temperature control is in the maximum heat position.

18   Slowly refill the radiator with the coolant, listed in this Chapter's Specifications, until coolant reaches the lip on the radiator filler neck. Add coolant to the reservoir up to the lower mark.

19   Install the radiator cap and run the engine in a well-ventilated area until the thermostat opens (coolant will begin flowing through the radiator and the upper radiator hose will become hot).

20   Rev the engine to approximately 2500 rpm for ten seconds, then let it idle; do this a few times.

21   Turn the engine off and let it cool. Add more coolant mixture to bring the level back up to the lip on the radiator filler neck.

22   Squeeze the upper radiator hose to expel air, then add more coolant mixture if necessary. Replace the radiator cap.

23   Start the engine, allow it to reach normal operating temperature and check for leaks. Verify the coolant level (see Section 4).

24   Reset the Maintenance Minder (see Section 30).

24 Evaporative emissions control (EVAP) system check (every 30,000 miles or 24 months)

1   The function of the EVAP system is to draw fuel vapors from the gas tank and fuel system, store them in a charcoal canister, then burn them during normal engine operation.

2   The most common symptom of a fault in the evaporative emissions system is a strong fuel odor. If a fuel odor is detected, inspect the charcoal canister, located underneath the vehicle, below the driver's door opening area,

behind a cover. Check the canister and all hoses for damage and deterioration.

3   The evaporative emissions control system is explained in more detail in Chapter 6.

25 Automatic transaxle fluid change (every 30,000 miles or 24 months)

Note: *Failure to use the fluid listed in this Chapter's Specifications will damage the transaxle and void the warranty.*

Draining

1   At the specified intervals, the automatic transaxle fluid should be drained and replaced.

2   Before beginning work, purchase the specified transaxle fluid (see this Chapter's Specifications).

3   Other tools necessary for this job include jackstands to support the vehicle in a raised position, a 3/8-inch drive ratchet, a large drain pan, newspapers and clean rags.

4   The fluid should be drained after the vehicle has been driven and brought to operating temperature. Hot fluid is more effective than cold fluid at removing built up sediment.

Warning: *Fluid temperature can exceed 350-degrees F in a hot transaxle. Wear protective gloves.*

5   Put the transaxle in Park and turn off the engine. Raise the vehicle and support it securely on jackstands.

6   Move the necessary equipment under the vehicle, being careful not to touch any of the hot exhaust components.

7   Place the drain pan under the drain plug and remove the drain plug (see illustration). Be sure the drain pan is in position, as fluid will come out with some force. Once the fluid is drained, reinstall the drain plug and tighten it to the torque listed in this Chapter's Specifications.

8   Lower the vehicle.

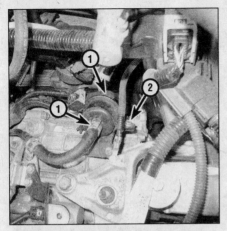

25.10 Automatic transaxle fluid filter details

1   Hoses
2   Hold-down clamp bolt

27.1a PCV valve location (intake manifold removed for clarity) - 2007 and 2008 models

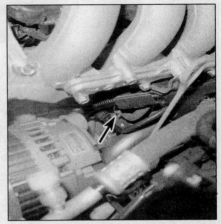

27.1b PCV valve location - 2009 and later models

Filter replacement

Note: *Although the manufacturer doesn't call for replacement of the automatic transaxle fluid filter during a routine transmission fluid change, it's a good idea to replace it (especially if the fluid looks dirty or contaminated).*

9   Remove the air filter housing (see Chapter 4).
10   Disconnect the hoses from the filter (see illustration).
11   Remove the hold-down clamp bolt and clamp, then remove the filter from its bracket.
12   Installation is the reverse of the removal procedure. Make sure the flange of the filter fits into the slot in the hold-down clamp. Tighten the clamp bolt securely.

Refilling

13   With the engine off, remove the dipstick and add new fluid to the transaxle through the dipstick hole (see Section 6). Use a funnel to prevent spills. It is best to add a little fluid at a time, checking the level with the dipstick.
14   Start the engine and move the shift selector into all positions from Park through Low then shift into Park and apply the parking brake.
15   Turn the engine off, then check the fluid level. Add fluid as needed (see Section 6).
16   Recheck the fluid level when it's at normal operating temperature, adding as necessary.
17   Reset the Maintenance Minder (see Section 30).
18   The old fluid drained from the transaxle cannot be reused in its present state and should be disposed of. Check with your local auto parts store, disposal facility or environmental agency to see if they will accept the fluid for recycling. After the fluid has cooled it can be drained into a container (capped plastic jugs, topped bottles, milk cartons, etc.) for transport to one of these disposal sites. Don't dispose of the fluid by pouring it on the ground or down a drain!

26   Manual transaxle lubricant change (every 60,000 miles or 48 months)

1   At the specified time intervals, the manual transaxle lubricant should be drained and replaced.
2   Before beginning work, purchase the specified transaxle lubricant as listed in this Chapter's Specifications).
3   Other tools necessary for this job include jackstands to support the vehicle in a raised position, a 1/2-inch drive ratchet, a drain pan, newspapers and clean rags.
4   Raise the vehicle and support it securely on jackstands.
5   Place the drain pan under the drain plug. Remove the check/fill plug, then remove the drain plug and allow the lubricant to drain into the pan (see Section 18).
Note: *On 2009 and later models, it is beneficial to remove the splash shield (otherwise the oil will drain onto it and make a mess).*
6   Reinstall the drain plug and tighten it to the torque listed in this Chapter's Specifications.
7   Add new lubricant until the level is up to the bottom of the check/fill plug hole.
8   Install the check/fill plug and tighten it to the torque listed in this Chapter's Specifications.
9   The old lubricant drained from the transaxle cannot be reused in its present state and should be disposed of. Check with your local auto parts store, disposal facility or environmental agency to see if they will accept the lubricant for recycling. After the lubricant has cooled it can be drained into a container (capped plastic jugs, topped bottles, milk cartons, etc.) for transport to one of these disposal sites. Don't dispose of the lubricant by pouring it on the ground or down a drain!
10   Reset the Maintenance Minder (see Section 30).

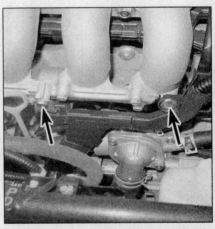

27.2 Remove the bolts and reposition the engine wiring harness for access to the PCV valve (2009 and later models)

27   Positive Crankcase Ventilation (PCV) valve check and replacement (every 30,000 miles or 24 months)

1   Locate the PCV valve just below the left (no.4) intake manifold runner (2008 and earlier models) or below the two center intake manifold runners (2009 and later models) (see illustrations).
2   If you're working on a 2009 or later model, remove the engine wiring harness holder bolts and move the harness out of the way (see illustration).
3   Disconnect the hose, then unscrew the PCV valve. Discard the sealing washer (a new one should be used during installation).
4   Installation is the reverse of removal. Be sure to use a new sealing washer.

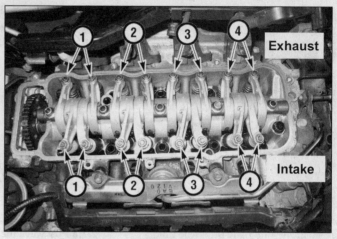

28.5 When the engine is at TDC for cylinder number 1, the "UP" mark on the camshaft sprocket will be visible, and the two lines on the sprocket will be parallel with the machined surface of the cylinder head

28.6 Valve layout

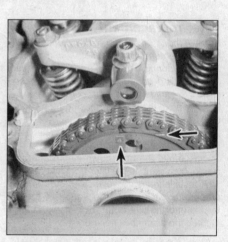

28.7 When the adjustment is correct, you will feel a slight drag as you pull the feeler gauge

28.9 When the number 3 cylinder is at TDC, the "3" mark will appear at 12 o'clock and the machined line on the cam sprocket will be parallel with the cylinder head surface

28.10 When the number 4 cylinder is at TDC, the "4" mark will appear at 12 o'clock and the machined line on the cam sprocket will be parallel with the cylinder head surface

28   Valve clearance check and adjustment (every 60,000 miles/48 months)

Note: *The manufacturer states that valve adjustment is only necessary as a routine maintenance item if the valves are noisy.*

Check

1   Valve clearances on these models generally do not need adjustment unless valvetrain components have been replaced, or a valve job has been performed.
2   The simplest check for proper valve adjustment is to listen carefully to the engine running with the hood open. If the valvetrain is noisy, adjustment is necessary.

Adjustment

3   The valve clearance must be checked and adjusted with the engine cold.

4   Remove the valve cover (see Chapter 2A).
5   Place the number one piston (closest to the drivebelt end of the engine) at Top Dead Center (TDC) on the compression stroke. This is accomplished by rotating the crankshaft in the normal direction of rotation (which is clockwise) until the white TDC mark on the crankshaft pulley aligns with the timing pointer on the timing chain cover and the UP mark on the camshaft sprocket is at the twelve o'clock position (see accompanying illustration and Chapter 2A).
6   With the engine in this position, the number one cylinder valve adjustment can be checked and adjusted (see illustrations).
7   Start with the intake valve clearance. Insert a feeler gauge of the correct thickness (see this Chapter's Specifications) between the valve stem and the rocker arm (see illustration). Withdraw it; you should feel a slight drag. If there's no drag or a heavy

drag, loosen the adjuster nut and back off the adjuster screw. Carefully tighten the adjuster screw until you can feel a slight drag on the feeler gauge as you withdraw it.
8   Hold the adjuster screw with a screwdriver (to keep it from turning) and tighten the locknut. Recheck the clearance to make sure it hasn't changed. Repeat the procedure in this Step and the previous Step on the other intake valve, then on the two exhaust valves.
Note: *After adjusting the second clearance on a pair of valves, re-check the clearance of the first one and readjust if necessary.*
9   Rotate the crankshaft pulley 180-degrees clockwise (the camshaft pulley will turn 90-degrees) until the number three cylinder is at TDC (see illustration). Check and adjust the number three cylinder valves.
10   Rotate the crankshaft pulley 180-degrees clockwise until the number four cylinder is at TDC (see illustration). Check and adjust the number four cylinder valves.

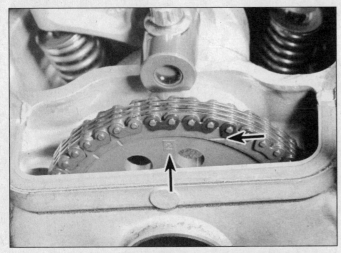

28.11 When the number 2 cylinder is at TDC, the "2" mark will appear at 12 o'clock and the machined line on the cam sprocket will be parallel with the cylinder head surface

30.2a SEL/RESET button - 2007 and 2008 models

11   Rotate the crankshaft pulley 180-degrees clockwise to bring the number two cylinder to TDC (see illustration). Check and adjust the number two cylinder valves.

12   Install the valve cover (see Chapter 2A).

29   Brake fluid change (every 36 months)

Warning: *Brake fluid can harm your eyes and damage painted surfaces, so use extreme caution when handling or pouring it. Do not use brake fluid that has been standing open or is more than one year old. Brake fluid absorbs moisture from the air. Excess moisture can cause a dangerous loss of braking effectiveness.*

1   At the specified interval, the brake fluid should be replaced. Since the brake fluid may drip or splash when pouring it, place plenty of rags around the master cylinder to protect any surrounding painted surfaces.

2   Before beginning work, purchase the specified brake fluid (see this Chapter's Specifications).

3   Remove the cap from the master cylinder reservoir.

4   Using a hand-operated suction pump or similar device, withdraw the fluid from the master cylinder reservoir.

5   Add new fluid to the master cylinder until it rises to the line indicated on the reservoir.

6   Bleed the brake system at all four brakes until new and uncontaminated fluid is expelled from each bleeder screw (see Chapter 9). Maintain the fluid level in the master cylinder as you perform the bleeding process. If you allow the master cylinder to run dry, air will enter the system.

7   Refill the master cylinder with fluid and check the operation of the brakes. The pedal should feel solid when depressed, with no sponginess.

Warning: *Do not operate the vehicle if you are at all in doubt about the effectiveness of the brake system.*

30   Maintenance Minder resetting

1   Turn the key to the On position.

2   Push the SEL/RESET button repeatedly until the engine oil life indicator is displayed (see illustrations).

3   Push the SEL/RESET button and hold it until the oil life indicator and other maintenance item codes blink, then release the button.

4   Push the button again and hold it for five seconds - the oil life indicator should now display 100%.

30.2b SEL/RESET button - 2009 and later models

Notes

Chapter 2 Part A Engine

Contents

Specifications

General

Firing order	1-3-4-2
Bore	
Standard	2.8740 to 2.8748 inches (73.00 to 73.03 mm)
Maximum bore	2.8767 inches (73.07mm)
Stroke 3.52 inches (89.4 mm)	
Displacement	91.3 cubic inches
Oil pressure	See Chapter 2B
Valve adjustment	See Chapter 1

FRONT OF VEHICLE ❶②③④

Cylinder locations

Camshaft

Endplay	
Standard	0.002 to 0.010 inch (0.05 to 0.25 mm)
Maximum	0.020 inch (0.5 mm)
Lobe height	
2008 and earlier models	
Intake	
Primary	1.39291 inches (35.3799 mm)
Secondary	1.20193 inches (30.5291 mm)
Exhaust	1.39321 inches (35.3877 mm)
2009 and later models	
Intake	
Primary	1.38744 inches (35.241 mm)
Secondary	1.42413 inches (36.173 mm)
Exhaust	1.39649 inches (35.471 mm)
Runout	
Standard	0.001 inch (0.03 mm)
Service limit	0.002 inch maximum (0.05 mm)
Journal oil clearance	
Standard	0.0018 to 0.0033 inch (0.046 to 0.084 mm)
Service limit	0.00394 inch maximum (0.100 mm)

Oil pump

Rotor-to-cover clearance

    Standard.. 0.001 to 0.002 inch (0.02 to 0.06 mm)

    Service limit

        2008 and earlier models .... 0.006 inch maximum (0.15 mm)

        2009 and later models.. 0.005 inch maximum (0.145 mm)

Tooth tip clearance

    Standard

        2008 and earlier models .... 0.001 to 0.006 inch (0.02 to 0.14 mm)

        2009 and later models.. 0.003 to 0.006 inch (0.06 to 0.14 mm)

    Service limit.. 0.008 inch maximum (0.20 mm)

Outer rotor-to-pump body clearance

    Standard

        2008 and earlier models .... 0.004 to 0.007 inch (0.10 to 0.18 mm)

        2009 and later models.. 0.004 to 0.006 inch (0.10 to 0.175 mm)

    Service limit.. 0.008 inch maximum (0.20 mm)

Flywheel

Runout

    Standard.. 0.002 inch (0.05 mm)

    Maximum... 0.006 inch (0.15 mm)

Torque specifications

Note: *One foot-pound (ft-lb) of torque is equivalent to 12 inch-pounds (in-lbs) of torque. Torque values below approximately 15 ft-lbs are expressed in inch-pounds, since most foot-pound torque wrenches are not accurate at these smaller values.*

	Ft-lbs (unless otherwise indicated)	Nm
Camshaft position sensor pulse plate bolt	25	34
Camshaft sprocket bolt...	41	56
Camshaft thrust cover bolts...	88 in-lbs	10
Crankshaft pulley bolt		
Original bolt		
Step 1	27	37
Step 2	Tighten an additional 90-degrees	
New bolt		
Step 1	130	176
Step 2	Loosen bolt 2 full turns	
Step 3	27	37
Step 4	Tighten an additional 90-degrees	
Cylinder head bolts		
Step 1	22	29
Step 2	Tighten an additional 130-degrees	
Driveplate-to-crankshaft bolts..	54	73
Intake manifold bolts/nuts		
Upper	17	24
Lower (bolts and nuts)	17	24
Support bracket...	108 in-lbs	12
Throttle body bolts	16	22
Exhaust manifold-to-cylinder head nuts/bolts..	33	44
Exhaust pipe-to-manifold bolts...	16	22
Flywheel-to-crankshaft bolts..	87	118
Oil pan drain plug	33	44
Oil pan bolts		
8 mm bolt	17	24
6 mm bolts	106 in-lbs	12
Oil pan-to-transaxle bolts	47	64
Oil pump pick-up tube to pump housing nuts		
2008 and earlier models	87 in-lbs	9.8
2009 and later models..	108 in-lbs	12
Oil pump pick-up screen to main bearing cap bolts		
2008 and earlier models	87 in-lbs	9.8
2009 and later models..	108 in-lbs	12
Oil pump housing-to-block bolts		
2008 and earlier models	87 in-lbs	9.8
2009 and later models..	108 in-lbs	12
Rocker arm assembly bolts		
2008 and earlier models	22	29
2009 and later models		
Step 1	84 in-lbs	9.8
Step 2	132 in-lbs	15

Torque specifications (continued)

Note: *One foot-pound (ft-lb) of torque is equivalent to 12 inch-pounds (in-lbs) of torque. Torque values below approximately 15 ft-lbs are expressed in inch-pounds, since most foot-pound torque wrenches are not accurate at these smaller values.*

	Ft-lbs (unless otherwise indicated)	Nm
Timing chain cover bolts		
8 mm bolts	23	31
6 mm bolts	106 in-lbs	12
Timing chain guide bolts	104 in-lbs	12
Timing chain tensioner arm pivot bolt	16	22
Timing chain tensioner bolts	104 in-lbs	12
Valve cover bolts		
2008 and earlier models	106 in-lbs	12
2009 and later models	84 in-lbs	9.8

1   General Information

1   This Part of Chapter 2A is devoted to in-vehicle repair procedures for the 1.5L four-cylinder engine. The engine incorporates the VTEC (Variable valve Timing and lift Electronic Control) system, which electronically alters valve timing to enhance engine performance. For more information on the VTEC system, see Section of this Chapter.

2   Engine designations include:

- *L15A1- 1.5L 16 valve SOHC VTEC 109horsepower engine - 2008 and earlier models*
- *L15A7- 1.5L 16 valve SOHC iVTEC 117 horsepower engine - 2009 and later models*

3   The engines are lightweight in design with an aluminum alloy block (with steel cylinder liners) and an aluminum alloy cylinder head. The crankshaft rides in a single carriage unit that houses the renewable insert-type main bearings.

4   The pistons have two compression rings and one oil control ring. The semi-floating piston pins are press-fitted into the small end of the connecting rod. The connecting rod big ends are equipped with renewable insert-type plain bearings.

5   The engine is liquid-cooled, utilizing a centrifugal impeller-type pump driven by the drivebelt to circulate coolant around the cylinders and combustion chambers and through the intake manifold.

6   Lubrication is handled by a rotor-type oil pump mounted on the front of the engine behind the timing chain lower sprocket. It is driven directly by the crankshaft. The oil is filtered continuously by a cartridge-type filter mounted on the oil pan.

7   Information concerning engine removal and installation and overhaul can be found in Part B of this Chapter.

8   The following repair procedures are based on the assumption that the engine is installed in the vehicle. If the engine has been removed from the vehicle and mounted on a stand, many of the steps outlined in this Part of Chapter 2A will not apply.

9   The Specifications included in this Part of Chapter 2A apply only to the procedures contained in this Chapter. Chapter 2B contains the Specifications necessary for certain engine block assembly procedures.

2   Repair operations possible with the engine in the vehicle

1   Clean the engine compartment and the exterior of the engine with some type of degreaser before any work is done. It will make the job easier and help keep dirt out of the internal areas of the engine.

2   Depending on the components involved, it may be helpful to remove the hood to improve access to the engine as repairs are performed (refer to Chapter 11 if necessary). Cover the fenders to prevent damage to the paint. Special pads are available, but an old bedspread or blanket will also work. The hood can be opened more by inserting the prop rod in the lower hole.

3   On 2009 and later models, many operations require the cowl cover and lower cowl to be removed (see Chapter 11). The cowl cover is the panel below the wiper arms at the rear of the engine compartment. There is an upper and lower cowl cover.

4   If vacuum, exhaust, oil or coolant leaks develop, indicating a need for gasket or seal replacement, the repairs can generally be made with the engine in the vehicle. The intake and exhaust manifold gaskets, oil pan gasket, crankshaft oil seals and cylinder head gasket are all accessible with the engine in place.

5   Exterior engine components, such as the intake and exhaust manifolds, the oil pan, the water pump, the starter motor, the alternator, and the fuel system components can be removed for repair with the engine in place.

6   Since the cylinder head can be removed without pulling the engine, camshaft and valve component servicing can also be accomplished with the engine in the vehicle. Replacement of the timing chain and sprockets is also possible with the engine in the vehicle.

7   In extreme cases caused by a lack of necessary equipment, repair or replacement of piston rings, pistons, connecting rods and rod bearings is possible with the engine in the vehicle. However, this practice is not recommended because of the cleaning and preparation work that must be done to the components involved.

3   Top Dead Center (TDC) for number one piston - locating

Note: *These engines are not equipped with a distributor. Piston position must be determined by feeling for compression at the number one spark plug hole, then aligning the ignition timing marks as described in Step 5.*

1   Top Dead Center (TDC) is the highest point in the cylinder that each piston reaches as it travels up-and-down during crankshaft rotation. Each piston reaches TDC on the compression stroke and again on the exhaust stroke, but TDC generally refers to piston position on the compression stroke.

2   Positioning the piston(s) at TDC is an essential part of many other repair procedures discussed in this manual.

3   Before beginning this procedure, be sure to place the transmission in Neutral and apply the parking brake or block the rear wheels. Remove the spark plugs (see Chapter 1) and install a compression gauge in the spark plug hole for cylinder no. 1.

4   In order to bring any piston to TDC, the crankshaft must be turned with a socket and ratchet or breaker bar. When looking at the front (timing belt or timing chain end) of the engine, normal crankshaft rotation is clockwise.

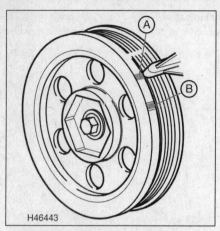

3.5 Align the white (TDC) mark (A) on the crankshaft pulley with the pointer on the timing belt cover. The red mark (B, 2007/2008 models only) is for the timing light

4.7a Press the new gasket into the groove in the valve cover

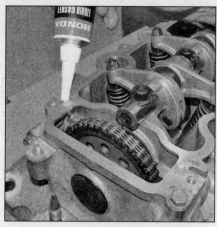

4.7b Apply beads of RTV sealant where the timing chain cover and cylinder head meet

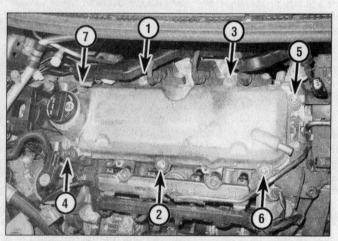

4.8a Valve cover bolt tightening sequence - 2008 and earlier models

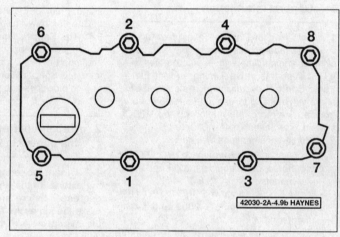

4.8b Valve cover bolt tightening sequence - 2009 and later models

5   Turn the crankshaft until compression registers on the gauge, then turn it slowly until the white TDC mark on the crankshaft pulley is aligned with the timing pointer (see illustration). The number one piston is now at TDC on the compression stroke.

Note: *On 2008 and earlier models, the red mark on the pulley is for verifying ignition timing and is 8 degrees advanced from the white mark. On 2009 and later models, the white mark is also for ignition timing verification.*

6   After the number one piston has been positioned at TDC on the compression stroke, TDC for any of the remaining pistons can be located by turning the crankshaft in its normal direction of rotation, in 180-degree (1/2-turn) increments, and following the firing order. Divide the crankshaft pulley into two equal sections with chalk marks at each point, each indicating 180-degrees of crankshaft rotation. Rotating the engine past TDC no. 1 to the next mark will place the engine at TDC for cylinder no. 3.

4   Valve cover - removal and installation

Removal

1   Remove the upper intake manifold (see Section 5).
2   On 2009 and later models, disconnect the ignition coil connectors and remove the harness and any brackets from the valve cover.
3   Wipe off the valve cover thoroughly to prevent debris from falling onto the exposed cylinder head or camshaft/valve train assembly.
4   Loosen the bolts a little at a time, in the reverse order of the tightening sequence (see illustrations 4.8a and 4.8b).
5   Lift off the valve cover and gasket. If the gasket is stuck to the cylinder head, tap it with a rubber mallet to break the seal. Do not pry

between the cover and cylinder head or you'll damage the gasket mating surfaces.

Installation

6   Remove the old gasket and clean the mating surfaces of the cylinder head and the valve cover. Clean the surfaces with a rag soaked in brake system cleaner.
7   Install a new molded rubber gasket into the groove around the valve cover perimeter (see illustration). Apply beads of RTV sealant to the gasket where the timing chain cover meets the cylinder head (see illustration)
8   Place the cover into position and tighten the bolts in the recommended sequence to the torque listed in this Chapter's Specifications (see illustrations).
9   The remainder of installation is the reverse of removal.

5.2 Engine cover fasteners

5.9 Upper intake manifold bolts (2009 and later models shown, earlier models similar)

1   *Plastic fasteners (twist 1/4-turn to release)*
2   *Bolts*

5   Intake manifold - removal and installation

Warning: *Gasoline is extremely flammable, so take extra precautions when you work on any part of the fuel system. Don't smoke or allow open flames or bare light bulbs near the work area, and don't work in a garage where a gas-type appliance (such as a water heater or clothes dryer) is present. If you spill any fuel on your skin, rinse it off immediately with soap and water. When you perform any kind of work on the fuel system, wear safety glasses and have a Class B type fire extinguisher on hand.*
Warning: *Wait until the engine is completely cool before beginning this procedure.*

Upper

Note: *The upper intake manifold can be removed along with the lower intake manifold as one unit if both need to be removed.*

Removal

1   Disconnect the cable from the negative terminal of the battery (see Chapter 5).
2   On 2008 and earlier models, remove the engine cover (see illustration).
3   On 2009 and later models, remove the cowl cover (see Chapter 11).
4   Remove the air filter housing (see Chapter 4).
5   Clearly label and detach any vacuum lines and electrical connectors which will interfere with removal of the manifold.
6   Remove the brake booster vacuum hose and disconnect the MAP sensor connector and harness from the harness brackets.
7   Remove the four bolts attaching the throttle body to the upper intake manifold (see

5.12 Install new upper-to-lower manifold gaskets

Chapter 4). With the throttle body connectors and coolant hoses still attached, position the throttle body to the side.
8   On 2009 and later models, remove the intake manifold support bracket mounting bolts. There are two that face downwards and one that faces inward below the throttle body mounting location.
9   Remove the bolts/nuts attaching the upper intake manifold to the lower intake manifold (see illustration).
10   Remove the upper intake manifold.

Installation

11   Clean the manifold mating surfaces with brake system cleaner.
12   Install new gaskets into the grooves in the mating surface of the upper intake manifold (see illustration).
13   Installation is reverse of removal. Tighten the fasteners a little at a time, working from

the center outwards, to the torque listed in this Chapter's Specifications .
14   Reconnect the battery (see Chapter 5).

Lower

Note: *You can remove the upper and lower intake manifolds together or separately. This procedure outlines removing both upper and lower as one unit.*

Removal

15   Follow steps 1 through 8 of the upper intake manifold removal procedure.
16   Remove the dipstick and disconnect the PCV hose from the lower intake manifold.
17   Remove the bolt(s) attaching the harness to the bottom of cylinder nos. 1 and 4 intake runners (some models have only one bolt at No. 4). Then slide the harness off the bracket to disengage the clip on the lower intake manifold in front of the dipstick tube.

5.18 Intake manifold-to-cylinder head fasteners (only some are visible)

5.19 Remove the old gasket and thoroughly clean the manifold and cylinder head

18   Remove the nuts and bolts attaching the intake manifold to the cylinder head and remove the manifold (see illustration).
19   Remove the intake manifold gasket from the cylinder head (see illustration).

Installation

20   Check the mating surfaces of the manifold for flatness with a precision straightedge and feeler gauges.
21   Inspect the manifold for cracks and distortion. If the manifold is cracked or warped, replace it or see if it can be resurfaced at an automotive machine shop.
22   Check carefully for any stripped or broken intake manifold bolts/studs. Replace any defective fasteners with new parts.
23   Remove all traces of old gasket material from the cylinder head and manifold mating surfaces.
24   Install the intake manifold with a new gasket, then install the fasteners and tighten them a little at a time, working from the center

outwards, to the torque listed in this Chapter's Specifications.
25   Reconnect the battery (see Chapter 5).
26   The remainder of installation is the reverse of removal.

6   Exhaust manifold - removal and installation

Note: *The following procedure is for 2008 and earlier models only. On 2009 and later models, the exhaust manifold is integrated into the cylinder head; the catalytic converter bolts directly to the cylinder head.*
Note: *Be sure to soak the fasteners with penetrating oil before attempting to unscrew them.*

Removal

1   Disconnect the cable from the negative terminal of the battery (see Chapter 5, Section 3).

2   Remove the engine cover (see Section 4).
3   Remove the exhaust manifold heat shield (see illustration).
4   Raise the front of the vehicle and support it securely on jackstands.
5   Remove the splash shield from under the engine.
6   Disconnect the oxygen sensor electrical connector.
7   Detach the catalytic converter from the exhaust manifold (see Chapter 6).
8   Unbolt the exhaust manifold support bracket from the manifold (see illustration).
9   Remove the exhaust manifold nuts and bolts and detach the exhaust manifold from the cylinder head (see illustration).

Installation

10   Discard the old gasket and use a scraper to clean the gasket mating surfaces on the exhaust manifold and cylinder head, then clean the surfaces with a rag soaked in brake system cleaner.

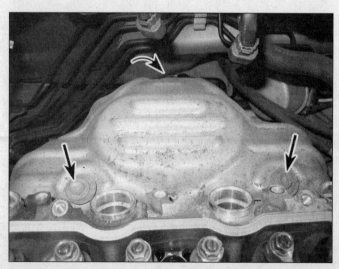

6.3 Exhaust manifold heat shield bolts (rear bolt not visible)

6.8 Exhaust manifold support bracket bolt

11 Place the exhaust manifold in position on the cylinder head and install new nuts and bolts. Starting at the center and working out to the ends, tighten the fasteners to the torque listed in this Chapter's Specifications.

12 Install the heat shield and tighten the bolts securely.

13 Connect the catalytic converter to the exhaust manifold, using new bolts. Tighten the bolts to the torque listed in the Chapter 6 Specifications .

14 The remainder of installation is the reverse of removal.

15 Reconnect the battery (see Chapter 5).

16 Start the engine and check for exhaust leaks.

7 Rocker arm assembly - removal, inspection and installation

Removal

1 Remove the valve cover (see Section 4).

2 Position the number one piston at Top Dead Center (see Section 3).

3 Loosen the rocker arm valve lash adjustment nuts and unscrew the adjustment screws (see Chapter 1, if necessary).

4 On 2008 and earlier models, use rubber bands to secure the companion intake rockers together before removal.

Note: *It is a good idea to bundle the rocker arms together with rubber bands on all models.*

This is important on rocker arms that have a piston between them to prevent the piston from pushing the rockers apart during removal.

5 Loosen the rocker arm shaft assembly mounting bolts two turns at a time, until the spring pressure is relieved. Follow the reverse of the tightening sequence (see illustrations 7.11a and 7.11b).

6 Lift the rocker arms and shaft assembly from the cylinder head. Note the dowel pin on the chain end.

Inspection

Caution: *The rocker arm pistons, located between the secondary intake rocker arms, are* spring loaded and can come apart once they are removed from the rocker arm shaft.

7 If you wish to disassemble and inspect the rocker arm assembly (a good idea as long as you have them off), slip the rocker arms, pistons and springs off the shafts from the chain end. On 2009 and later models you must remove the rocker shaft bridge retaining bolt to remove the bridge. Mark the relationship of the components to keep them in order. They must be reassembled in the same positions they were removed from (see illustrations).

8 Thoroughly clean the components and inspect them for wear and damage. Check

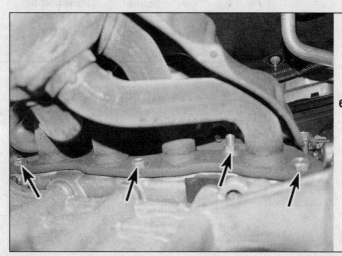

6.9 Exhaust manifold-to-cylinder head fasteners (not all are visible)

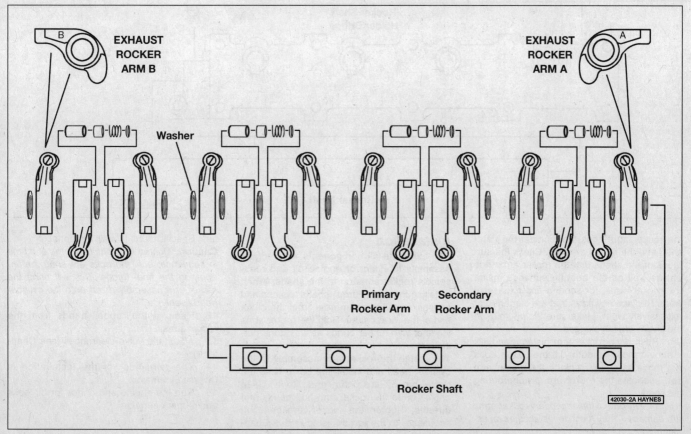

7.7a Exploded view of the rocker arm assembly - 2008 and earlier models

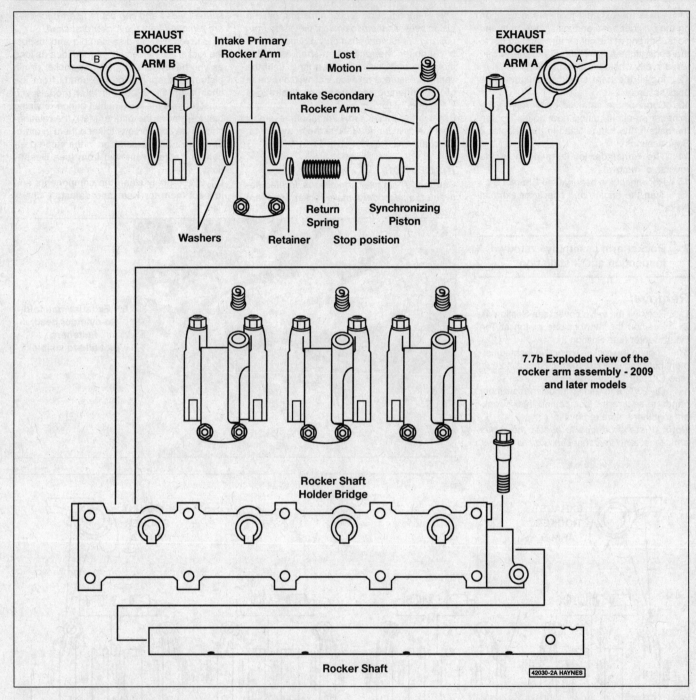

EXHAUST ROCKER ARM B

Intake Primary Rocker Arm

Lost Motion

EXHAUST ROCKER ARM A

Intake Secondary Rocker Arm

Return Spring

Synchronizing Piston

Washers

Retainer

Stop position

7.7b Exploded view of the rocker arm assembly - 2009 and later models

Rocker Shaft Holder Bridge

Rocker Shaft

42030-2A HAYNES

the rocker arm faces that contact the camshaft and the rocker arm tips. Check the surfaces of the shafts that the rocker arms ride on, as well as the bearing surfaces inside the rocker arms, for scoring and excessive wear. Replace any parts that are damaged or excessively worn. Make sure the oil holes in the shafts are not plugged.

9   Push each rocker arm piston manually, it should move smoothly. If the piston does not move smoothly, replace the rocker arm set. Lubricate the rocker arm pistons during assembly.

Note: *If any one of the secondary rocker arms are damaged, they must be replaced as an assembly.*

Installation

10   Lubricate all components with engine assembly lubricant or engine oil and reassemble rocker arms on to the shafts. When installing the rocker arms, shafts, pistons and springs, install them in order from the chain end of the rocker shaft. Hold the rocker arms together with rubber bands as was done during removal.

11   Install the rocker arm assembly to the cylinder head and install the bolts. Note the dowel pin on the chain end. Apply clean engine oil to the rocker arm bolt beads and threads. Tighten the rocker arm bolts, in sequence, to the torque listed in this Chap-

ter's Specifications (see illustrations).

Caution: *Tighten the bolts two turns at a time in sequence, until the bolts are snug, before applying the final torque (this will bring the rocker arm assembly down onto the cylinder head evenly).*

12   Remove the rubber bands from the rocker arms.

13   Adjust the valve clearances (see Chapter 1).

14   The remainder of the installation is reverse of removal.

15   Run the engine and check for oil leaks and proper operation.

7.11a Rocker arm bolt tightening sequence - 2008 and earlier models

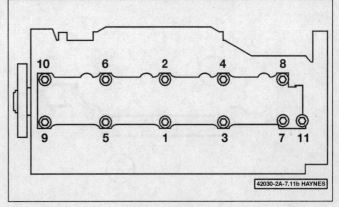

7.11b Rocker arm assembly bolt tightening sequence - 2009 and later models

8.7 Idler pulley mounting bolt (2008 and earlier models)

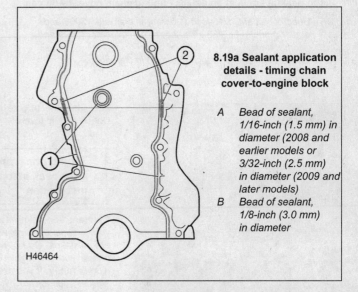

8.19a Sealant application details - timing chain cover-to-engine block

A   Bead of sealant, 1/16-inch (1.5 mm) in diameter (2008 and earlier models or 3/32-inch (2.5 mm) in diameter (2009 and later models)

B   Bead of sealant, 1/8-inch (3.0 mm) in diameter

8 Timing chain cover - removal and installation

Removal

1   Disconnect the cable from the negative battery terminal (see Chapter 5).

2   Loosen the right front wheel lug nuts.

3   Raise the front of the vehicle and support it securely on jackstands. Remove the right front wheel.

4   Remove the splash shield from below the engine compartment (see Section 5).

5   Remove the drivebelt (see Chapter 1).

6   Remove the alternator bracket-to-timing chain cover bolts, then loosen the alternator pivot bolt (see Chapter 5) and swing the alternator and bracket towards the front of the car.

7   On 2008 and earlier models, remove the mounting bolt and idler pulley from the cover (see illustration). On 2009 and later models, remove the belt tensioner assembly.

8   Remove the valve cover (Section 4).

9   Remove the water pump pulley (see Chapter 3).

10   Remove the crankshaft pulley (see Section 10).

11   Drain the engine oil (see Chapter 1).

12   On 2008 and earlier models, remove the oil pan (see Section 13).

13   On 2008 and earlier models, disconnect the crankshaft position sensor connector and harness clips from the timing chain cover.

14   Support the engine with a floor jack. Place a wood block between the jack pad and the engine block to avoid damaging the crankshaft or oil pump pickup (2008 and earlier models) or oil pan (2009 and later models).

15   Detach the ground cable, then remove the right-side engine mount and bracket assembly (see Section 17).

16   Remove the timing chain cover bolts and detach the cover from the engine.

Note: *Mark the bolt locations for installation as the bolts are not the same size, design or length.*

Caution: *The cover is installed using a bead of RTV sealant, so it will probably be stuck to the engine block. Start by pulling it at the top, working downwards until until it is free. If it won't come loose, try to jar it loose with a* hammer and block of wood. Prying between the mating surfaces could damage them, leading to oil leaks.

Installation

17   Inspect and clean all sealing surfaces of the timing chain cover, cylinder block and oil pan.

Caution: *Be very careful when scraping on aluminum engine parts. Aluminum is soft and gouges easily. Severely gouged parts may require replacement.*

18   If necessary, replace the crankshaft oil seal in the timing chain cover (see Section 10).

19   Apply RTV sealant to the mating surfaces on the timing chain cover (see illustrations).

Note: *If using Honda brand sealant, the timing chain cover must be installed within four minutes of application.*

Caution: *On 2009 and later models, when installing the timing chain cover, set the oil pan mating surface against the oil pan first, then tilt the timing chain cover against the block. DO NOT allow the oil pan sealing area to slide.*

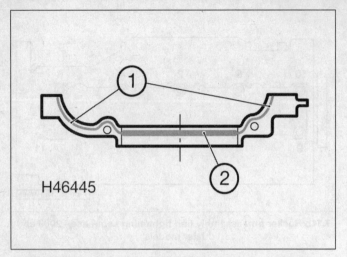

8.19b Sealant application details - timing chain cover-to-oil pan

1   *Bead of sealant, 1/16-inch (1.5 mm) in diameter (2008 and earlier models) or 3/32-inch (2.5 mm) in diameter (2009 and later models)*
2   *Bead of sealant, 3/16-inch (5.0 mm) in diameter*

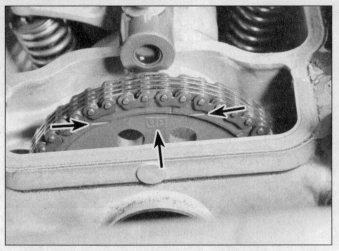

9.4 When the engine is at TDC for cylinder number 1, the "UP" mark on the camshaft sprocket will be visible, and the two lines on the sprocket will be parallel with the machined surface of the cylinder head

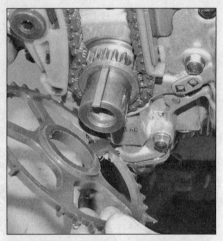

9.6 Remove the CKP sensor pulse plate (2008 and earlier models only)

20   Install the timing chain cover and fasteners. Make sure the fasteners are in their original locations. Tighten the fasteners by hand until the cover is contacting the block around its entire periphery.
21   Tighten the bolts to the torque listed in this Chapter's Specifications.
22   Reinstall the remaining parts in the reverse order of removal.
Note: *If using Honda sealant, allow 30 minutes for the sealant to cure before adding engine oil.*
23   Fill the crankcase with the recommended oil (see Chapter 1).
24   Reconnect the battery (see Chapter 5).
Note: *If using Honda sealant, wait 3 hours before running engine for sealant to completely cure.*

25   Start the engine and check for leaks. Check all fluid levels.

9   Timing chain and sprockets - removal, inspection and installation

Caution: *The timing system is complex. Severe engine damage will occur if you make any mistakes. Do not attempt this procedure unless you are highly experienced with this type of repair. If you are at all unsure of your abilities, consult an expert. Double-check all your work and be sure everything is correct before you attempt to start the engine.*
Caution: *Don't touch the timing chain with a magnet or allow it to get near magnetic fields.*

Removal

1   Disconnect the cable from the negative battery terminal (see Chapter 5).
2   Set the engine to TDC number 1 (see Section 3).
3   Remove the valve cover (see Section 4).
4   Verify that the camshaft is set to TDC number 1 (UP mark is shown and TDC line is level with the cylinder head surface) (see illustration).
5   Remove the timing chain cover (see Section 8).
6   On 2008 and earlier models, remove the Crankshaft Position Sensor pulse plate from the front of the crankshaft (see illustration).
7   Measure the distance between the chain at the closest part (between the tensioner and the guide). The standard measurement is 3/4-inch (19 mm). If less than 19/32-inch" (15 mm), replace the chain and the tensioner.
8   Apply some clean engine oil to the

timing chain tensioner slider, then insert a screwdriver into the tensioner from the top and apply even pressure towards the chain. While applying pressure, remove the upper tensioner bolt and loosen the lower bolt (see illustration).
9   Release pressure from the screwdriver and remove the timing chain tensioner lower bolt and the tensioner (see illustrations).
10   Remove the tensioner arm pivot bolt and the arm (see illustration). Remove the two bolts retaining the chain guide on the right side of the chain and remove the guide (see illustration).
11   To remove the camshaft sprocket, hold the camshaft with an open-end wrench and loosen the camshaft sprocket bolt. Remove the bolt and slide the camshaft sprocket, crankshaft sprocket and chain off the camshaft and crankshaft.
Warning: *Do not turn the crankshaft or camshaft once the timing chain has been removed to prevent damage to the engine.*

Inspection

Note: *If chain is out of specification as mentioned earlier, the chain, tensioner, tensioner arm, and chain guide must be replaced.*
12   Clean all parts with clean solvent, then dry with compressed air.
13   Inspect the chain tensioner for excessive wear or other damage.
14   Inspect the timing chain guide and tensioner arm for deep grooves, excessive wear, or other damage.
15   Inspect the timing chain for excessive wear or damage.
16   Inspect the crankshaft and camshaft sprocket for chipped or broken teeth, excessive wear, or damage. Replace any component that is in questionable condition.

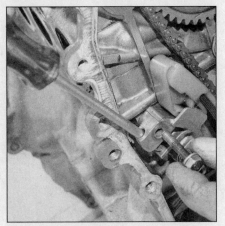

9.8 Hold the tensioner with a screwdriver and remove the upper tensioner bolt

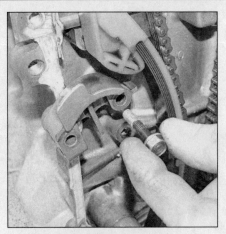

9.9a Take out the lower bolt. . .

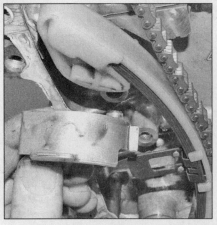

9.9b . . . and remove the tensioner

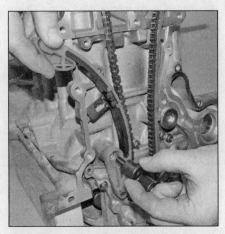

9.10a Remove the lower bolt and take off the tensioner arm

9.10b Unbolt and remove the stationary chain guide

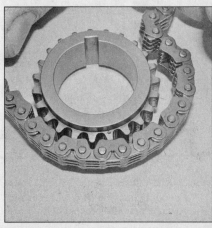

9.19 The single plated link must align with the mark on the crankshaft sprocket

Installation

Note: *Notice the chain has colored links for installation.*

17 Make sure the timing mark (triangle) on the crankshaft sprocket is still aligned with the pointer on the engine block.

18 Make sure the "UP" mark on the camshaft sprocket is at the top and the two index marks are in line with the top edge of the cylinder head.

19 Install the timing chain around the crankshaft sprocket with the plated link on the chain aligned with the dot (indentation) on the crankshaft sprocket (see illustration).

20 Install the timing chain over the camshaft sprocket with the marks aligned with the three colored chain links (see illustrations).

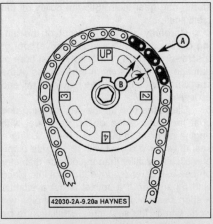

9.20a The center plated link (A) must be positioned between the two timing marks (B) on the camshaft sprocket - 2008 and earlier models

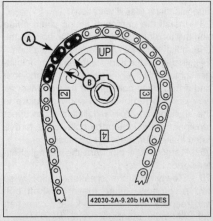

9.20b The center plated link (A) must be positioned between the two timing marks (B) on the camshaft sprocket - 2009 and later models

9.21a Install the chain and sprockets as an assembly

9.21b When installed, the plated link and the mark on the camshaft sprocket should line up with the pointer on the oil pump

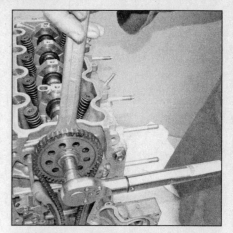

9.22 Use a wrench to prevent the camshaft from turning while tightening the sprocket bolt

11.7 Pry out the plastic plug for access to the camshaft sprocket bolt

21   Guide the sprockets and chain into position and install the sprockets onto the crankshaft and camshaft (see illustrations).
22   Install the camshaft sprocket bolt. Hold the camshaft with a wrench and tighten the bolt to the torque listed in this Chapter's Specifications (see illustration).
23   Install the camshaft timing chain guide and the tensioner arm. Tighten the bolts to the torque listed in this Chapter's Specifications.
24   Install the tensioner with the lower bolt finger tight. Apply fresh engine oil to the tensioner and arm contact point. Insert a screwdriver as was done in removal and apply pressure to the tensioner to allow installation of the upper tensioner bolt. Tighten the bolts to the torque listed in this Chapter's Specifications.
25   Remove the pin from the timing chain tensioner.
26   Slowly turn the crankshaft clockwise two revolutions using the crankshaft bolt and recheck the timing marks and camshaft sprocket index marks for proper alignment.
Caution: *If the crankshaft binds or seems to hit something, do not force it, as the valves may be hitting the pistons. If this happens, valve timing is incorrect. Remove the chain*

and repeat the installation procedure and verify that the installation is correct.
27   The remainder of installation is the reverse of the removal Steps.
28   Reconnect the battery negative cable (see Chapter 5).
29   Run the engine and check for leaks.

---

10   Crankshaft pulley and front oil seal - replacement

---

1   Disconnect the cable from the negative battery terminal (see Chapter 5).
2   Raise the vehicle and support it securely on jackstands. Remove the wheel and the splash shield from below the engine compartment.
3   Loosen the crankshaft pulley bolt. A special tool that engages with the recessed hex in the pulley opening is available to prevent the crankshaft from turning while unscrewing the bolt. If you can't obtain one of these tools, remove the flywheel/driveplate inspection cover and wedge a screwdriver into the starter ring gear teeth. Slip the pulley off the crankshaft.
4   Carefully pry the seal out of the timing chain cover with a seal removal tool or a screwdriver. Don't scratch the seal bore or damage the crankshaft in the process (if the crankshaft is damaged, the new seal will end up leaking).
5   Clean the bore in the seal housing and coat the outer edge of the new seal with engine oil or multi-purpose grease. Using a seal driver or a socket with an outside diameter slightly smaller than the outside diameter of the seal, carefully drive the seal into place with a hammer. If a socket is not available, a short section of a large diameter pipe will work. Check the seal after installation to be sure the spring did not pop out.
6   Lubricate the lip of the seal with a thin film of engine oil or multi-purpose grease. Lubricate the pulley bolt threads and surface between washer and bolt head with clean

engine oil, then install the crankshaft pulley and tighten to the torque listed in this Chapter's Specifications .
7   The remainder of installation is the reverse of removal.
8   Run the engine and check for leaks.

---

11   Camshaft - removal, inspection and installation

Removal

1   Disconnect the negative battery cable (see Chapter 5).
2   Remove the air filter housing (see Chapter 4).
3   Remove the valve cover (see Section 4).
4   Set the engine at TDC (see Section 3). Make sure UP is shown on the camshaft sprocket and the alignment marks are level with the surface of the cylinder head.
5   Place a reference mark on the timing chain and the camshaft gear for installation purposes.
6   Lubricate the timing chain tensioner wih fresh engine oil through the left side of the timing chain (looking from the front of the engine).
7   Pry out the cam plug on the front of the cylinder head (see illustration).
8   Remove the bolt near the center of the timing chain cover to reveal the access hole for securing the timing chain tensioner arm for service (see illustration).
Note: *Obtain a 6 x 1.0 mm bolt and have it ready to install into the access hole during the next step.*
9   While holding the crankshaft pulley bolt securely so the engine will not turn, rotate the camshaft clockwise using the camshaft sprocket bolt accessed through the cam plug opening. Rotate the camshaft enough to allow the 6 x 1.0 mm bolt to be installed in the access hole and threaded into the block (see illustrations). Once the bolt is threaded in, release the tension on the camshaft.

11.8 Timing chain tensioner access bolt

11.9a Turning the cam sprocket moves the slotted bracket in the tensioner to reveal a hole . . .

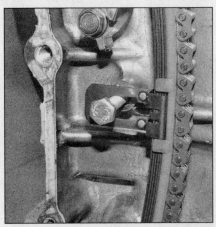

11.9b . . . into which a locking bolt can be installed (timing chain cover removed for clarity)

11.10 Secure the timing chain to the camshaft sprocket with a tie-strap

11.11 Hold the camshaft with a wrench while the sprocket bolt is loosened

11.12 Two lengths of stiff wire can be used to support the camshaft sprocket and prevent the timing chain from becoming disengaged from the crankshaft sprocket

Note: *DO NOT exceed 41 ft-lbs (56 Nm) when rotating the camshaft.*

10   Use a plastic tie-strap to secure the timing chain to the sprocket (see illustration).

11   While holding the camshaft using an open end wrench behind the camshaft sprocket, loosen and remove the camshaft sprocket bolt (see illustration).

12   Remove the sprocket from the camshaft and secure it to the cylinder head (see illustration).

Caution: *Do not allow the timing chain to fall off the crankshaft sprocket. If it does, the oil pan (2008 and earlier models) or timing chain cover (2009 and later models) will have to be removed to align it.*

13   Remove the rocker arm assembly (see Section 7).

14   Remove the Camshaft Position Sensor (see Chapter 6).

15   Remove the camshaft thrust cover from the end of the cylinder head (see illustrations).

11.15a Remove the thrust cover bolts . . .

11.15b . . . then pull the thrust cover out of the cylinder head. Be sure to replace the O-ring with a new one before installation

11.17 Keep the camshaft as horizontal as possible while removing it

16   On 2009 and later models, use the same open end wrench to prevent the camshaft from turning and remove the camshaft position sensor pulse plate from the end of the camshaft through the thrust cover opening using an Allen wrench.

17   Slide the camshaft out of the head from the thrust cover end (see illustration).

Inspection

18   Check the camshaft bearing journals for scoring and signs of wear. If they are worn, replace the cylinder head with a new or rebuilt assembly.

19   Check the cam lobes for wear:

a) *Check the toe and ramp areas of each cam lobe for score marks and uneven wear. Also check for flaking and pitting.*

b) *If there's wear on the toe or the ramp, replace the camshaft, but first try to find the cause of the wear. Look for abrasive substances in the oil and inspect the oil pump and oil passages for blockage. Lobe wear is usually caused by inadequate lubrication or dirty oil.*

c) *Using a micrometer, measure the cam lobe height. If lobe wear is indicated, replace the camshaft.*

20   Inspect the rocker arms for wear, galling and pitting of the contact surfaces (see Section 7).

21   If any of the conditions described above are noted, the cylinder head is probably getting insufficient lubrication or dirty oil. Make sure you track down the cause of this problem (low oil level, low oil pump capacity, clogged oil passage, etc.) before installing a new cylinder head, camshaft or rocker arm assembly.

Installation

22   Thoroughly clean the camshaft, the bearing surfaces in the head and caps and the rocker arms. Wipe off all components with a clean, lint-free cloth.

23   Lubricate the camshaft bearing surfaces in the head and the bearing journals and lobes on the camshaft with camshaft assembly lubricant.

Caution: *Failure to adequately lubricate the camshaft and related components can cause serious damage to bearing and friction surfaces during the first few seconds after engine start-up, when the oil pressure is low or non-existent.*

24   Install the camshaft through the thrust cover opening. Use care not to damage the bearing surfaces during installation.

25   On 2009 and later models, install the camshaft position sensor pulse plate and tighten it to the torque listed in this Chapter's Specifications .

26   Install the thrust cover using a new O-ring and tighten the bolts to the torque listed in this Chapter's Specifications .

27   Install the camshaft position sensor. Install and lubricate the NEW O-ring prior to installation.

28   Install the camshaft sprocket, tightening the bolt to the torque listed in this Chapter's Specifications.

29   Remove the bolt securing the timing chain tensioner arm by holding the crankshaft pulley bolt and applying counter clockwise tension to the camshaft sprocket bolt. Install the cam plug using a new o-ring and install the access hole bolt.

30   Rotate the camshaft as necessary and position the camshaft sprocket with the " UP " mark stamped on the sprocket at the twelve o'clock position.

31   Make sure the camshaft and crankshaft marks are still set to TDC for cylinder number 1, then install the rocker arm assembly (see Section 7).

32   Rotate the crankshaft clockwise slowly by hand through two complete revolutions and recheck the alignment marks on the sprockets. The timing marks should still be aligned. If they're not, reset all the timing marks again.

Caution: *If you feel resistance while rotating the crankshaft, stop immediately and find out why!*

33   The remainder of installation is the reverse of removal.

34   Reconnect the negative battery cable (see Chapter 5).

35   Run the engine and check for leaks.

12   Cylinder head - removal and installation

Warning: *Allow the engine to cool completely before beginning this procedure.*

Removal

1   Relieve the fuel system pressure (see Chapter 4), then disconnect the cable from the negative terminal of the battery (see Chapter 5).

2   Position the number one piston at Top Dead Center (see Section 3).

3   Drain the cooling system and remove the spark plugs (see Chapter 1).

4   Remove the air filter housing (see Chapter 4).

5   Disconnect the heater hoses, the upper and lower radiator hoses and the bypass hose from the water outlet/thermostat housing.

6   Remove the drivebelt (see Chapter 1).

7   Disconnect the EVAP canister hose, the brake booster vacuum hose, the PCV hose and intake breather hose.

8   Remove the intake manifold (see Section 5).

9   On 2008 and earlier models, remove the exhaust manifold (see Section 6). On 2009 and later models, disconnect the catalytic converter from the cylinder head.

10   Disconnect the electrical connectors from the fuel injector connectors, the ECT sensor, the TP sensor, the MAP sensor, oxygen sensor, EGR sensor, the CKP sensor, the CMP sensor, and the VTEC solenoid. Label each connector to prevent incorrect reassembly.Remove the harness clamps and holders from the transaxle end of the cylinder head. Remove the ground cable.

11   Remove the fuel rail (see Chapter 4).

12   Remove the coolant bypass hose from the coolant housing and remove the coolant pipe that runs across the front of the engine block.

13   Remove the timing chain and sprocket (see Section 9).

14   Remove the rocker arm assembly (see Section 7).

15   Loosen the cylinder head bolts in 1/4-turn increments until they can be removed by hand. Work in a pattern that's the reverse of the tightening sequence to avoid warping the cylinder head (see illustration 12.23).

Caution: *Discard the old bolts and obtain new ones (re-using the old bolts is not recommended, the final tightening stage assumes that new bolts are being installed).*

16   Lift the cylinder head off the engine. If resistance is felt, don't pry between the head and block gasket mating surfaces - damage to the mating surfaces will result. Set the head on blocks of wood to prevent damage to the gasket sealing surfaces.

17   Have an automotive machine shop inspect the cylinder head for for cracks and check for warpage.

Installation

18   The mating surfaces of the cylinder head and block must be perfectly clean when the head is installed.

19   Use a gasket scraper to remove all traces of carbon and old gasket material, then clean the mating surfaces with brake system cleaner. If there's oil on the mating surfaces when the cylinder head is installed, the gasket may not seal correctly and leaks may develop. When working on the engine block, stuff the cylinders with clean shop rags to keep out debris. Use a vacuum cleaner to remove material that falls into the cylinders. Since the cylinder head and engine block are

made of aluminum, aggressive scraping can cause damage. Be extra careful not to nick or gouge the mating surfaces with the scraper.

20 Check the block and cylinder head mating surfaces for nicks, deep scratches and other damage. If damage is slight, it can be removed with a file; if it's excessive, machining may be the only alternative.

21 Use a tap of the correct size to chase the threads in the cylinder head bolt holes. Use a wire brush to remove corrosion and clean the bolt threads. Dirt, corrosion, sealant and damaged threads will affect torque readings.

22 Place a new gasket on the engine block. Check to see if there are any markings (such as "TOP") on the gasket to indicate how it is to be installed. Those identification marks must face UP. Set the cylinder head in position.

23 Lubricate the threads and the seats of the NEW cylinder head bolts with clean engine oil, then install them. Tighten the bolts in the recommended sequence, in stages, to the torque listed in this Chapter's Specifications (see illustrations). Because of the critical function of cylinder head bolts, the manufacturer specifies the following conditions for tightening them:

a) A beam-type or dial-type torque wrench is preferable to a pre-set (click-stop) torque wrench. If you use a pre-set torque wrench, tighten slowly and be careful not to overtighten the bolts.

b) If a bolt makes any sound while you're tightening it (squeaking, clicking, etc.), loosen it completely and tighten it again in the specified stages.

24 Install the timing chain (see Section 9) and rocker arm assembly (see Section 7).

25 Rotate the crankshaft clockwise slowly by hand through two complete revolutions and recheck the alignment marks on the sprockets.

Caution: *If you feel any resistance while turning the engine over, stop and re-check the camshaft timing. The valves might be hitting*

the pistons.

26 It is recommended to install a new thermostat of the proper heat specification for the vehicle during installation.

27 Reinstall the remaining parts in the reverse order of removal. Use a new O-ring on the coolant pipe and any other components using O-rings.

28 Refill the cooling system and change the engine oil and filter (see Chapter 1).

29 Reconnect the battery (see Chapter 5).

30 Run the engine until normal operating temperature is reached. Check for leaks and proper operation.

Note: *The idle speed and crankshaft position sensor pattern clear/learn procedure may need to be performed after replacing the head and/or head gasket (this would be indicated by a Check Engine light). This requires specialized diagnostic equipment available at a dealer or independent repair shop.*

13 Oil pan - removal and installation

Removal

1 Disconnect the cable from the negative terminal of the battery (see Chapter 5).

2 Raise the vehicle and support it securely on jackstands. Remove the splash shield from under the engine.

3 Drain the engine oil and replace the oil filter (see Chapter 1).

4 On 2009 and later models, remove the bolts attaching the air conditioning compressor to the engine and position it aside (see Chapter 3). Support the compressor with rope or wire.

Warning: *Do not disconnect the refrigerant lines.*

5 Remove the driveaxle heat shield.

6 On 2009 and later automatic transaxle equipped vehicles, remove the shift cable cover (see Chapter 7B). On manual transaxle

equipped vehicles, remove the torque rod bracket (see Chapter 7A).

7 Remove the dipstick, then remove the bolt securing the dipstick tube to the engine block. Use a twisting motion to remove the dipstick tube from the engine.

8 On 2009 and later models, remove the Crankshaft Position Sensor (CKP) cover and disconnect the CKP connector (see Chapter 6).

9 Remove the flywheel or driveplate inspection cover.

10 Remove the two (manual transaxle) or three (automatic transaxle) oil pan-to-transaxle bolts. Remove the remaining oil pan bolts. Note the location for installation as the bolts are different lengths.

11 Tap on the pan with a soft-face hammer to break the gasket seal and detach the oil pan from the engine.

12 Remove the oil pan from the engine. Use care not to spill any remaining oil during removal.

Installation

13 Using a gasket scraper, remove all traces of old gasket and/or sealant from the engine block and the oil pan. Also make sure the threaded bolt holes in the block are clean.

Caution: *Be very careful when scraping on aluminum engine parts. Aluminum is soft and gouges easily. Severely gouged parts may require replacement.*

14 Clean the oil pan with solvent and dry it thoroughly.

15 Clean the mating surfaces on the engine block and the oil pan with brake system cleaner to remove any oil residue which will prevent the new gasket from sealing properly.

16 Install a new oil pan gasket at the transaxle end and replace the O-ring on the oil filter side of the pan. Also install the dowel pins (see illustrations).

17 Apply a bead of RTV sealant to the

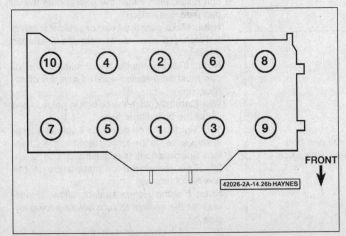

12.23 Cylinder head bolt TIGHTENING sequence

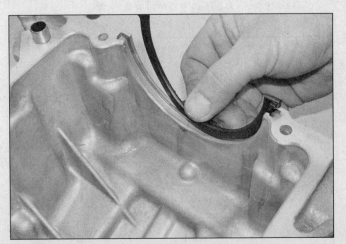

13.16a Install a new U-shaped gasket to the oil pan groove

13.16b Install a new O-ring to the oil filter supply passage, and insert the dowel into its hole

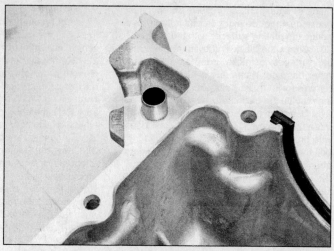

13.16c Install the other dowel into its hole in the transaxle-end of the pan

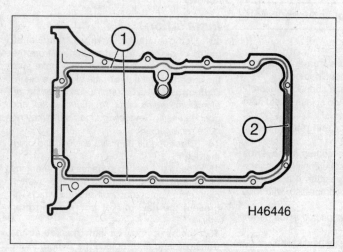

H46446

13.17a Oil pan sealant application details

13.17b Run the bead of sealant around the inboard side of the bolt holes

1　Bead of sealant, 1/16-inch (1.5 mm) in diameter (2008 and earlier models) or 3/32-inch (2.5 mm) in diameter (2009 and later models)
2　Bead of sealant, 3/16-inch (5 mm) in diameter

13.19 Oil pan bolt tightening sequence

H46447

perimeter of the oil pan along the inside of the bolt holes, then install the gasket onto the oil pan (see illustrations).

Note: *Make sure the bead of sealant extends 5/8-inch (15 mm) down onto the U-shaped gasket.*

Note: *If using Honda brand sealant, the oil pan must be installed within 4 minutes of application.*

18　Carefully place the oil pan in position and install the bolts finger tight.

19　Tighten the oil pan bolts a little at a time, in sequence, to the torque listed in this Chapter's Specifications (see illustration).

20　The remainder of installation is the reverse of removal.

Note: *If using Honda sealant, allow 30 minutes for the sealant to cure before adding engine oil.*

21　Fill the crankcase with the recommended oil and install a new oil filter (see Chapter 1).

22　Reconnect the battery (see Chapter 5).

Note: *If using Honda sealant, wait 3 hours be-*

14.3 Oil pump mounting bolts

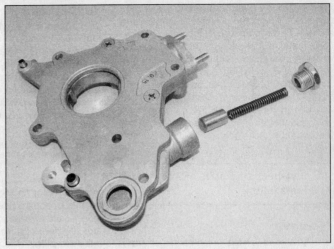

14.5 Pressure relief valve plug, spring and plunger

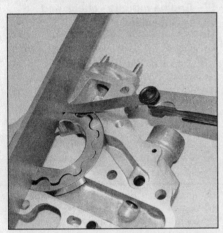

14.6a Use a feeler gauge and straight-edge to check the clearance between the rotors and the cover

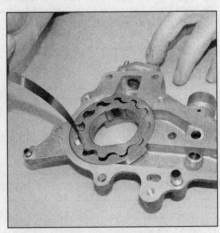

14.6b Use a feeler gauge to check the tooth-tip clearance between the inner and outer rotors

14.6c Use a feeler gauge to check the outer rotor-to-pump body clearance

fore running engine for sealant to completely cure.

23   Start the engine and check for leaks. Check all fluid levels.

14   Oil pump - removal, inspection and installation

Removal

1   Remove the timing chain (see Section 9).

2   Remove the oil pick-up tube and screen from the pump housing and the main bearing cap bridge.

3   Remove the bolts from the oil pump housing and separate the assembly from the engine (see illustration).

Inspection

4   Remove the screws and remove the oil pump cover. You may need to use an impact screwdriver to loosen the pump cover screws

without stripping the heads.

5   Remove the pressure relief valve plug and extract the spring and pressure relief valve plunger from the pump housing (see illustration). Check the spring for distortion and the relief valve plunger for scoring. Replace parts as necessary.

6   Check the oil pump rotor-to-cover clearance, tooth tip clearance and rotor-to-body clearance (see illustrations). Compare your measurements to the values listed in this Chapter's Specifications. Replace the pump if any of the measurements exceed the specified limits.

7   Install the pump rotors. Pack the spaces between the rotors with petroleum jelly (this will prime the pump).

8   Apply thread-locking compound to the pump cover screws, install the cover and tighten the screws. Install the oil pressure relief valve and spring assembly. Use a new sealing washer on the plug and tighten the plug securely.

14.9 Install a new O-ring into the back of vthe oil pump

Installation

9   Install a new O-ring in the pump housing (see illustration).

10   Apply a thin coat of anaerobic sealant to the pump housing-to-block sealing surface.

11   Install the pump housing to the engine block and tighten the bolts to the torque listed in this Chapter's Specifications.
12   Install the oil pick-up tube and screen, using a new gasket. Tighten the bolts to the torque listed in this Chapter's Specifications. Install the oil pan (see Section 13).
13   The remainder of installation is the reverse of removal. Add the specified type and quantity of oil (see Chapter 1), run the engine and check for leaks.

15   Flywheel/driveplate - removal and installation

Removal

1   Raise the vehicle and support it securely on jackstands, then remove the transaxle from the vehicle (see Chapter 7A, 7B).
2   If the vehicle is equipped with a manual transaxle, remove the pressure plate and clutch disc (see Chapter 8). Now is a good time to check/replace the clutch components and pilot bearing.
3   Remove the bolts that secure the flywheel/driveplate to the crankshaft. To prevent the crankshaft from turning, wedge a screwdriver in the ring gear teeth (manual transaxle models), or insert a long punch through one of the holes in the driveplate and allow it to rest against a projection on the engine block (automatic transaxle models).
4   Remove the flywheel/driveplate from the crankshaft. Since the flywheel is fairly heavy, be sure to support it while removing the last bolt.

Inspection

5   Clean the flywheel to remove grease and oil. Inspect the surface for cracks, rivet grooves, burned areas and score marks. Light scoring can be removed with emery cloth. Check for cracked and broken ring gear teeth. Lay the flywheel on a flat surface and use a straightedge to check for warpage.
6   Clean and inspect the mating surfaces of the flywheel/driveplate and the crankshaft. If the rear main oil seal is leaking, replace it before reinstalling the flywheel/driveplate (see Section 16).
7   If necessary, check flywheel runout and compare your findings with the values listed in this Chapter's Specifications . If not within specifications or wear grooves are deep, have the flywheel resurfaced as necessary at a machine shop.

Installation

8   Position the flywheel/driveplate against the crankshaft. Note that some engines have an alignment dowel or staggered bolt holes to ensure correct installation. Before installing the bolts, apply thread-locking compound to the threads.
9   Prevent the flywheel/driveplate from turning by using one of the methods described in Step 3. Using a criss-cross pattern, tighten the bolts to the torque listed in this Chapter's Specifications.
10   The remainder of installation is the reverse of the removal procedure.

16   Rear main oil seal - replacement

1   The transaxle must be removed from the vehicle for this procedure (see Chapter 7A, 7B).

2   Remove the flywheel/driveplate (see Section 15).
3   Before removing the seal, it is very important that the clearance between the seal and the outside edge of the retainer or block is checked. The new seal must not be driven in past this measurement.
4   Use a screwdriver or seal removal tool to carefully pry the seal out.
5   Apply a film of clean oil to the crankshaft seal journal and the lip of the new seal and carefully tap the seal into place. The lip is stiff, so carefully work it onto the seal journal of the crankshaft with a smooth object like the end of a socket extension. Using a seal driver, tap the seal into place to the previously recorded depth.
6   The remaining steps are the reverse of removal.
7   Run the engine and check for oil leaks.

17   Engine mounts - check and replacement

1   Engine mounts seldom require attention, but broken or deteriorated mounts should be replaced immediately or the added strain placed on the driveline components may cause damage or wear.

Check

2   During the check, the engine must be raised slightly to remove the weight from the mounts.
3   Raise the vehicle and support it securely on jackstands, then position a jack under the engine oil pan. Place a large wood block between the jack head and the oil pan, then

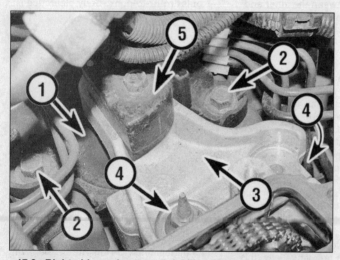

17.8a Right-side engine mount details - 2008 and earlier models

1   *Mount*
2   *Mount-to-chassis bolts (two on manual transaxle models, three on automatic transaxle models)*
3   *Mount bracket*
4   *Bracket-to-engine nuts (rear nut accessed from underneath)*
5   *Damper weight (mount-to-bracket nut underneath)*

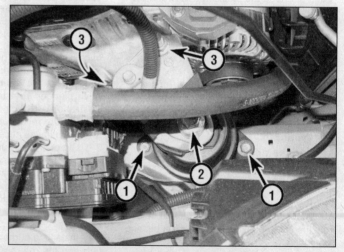

17.8b Right-side engine mount details - 2009 and later models

1   *Mount-to-chassis bolts*
2   *Mount-to-bracket bolt*
3   *Bracket-to-engine nuts (rear nut accessed from underneath)*

carefully raise the engine just enough to take the weight off the mounts.

Warning: *DO NOT place any part of your body under the engine when it's supported only by a jack!*

4   Check the mount insulators to see if the rubber is cracked, hardened or separated from the metal in the center of the mount.

5   Check for relative movement between the mount plates and the engine or frame (use a large screwdriver or prybar to attempt to move the mounts). If movement is noted, lower the engine and tighten the mount fasteners.

Replacement

6   Disconnect the cable from the negative terminal of the battery (see Chapter 5). Raise the vehicle and support it securely on jackstands (if not already done). Support the engine as described in Step 3.

7   Remove the fasteners, raise the engine with the jack and detach the mount from the frame bracket and engine (see illustrations).

8   Install the new mount, making sure it is correctly positioned in its bracket (see illustrations). Install the fasteners and tighten them securely.

9   Install the new mount, making sure it is correctly positioned in its bracket. Install the fasteners and tighten them securely.

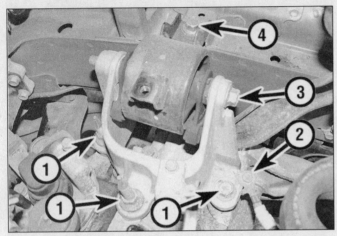

17.8c Left-side transaxle mount details - 2008 and earlier models

1	Mount-to-transaxle fasteners	3	Mount through-bolt
2	Ground strap bolt	4	Mount-to-chassis bolt

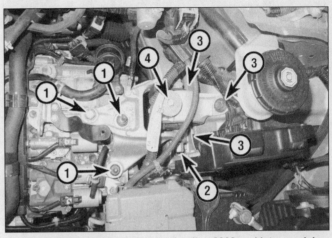

17.8d Left-side transaxle mount details - 2009 and later models

1   Mount-to-transaxle fasteners
2   Mount through-bolt
3   Mount-to-chassis bolts (manual transaxle models do not have the upper center bolt)
4   Damper weight

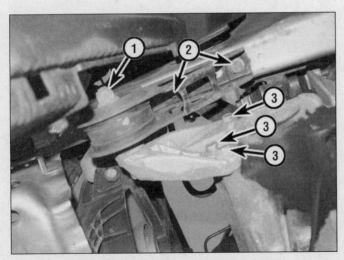

17.8e Left-front front transaxle mount details

1   Mount-to-bracket nut
2   Mount-to-chassis bolts
3   Mount bracket-to-transaxle bolts

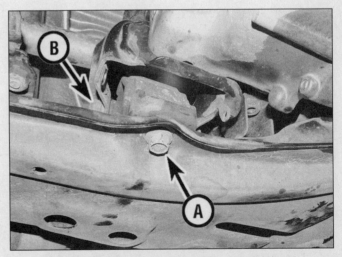

7.8f Rear transaxle mount-to-subframe bolt (A) and through-bolt (B) (2008 and earlier models shown)

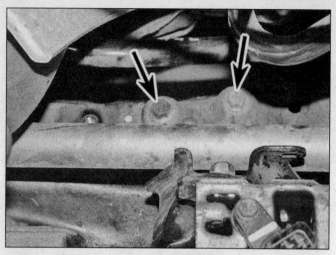

17.8g Rear transaxle mount-to-subframe bolts, seen from above
(2008 and earlier models shown)

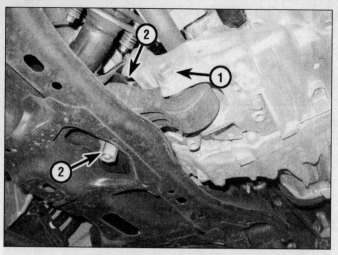

17.8h Rear roll restrictor (torque rod) details
(2009 and later models)

Notes

Notes

Chapter 2 Part B
General engine overhaul procedures

Contents

Specifications

General

Engine designation
  2008 and earlier models L15A1
  2009 and later models L15A7
Displacement .... 91.3 cubic inches
Compression ratio 10.4:1
Rear main seal installed height
  2008 and earlier models .... 0.28 to 0.31 inches (7 to 8 mm) (1)
  2009 and later models .... 0.008 to 0.047 inches (0.2 to 1.2 mm) (2)
Crankshaft endplay
  Standard .... 0.004 to 0.014 inches (0.10 to 0.35 mm)
  Maximum .... 0.018 inch (0.45 mm)
Cylinder compression pressure
  Minimum .... 132 psi
  Maximum variation between cylinders .... 29 psi
Oil pressure (minimum, warm engine)
  Idle .... 10 psi
  3000 rpm .... 50 psi
Main bearing oil clearance
  Standard .... 0.00071 to 0.00142 inch (0.018 to 0.036 mm)
  Maximum .... 0.00197 inch (0.050 mm)

(1) Measured from seal to flywheel/driveplate mating surface.
(2) Measured from seal to edge of rear main seal bore in block.

Torque specifications

	Ft-lbs (unless otherwise indicated)	Nm

Note: *One foot-pound (ft-lb) of torque is equivalent to 12 inch-pounds (in-lbs) of torque. Torque values below approximately 15 ft-lbs are expressed in inch-pounds, since most foot-pound torque wrenches are not accurate at these smaller values.*

	Ft-lbs (unless otherwise indicated)	Nm
Connecting rod cap bolts		
Step 1	85 in-lbs	9.8
Step 2	Tighten an additional 90-degrees	
Main bearing cap bridge bolts		
Step 1	18	25
Step 2	Tighten an additional 40-degrees	
Crankshaft pulse plate bolts (2009 and later models)	168 in-lbs	19

Note: *Refer to Chapter 2A for additional torque specifications.*

1 General information - engine overhaul

1   Included in this portion of Chapter 2 are general information and diagnostic testing procedures for determining the overall mechanical condition of your engine.

2   The information ranges from advice concerning preparation for an overhaul and the purchase of replacement parts and/or components to detailed, step-by-step procedures covering removal and installation.

3   The following Sections have been written to help you determine whether your engine needs to be overhauled and how to remove and install it once you've determined it needs to be rebuilt. For information concerning in-vehicle engine repair, see Chapter.

4   The Specifications included in this Part are general in nature and include only those necessary for testing the oil pressure and engine compression, and bottom-end torque specifications. Refer to Chapter 2A for additional engine Specifications.

5   It's not always easy to determine when, or if, an engine should be completely overhauled, because a number of factors must be considered.

6   High mileage is not necessarily an indication that an overhaul is needed, while low mileage doesn't preclude the need for an overhaul. Frequency of servicing is probably the most important consideration. An engine that's had regular and frequent oil and filter changes, as well as other required maintenance, will most likely give many thousands of miles of reliable service. Conversely, a neglected engine may require an overhaul very early in its service life.

7   Excessive oil consumption is an indication that piston rings, valve seals and/or valve guides are in need of attention. Make sure that oil leaks aren't responsible before deciding that the rings and/or guides are bad. Perform a cylinder compression check to determine the extent of the work required (see Section 3). Also, check the vacuum readings under various conditions (see Section 4).

8   Check the oil pressure with a gauge installed in place of the oil pressure sending unit (see Section 2) and compare it to this Chapter's Specifications. If it's extremely low, the bearings and/or oil pump are probably worn out.

9   Loss of power, rough running, knocking or metallic engine noises, excessive valve train noise and high fuel consumption rates may also point to the need for an overhaul, especially if they're all present at the same time. If a complete tune-up doesn't remedy the situation, major mechanical work is the only solution.

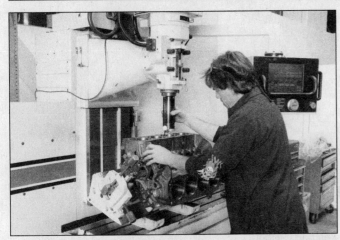

1.10a An engine block being bored. An engine rebuilder will use special machinery to recondition the cylinder bores

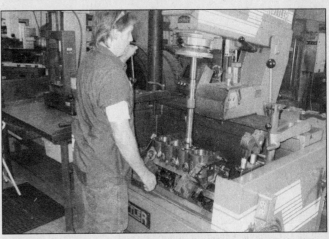

1.10b If the cylinders are bored, the machine shop will normally hone the engine on a machine like this

10   An engine overhaul involves restoring the internal parts to the specifications of a new engine. During an overhaul, the piston rings are replaced and the cylinder walls are reconditioned (rebored and/or honed) (see illustrations). If a rebore is done by an automotive machine shop, new oversize pistons will also be installed. The main bearings, connecting rod bearings and camshaft bearings are generally replaced with new ones and, if necessary, the crankshaft may be reground to restore the journals (see illustration). Generally, the valves are serviced as well, since they're usually in less-than-perfect condition at this point. While the engine is being overhauled, other components, such as the distributor, starter and alternator, can be rebuilt as well. The end result should be similar to a new engine that will give many trouble free miles.

Note: *Critical cooling system components such as the hoses, drivebelts, thermostat and water pump should be replaced with new parts when an engine is overhauled. The radiator should be checked carefully to ensure that it isn't clogged or leaking (see Chapter 3). If you purchase a rebuilt engine or short block, some rebuilders will not warranty their engines unless the radiator has been professionally flushed. Also, we don't recommend overhauling the oil pump - always install a new one when an engine is rebuilt.*

11   Overhauling the internal components on today's engines is a difficult and time-consuming task which requires a significant amount of specialty tools and is best left to a professional engine rebuilder (see illustrations). A competent engine rebuilder will handle the inspection of your old parts and offer advice concerning the reconditioning or replacement of the original engine, never purchase parts or have machine work done on other components until the block has been thoroughly inspected by a professional machine shop. As a general rule, time is the primary cost of an overhaul, especially since the vehicle may be tied up for a minimum of two weeks or more. Be aware that some engine builders only have the capability to rebuild the engine you bring them while other rebuilders have a large inventory of rebuilt exchange engines in stock. Also be aware that many machine

1.10c A crankshaft having a main bearing journal ground

shops could take as much as two weeks time to completely rebuild your engine depending on shop workload. Sometimes it makes more sense to simply exchange your engine for another engine that's already rebuilt to save time.

1.11a A machinist checks for a bent connecting rod, using specialized equipment

1.11b A bore gauge being used to check the main bearing bore

1.11c Uneven piston wear like this indicates a bent connecting rod

2.2a Oil pressure sending unit location on 2008 and earlier models (accessible from below)

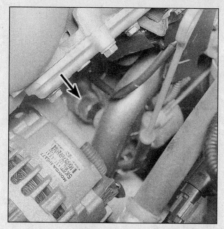

2.2b Oil pressure sending unit location on 2009 and later models (accessible from above)

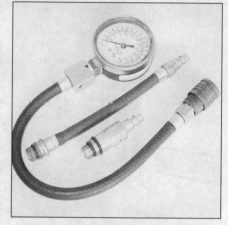

3.5 Use a compression gauge with a threaded fitting for the spark plug hole, not the type that requires hand pressure to maintain the seal

2   Oil pressure check

1   Low engine oil pressure can be a sign of an engine in need of rebuilding. A low oil pressure indicator (often called an "idiot light") is not a test of the oiling system. Such indicators only come on when the oil pressure is dangerously low. Even a factory oil pressure gauge in the instrument panel is only a relative indication, although much better for driver information than a warning light. A better test is with a mechanical (not electrical) oil pressure gauge.

2   Locate the oil pressure sending unit on the front side of the engine block above the oil filter (see illustrations).

3   Unscrew and remove the oil pressure sending unit and screw in the hose for your oil pressure gauge. If necessary, install an adapter fitting. Use Teflon tape or thread sealant on the threads of the adapter and/or the fitting on the end of your gauge's hose.

4   Check the oil pressure with the engine running (normal operating temperature) at the specified engine speed, and compare it to this Section. If it's extremely low, the bearings and/or oil pump may be worn out, also check the pressure relief spring and oil pickup screen for restrictions. An oil filter that has not been changed regularly can also cause a restriction resulting in low oil pressure.

3   Cylinder compression check

1   A compression check will tell you what mechanical condition the upper end of your engine (pistons, rings, valves, head gaskets) is in. Specifically, it can tell you if the compression is down due to leakage caused by worn piston rings, defective valves and seats or a blown head gasket.

Note: *The engine should be at normal operating temperature and the battery must be fully charged for this check.*

2   Begin by cleaning the area around the spark plugs before you remove them (compressed air should be used, if available). The idea is to prevent dirt from getting into the cylinders as the compression check is being done.

3   Remove the ignition coil assemblies (see Chapter 5). Also disable the fuel pump by removing the PGM-FI relay no. 2 from the under-dash fuse/relay box (see Chapter 4).

4   Remove all of the spark plugs (see Chapter 1).

5   Install a compression gauge in the spark plug hole (see illustration).

6   Depress the accelerator pedal to the floor and crank the engine over at least seven compression strokes and watch the gauge. The compression should build up quickly in a healthy engine. Low compression on the first stroke, followed by gradually increasing pressure on successive strokes, indicates worn piston rings. A low compression reading on the first stroke, which doesn't build up during successive strokes, indicates leaking valves or a blown head gasket (a cracked head could also be the cause). Deposits on the undersides of the valve heads can also cause low compression. Record the highest gauge reading obtained.

7   Repeat the procedure for the remaining cylinders and compare the results to this Chapter's Specifications.

8   Add some engine oil (about three squirts from a plunger-type oil can) to each cylinder, through the spark plug hole, and repeat the test.

9   If the compression increases after the oil is added, the piston rings are definitely worn. If the compression doesn't increase significantly, the leakage is occurring at the valves or head gasket. Leakage past the valves may be caused by burned valve seats and/or faces or warped, cracked or bent valves.

10   If two adjacent cylinders have equally low compression, there's a strong possibility that the head gasket between them is blown.

The appearance of coolant in the combustion chambers or the crankcase would verify this condition.

11   If one cylinder is slightly lower than the others, and the engine has a slightly rough idle, a worn lobe on the camshaft could be the cause.

12   If the compression is unusually high, the combustion chambers are probably coated with carbon deposits. If that's the case, the cylinder head(s) should be removed and decarbonized.

13   If compression is way down or varies greatly between cylinders, it would be a good idea to have a leak-down test performed by an automotive repair shop. This test will pinpoint exactly where the leakage is occurring and how severe it is.

4   Vacuum gauge diagnostic checks

1   A vacuum gauge provides inexpensive but valuable information about what is going on in the engine. You can check for worn rings or cylinder walls, leaking head or intake manifold gaskets, incorrect carburetor adjustments, restricted exhaust, stuck or burned valves, weak valve springs, improper ignition or valve timing and ignition problems.

2   Unfortunately, vacuum gauge readings are easy to misinterpret, so they should be used in conjunction with other tests to confirm the diagnosis.

3   Both the absolute readings and the rate of needle movement are important for accurate interpretation. Most gauges measure vacuum in inches of mercury (in-Hg). The following references to vacuum assume the diagnosis is being performed at sea level. As elevation increases (or atmospheric pressure decreases), the reading will decrease. For every 1,000 foot increase in elevation above approximately 2,000 feet, the gauge readings will decrease about one inch of mercury.

4   Connect the vacuum gauge directly to

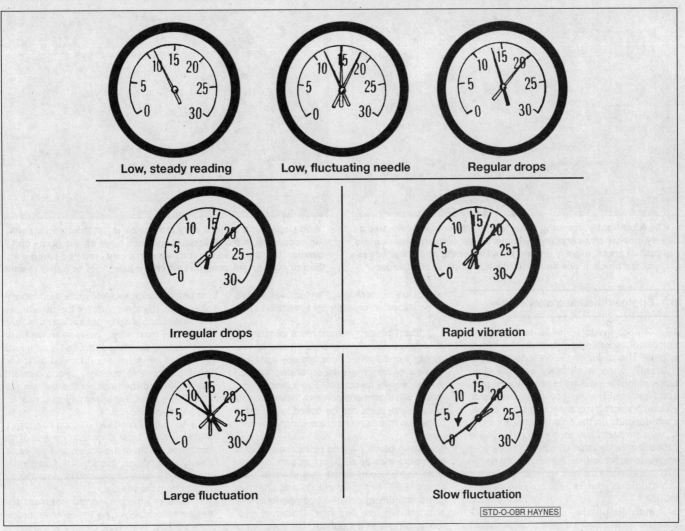

Low, steady reading   **Low, fluctuating needle**   **Regular drops**

Irregular drops   **Rapid vibration**

Large fluctuation   **Slow fluctuation**

STD-O-OBR HAYNES

4.6 Typical vacuum gauge readings

the intake manifold vacuum, not to ported (throttle body) vacuum. Some models are equipped with a vacuum fitting built into the brake booster vacuum hose grommet at the brake booster. Other models are equipped with a vacuum hose fitting on the intake manifold. Use a T-fitting to access the vacuum signal. Be sure no hoses are left disconnected during the test or false readings will result.

5 Before you begin the test, allow the engine to warm up completely. Block the wheels and set the parking brake. With the transaxle in Park, start the engine and allow it to run at normal idle speed.

Warning: *Keep your hands and the vacuum gauge clear of the fans.*

6 Read the vacuum gauge; an average, healthy engine should normally produce about 17 to 22 in-Hg with a fairly steady needle (see illustration). Refer to the following vacuum gauge readings and what they indicate about the engine's condition:

7 A low, steady reading usually indicates a leaking gasket between the intake manifold and cylinder head(s) or throttle body, a leaky vacuum hose, late ignition timing or incorrect camshaft timing. Check ignition timing with a timing light and eliminate all other possible causes, utilizing the tests provided in this Chapter before you remove the timing chain cover to check the timing marks.

8 If the reading is three to eight inches below normal and it fluctuates at that low reading, suspect an intake manifold gasket leak at an intake port or a faulty fuel injector.

9 If the needle has regular drops of about two-to-four inches at a steady rate, the valves are probably leaking. Perform a compression check or leak-down test to confirm this.

10 An irregular drop or down-flick of the needle can be caused by a sticking valve or an ignition misfire. Perform a compression check (see Section 3) or leak-down test and read the spark plugs.

11 A rapid vibration of about four in-Hg vibration at idle combined with exhaust smoke indicates worn valve guides. Perform a leak-down test to confirm this. If the rapid vibration occurs with an increase in engine speed, check for a leaking intake manifold gasket or head gasket, weak valve springs, burned valves or ignition misfire.

12 A slight fluctuation, say one inch up and down, may mean ignition problems. Check all the usual tune-up items and, if necessary, run the engine on an ignition analyzer.

13 If there is a large fluctuation, perform a compression or leak-down test to look for a weak or dead cylinder or a blown head gasket.

14 If the needle moves slowly through a wide range, check for a clogged PCV system, incorrect idle fuel mixture, throttle body or intake manifold gasket leaks.

15 Check for a slow return after revving the engine by quickly snapping the throttle open until the engine reaches about 2,500 rpm and let it shut. Normally the reading should drop to near zero, rise above normal idle reading (about 5 in-Hg over) and then return to the previous idle reading. If the vacuum returns slowly and doesn't peak when the throttle is snapped shut, the rings may be worn. If there is a long delay, look for a restricted exhaust system (often the muffler or catalytic converter). An easy way to check this is to temporarily disconnect the exhaust ahead of the suspected part and redo the test.

6.5a After tightly wrapping water-vulnerable components, use a spray cleaner on everything, with particular concentration on the greasiest areas, usually around the valve cover and lower edges of the block. If one section dries out, apply more cleaner

6.5b Depending on how dirty the engine is, let the cleaner soak in according to the directions and then hose off the grime and cleaner. Get the rinse water down into every area you can get at; then dry important components with a hair dryer or paper towels

5   Engine rebuilding alternatives

1   The do-it-yourselfer is faced with a number of options when purchasing a rebuilt engine. The major considerations are cost, warranty, parts availability and the time required for the rebuilder to complete the project. The decision to replace the engine block, piston/connecting rod assemblies and crankshaft depends on the final inspection results of your engine. Only then can you make a cost effective decision whether to have your engine overhauled or simply purchase an exchange engine for your vehicle.

2   Some of the rebuilding alternatives include:

3   **Individual parts** - If the inspection procedures reveal that the engine block and most engine components are in reusable condition, purchasing individual parts and having a rebuilder rebuild your engine may be the most economical alternative. The block, crankshaft

6.7 Get an engine stand sturdy enough to firmly support the engine while you're working on it. Stay away from three-wheeled models; they have a tendency to tip over more easily, so get a four-wheeled unit

and piston/connecting rod assemblies should all be inspected carefully by a machine shop first.

4   **Short block** - A short block consists of an engine block with a crankshaft and piston/connecting rod assemblies already installed. All new bearings are incorporated and all clearances will be correct. The existing camshafts, valve train components, cylinder head and external parts can be bolted to the short block with little or no machine shop work necessary.

5   **Long block** - A long block consists of a short block plus an oil pump, oil pan, cylinder head, valve cover, camshaft and valve train components, timing sprockets and chain or gears and timing cover. All components are installed with new bearings, seals and gaskets incorporated throughout. The installation of manifolds and external parts is all that's necessary.

6   **Low mileage used engines** - Some companies now offer low mileage used engines which is a very cost effective way to get your vehicle up and running again. These engines often come from vehicles which have been in totaled in accidents or come from other countries which have a higher vehicle turn over rate. A low mileage used engine also usually has a similar warranty like the newly remanufactured engines.

7   Give careful thought to which alternative is best for you and discuss the situation with local automotive machine shops, auto parts dealers and experienced rebuilders before ordering or purchasing replacement parts.

6   Engine removal - methods and precautions

1   If you've decided that an engine must be removed for overhaul or major repair work, several preliminary steps should be taken. Read all removal and installation procedures carefully prior to committing to this job.

2   Locating a suitable place to work is

extremely important. Adequate work space, along with storage space for the vehicle, will be needed. If a shop or garage isn't available, at the very least a flat, level, clean work surface made of concrete or asphalt is required.

3   These engines are removed by lowering the engine to the floor, along with the transaxle, and then raising the vehicle sufficiently to slide the assembly out; this will require a vehicle hoist.

4   An engine hoist will also be necessary. Make sure the hoist is rated in excess of the combined weight of the engine and transaxle. Safety is of primary importance, considering the potential hazards involved in removing the engine from the vehicle.

5   Cleaning the engine compartment and engine before beginning the removal procedure will help keep tools clean and organized (see illustrations).

6   If you're a novice at engine removal, get at least one helper. One person cannot easily do all the things you need to do to remove a big heavy engine and transaxle assembly from the engine compartment. Also helpful is to seek advice and assistance from someone who's experienced in engine removal.

7   Plan the operation ahead of time. Arrange for or obtain all of the tools and equipment you'll need prior to beginning the job (see illustration). Some of the equipment necessary to perform engine removal and installation safely and with relative ease are (in addition to a vehicle hoist and an engine hoist) a heavy duty floor jack (preferably fitted with a transmission jack head adapter), complete sets of wrenches and sockets as described in the front of this manual, wooden blocks, plenty of rags and cleaning solvent for mopping up spilled oil, coolant and gasoline.

8   Plan for the vehicle to be out of use for quite a while. A machine shop can do the work that is beyond the scope of the home mechanic. Machine shops often have a busy schedule, so before removing the engine, consult the shop for an estimate of how long it will take to rebuild or repair the components that may need work.

7 Engine - removal and installation

Warning: *Gasoline is extremely flammable, so take extra precautions when you work on any part of the fuel system. Don't smoke or allow open flames or bare light bulbs near the work area, and don't work in a garage where a gas-type appliance (such as a water heater or clothes dryer) is present. Since gasoline is carcinogenic, wear fuel-resistant gloves when there's a possibility of being exposed to fuel, and, if you spill any fuel on your skin, rinse it off immediately with soap and water. Mop up any spills immediately and do not store fuel-soaked rags where they could ignite. The fuel system is under constant pressure, so, if any fuel lines are to be disconnected, the fuel pressure in the system must be relieved first (see Chapter 4 for more information). When you perform any kind of work on the fuel system, wear safety glasses and have a Class B type fire extinguisher on hand.*

Warning: *The air conditioning system is under high pressure. Do not loosen any hose fittings or remove any components until after the system has been discharged. Air conditioning refrigerant must be properly discharged into an EPA-approved recovery/recycling unit at a dealer service department or an automotive air conditioning repair facility. Always wear eye protection when disconnecting air conditioning system fittings.*

Warning: *The engine must be completely cool before beginning this procedure.*

Note: *Engine removal on these vehicles is a difficult job, especially for a do-it-yourselfer working at home. The manufacturer states that the engine and transaxle have to be removed as a unit from the bottom of the vehicle, not the top. With a floor jack and jackstands, it can't be raised high enough or supported safely enough for the engine/transaxle to slide out from underneath. The manufacturer recommends that removal of the engine/transaxle only be performed with a frame-contact type hoist.*

Note: *During this procedure you'll have to adjust the height of the vehicle with the vehicle hoist to perform certain operations.*

Removal

1 Park the car on a vehicle hoist, then raise the hoist arms to contact the jacking points on each side of the vehicle, but don't raise the vehicle yet.

2 Remove the engine cover if equipped.

3 Relieve the fuel system pressure (see Chapter 4), then remove the battery and battery tray (see Chapter 5).

4 Drain the engine oil and engine coolant (see Chapter 1).

5 Loosen the front wheel lug nuts. Raise the vehicle on the hoist. Remove the front wheels and the splash shields under the vehicle.

6 Drain the transaxle fluid (see Chapter 1). On manual transaxle models, disconnect the hydraulic line from the release cylinder fitting at the transaxle.

7 Remove the air filter housing (see Chapter 4).

8 On 2009 and later models, remove the cowl cover and lower cowl (see Chapter 11 Section 25).

9 On 2008 and earlier models, working from the passengers footwell, remove the under-dash cover and disconnect the PCM electrical connectors, the dash harness connector and throttle actuator connector (attached to the PCM).

10 On 2008 and earlier models, loosen the two lower and one upper blower case nuts securing the blower case to the firewall.

11 On 2008 and earlier models, working from the engine compartment, disconnect the main harness from the cowl. Detach the main harness grommet from the firewall and feed the PCM connectors, dash harness and throttle actuator connectors through the firewall from the passenger compartment. It may be helpful to have an assistant for this operation.

12 On 2009 and later models, disconnect the two PCM connectors and one engine harness connector.

13 On 2008 and earlier models, disconnect the starter cable and battery cable from the underhood fuse box. Detach the battery cable harness from the strut tower.

14 Disconnect the brake booster vacuum line from the upper intake manifold. On 2008 and earlier models, disconnect the MAP sensor connector and remove the bolt attaching the harness to the upper intake manifold.

15 Disconnect the two electrical connectors and three hoses (two are coolant hoses) from the throttle body.

16 Disconnect the fuel supply line below the throttle body by removing the connection cover and pressing in on the retainer tabs to remove the hose.

17 On manual transaxle models, remove the hairpin clips and washers and disconnect the shift cables from the transaxle. Remove the bolts and remove the shift cables and bracket together from the transaxle.

18 On manual transaxle models, remove the clutch release cylinder and hydraulic line bracket from the transaxle and position it aside.
Caution: *DO NOT press the clutch pedal while the release cylinder is removed. If the clutch pedal is pressed, the release cylinder will extend and come apart.*

19 Disconnect the downstream oxygen sensor electrical connector (see Chapter 6).

20 Remove the drivebelt (see Chapter 1).

21 Raise the vehicle.

22 Remove the under-vehicle splash shield.

23 Remove the catalytic converter (see Chapter 6).

24 On automatic transaxle models, remove the shift lever cover and disconnect the shift cable and bracket from the transaxle (see Chapter 7B).

25 Remove the air conditioning compressor without disconnecting the hoses and position the compressor aside (see Chapter 3).
Note: *Support the compressor with rope or mechanic's wire.*

26 Remove the driveaxles and, on automatic transaxle models, the intermediate shaft (see Chapter 8).

27 Lower the vehicle.

28 Remove the condenser and radiator fans (see Chapter 3 Section 5).

29 On automatic transaxle models, disconnect the oil cooler hoses from the transaxle. Place a drain pan to catch any fluid that spills. Plug the hoses to prevent contamination.

30 Remove the upper and lower radiator hoses and heater hoses (see Chapter 3).

31 Attach an engine support fixture to the engine at the transaxle end. Use a bolt threaded into the engine for the chain to attach to if a hook is not provided.
Note: *Engine support fixtures can be obtained at most equipment rental yards and some auto parts stores.*

32 Raise the vehicle.

33 Remove the front subframe (see Chapter 10).

34 Lower the vehicle.

35 Support the engine/transaxle assembly from above with an engine hoist. Attach the hoist chain to lift brackets bolted to opposite corners of the cylinder head. Make certain that the chains are connected to components that are solid enough to support the weight of the entire assembly. Use washers under bolt heads to prevent pull-through. The chains must be attached so they don't apply force to components that could be damaged.
Warning: *Don't put any part of your body under the engine or transaxle when it's supported only by a hoist or other lifting device.*

36 Take up the slack in the chain until there is slight tension on the hoist. Make sure it's connected so that the engine/transaxle is balanced.
Note: *The chain must be long enough to allow the hoist to lower the engine/transaxle assembly to the ground without letting the hoist arm contact the vehicle.*

37 Remove the transaxle mount(s) (see Chapter 2A).

38 Check that there is nothing connecting the engine/transaxle to the vehicle. Label and disconnect anything remaining.

39 Lower the engine/transaxle assembly slowly to the floor (see illustration).

7.39 Lowering the engine/transaxle assembly

40   Disconnect the engine hoist after blocking the engine so it can't tip.
41   Raise the vehicle on the hoist.
42   Reconnect the chain of the engine hoist to the engine/transaxle to support it. The assembly can now be moved from under the vehicle to another work area.
43   Separate the transaxle from the engine. Be careful to support the engine and the transaxle securely so they can't fall.
44   Mount the engine on an engine stand using the hoist.

Installation

45   Installation is the reverse of removal noting these points:

a) Check the engine and transaxle mounts. If they're worn or damaged, replace them.
b) Attach the transaxle to the engine (see Chapter 7A or 7B).
c) Tighten the subframe mounting bolts to the torque listed in the Chapter 10 Specifications.
d) Tighten the wheel lug nuts to the torque listed in the Chapter 1 Specifications.
e) Tighten the driveaxle/hub nuts to the torque listed in the Chapter 8 Specifications.
f) Tighten the steering and suspension fasteners to the torque values listed in the Chapter 10 Specifications.
g) Refill the engine coolant, oil, clutch fluid and transaxle fluid (see Chapter 1).
h) Recheck all fluid levels (see Chapter 1).

8   Engine overhaul - disassembly sequence

1   It's much easier to remove the external components if it's mounted on a portable engine stand. A stand can often be rented quite cheaply from an equipment rental yard. Before the engine is mounted on a stand, the flywheel/driveplate should be removed from the engine.
2   If a stand isn't available, it's possible to

remove the external engine components with it blocked up on the floor. Be extra careful not to tip or drop the engine when working without a stand.
3   If you're going to obtain a rebuilt engine, all external components must come off first, to be transferred to the replacement engine. These components include:

• Flywheel/driveplate
• Ignition coils and wiring harnesses
• Emissions-related components
• Engine mounts and mount brackets
• Intake/exhaust manifolds
• Fuel injection components
• Oil filter and oil cooler
• Spark plugs
• Thermostat and housing assembly
• Water pump

Note: When removing the external components from the engine, pay close attention to details that may be helpful or important during installation. Note the installed position of gaskets, seals, spacers, pins, brackets, washers, bolts and other small items.
4   If you're going to obtain a short block (assembled engine block, crankshaft, pistons and connecting rods), then remove the timing chain, cylinder head, oil pan, oil pump pick-up tube, oil pump and water pump from your engine so that you can turn in your old short block to the rebuilder as a core. See Section 5 for additional information regarding the different possibilities to be considered.

9   Pistons and connecting rods - removal and installation

Removal

Note: Prior to removing the piston/connecting rod assemblies, remove the cylinder head, oil pan and oil pump (see Chapter 2A).
1   Use your fingernail to feel if a ridge has formed at the upper limit of ring travel (about 1/4-inch down from the top of each cylinder). If carbon deposits or cylinder wear have produced ridges, they must be completely

removed with a special tool (see illustration). Follow the manufacturer's instructions provided with the tool. Failure to remove the ridges before attempting to remove the piston/connecting rod assemblies may result in piston breakage.
2   After the cylinder ridges have been removed, turn the engine so the crankshaft is facing up. Check the crankshaft endplay (see Section 10), then remove the main bearing cap bridge (see Section 10).
3   Before the connecting rods are removed, check the connecting rod endplay with feeler gauges. Slide them between the first connecting rod and the crankshaft throw until the play is removed (see illustration). Repeat this procedure for each connecting rod. The endplay is equal to the thickness of the feeler gauge(s). Check with an automotive machine shop for the endplay service limit (a typical endplay should measure between 0.005 to 0.015 inch [0.127 to 0.381 mm]). If the play exceeds the service limit, new connecting rods will be required. If new rods (or a new crankshaft) are installed, the endplay may fall under the minimum allowable. If it does, the rods will have to be machined to restore it. If necessary, consult an automotive machine shop for advice.
4   Check the connecting rods and caps for identification marks. If they aren't plainly marked, use paint or marker (see illustration) to clearly identify each rod and cap (1, 2, 3, etc., depending on the cylinder they're associated with). Do not interchange the rod caps. Install the exact same rod cap onto the same connecting rod.
Caution: Do not use a punch and hammer to mark the connecting rods or they may be damaged.
5   Loosen each of the connecting rod cap bolts 1/2-turn at a time until they can be removed by hand.
Caution: Obtain new connecting rod bolts; the old ones shouldn't be re-used.
6   Remove the number one connecting rod cap and bearing insert. Don't drop the bearing insert out of the cap.

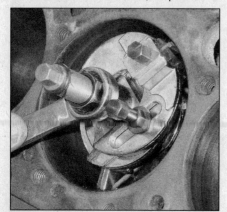

9.1 Before you try to remove the pistons, use a ridge reamer to remove the raised material (ridge) from the top of the cylinders

9.3 Checking the connecting rod endplay (side clearance)

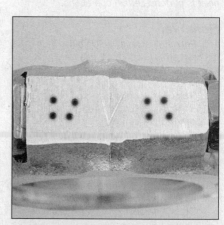

9.4 If the connecting rods or caps are not marked, use permanent ink or paint to mark the caps to the rods by cylinder number (for example, this would be number 4 cylinder connecting rod)

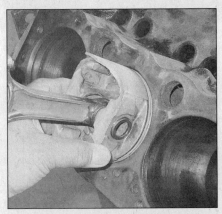

9.13 Install the piston ring into the cylinder then push it down into position using a piston so the ring will be square in the cylinder

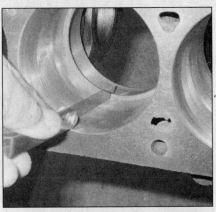

9.14 With the ring square in the cylinder, measure the ring end gap with a feeler gauge

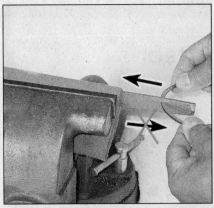

9.15 If the ring end gap is too small, clamp a file in a vise as shown and file the piston ring ends - be sure to remove all raised material

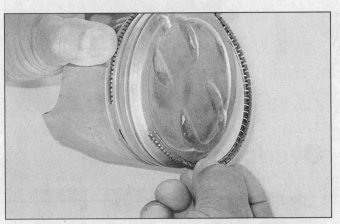

9.19a Installing the spacer/expander in the oil ring groove

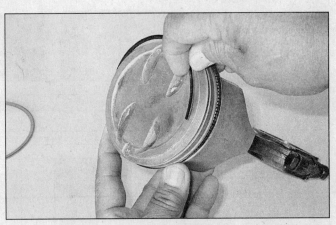

9.19b DO NOT use a piston ring installation tool when installing the oil control side rails

7   Remove the bearing insert and push the connecting rod/piston assembly out through the top of the engine. Use a wooden or plastic hammer handle to push on the upper bearing surface in the connecting rod. If resistance is felt, double-check to make sure that all of the ridge was removed from the cylinder.

8   Repeat the procedure for the remaining cylinders.

9   After removal, reassemble the connecting rod caps and bearing inserts in their respective connecting rods and install the cap bolts finger tight. Leaving the old bearing inserts in place until reassembly will help prevent the connecting rod bearing surfaces from being accidentally nicked or gouged.

10   The pistons and connecting rods are now ready for inspection and overhaul at an automotive machine shop.

Piston ring installation

11   Before installing the new piston rings, the ring end gaps must be checked. It's assumed that the piston ring side clearance has been checked and verified correct.

12   Lay out the piston/connecting rod assemblies and the new ring sets so the ring sets will

be matched with the same piston and cylinder during the end gap measurement and engine assembly.

13   Insert the top (number one) ring into the first cylinder and square it up with the cylinder walls by pushing it in with the top of the piston (see illustration). The ring should be near the bottom of the cylinder, at the lower limit of ring travel.

14   To measure the end gap, slip feeler gauges between the ends of the ring until a gauge equal to the gap width is found (see illustration). The feeler gauge should slide between the ring ends with a slight amount of drag. A typical ring gap should fall between 0.010 and 0.020 inch (0.25 to 0.50 mm) for compression rings and up to 0.030 inch (0.76 mm) for the oil ring steel rails. If the gap is larger or smaller than specified, double-check to make sure you have the correct rings before proceeding.

15   If the gap is too small, it must be enlarged or the ring ends may come in contact with each other during engine operation, which can cause serious damage to the engine. If necessary, increase the end gaps by filing the ring ends very carefully with a fine file. Mount the file in a vise equipped with soft jaws, slip

the ring over the file with the ends contacting the file face and slowly move the ring to remove material from the ends. When performing this operation, file only by pushing the ring from the outside end of the file towards the vise (see illustration).

16   Excess end gap isn't critical unless it's greater than 0.040 inch (1.01 mm). Again, double-check to make sure you have the correct ring type.

17   Repeat the procedure for each ring that will be installed in the first cylinder and for each ring in the remaining cylinders. Remember to keep rings, pistons and cylinders matched up.

18   Once the ring end gaps have been checked/corrected, the rings can be installed on the pistons.

19   The oil control ring (lowest one on the piston) is usually installed first. It's composed of three separate components. Slip the spacer/expander into the groove (see illustration). If an anti-rotation tang is used, make sure it's inserted into the drilled hole in the ring groove. Next, install the lower side rail in the same manner (see illustration). Don't use a piston ring installation tool on the oil ring side rails, as they may be damaged. Instead,

ENGINE BEARING ANALYSIS

Debris

Babbitt bearing embedded with debris from machinings

Microscopic detail of debris

Microscopic detail of gouges

Overplated copper alloy bearing gouged by cast iron debris

Aluminum bearing embedded with glass beads

Microscopic detail of glass beads

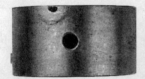

Damaged lining caused by dirt left on the bearing back

Misassembly

Result of a lower half assembled as an upper - blocking the oil flow

Excessive oil clearance is indicated by a short contact arc

Polished and oil-stained backs are a result of a poor fit in the housing bore

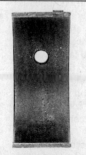

Result of a wrong, reversed, or shifted cap

Overloading

Damage from excessive idling which resulted in an oil film unable to support the load imposed

Damaged upper connecting rod bearings caused by engine lugging; the lower main bearings (not shown) were similarly affected

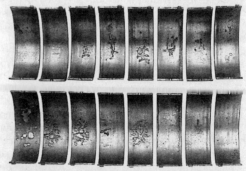

The damage shown in these upper and lower connecting rod bearings was caused by engine operation at a higher-than-rated speed under load

Misalignment

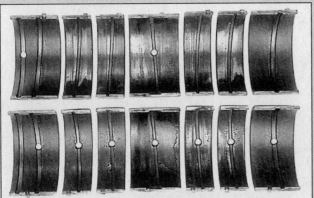

A warped crankshaft caused this pattern of severe wear in the center, diminishing toward the ends

A poorly finished crankshaft caused the equally spaced scoring shown

A tapered housing bore caused the damage along one edge of this pair

A bent connecting rod led to the damage in the "V" pattern

Lubrication

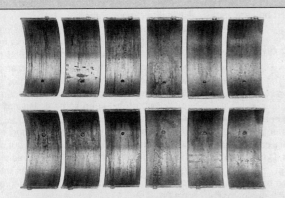

Result of dry start: The bearings on the left, farthest from the oil pump, show more damage

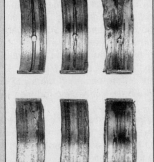

Result of a low oil supply or oil starvation

Severe wear as a result of inadequate oil clearance

Corrosion

Microscopic detail of corrosion

Corrosion is an acid attack on the bearing lining generally caused by inadequate maintenance, extremely hot or cold operation, or inferior oils or fuels

Microscopic detail of cavitation

Example of cavitation - a surface erosion caused by pressure changes in the oil film

Damage from excessive thrust or insufficient axial clearance

Bearing affected by oil dilution caused by excessive blow-by or a rich mixture

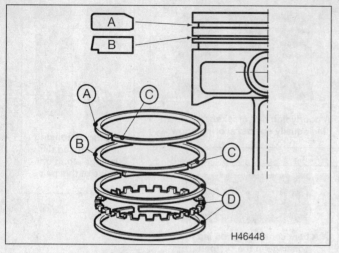

9.22a Piston ring details

A   *First compression ring*
B   *Second compression ring*
C   *Markings (R1 and R)*
D   *Oil control rings*
     and expander

9.22b Use a piston ring installation tool to install the compression rings - on some engines the number two compression ring has a directional mark that must face toward the top of the piston

place one end of the side rail into the groove between the spacer/expander and the ring land, hold it firmly in place and slide a finger around the piston while pushing the rail into the groove. Finally, install the upper side rail.

20   After the three oil ring components have been installed, check to make sure that both the upper and lower side rails can be rotated smoothly inside the ring grooves.

21   The number two (middle) ring is installed next. It's usually stamped with a mark which must face up, toward the top of the piston. Do not mix up the top and middle rings, as they have different cross-sections.

Note: *Always follow the instructions printed on the ring package or box - different manufacturers may require different approaches.*

22   Identify the compression rings: The top compression ring is marked R1 and the second compression ring is marked R (see illustration). Use a piston ring installation tool to slip the ring into the middle groove on the piston (see illustration). Don't expand the ring any more than necessary to slide it over the piston.

Note: *Be careful not to confuse the number one and number two rings.*

23   Install the number one (top) ring in the same manner.

24   Repeat the procedure for the remaining pistons and rings.

Installation

25   Before installing the piston/connecting rod assemblies, the cylinder walls must be perfectly clean, the top edge of each cylinder bore must be chamfered, and the crankshaft (without the main bearing bridge installed) must be in place.

Note: *Position the engine on a 45-degree angle with the crankshaft facing up.*

26   Remove the cap from the end of the number one connecting rod (refer to the marks made during removal). Remove the

original bearing inserts and wipe the bearing surfaces of the connecting rod and cap with a clean, lint-free cloth. They must be kept spotlessly clean.

Connecting rod bearing oil clearance check

27   Clean the back side of the new upper bearing insert, then lay it in place in the connecting rod.

28   Make sure the tab on the bearing fits into the recess in the rod. Don't hammer the bearing insert into place and be very careful not to nick or gouge the bearing face. Don't lubricate the bearing at this time.

29   Clean the back side of the other bearing insert and install it in the rod cap. Again, make sure the tab on the bearing fits into the recess in the cap, and don't apply any lubricant. It's critically important that the mating surfaces of the bearing and connecting rod are perfectly clean and oil free when they're assembled.

30   Position the piston ring gaps at the intervals around the piston as shown (see illustration).

31   Lubricate the piston and rings with clean engine oil and attach a piston ring compressor to the piston. Leave the skirt protruding about 1/4-inch to guide the piston into the cylinder. The rings must be compressed until they're flush with the piston.

32   Rotate the crankshaft until the number one connecting rod journal is at BDC (bottom dead center) and apply a liberal coat of engine oil to the cylinder walls.

33   With the arrow mark on the piston facing the front (timing chain end) of the engine, gently insert the piston/connecting rod assembly into the number one cylinder bore and rest the bottom edge of the ring compressor on the engine block (see illustration).

Note: *Some engines have an arrow or dimples or groove on the top of the piston. All of these are marks that indicate the front of the piston.*

34   Tap the top edge of the ring compressor to make sure it's contacting the block around its entire circumference.

35   Gently tap on the top of the piston with the end of a wooden or plastic hammer handle (see illustration) while guiding the end of the connecting rod into place on the crankshaft journal. The piston rings may try to pop out of the ring compressor just before entering the cylinder bore, so keep some downward pressure on the ring compressor. Work slowly, and if any resistance is felt as the piston enters the cylinder, stop immediately. Find out what's hanging up and fix it before proceeding. Do not, for any reason, force the piston into the cylinder - you might break a ring and/or the piston.

36   Once the piston/connecting rod assembly is installed, the connecting rod bearing oil clearance must be checked before the rod cap is permanently installed.

37   Cut a piece of the appropriate size Plastigage slightly shorter than the width of the connecting rod bearing and lay it in place on the number one connecting rod journal, parallel with the journal axis (see illustration).

38   Clean the connecting rod cap bearing face and install the rod cap. Make sure the mating mark on the cap is on the same side as the mark on the connecting rod (see illustration 9.4).

39   Install the old rod bolts and tighten them to the torque listed in this Chapter's Specifications. DO NOT rotate the crankshaft at any time during this operation.

Note: *Use a thin-wall socket to avoid erroneous torque readings that can result if the socket is wedged between the rod cap and the bolt. If the socket tends to wedge itself between the fastener and the cap, lift up on it slightly until it no longer contacts the cap.*

40   Remove the fasteners and detach the rod cap, being careful not to disturb the Plastigage. If the connecting rod fasteners have

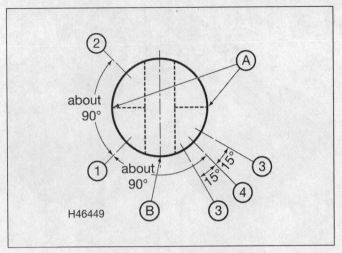

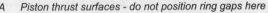

9.30 Piston ring end gap positioning

9.33 With the engine positioned at an angle and the crankshaft in place, insert the piston and rod assembly with the rings compressed

A   Piston thrust surfaces - do not position ring gaps here
B   Piston pin axis - do not position ring gaps here
1   Top ring gap   3   Oil ring gaps
2   Second ring gap   4   Oil ring spacer gap

9.35 Use a plastic or wooden hammer handle to push the piston into the cylinder (typical)

9.37 Place Plastigage on each connecting rod bearing journal parallel to the crankshaft centerline

9.41 Use the scale on the Plastigage package to determine the bearing oil clearance - be sure to measure the widest part of the Plastigage and use the correct scale; it comes with both standard and metric scales

any type of wear or distortion they cannot be reused.

41   Compare the width of the crushed Plastigage to the scale printed on the Plastigage envelope to obtain the oil clearance (see illustration). The connecting rod bearing oil clearance is usually about 0.001 to 0.002 inch. Consult an automotive machine shop for the clearance specified for the rod bearings on your engine.

42   If the clearance is not as specified, the bearing inserts may be the wrong size (which means different ones will be required). Before deciding that different inserts are needed, make sure that no dirt or oil was between the bearing inserts and the connecting rod or cap when the clearance was measured. Also, recheck the journal diameter. If the Plastigage was wider at one end than the other, the journal may be tapered. If the clearance still

exceeds the limit specified, the bearing will have to be replaced with an undersize bearing.

Caution: *When installing a new crankshaft, always use a standard size bearing.*

Final installation

43   Carefully scrape all traces of the Plastigage material off the rod journal and/or bearing face. Be very careful not to scratch the bearing - use your fingernail or the edge of a plastic card.

44   Make sure the bearing faces are perfectly clean, then apply a uniform layer of clean moly-base grease or engine assembly lube to both of them. You'll have to push the piston into the cylinder to expose the face of the bearing insert in the connecting rod.

45   Slide the connecting rod back into place on the journal, install the rod cap, install the

new bolts and tighten them to the torque listed in this Chapter's Specifications.

46   Repeat the entire procedure for the remaining pistons/connecting rods, then install the main bearing cap bridge.

47   The important points to remember are:

• *Keep the back sides of the bearing inserts and the insides of the connecting rods and caps perfecltly clean when assembling them.*

• *Make sure you have the correct piston/rod assembly for each cylinder.*

• *The mark on the piston must face the front (timing chain end) of he engine.*

• *Lubricate the cylinder walls liberally with clean oil.*

• *Lubricate the bearing faces when installing the old rod caps after the oil clearance has been checked.*

10.1 Checking crankshaft endplay with a dial indicator

10.3 Checking the crankshaft endplay with feeler gauges at the thrust bearing journal

10   Crankshaft - removal and installation

Removal

Note: *The crankshaft can be removed only after the engine has been removed from the vehicle. It's assumed that the flywheel or driveplate, crankshaft pulley, timing chain, oil pan, baffle plate, oil screen, oil pump body, crankshaft position sensor, oil filter and piston/ connecting rod assemblies have already been removed..*

1   Before the crankshaft is removed, measure the endplay. Mount a dial indicator with the indicator in line with the crankshaft and just touching the end of the crankshaft as shown (see illustration).

2   Pry the crankshaft all the way to the rear and zero the dial indicator. Next, pry the crankshaft to the front as far as possible and check the reading on the dial indicator. The distance traveled is the endplay. Check the measured endplay against specification in this Section. If it is greater than that, check the crankshaft thrust surfaces for wear after it's removed. If no wear is evident, new main bearings should correct the endplay.

3   If a dial indicator isn't available, feeler gauges can be used. Gently pry the crankshaft all the way to the front of the engine. Slip feeler gauges between the crankshaft and the front face of the thrust bearing or washer to determine the clearance (see illustration).

4   Loosen the main bearing cap bridge bolts 1/4-turn at a time each, until they can be removed by hand. Follow the reverse of the tightening sequence (see illustration 10.19).

5   Remove the bolts and the main bearing cap bridge. Try not to drop the bearing inserts if they come out with the main bearing cap bridge.

Note: *Obtain new bolts, but save the old ones for the main bearing oil clearance check.*

6   Carefully lift the crankshaft out of the engine. On 2009 and later models, unscrew the bolts and remove the Crankshaft Position Sensor (CKP) pulse plate from the rear of the crankshaft.

Note: *With the bearing inserts in place inside the engine block and main bearing bridge, reinstall the bridge assembly onto the engine block and tighten the bolts finger tight.*

Installation

7   Crankshaft installation is the first step in engine reassembly. It's assumed at this point that the engine block and crankshaft have been cleaned, inspected and repaired or reconditioned.

8   Position the engine block with the bottom facing up, or at least a 45-degree angle.

9   Remove the bolts and lift off the main bearing cap bearing bridge assembly.

10   If they're still in place, remove the original bearing inserts from the block and from the main bearing bridge. Wipe the bearing surfaces of the block and main bearing bridge saddle with a clean, lint-free cloth. They must be kept spotlessly clean. This is critical for determining the correct bearing oil clearance.

Main bearing oil clearance check

11   Without mixing them up, clean the back sides of the new upper main bearing inserts (with grooves and oil holes) and lay one in each main bearing saddle in the engine block. Each upper bearing (engine block) has an oil groove and oil hole in it. Clean the back sides of the lower main bearing inserts and lay them in the corresponding location in the main bearing bridge. Make sure the tab on the bearing insert fits into the recess in the block or main bearing caps. Also install the thrust washers (see illustrations).

Caution: *The oil holes in the block must line up with the oil holes in the engine block inserts. The thrust washer or thrust bearing insert must be installed in the correct location.*

Caution: *Do not hammer the bearing insert into place and don't nick or gouge the bearing faces. DO NOT apply any lubrication at this time.*

Caution: *The thrust bearing is located on the 4th journal in the engine block (upper).*

12   Clean the faces of the bearing inserts in the block and the crankshaft main bearing journals with a clean, lint-free cloth.

13   Check or clean the oil holes in the crankshaft, as any dirt here can go only one way - straight through the new bearings.

14   Once you're certain the crankshaft is clean, carefully lay it in position in the cylinder block.

15   Before the crankshaft can be permanently installed, the main bearing oil clearance must be checked.

16   Cut several strips of the appropriate size of Plastigage. They must be slightly shorter than the width of the main bearing journal.

17   Place one piece on each crankshaft main bearing journal, parallel with the journal axis as shown (see illustration).

18   Clean the faces of the bearing inserts in the lower crankcase or main bearing caps. Hold the bearing inserts in place and install the main bearing cap bridge onto the crankshaft and cylinder block. DO NOT disturb the Plastigage.

19   Apply clean engine oil to all bolt threads prior to installation, then install all bolts finger-tight. Tighten the main bearing bridge bolts in the sequence shown (see illustration) progressing in steps, to the torque listed in this Section. DO NOT rotate the crankshaft at any time during this operation.

Note: *Use the old main bearing cap bridge bolts at this time.*

20   Remove the bolts in the reverse order of the tightening sequence and carefully lift the main bearing bridge straight up and off the block. Do not disturb the Plastigage or rotate the crankshaft.

21   Compare the width of the crushed Plasti-

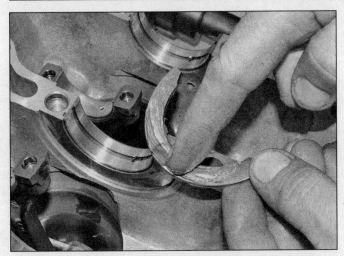

10.11a Apply grease to the back side f the thrust washers to helpthem stick. . .

10.11b. . . then lay them in place on the sides of the No. 4 bearing journal, with the grooves facing away from the journal

10.17 Place the Plastigage onto the crankshaft bearing journal as shown

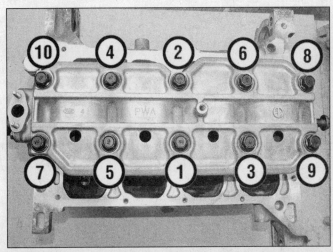

10.19 Main bearing cap bridge bolt tightening sequence

gage on each journal to the scale printed on the Plastigage envelope to determine the main bearing oil clearance (see illustration). Check the oil clearance for the engine in this Section.

22   If the clearance is not as specified, the bearing inserts may be the wrong size (which means different ones will be required). Before deciding if different inserts are needed, make sure that no dirt or oil was between the bearing inserts and the caps or block when the clearance was measured. If the Plastigage was wider at one end than the other, the crankshaft journal may be tapered. If the clearance still exceeds the limit specified, the bearing insert(s) will have to be replaced with an undersize bearing insert(s).

Caution: *When installing a new crankshaft always install a standard bearing insert set.*

23   Carefully scrape all traces of the Plasti-

10.21 Use the scale on the Plastigage package to determine the bearing oil clearance - be sure to measure the widest part of the Plastigage and use the correct scale; it comes with both standard and metric scales

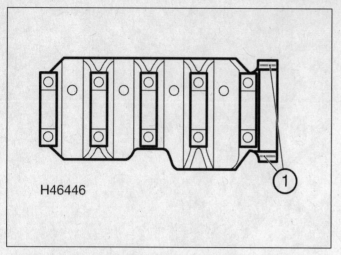

10.29a Apply liquid gasket to the main bearing cap bridge in the indicated area before installing

1   *Bead of liquid gasket, 1/6-inch (1.5 mm) in diameter*

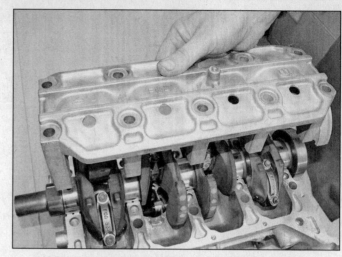

10.29b Install the main bearing cap bridge assembly. . .

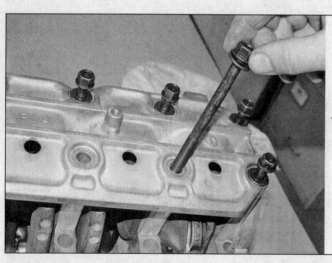

10.29c. . . then oil and install the new bolts

gage material off the main bearing journals and/or the bearing insert faces. Be sure to remove all residue from the oil holes. Use your fingernail or the edge of a plastic card - don't nick or scratch the bearing faces.

Final installation

24   Carefully lift the crankshaft out of the cylinder block. On 2009 and later models, install the crankshaft position sensor (CKP) pulse plate and mounting bolts, then tighten the bolts to the torque listed in this Section.

25   Clean the bearing insert faces in the cylinder block, then apply a thin, uniform layer of moly-base grease or engine assembly lube to each of the bearing surfaces. Be sure to coat the thrust faces as well as the journal face of the thrust bearing.

26   Make sure the crankshaft journals are clean, then lay the crankshaft back in place in the cylinder block.

27   Attach the connecting rods/caps to the crankshaft as previously described.

28   Clean the bearing insert faces and apply the same lubricant to them. Clean the engine block and the mating surface of the main bearing caps thoroughly. The surfaces must be free of oil residue.

29   Apply liquid gasket (not RTV sealant) to the lower main bearing bridge (see illustration), then install the lower main bearing bridge (see illustrations).

Caution: *Once the liquid gasket has been applied, the bearing bridge must be installed within a few minutes or the gasket must be removed, parts cleaned and applied again.*

30   Prior to installation, apply clean engine oil to all bolt threads, wiping off any excess, then install the new bolts finger-tight.

31   Tighten the bolts to the torque listed in this Chapter's Specifications following the correct torque sequence (see illustration 10.19).

32   Recheck the crankshaft endplay with a feeler gauge or a dial indicator. The endplay should be correct if the crankshaft thrust faces aren't worn or damaged and if new bearings have been installed.

33   Rotate the crankshaft a number of times by hand to check for any obvious binding. It should rotate with a running torque of 50 in-lbs or less. If the running torque is too high, correct the problem at this time.

34   Install the new rear main oil seal (see Chapter 2A).

11   Engine overhaul - reassembly sequence

1   Before beginning engine reassembly, make sure you have all the necessary new parts, gaskets and seals as well as the following items on hand:

   Common hand tools
   A 1/2-inch drive torque wrench
   New engine oil
   Oil filter
   Gasket sealant
   Thread locking compound

2   If you obtained a short block it will be necessary to install the cylinder head, the oil pump and pick-up tube, the oil pan, the water pump, the timing chain and timing cover, and the valve cover (see Chapter). In order to save time and avoid problems, the external components must be installed in the following

general order:

Thermostat and housing cover
Water pump
Intake and exhaust manifolds
Fuel injection components
Emission control components
Spark plugs
Ignition coils
Oil filter
Engine mounts and mount brackets
Flywheel/driveplate

12 Initial start-up and break-in after overhaul

Warning: *Have a fire extinguisher handy when starting the engine for the first time.*

1   Once the engine has been installed in the vehicle, double-check the engine oil and coolant levels.

2   With the spark plugs out of the engine and the and the fuel pump disabled (see Chapter 4, Section 3), crank the engine until oil pressure registers on the gauge or the light goes out.

3   Install the spark plugs and ignition coils, and reinstall the fuel pump fuse.

4   Start the engine. It may take a few moments for the fuel system to build up pressure, but the engine should start without a great deal of effort.

5   After the engine starts, it should be allowed to warm up to normal operating temperature. While the engine is warming up, make a thorough check for fuel, oil and coolant leaks.

6   Shut the engine off and recheck the engine oil and coolant levels.

7   Drive the vehicle to an area with minimum traffic, accelerate from 30 to 50 mph, then allow the vehicle to slow to 30 mph with the throttle closed. Repeat the procedure 10 or 12 times. This will load the piston rings and cause them to seat properly against the cylinder walls. Check again for oil and coolant leaks.

8   Drive the vehicle gently for the first 500 miles (no sustained high speeds) and keep a constant check on the oil level. It is not unusual for an engine to use oil during the break-in period.

9   At approximately 500 to 600 miles, change the oil and filter.

10   For the next few hundred miles, drive the vehicle normally. Do not pamper it or abuse it.

11   After 2000 miles, change the oil and filter again and consider the engine broken in.

COMMON ENGINE OVERHAUL TERMS

B

Backlash - The amount of play between two parts. Usually refers to how much one gear can be moved back and forth without moving the gear with which it's meshed.

Bearing Caps - The caps held in place by nuts or bolts which, in turn, hold the bearing surface. This space is for lubricating oil to enter.

Bearing clearance - The amount of space left between shaft and bearing surface. This space is for lubricating oil to enter.

Bearing crush - The additional height which is purposely manufactured into each bearing half to ensure complete contact of the bearing back with the housing bore when the engine is assembled.

Bearing knock - The noise created by movement of a part in a loose or worn bearing.

Blueprinting - Dismantling an engine and reassembling it to EXACT specifications.

Bore - An engine cylinder, or any cylindrical hole; also used to describe the process of enlarging or accurately refinishing a hole with a cutting tool, as to bore an engine cylinder. The bore size is the diameter of the hole.

Boring - Renewing the cylinders by cutting them out to a specified size. A boring bar is used to make the cut.

Bottom end - A term which refers collectively to the engine block, crankshaft, main bearings and the big ends of the connecting rods.

Break-in - The period of operation between installation of new or rebuilt parts and time in which parts are worn to the correct fit. Driving at reduced and varying speed for a specified mileage to permit parts to wear to the correct fit.

Bushing - A one-piece sleeve placed in a bore to serve as a bearing surface for shaft, piston pin, etc. Usually replaceable.

C

Camshaft - The shaft in the engine, on which a series of lobes are located for operating the valve mechanisms. The camshaft is driven by gears or sprockets and a timing chain. Usually referred to simply as the cam.

Carbon - Hard, or soft, black deposits found in combustion chamber, on plugs, under rings, on and under valve heads.

Cast iron - An alloy of iron and more than two percent carbon, used for engine blocks and heads because it's relatively inexpensive and easy to mold into complex shapes.

Chamfer - To bevel across (or a bevel on) the sharp edge of an object.

Chase - To repair damaged threads with a tap or die.

Combustion chamber - The space between the piston and the cylinder head, with the piston at top dead center, in which air-fuel mixture is burned.

Compression ratio - The relationship between cylinder volume (clearance volume) when the piston is at top dead center and cylinder volume when the piston is at bottom dead center.

Connecting rod - The rod that connects the crank on the crankshaft with the piston. Sometimes called a con rod.

Connecting rod cap - The part of the connecting rod assembly that attaches the rod to the crankpin.

Core plug - Soft metal plug used to plug the casting holes for the coolant passages in the block.

Crankcase - The lower part of the engine in which the crankshaft rotates; includes the lower section of the cylinder block and the oil pan.

Crank kit - A reground or reconditioned crankshaft and new main and connecting rod bearings.

Crankpin - The part of a crankshaft to which a connecting rod is attached.

Crankshaft - The main rotating member, or shaft, running the length of the crankcase, with offset throws to which the connecting rods are attached; changes the reciprocating motion of the pistons into rotating motion.

Cylinder sleeve - A replaceable sleeve, or liner, pressed into the cylinder block to form the cylinder bore.

D

Deburring - Removing the burrs (rough edges or areas) from a bearing.

Deglazer - A tool, rotated by an electric motor, used to remove glaze from cylinder walls so a new set of rings will seat.

E

Endplay - The amount of lengthwise movement between two parts. As applied to a crankshaft, the distance that the crankshaft can move forward and back in the cylinder block.

F

Face - A machinist's term that refers to removing metal from the end of a shaft or the face of a larger part, such as a flywheel.

Fatigue - A breakdown of material through a large number of loading and unloading cycles. The first signs are cracks followed shortly by breaks.

Feeler gauge - A thin strip of hardened steel, ground to an exact thickness, used to check clearances between parts.

Free height - The unloaded length or height of a spring.

Freeplay - The looseness in a linkage, or an assembly of parts, between the initial application of force and actual movement. Usually perceived as slop or slight delay.

Freeze plug - See Core plug.

G

Gallery - A large passage in the block that forms a reservoir for engine oil pressure.

Glaze - The very smooth, glassy finish that develops on cylinder walls while an engine is in service.

H

Heli-Coil - A rethreading device used when threads are worn or damaged. The device is installed in a retapped hole to reduce the thread size to the original size.

I

Installed height - The spring's measured length or height, as installed on the cylinder head. Installed height is measured from the spring seat to the underside of the spring retainer.

J

Journal - The surface of a rotating shaft which turns in a bearing.

K

Keeper - The split lock that holds the valve spring retainer in position on the valve stem.

Key - A small piece of metal inserted into matching grooves machined into two parts fitted together - such as a gear pressed onto a shaft - which prevents slippage between the two parts.

Knock - The heavy metallic engine sound, produced in the combustion chamber as a result of abnormal combustion - usually detonation. Knock is usually caused by a loose or worn bearing. Also referred to as detonation, pinging and spark knock. Connecting rod or main bearing knocks are created by too much oil clearance or insufficient lubrication.

L

Lands - The portions of metal between the piston ring grooves.

Lapping the valves - Grinding a valve face and its seat together with lapping compound.

Lash - The amount of free motion in a gear train, between gears, or in a mechanical assembly, that occurs before movement can begin. Usually refers to the lash in a valve train.

Lifter - The part that rides against the cam to transfer motion to the rest of the valve train.

M

Machining - The process of using a machine to remove metal from a metal part.

Main bearings - The plain, or babbit, bearings that support the crankshaft.

Main bearing caps - The cast iron caps, bolted to the bottom of the block, that support the main bearings.

O

O.D. - Outside diameter.

Oil gallery - A pipe or drilled passageway in the engine used to carry engine oil from one area to another.

Oil ring - The lower ring, or rings, of a piston; designed to prevent excessive amounts of oil from working up the cylinder walls and into the combustion chamber. Also called an oil-control ring.

Oil seal - A seal which keeps oil from leaking out of a compartment. Usually refers to a dynamic seal around a rotating shaft or other moving part.

O-ring - A type of sealing ring made of a special rubberlike material; in use, the O-ring is compressed into a groove to provide the sealing action.

Overhaul - To completely disassemble a unit, clean and inspect all parts, reassemble it with the original or new parts and make all adjustments necessary for proper operation.

P

Pilot bearing - A small bearing installed in the center of the flywheel (or the rear end of the crankshaft) to support the front end of the input shaft of the transmission.

Pip mark - A little dot or indentation which indicates the top side of a compression ring.

Piston - The cylindrical part, attached to the connecting rod, that moves up and down in the cylinder as the crankshaft rotates. When the fuel charge is fired, the piston transfers the force of the explosion to the connecting rod, then to the crankshaft.

Piston pin (or wrist pin) - The cylindrical and usually hollow steel pin that passes through the piston. The piston pin fastens the piston to the upper end of the connecting rod.

Piston ring - The split ring fitted to the groove in a piston. The ring contacts the sides of the ring groove and also rubs against the cylinder wall, thus sealing space between piston and wall. There are two types of rings: Compression rings seal the compression pressure in the combustion chamber; oil rings scrape excessive oil off the cylinder wall.

Piston ring groove - The slots or grooves cut in piston heads to hold piston rings in position.

Piston skirt - The portion of the piston below the rings and the piston pin hole.

Plastigage - A thin strip of plastic thread, available in different sizes, used for measuring clearances. For example, a strip of plastigage is laid across a bearing journal and mashed as parts are assembled. Then parts are disassembled and the width of the strip is measured to determine clearance between journal and bearing. Commonly used to measure crankshaft main-bearing and connecting rod bearing clearances.

Press-fit - A tight fit between two parts that requires pressure to force the parts together. Also referred to as drive, or force, fit.

Prussian blue - A blue pigment; in solution, useful in determining the area of contact between two surfaces. Prussian blue is commonly used to determine the width and location of the contact area between the valve face and the valve seat.

R

Race (bearing) - The inner or outer ring that provides a contact surface for balls or rollers in bearing.

Ream - To size, enlarge or smooth a hole by using a round cutting tool with fluted edges.

Ring job - The process of reconditioning the cylinders and installing new rings.

Runout - Wobble. The amount a shaft rotates out-of-true.

S

Saddle - The upper main bearing seat.

Scored - Scratched or grooved, as a cylinder wall may be scored by abrasive particles moved up and down by the piston rings.

Scuffing - A type of wear in which there's a transfer of material between parts moving against each other; shows up as pits or grooves in the mating surfaces.

Seat - The surface upon which another part rests or seats. For example, the valve seat is the matched surface upon which the valve face rests. Also used to refer to wearing into a good fit; for example, piston rings seat after a few miles of driving.

Short block - An engine block complete with crankshaft and piston and, usually, camshaft assemblies.

Static balance - The balance of an object while it's stationary.

Step - The wear on the lower portion of a ring land caused by excessive side and back-clearance. The height of the step indicates the ring's extra side clearance and the length of the step projecting from the back wall of the groove represents the ring's back clearance.

Stroke - The distance the piston moves when traveling from top dead center to bottom dead center, or from bottom dead center to top dead center.

Stud - A metal rod with threads on both ends.

T

Tang - A lip on the end of a plain bearing used to align the bearing during assembly.

Tap - To cut threads in a hole. Also refers to the fluted tool used to cut threads.

Taper - A gradual reduction in the width of a shaft or hole; in an engine cylinder, taper usually takes the form of uneven wear, more pronounced at the top than at the bottom.

Throws - The offset portions of the crankshaft to which the connecting rods are affixed.

Thrust bearing - The main bearing that has thrust faces to prevent excessive endplay, or forward and backward movement of the crankshaft.

Thrust washer - A bronze or hardened steel washer placed between two moving parts. The washer prevents longitudinal movement and provides a bearing surface for thrust surfaces of parts.

Tolerance - The amount of variation permitted from an exact size of measurement. Actual amount from smallest acceptable dimension to largest acceptable dimension.

U

Umbrella - An oil deflector placed near the valve tip to throw oil from the valve stem area.

Undercut - A machined groove below the normal surface.

Undersize bearings - Smaller diameter bearings used with re-ground crankshaft journals.

V

Valve grinding - Refacing a valve in a valve-refacing machine.

Valve train - The valve-operating mechanism of an engine; includes all components from the camshaft to the valve.

Vibration damper - A cylindrical weight attached to the front of the crankshaft to minimize torsional vibration (the twist-untwist actions of the crankshaft caused by the cylinder firing impulses). Also called a harmonic balancer.

W

Water jacket - The spaces around the cylinders, between the inner and outer shells of the cylinder block or head, through which coolant circulates.

Web - A supporting structure across a cavity.

Woodruff key - A key with a radiused backside (viewed from the side).

Notes

Chapter 3
Cooling, heating and air conditioning systems

Contents

Specifications

General

Radiator cap pressure rating	Refer to pressure specification on cap
Cooling system capacity...	See Chapter 1
Refrigerant type..	R-134a
Refrigerant capacity..	1.0 lbs (453 grams)
Refrigerant oil capacities	
Compressor...	2-2/3 to 3 ounces (80 to 90 mL)
Condenser...	5/6 ounce (25 mL)
Receiver-drier..	1/3 ounce (10 mL)
Evaporator...	1-1/6 ounces (35 mL)
Refrigerant line...	1/3 ounce (10 mL)

Torque specifications

	Ft-lbs (unless otherwise indicated)	Nm

Note: *One foot-pound (ft-lb) of torque is equivalent to 12 inch-pounds (in-lbs) of torque. Torque values below approximately 15 foot-pounds are expressed in inch-pounds, because most foot-pound torque wrenches are not accurate at these smaller values.*

	Ft-lbs (unless otherwise indicated)	Nm
Thermostat housing inlet bolts..	108 in-lbs	12
Water pump mounting bolts	108 in-lbs	12
Water pump pulley bolts		
2008 and earlier models..	120 in-lbs	14
2009 and later models...	144 in-lbs	16
Refrigerant line-to-air conditioning compressor bolts	86 in-lbs	9.8
Air conditioning compressor mounting bolts..............................	16	22

2.2 The cooling system pressure tester is connected in place of the pressure cap. then pumped up to pressurize the system

2.5a The combustion leak detector consists of a bulb, syringe and test fluid

2.5b Place the tester over the cooling system filler neck and use the bulb to draw a sample into the tester

1   General information

Warning: *Do not allow antifreeze to come in contact with your skin or painted surfaces of the vehicle. Rinse off spills immediately with plenty of water. Antifreeze is highly toxic if ingested. Never leave antifreeze lying around in an open container or in puddles on the floor; children and pets are attracted by it's sweet smell and may drink it. Check with local authorities about disposing of used antifreeze. Many communities have collection centers which will see that antifreeze is disposed of safely. Never dump used antifreeze on the ground or pour it into drains.*

Engine cooling system

1   All modern vehicles employ a pressurized engine cooling system with thermostatically controlled coolant circulation. The cooling system consists of a radiator, an expansion tank or coolant reservoir, a pressure cap (located on the expansion tank or radiator), a thermostat, a cooling fan, and a water pump.

2   The water pump circulates coolant through the engine. The coolant flows around each cylinder and around the intake and exhaust ports, near the spark plug areas and in close proximity to the exhaust valve guides.

3   A thermostat controls engine coolant temperature. During warm up, the closed thermostat prevents coolant from circulating through the radiator. As the engine nears normal operating temperature, the thermostat opens and allows hot coolant to travel through the radiator, where it's cooled before returning to the engine.

Heating system

4   The heating system consists of a blower fan and heater core located in a housing under the dash, the hoses connecting the heater core to the engine cooling system and the heater/air conditioning control head on the dashboard. Hot engine coolant is circulated through the heater core. When the heater mode is activated, a flap door in the housing opens to expose the heater core to the passenger compartment through air ducts. A fan switch on the control head activates the blower motor, which forces air through the core, heating the air.

Air conditioning system

5   The air conditioning system consists of a condenser mounted in front of the radiator, an evaporator mounted adjacent to the heater core, a compressor mounted on the engine, a receiver-drier or accumulator and the plumbing connecting all of the above components.

6   A blower fan forces the warmer air of the passenger compartment through the evaporator core (sort of a radiator-in-reverse), transferring the heat from the air to the refrigerant. The liquid refrigerant boils off into low pressure vapor, taking the heat with it when it leaves the evaporator.

2   Troubleshooting

Coolant leaks

1   A coolant leak can develop anywhere in the cooling system, but the most common causes are:

a) A loose or weak hose clamp
b) A defective hose
c) A faulty pressure cap
d) A damaged radiator
e) A bad heater core
f) A faulty water pump
g) A leaking gasket at any joint that carries coolant

2   Coolant leaks aren't always easy to find. Sometimes they can only be detected when the cooling system is under pressure. Here's where a cooling system pressure tester comes in handy. After the engine has cooled completely, the tester is attached in place of the pressure cap, then pumped up to the pressure value equal to that of the pressure cap rating (see illustration). Now, leaks that only exist when the engine is fully warmed up will become apparent. The tester can be left connected to locate a nagging slow leak.

Coolant level drops, but no external leaks

3   If you find it necessary to keep adding coolant, but there are no external leaks, the probable causes include:

a) A blown head gasket
b) A leaking intake manifold gasket (only on engines that have coolant passages in the manifold)
c) A cracked cylinder head or cylinder block

4   Any of the above problems will also usually result in contamination of the engine oil, which will cause it to take on a milkshake-like appearance. A bad head gasket or cracked head or block can also result in engine oil contaminating the cooling system.

5   Combustion leak detectors (also known as block testers) are available at most auto parts stores. These work by detecting exhaust gases in the cooling system, which indicates a compression leak from a cylinder into the coolant. The tester consists of a large bulb-type syringe and bottle of test fluid (see illustration). A measured amount of the fluid is added to the syringe. The syringe is placed over the cooling system filler neck and, with the engine running, the bulb is squeezed and a sample of the gases present in the cooling system are drawn up through the test fluid (see illustration). If any combustion gases are present in the sample taken, the test fluid will change color.

6   If the test indicates combustion gas is present in the cooling system, you can be sure that the engine has a blown head gasket or a crack in the cylinder head or block, and will require disassembly to repair.

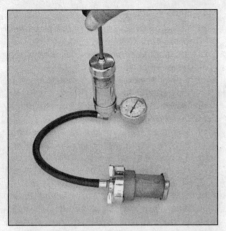

2.8 Checking the cooling system pressure cap with a cooling system pressure tester

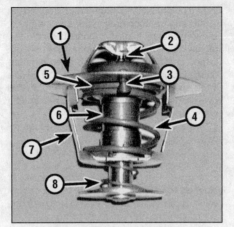

2.10 Typical thermostat:

1	*Flange*	*5*	*Valve seat*
2	*Piston*	*6*	*Valve*
3	*Jiggle valve*	*7*	*Frame*
4	*Main coil*	*8*	*Secondary*
	spring		*coil spring*

2.28 The water pump weep hole is generally located on the underside of the pump

Pressure cap

Warning: *Wait until the engine is completely cool before beginning this check.*

7   The cooling system is sealed by a spring-loaded cap, which raises the boiling point of the coolant. If the cap's seal or spring are worn out, the coolant can boil and escape past the cap. With the engine completely cool, remove the cap and check the seal; if it's cracked, hardened or deteriorated in any way, replace it with a new one.

8   Even if the seal is good, the spring might not be; this can be checked with a cooling system pressure tester (see illustration). If the cap can't hold a pressure within approximately 1-1/2 lbs of its rated pressure (which is marked on the cap), replace it with a new one.

9   The cap is also equipped with a vacuum relief spring. When the engine cools off, a vacuum is created in the cooling system. The vacuum relief spring allows air back into the system, which will equalize the pressure and prevent damage to the radiator (the radiator tanks could collapse if the vacuum is great enough). If, after turning the engine off and allowing it to cool down you notice any of the cooling system hoses collapsing, replace the pressure cap with a new one.

Thermostat

10   Before assuming the thermostat or water control valve (see illustration) is responsible for a cooling system problem, check the coolant level (see Chapter 1), drivebelt tension (see Chapter 1) and temperature gauge (or light) operation.

11   If the engine takes a long time to warm up (as indicated by the temperature gauge or heater operation), the thermostat is probably stuck open. Replace the thermostat or water control valve with a new one.

12   If the engine runs hot or overheats, a thorough test of the thermostat should be performed.

13   Definitive testing of the thermostat or water control valve can only be made when it is removed from the vehicle. If the thermostat is stuck in the open position at room temperature, it is faulty and must be replaced.

Caution: *Do not drive the vehicle without a thermostat. The computer may stay in open loop and emissions and fuel economy will suffer.*

14   To test a thermostat, suspend the (closed) thermostat on a length of string or wire in a pot of cold water.

15   Heat the water on a stove while observing thermostat. The thermostat should fully open before the water boils.

16   If the thermostat doesn't open and close as specified, or sticks in any position, replace it.

Cooling fan

Electric cooling fan

17   If the engine is overheating and the cooling fan is not coming on when the engine temperature rises to an excessive level, unplug the fan motor electrical connector(s) and connect the motor directly to the battery with fused jumper wires. If the fan motor doesn't come on, replace the motor.

18   If the radiator fan motor is okay, but it isn't coming on when the engine gets hot, the fan relay might be defective. A relay is used to control a circuit by turning it on and off in response to a control decision by the Powertrain Control Module (PCM). These control circuits are fairly complex, and checking them should be left to a qualified automotive technician. Sometimes, the control system can be fixed by simply identifying and replacing a bad relay.

19   Locate the fan relays in the engine compartment fuse/relay box.

20   Test the relay (see Chapter 12).

21   If the relay is okay, check all wiring and connections to the fan motor. Refer to the

wiring diagrams in Chapter 13. If no obvious problems are found, the problem could be the Engine Coolant Temperature (ECT) sensor or the Powertrain Control Module (PCM). Have the cooling fan system and circuit diagnosed by a dealer service department or repair shop with the proper diagnostic equipment.

Belt-driven cooling fan

22   Disconnect the cable from the negative terminal of the battery and rock the fan back and forth by hand to check for excessive bearing play.

23   With the engine cold (and not running), turn the fan blades by hand. The fan should turn freely.

24   Visually inspect for substantial fluid leakage from the clutch assembly. If problems are noted, replace the clutch assembly.

25   With the engine completely warmed up, turn off the ignition switch and disconnect the negative battery cable from the battery. Turn the fan by hand. Some drag should be evident. If the fan turns easily, replace the fan clutch.

Water pump

26   A failure in the water pump can cause serious engine damage due to overheating.

Drivebelt-driven water pump

27   There are two ways to check the operation of the water pump while it's installed on the engine. If the pump is found to be defective, it should be replaced with a new or rebuilt unit.

28   Water pumps are equipped with weep (or vent) holes (see illustration). If a failure occurs in the pump seal, coolant will leak from the hole.

29   If the water pump shaft bearings fail, there may be a howling sound at the pump while it's running. Shaft wear can be felt with the drivebelt removed if the water pump pul-

ley is rocked up and down (with the engine off). Don't mistake drivebelt slippage, which causes a squealing sound, for water pump bearing failure.

Timing chain or timing belt-driven water pump

30   Water pumps driven by the timing chain or timing belt are located underneath the timing chain or timing belt cover.

31   Checking the water pump is limited because of where it is located. However, some basic checks can be made before deciding to remove the water pump. If the pump is found to be defective, it should be replaced with a new or rebuilt unit.

32   One sign that the water pump may be failing is that the heater (climate control) may not work well. Warm the engine to normal operating temperature, confirm that the coolant level is correct, then run the heater and check for hot air coming from the ducts.

33   Check for noises coming from the water pump area. If the water pump impeller shaft or bearings are failing, there may be a howling sound at the pump while the engine is running.

Note: *Be careful not to mistake drivebelt noise (squealing) for water pump bearing or shaft failure.*

34   It you suspect water pump failure due to noise, wear can be confirmed by feeling for play at the pump shaft. This can be done by rocking the drive sprocket on the pump shaft up and down. To do this you will need to remove the tension on the timing chain or belt as well as access the water pump.

All water pumps

35   In rare cases or on high-mileage vehicles, another sign of water pump failure may be the presence of coolant in the engine oil. This condition will adversely affect the engine in varying degrees.

Note: *Finding coolant in the engine oil could indicate other serious issues besides a failed water pump, such as a blown head gasket or a cracked cylinder head or block.*

36   Even a pump that exhibits no outward signs of a problem, such as noise or leakage, can still be due for replacement. Removal for close examination is the only sure way to tell. Sometimes the fins on the back of the impeller can corrode to the point that cooling efficiency is diminished significantly.

Heater system

37   Little can go wrong with a heater. If the fan motor will run at all speeds, the electrical part of the system is okay. The three basic heater problems fall into the following general categories:

a) *Not enough heat*
b) *Heat all the time*
c) *No heat*

38   If there's not enough heat, the control valve or door is stuck in a partially open position, the coolant coming from the engine isn't hot enough, or the heater core is restricted.

If the coolant isn't hot enough, the thermostat in the engine cooling system is stuck open, allowing coolant to pass through the engine so rapidly that it doesn't heat up quickly enough. If the vehicle is equipped with a temperature gauge instead of a warning light, watch to see if the engine temperature rises to the normal operating range after driving for a reasonable distance.

39   If there's heat all the time, the control valve or the door is stuck wide open.

40   If there's no heat, coolant is probably not reaching the heater core, or the heater core is plugged. The likely cause is a collapsed or plugged hose, core, or a frozen heater control valve. If the heater is the type that flows coolant all the time, the cause is a stuck door or a broken or kinked control cable.

Air conditioning system

41   If the cool air output is inadequate: Inspect the condenser coils and fins to make sure they're clear

a) *Check the compressor clutch for slippage*
b) *Check the blower motor for proper operation*
c) *Inspect the blower discharge passage for obstructions*
d) *Check the system air intake filter for clogging*

42   If the system provides intermittent cooling air:

a) *Check the circuit breaker, blower switch and blower motor for a malfunction*
b) *Make sure the compressor clutch isn't slipping*
c) *Inspect the plenum door to make sure it's operating properly*
d) *Inspect the evaporator to make sure it isn't clogged*
e) *If the unit is icing up, it may be caused by excessive moisture in the system, incorrect super heat switch adjustment or low thermostat adjustment*

43   If the system provides no cooling air:

a) *Inspect the compressor drivebelt; make sure it's not loose or broken*
b) *Make sure the compressor clutch engages; if it doesn't, check for a blown fuse*
c) *Inspect the wire harness for broken or disconnected wires*
d) *If the compressor clutch doesn't engage, bridge the terminals of the AC pressure switch(es) with a jumper wire; if the clutch now engages, and the system is properly charged, the pressure switch is bad*
e) *Make sure the blower motor is not disconnected or burned out*
f) *Make sure the compressor isn't partially or completely seized*
g) *Inspect the refrigerant lines for leaks*
h) *Check the components for leaks*
i) *Inspect the receiver-drier/accumulator or expansion valve/tube for clogged screens*

44   If the system is noisy:

a) *Look for loose panels in the passenger compartment*
b) *Inspect the compressor drivebelt; it may be loose or worn*
c) *Check the compressor mounting bolts; they should be tight*
d) *Listen carefully to the compressor; it may be worn out*
e) *Listen to the idler pulley and bearing, and the clutch; either may be defective*
f) *The winding in the compressor clutch coil or solenoid may be defective*
g) *The compressor oil level may be low*
h) *The blower motor fan bushing or the motor itself may be worn out*
i) *If there is an excessive charge in the system, you'll hear a rumbling noise in the high pressure line, a thumping noise in the compressor, or see bubbles or cloudiness in the sight glass*
j) *If there's a low charge in the system, you might hear hissing in the evaporator case at the expansion valve, or see bubbles or cloudiness in the sight glass*

---

3   Air conditioning and heating system - check and maintenance

---

Air conditioning system

Warning: *The air conditioning system is under high pressure. Do not loosen any hose fittings or remove any components until after the system has been discharged. Air conditioning refrigerant should be properly discharged into an EPA-approved recovery/recycling unit at a dealer service department or an automotive air conditioning repair facility. Always wear eye protection when disconnecting air conditioning system fittings.*

Caution: *All models covered by this manual use environmentally friendly R-134a. This refrigerant (and its appropriate refrigerant oils) are not compatible with R-12 refrigerant system components and must never be mixed or the components will be damaged.*

Caution: *When replacing entire components, additional refrigerant oil should be added equal to the amount that is removed with the component being replaced. Be sure to read the can before adding any oil to the system, to make sure it is compatible with the R-134a system.*

1   The following maintenance checks should be performed on a regular basis to ensure that the air conditioning continues to operate at peak efficiency:

a) *Inspect the condition of the compressor drivebelt. If it is worn or deteriorated, replace it (see Chapter 1).*
b) *Check the drivebelt tension (see Chapter 1).*
c) *Inspect the system hoses. Look for cracks, bubbles, hardening and deterioration. Inspect the hoses and all fittings for oil bubbles or seepage. If there is any evidence of wear, damage or leakage, replace the hose(s).*

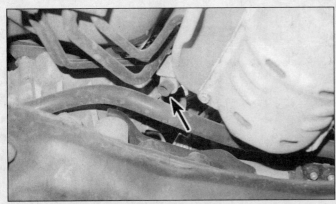

3.1a The evaporator drain hose extends through the floor to allow collected water to run out. This is a 2007/2008 model. . .

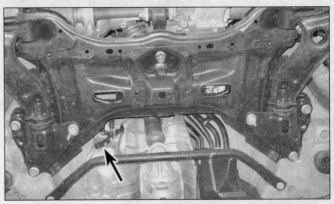

3.1b. . . and this is a 2009 or later model

3.9 Insert a thermometer in the center vent, turn on the air conditioning system and wait for it to cool down; depending on the humidity, the output air should be 30 to 40 degrees cooler than the ambient air temperature

3.11 R-134a automotive air conditioning charging kit

d) *Inspect the condenser fins for leaves, bugs and any other foreign material that may have embedded itself in the fins. Use a fin comb or compressed air to remove debris from the condenser.*

e) *Make sure the system has the correct refrigerant charge.*

f) *If you hear water sloshing around in the dash area or have water dripping on the carpet, check the evaporator housing drain tube (see illustrations) and insert a piece of wire into the opening to check for blockage.*

2   It's a good idea to operate the system for about ten minutes at least once a month. This is particularly important during the winter months because long term non-use can cause hardening, and subsequent failure, of the seals. Note that using the Defrost function operates the compressor.

3   If the air conditioning system is not working properly, proceed to Step 6 and perform the general checks outlined below.

4   Because of the complexity of the air conditioning system and the special equipment necessary to service it, in-depth troubleshooting and repairs beyond checking the refrigerant charge and the compressor clutch opera-

tion are not included in this manual. However, simple checks and component replacement procedures are provided in this Chapter. For more complete information on the air conditioning system, refer to the Haynes Automotive Heating and Air Conditioning Manual.

5   The most common cause of poor cooling is simply a low system refrigerant charge. If a noticeable drop in system cooling ability occurs, one of the following quick checks will help you determine if the refrigerant level is low.

Checking the refrigerant charge

6   Warm the engine up to normal operating temperature.

7   Place the air conditioning temperature selector at the coldest setting and put the blower at the highest setting.

8   After the system reaches operating temperature, feel the larger pipe exiting the evaporator at the firewall. The outlet pipe should be cold (the tubing that leads back to the compressor). If the evaporator outlet pipe is warm, the system probably needs a charge.

9   Insert a thermometer in the center air distribution duct (see illustration) while operating the air conditioning system at its maxi-

mum setting - the temperature of the output air should be 30 to 40 degrees F below the ambient air temperature (down to approximately 40 degrees F). If the ambient (outside) air temperature is very high, say 110 degrees F, the duct air temperature may be as high as 60 degrees F, but generally the air conditioning is 30 to 40 degrees F cooler than the ambient air.

10   Further inspection or testing of the system requires special tools and techniques and is beyond the scope of the home mechanic.

Adding refrigerant

Caution: *Make sure any refrigerant, refrigerant oil or replacement component you purchase is designated as compatible with R-134a systems.*

11   Purchase an R-134a automotive charging kit at an auto parts store (see illustration). A charging kit includes a can of refrigerant, a tap valve and a short section of hose that can be attached between the tap valve and the system low side service valve.

Caution: *Never add more than one can of refrigerant to the system. If more refrigerant than that is required, the system should be evacuated and leak tested.*

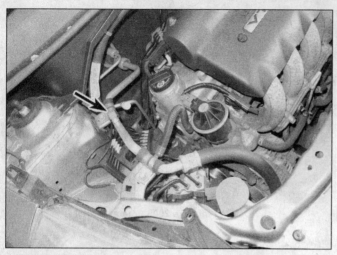

3.13a Location of the low-side charging port - 2007/2008 models

3.13b Location of the low-side charging port - 2009 and later models

12 Back off the valve handle on the charging kit and screw the kit onto the refrigerant can, making sure first that the O-ring or rubber seal inside the threaded portion of the kit is in place.

Warning: *Wear protective eyewear when dealing with pressurized refrigerant cans.*

13 Remove the dust cap from the low-side charging port and attach the hose's quick-connect fitting to the port (see illustrations). The fittings on the charging kit are designed to fit only on the low side of the system.

Warning: *DO NOT hook the charging kit hose to the system high side!*

14 Warm up the engine and turn on the air conditioning. Keep the charging kit hose away from the fan and other moving parts.

Note: *The charging process requires the compressor to be running. If the clutch cycles off, you can put the air conditioning switch on High and leave the car doors open to keep the clutch on and compressor working. The compressor can be kept on during the charging by removing the connector from the pressure switch and bridging it with a paper clip or jumper wire during the procedure.*

15 Turn the valve handle on the kit until the stem pierces the can, then back the handle out to release the refrigerant. You should be able to hear the rush of gas. Keep the can upright at all times, but shake it occasionally. Allow stabilization time between each addition.

Note: *The charging process will go faster if you wrap the can with a hot-water-soaked rag to keep the can from freezing up.*

16 If you have an accurate thermometer, you can place it in the center air conditioning duct inside the vehicle and keep track of the output air temperature. A charged system that is working properly should cool down to approximately 40 degrees F. If the ambient (outside) air temperature is very high, say 110 degrees F, the duct air temperature may be as high as 60 degrees F, but generally the air conditioning is 30 to 40 degrees F cooler than the ambient air.

17 When the can is empty, turn the valve handle to the closed position and release the connection from the low-side port. Reinstall the dust cap.

18 Remove the charging kit from the can and store the kit for future use with the piercing valve in the UP position, to prevent inadvertently piercing the can on the next use.

Heating systems

19 If the carpet under the heater core is damp, or if antifreeze vapor or steam is coming through the vents, the heater core is leaking. Remove it (see Section 11) and install a new unit (most radiator shops will not repair a leaking heater core).

20 If the air coming out of the heater vents isn't hot, the problem could stem from any of the following causes:

a) *The thermostat is stuck open, preventing the engine coolant from warming up enough to carry heat to the heater core. Replace the thermostat (see Section 4).*

b) *There is a blockage in the system, preventing the flow of coolant through the heater core. Feel both heater hoses at the firewall. They should be hot. If one of them is cold, there is an obstruction in one of the hoses or in the heater core, or the heater control valve is shut. Detach the hoses and back flush the heater core with a water hose. If the heater core is clear but circulation is impeded, remove the two hoses and flush them out with a water hose.*

c) *If flushing fails to remove the blockage from the heater core, the core must be replaced (see Section 11).*

Eliminating air conditioning odors

21 Unpleasant odors that often develop in air conditioning systems are caused by the growth of a fungus, usually on the surface of the evaporator core. The warm, humid environment there is a perfect breeding ground for mildew to develop.

22 The evaporator core on most vehicles is difficult to access, and factory dealerships have a lengthy, expensive process for eliminating the fungus by opening up the evaporator case and using a powerful disinfectant and rinse on the core until the fungus is gone. You can service your own system at home, but it takes something much stronger than basic household germ-killers or deodorizers.

23 Aerosol disinfectants for automotive air conditioning systems are available in most auto parts stores, but remember when shopping for them that the most effective treatments are also the most expensive. The basic procedure for using these sprays is to start by running the system in the RECIRC mode for ten minutes with the blower on its highest speed. Use the highest heat mode to dry out the system and keep the compressor from engaging by disconnecting the wiring connector at the compressor.

24 The disinfectant can usually comes with a long spray hose. Insert the nozzle into an intake port inside the cabin, and spray according to the manufacturer's recommendations. Follow the manufacturer's recommendations for the length of spray and waiting time between applications.

25 Once the evaporator has been cleaned, the best way to prevent the mildew from coming back again is to make sure your evaporator housing drain tube is clear (see illustration 3.1).

Automatic heating and air conditioning systems

26 Some vehicles are equipped with an optional automatic climate control system. This system has its own computer that receives inputs from various sensors in the heating and air conditioning system. This computer, like the PCM, has self-diagnostic capabilities to help pinpoint problems or faults within the system. Vehicles equipped with automatic heating and air conditioning systems are very complex and considered

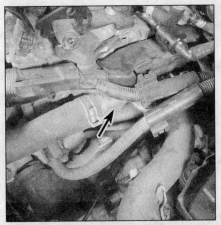

4.6a On 2007/2008 models, the thermostat housing is located on the left end (driver's side) of the engine

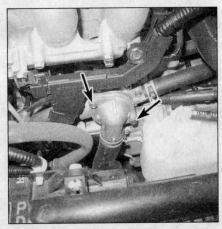

4.6b Thermostat housing bolts (2009 and later models)

4.9a The thermostat sealing ring fits around the edge of the flange

4.9b When installing the thermostat, be sure to position the jiggle valve at the top

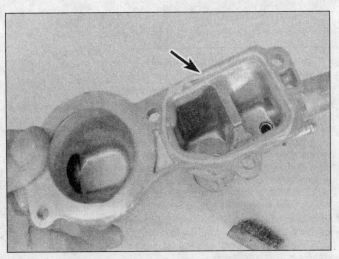

4.10 On 2007/2008 models, apply a bead of RTV sealant around the water outlet portion of the thermostat housing

beyond the scope of the home mechanic. Vehicles equipped with automatic heating and air conditioning systems should be taken to dealer service department or other qualified facility for repair.

4   Thermostat - replacement

Warning: *See the antifreeze Warning in Section 1.*
Warning: *Wait until the engine is completely cool before beginning this procedure.*
1   Drain the cooling system (see Chapter 1). If the coolant is relatively new, or is in good condition (see Section 2), save it and re-use it.
2   Remove the splash guard underneath the engine.
Note: *This is so any coolant that spills out when the thermostat housing and thermostat is removed won't collect on the splash shield. If you surround the housing with rags to ab-*

sorb spilling coolant, this step isn't necessary.

2008 and earlier models
3   Remove the air filter housing (see Chapter 4 Section 9).
4   Remove the wire harness bracket, ground strap bolt, and the harness clamps from above the thermostat housing.
5   Disconnect the coolant hoses from the thermostat housing.

All models
6   Remove the thermostat housing cover mounting bolts and remove the cover (see illustrations). If the cover is stuck, tap it with a soft-face hammer to jar it loose. Be prepared for some coolant to spill as the gasket seal is broken. Clean the mating surfaces of all gasket or sealant.
7   Remove the thermostat.
8   Remove all traces of old gasket from the thermostat housing mating surfaces, fasteners and bolt holes.

Installation
9   Install a new sealing ring onto the thermostat (see illustration), then insert the thermostat into the housing. Make sure that the air bleed valve (pin, or jiggle valve) is positioned at the top (see illustration), and the spring end of the valve is directed toward the engine.
10   On 2008 and earlier models, apply RTV sealant to the mating surface of the thermostat housing cover (see illustration).
11   The remainder of installation is the reverse of removal. Tighten the thermostat housing bolts to the torque values listed in this Chapter's Specifications
12   On 2008 and earlier models, wait until the recommended time has passed for the RTV sealant to cure before refilling the cooling system.
13   Refill the cooling system (see Chapter 1).
14   Start the engine and allow it to reach normal operating temperature, then check for leaks and proper thermostat operation.

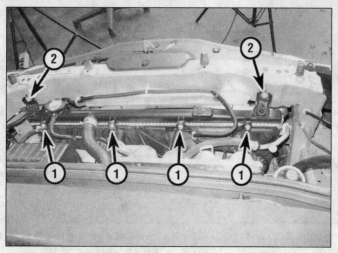

5.5 Engine cooling fan and radiator details - 2009 and later models

1   Fan/shroud   2   Radiator upper
    mounting bolts   bracket bolts

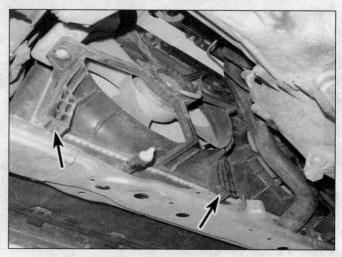

5.11 Properly seated shroud mounts

5   Engine cooling fans - removal and installation

Warning: *The engine must be completely cool before beginning this procedure.*
Warning: *The models covered by this manual are equipped with a Supplemental Restraint System (SRS), more commonly known as airbags. Always disarm the airbag system before working in the vicinity of any airbag system component to avoid the possibility of accidental deployment of the airbag, which could cause personal injury (see Chapter 12). Do not use a memory saving device to preserve the PCM's memory when working on or near airbag system components.*
Warning: *See the antifreeze Warning in Section 1 .*

Removal

2008 and ealier models

1   Remove the radiator (see Section 6).
2   Lift up and remove the radiator fan and shrouds from the vehicle.

2009 and later models

3   Remove the coolant reservoir (see Section 6).
4   Disconnect the electrical connector for the radiator fan and the air conditioning condenser fan.
5   Remove the upper radiator brackets (see illustration).
6   Remove the fasteners holding the air conditioning condenser fan shroud to the passenger side of the engine compartment and remove the fan and shroud assembly from the vehicle.
7   Remove the fasteners holding the radiator fan to the driver's side of the engine compartment and remove the fan and shroud assembly from the vehicle.

All models

8   Remove the nuts for each fan blade assembly and remove them from their motor shafts.
9   Inspect the fans for cracks, chips or other damage and replace as necessary.
10 Remove the fan motor-to-fan support retaining bolts, then remove the motor.

Installation

11 Installation is the reverse of removal. Make sure the fan shrouds seat properly at the bottom (see illustration).
12 On 2008 and earlier models, refill the cooling system (see Chapter 1).

6   Radiator and coolant reservoir - removal and installation

Warning: *The engine must be completely cool before beginning this procedure.*
Warning: *The models covered by this manual are equipped with a Supplemental Restraint System (SRS), more commonly known as airbags. Always disarm the airbag system before working in the vicinity of any airbag system component to avoid the possibility of accidental deployment of the airbag, which could cause personal injury (see Chapter 12). Do not use a memory saving device to preserve the PCM's memory when working on or near airbag system components.*
Warning: *See the antifreeze Warning in Section 1.*

Radiator

Removal

1   Remove the battery (see Chapter 5).
2   Drain the engine coolant (see Chapter 1).
3   Remove the coolant reservoir (see Step 26).

2008 and earlier models

4   Remove the front bumper cover (see Chapter 11).
5   Remove the air filter housing and bracket (see Chapter 4).
6   Remove the hood latch (see Chapter 11).
7   Remove the center radiator support bracket.
8   Remove the upper air conditioning condenser brackets (see Section 13).
9   Remove the fasteners holding the radiator air guide from the upper radiator support and remove the air guide.

All models

10 Remove the splash shield below the engine bay.
11 Disconnect the upper and lower radiator hoses from the radiator. If a hose is stuck, grasp it near the end with a pair of large adjustable pliers and twist it to break the seal, then pull it off. If the hose is old or deteriorated, cut it off and install a new one.
12 Disconnect the electrical connector from Engine Coolant Temperature (ETC) sensor no. 2 at the bottom of the radiator.
13 Disconnect the automatic transmission fluid (ATF) cooler hose from the lower part of the radiator (if equipped).
14 Disconnect the electrical connectors for the radiator and air conditioning condenser fans. Remove the harness clamps for the connectors and move the wires aside.
15 On 2008 and earlier models disconnect the air conditioning compressor clutch electrical connector from the air conditioning condenser fan shroud. Also remove the air conditioning condenser fan shroud mounting bolt.
16 Remove the upper radiator brackets (see accompanying illustration and illustration 5.5).
17 Push the air conditioning condenser towards the front of the vehicle to make room for the radiator removal.
18 Remove the radiator from the vehicle.

6.16 Radiator mounting bracket bolt (left side, 2007/2008 models)

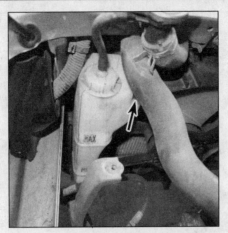

6.28a Coolant reservoir mounting bolt (2008 and earlier models; not visible here, location given)

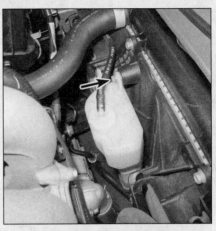

6.28b Coolant reservoir mounting bolt (2009 and later models)

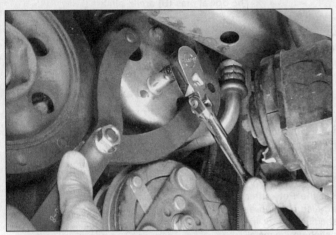

7.5 If the drivebelt won't prevent the water pump pulley from turning when loosening the bolts, use a pin spanner to hold it

7.6 Drivebelt idler pulley bolt (seen from above) - 2007/2008 models

Caution: *Avoid damaging the radiator or condenser fins and tanks during radiator removal.*

19   Inspect the radiator for any leaks or damage. If repairs are needed take it to a radiator shop or dealer service department to perform the work, as special techniques are required.

20   Bugs and dirt can be removed from the radiator with a soft brush followed by forcing water from a garden hose through the core from the engine side. Do not bend the cooling fins as this is done.

Installation

21   Installation of the radiator is the reverse of removal. Discard the old O-ring for the ECT sensor and drain plug and re-install with new O-rings.

22   Tighten all fasteners to the torque values listed in this Chapter's Specifications.

23   Ensure that the cooling fan shroud mounts are seated properly at the top and bottom of the radiator (see illustration 5.11).

24   Refill the cooling system (see Chapter 1).

25   Reconnect the battery (see Chapter 5). Allow the engine to reach normal operating temperature, indicated by the upper radiator hose becoming hot. Allow the engine to cool completely, the recheck the coolant level and add more if required.

Coolant reservoir

26   If you're working on a 2007/2008 model, remove the air filter housing (see Chapter 4). Also remove the air filter housing mounting bracket.

27   Disconnect the overflow hose from the fitting by the radiator cap.

28   Remove the coolant reservoir mounting bolt (see illustrations).

29   Remove the coolant reservoir from the vehicle.

30   Pour the coolant into a container. Wash out the reservoir using soapy water and a long brush to make the coolant level easier to read. Inspect the reservoir for cracks and chafing. Replace it if any are found.

31   Installation is the reverse of removal.

7   Water pump - replacement

Warning: *Wait until the engine is completely cool before beginning this procedure.*

Warning: *See the antifreeze Warning in Section 1.*

1   Disconnect the cable from the negative terminal of the battery (see Chapter 5). Loosen the right front wheel lug nuts, raise the front of the vehicle and support it securely on jackstands. Remove the wheel.

2   Remove the under-vehicle splash shield.

3   Drain the cooling system (see Chapter 1). If the coolant is relatively new, or is in good condition, save it and re-use it.

4   Remove the right inner fender splash shield (seeChapter 11).

5   Loosen the water pump pulley mounting bolts (see illustration).

6   Remove the drivebelt (see Chapter 1). On 2008 and earlier models, remove the idler pulley mounting bolt and remove the idler pulley (see illustration).

7   Remove the water pump pulley mount-

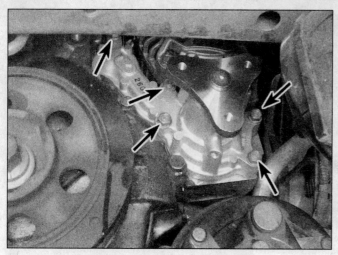

7.8 Water pump mounting bolts

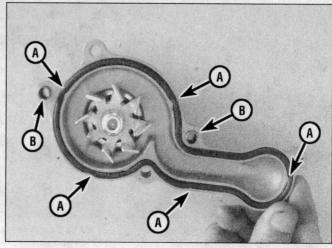

7.10 Seat the new O-ring seal into the pump groove, pushing it
into the dimpled areas (A) so it doesn't fall out. Also make sure
the dowel pins (B) are in place

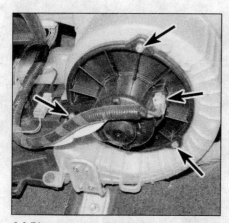

9.3 Blower motor electrical connector and
mounting screws

ing bolts and remove the pulley.
8   Remove the water pump bolts and separate the pump from the pump housing (see
illustration). If the pump is stuck, gently tap it
with a soft faced hammer to break the gasket
seal.
Caution: *When the pump is removed, coolant
will spill out. Have a container ready to catch
the excess coolant.*
9   Clean the water pump and timing chain
cover mating surfaces.
10   Install a new O-ring into the water pump
groove (see illustration).
11   Guide the pump into place on the timing
chain cover and install the bolts.
12   Tighten the pump-to-housing bolts to the
torque values listed in this Chapter's Specifications.
13   The remainder of installation is the
reverse of removal.
14   Refill the cooling system (see Chapter 1).
15   Reconnect the battery (see Chapter 5).
16   Start the engine and check for any leaks.
Re-check the coolant level and add some, if
necessary.

8   Engine Coolant Temperature (ECT) sensor - check and replacement

Warning: *Wait until the engine is completely
cool before beginning this procedure.*
1   The coolant temperature indicator system consists of a warning light or a temperature gauge on the dash and a pair of Engine
Coolant Temperature (ECT) sensors. The
Engine Coolant Temperature (ECT) sensors
are information sensors for the Powertrain
Control Module (PCM) and also function as
the coolant temperature sending unit for the
temperature gauge. Information on the installation and installation of the Engine Coolant
Temperature (ECT) sensors can be found
Chapter 6 .

9   Blower motor - removal and installation

Warning: *The models covered by this manual
are equipped with a Supplemental Restraint
System (SRS), more commonly known as airbags. Always disarm the airbag system before
working in the vicinity of any airbag system
component to avoid the possibility of accidental deployment of the airbag, which could
cause personal injury (see Chapter 12). Do
not use a memory saving device to preserve
the PCM's memory when working on or near
airbag system components.*
1   Disconnect the cable from the negative
terminal of the battery (see Chapter 5).
2   Remove the passenger's side under-
dash panel.
3   Disconnect the electrical connector from
the blower motor (see illustration).
4   Remove the blower motor mounting
screws and remove the blower motor from the
housing.

5   Installation is the reverse of removal.
6   Reconnect the battery (see Chapter 5).

10 Heater and air conditioning control assembly - removal and installation

Warning: *The models covered by this manual
are equipped with a Supplemental Restraint
System (SRS), more commonly known as airbags. Always disarm the airbag system before
working in the vicinity of any airbag system
component to avoid the possibility of accidental deployment of the airbag, which could
cause personal injury (see Chapter 12). Do
not use a memory saving device to preserve
the PCM's memory when working on or near
airbag system components.*

Removal
1   Disconnect the cable from the negative
terminal of the battery (see Chapter 5).
2   Remove the center dash panel from the
instrument panel (see Chapter 11).

2008 and earlier models
3   Remove the rear defogger, air conditioning switch and passenger airbag indicator
from the center panel.
4   Remove the knobs from the control
assembly.
5   Remove the mounting screws and
detach the heater and air conditioning control
panel from the center panel.

2009 and later models
6   Remove the instrument cluster trim panel
(see Chapter 11).
7   Remove the mounting screw and detach
the control panel from the instrument panel.

All models
8   The ventilation cables must be disconnected from the heating and air conditioning

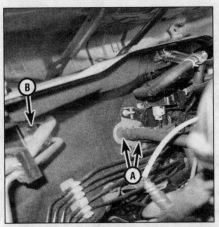

11.4 Heater hoses (A) at heater tubes at the firewall, and refrigerant line fitting bolt (B) at evaporator (2009 and later models)

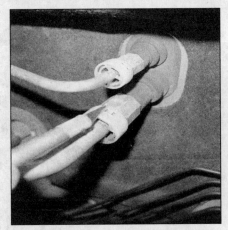

11.5a Slice the joint caps open and remove them from the fittings. . .

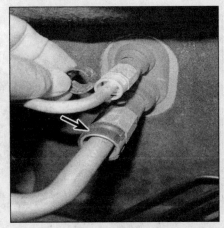

11.5b. . . remove the retaining stops from the fittings. . .

assembly to completely detach the heating and air conditioning control panel.

9   Open the glove box, pinch the sides of the glove box in and allow it to hang all the way down.

10   Set the air mix knob to maximum cool.

11   Locate the linkage for the air mix control on the heating and air conditioning assembly. Pry open the clamp and disconnect the cable.

12   Set the mode control dial to vent.

13   Locate the linkage for the mode control on the heating and air conditioning assembly. Pry open the clamp and disconnect the cable.

14   On 2008 and earlier models, set the recirculation control lever to recirculate. On 2009 and later models set the recirculation control lever to fresh.

15   Locate the linkage for the recirculation control on the heating and air conditioning assembly. Pry open the clamp and disconnect the cable.

16   Remove the heater and air conditioning control assembly from the vehicle.

Installation

17   On 2008 and earlier models, turn the air mix linkage completely counterclockwise and hold it in place.

18   Snap the air mix control cable housing back into the linkage clamp.

19   On 2008 and earlier models turn the mode linkage completely counter clockwise and hold it in place.

20   Snap the air mix control cable housing back into linkage the clamp.

21   Turn the recirculation linkage completely clockwise and hold it in place. Snap the air mix control cable housing back into the clamp.

22   Check that all control cables work properly, if any are found to work incorrectly they must be replaced. The cable can be disconnected from the heater and air conditioner controller using snap ring pliers to spread open the clip and remove the end of the cable. Replace the cable with a new one.

23   The remainder of the installation is the

reverse of removal.

24   Reconnect the battery (see Chapter 5).

11   Heater core - removal and installation

Warning: *Wait until the engine is completely cool before beginning this procedure.*

Warning: *The air conditioning system is under high pressure. Do not loosen any fittings or remove any components until after the system has been discharged. Air conditioning refrigerant should be properly discharged into an EPA-approved container at a dealer service department or an automotive air conditioning repair facility. Always wear eye protection when disconnecting air conditioning system fittings.*

Warning: *The models covered by this manual are equipped with a Supplemental Restraint System (SRS), more commonly known as airbags. Always disarm the airbag system before working in the vicinity of any airbag system component to avoid the possibility of accidental deployment of the airbag, which could cause personal injury (see Chapter 12). Do not use a memory saving device to preserve the PCM's memory when working on or near airbag system components.*

Note: *Replacement of the heater core is a difficult procedure for the home mechanic, involving removal of the entire dashboard, console, and many wiring connectors. If you attempt it at home, keep track of the assemblies by taking notes and keeping screws and other hardware in small, marked plastic bags for reassembly.*

Removal

1   Have the refrigerant discharged at a dealer service department or an automotive air conditioning repair facility.

2   Disconnect the cable from the negative terminal of the battery (see Chapter 5).

3   Drain the cooling system (see Chapter 1).

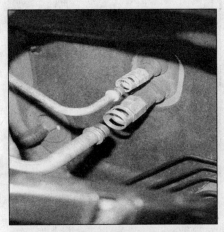

11.5c. . . then disconnect the refrigerant lines

If the coolant is relatively new, or is in good condition, save it and re-use it.

Note: *Plug all open fittings of disconnected lines to prevent entry of dirt and moisture into the lines.*

4   Loosen the hose clamps holding the heater hoses to the heater core tubes and slide the hoses off the tubes (see illustration). Prepare towels or rags underneath the ends of the heater hoses to catch spilled coolant. Plug the heater core tubes to prevent spillage.

Note: *Some models might have a plastic cover over the heater hose clamps; pry the cover open and discard it (it isn't necessary to reinstall it).*

5   On 2008 and earlier models cut the joint caps at the refrigerant line fittings where they connect to the evaporator at the firewall, then remove the fitting stops and disconnect the refrigerant lines from the evaporator core (see illustrations). Discard the old O-rings and joint caps.

6   On 2009 and later models, remove the bolt holding the refrigerant line fitting to the

11.10 Heater core cover screws

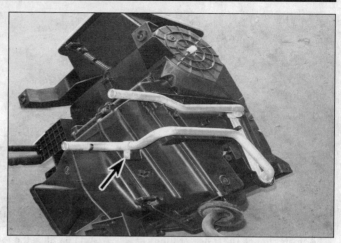

11.11 Heater core pipe bracket screw

11.12 Remove the heater core from the housing

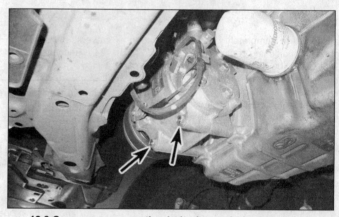

12.8 Compressor mounting bolts (upper bolts not visible)

evaporator core and disconnect the lines (see illustration 11.4).

7   Remove the instrument panel (see Chapter 11).

8   Disconnect the evaporator drain hose from the heater core.

9   Remove the mounting nuts holding the heating and air conditioning housing, then remove the housing from the vehicle.
Note: *Some of the nuts are accessed from the engine compartment side of the firewall.*

10   Remove the screws holding the heater core cover and remove the cover (see illustration).

11   Remove the heater core pipe bracket screw(s) (see illustration).

12   Slide the heater core out from the HVAC housing (see illustration).

Installation

13   Installation is the reverse of removal, noting the following:
Note: *Do not use old O-rings for the refrigerant lines; replace with new ones and apply R134a-compatible refrigerant oil to them before installation.*

14   Reconnect the battery (see Chapter 5).

15   Refill the cooling system (see Chapter 1).

16   Check the operation of all electrical com-

ponents of the steering column and dash.

17   Have the air conditioning system recharged by the shop that discharged it.

***

12   Air conditioning compressor - removal and installation

Warning: *The air conditioning system is under high pressure. Do not loosen any fittings or remove any components until after the system has been discharged. Air conditioning refrigerant should be properly discharged into an EPA-approved container at a dealer service department or an automotive air conditioning repair facility. Always wear eye protection when disconnecting air conditioning system fittings.*

Warning: *Wait until the engine is completely cool before beginning this procedure.*

1   Have the refrigerant discharged at a dealer service department or an automotive air conditioning repair facility.

2   Disconnect the cable from the negative terminal of the battery (see Chapter 5).

3   Loosen the right front wheel lug nuts. Raise the vehicle and support it securely on jackstands. Remove the right inner fender splash shield.

4   Remove the under-vehicle splash shield.

5   Remove the drivebelt (see Chapter 1).

6   Disconnect the compressor clutch electrical connector.

7   Remove the fitting bolts and disconnect the refrigerant lines from the compressor. Discard the old O-rings.
Note: *Plug all open fittings to prevent entry of dirt and moisture into the lines.*

8   Remove the compressor mounting bolts and lower the compressor from the engine compartment (see illustration).
Caution: *Avoid damaging the radiator fins during removal of the air conditioning compressor from the vehicle.*
Note: *If a new compressor is being installed, the clutch assembly may have to be transferred to the new compressor. The removal of the clutch assembly will require the use of several special tools; this procedure should be performed by an air conditioning shop or other repair facility.*

Installation

9   Follow the instructions with the compressor regarding draining out excess refrigerant oil or adding oil to the compressor. Refrigerant oil capacities are listed in this Chapter's Specifications.

10   Installation is the reverse of removal.

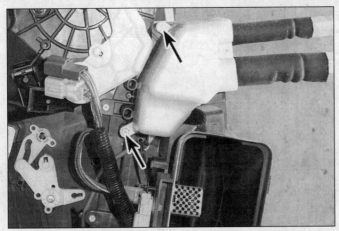

14.7 Expansion valve cover screws (2007/2008 models shown)

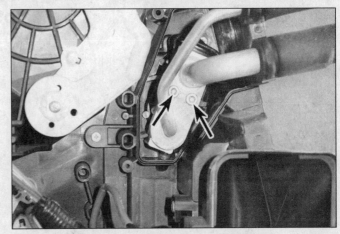

14.8 Refrigerant line/expansion valve bolts

Tighten the compressor mounting bolts to the torque value listed in this Chapter's Specifications.

Note: *To prevent leaks in the air conditioning system, do not use old O-rings for the refrigerant lines. Replace them with new ones and apply R-134a refrigerant oil to them before installation.*

11   Reconnect the battery (see Chapter 5).

12   Have the system evacuated, charged and leak tested by the shop that discharged it.

---

13   Air conditioning condenser - removal and installation

Warning: *The models covered by this manual are equipped with a Supplemental Restraint System (SRS), more commonly known as airbags. Always disarm the airbag system before working in the vicinity of any airbag system component to avoid the possibility of accidental deployment of the airbag, which could cause personal injury (see Chapter 12). Do not use a memory saving device to preserve the PCM's memory when working on or near airbag system components.*

Warning: *The air conditioning system is under high pressure. Do not loosen any fittings or remove any components until after the system has been discharged. Air conditioning refrigerant should be properly discharged into an EPA-approved container at a dealer service department or an automotive air conditioning repair facility. Always wear eye protection when disconnecting air conditioning system fittings.*

Note: *This air conditioning system doesn't have a separate receiver-drier. The condenser has an attached liquid tank that isn't serviced separately.*

1   Have the refrigerant discharged at a dealer service department or an automotive air conditioning repair facility.

2   On 2008 and earlier models, remove the front bumper cover. On 2009 and later models, remove the grille cover (see Chapter 11).

3   Remove the refrigerant line fasteners and detach the lines from the condenser. Discard the old O-rings.

Note: *Plug all open fittings to prevent entry of dirt and moisture into the lines.*

2009 and later models

4   Remove the radiator upper mounting brackets.

5   Disconnect the electrical connector for the air conditioning condenser fan. Detach the wire harness clamp from the fan shroud and move the electrical connector aside.

All models

6   Remove the mounting brackets at the top of the air conditioning condenser.

7   Lift the air conditioning condenser up and remove it from the vehicle.

Caution: *Avoid damaging the condenser fins and tanks during removal.*

Installation

8   Installation is the reverse of removal.

9   If installing a new condenser, add the specified amount of R-134a-compatible refrigerant oil (see this Chapter's Specifications).

Note: *To prevent leaks in the air conditioning system, do not use old O-rings for the refrigerant lines. Replace them with new ones and apply R-134a-compatible refrigerant oil to them before installation.*

10   Have the system evacuated, charged and leak tested by the shop that discharged it.

---

14   Expansion valve - removal and installation

Warning: *The air conditioning system is under high pressure. Do not loosen any fittings or remove any components until after the system has been discharged. Air conditioning refrigerant should be properly discharged into an EPA-approved container at a dealer service department or an automotive air conditioning repair facility. Always wear eye protection*

when disconnecting air conditioning system fittings.

Removal

1   Have the refrigerant discharged at a dealer service department or an automotive air conditioning repair facility.

2   On 2008 and later models disconnect the air conditioning lines from the evaporator core. Cut the joint caps holding the tube to the evaporator at the designated areas and remove the stops, disconnect the air conditioning lines from the evaporator core. Discard the old O-rings and joint caps.

2009 and later models

3   Remove the glove box (see Chapter 11) and the glove box frame, then cut the plastic brace from the glove box aperture.

4   Disconnect the electrical connector from the blower motor.

5   Remove the passenger's heater duct.

6   Remove the blower motor and housing as a unit.

All models

7   Remove the screws on the expansion valve cover and remove the cover (see illustration). On 2009 and later models remove the seals from the cover, discard the old seals and replace upon installation.

8   Remove the refrigerant line/expansion valve bolts and disconnect the refrigerant lines (see illustration).

9   Remove the expansion valve. Discard the O-rings.

Installation

10   Installation is the reverse of removal. Tighten the expansion valve bolts to the torque listed in this Chapter's Specifications.

Note: *To prevent leaks in the air conditioning system, do not use old O-rings. Replace them with new ones and apply R-134a-compatible refrigerant oil to them before installation.*

11   Have the system evacuated, charged and leak tested by the shop that discharged it.

Notes

Chapter 4
Fuel and exhaust systems

Contents

Specifications

Fuel system pressure, at idle (approximate) .... 47 to 54 psi (324 to 372 kpa)

Torque specifications

Note: *One foot-pound (ft-lb) of torque is equivalent to 12 inch-pounds (in-lbs) of torque. Torque values below approximately 15 ft-lbs are expressed in inch-pounds, since most foot-pound torque wrenches are not accurate at these smaller values.*

	Ft-lbs (unless otherwise indicated)	Nm
Fuel rail mounting nuts	106 in-lbs	12
Throttle body mounting fasteners	17	23
Fuel pump lock ring		
2008 and earlier models	69	93
2009 and later models	51	70

1 General information

Fuel system warnings

1   Gasoline is extremely flammable and repairing fuel system components can be dangerous. Consider your automotive repair knowledge and experience before attempting repairs which may be better suited for a professional mechanic.

- *Don't smoke or allow open flames or bare light bulbs near the work area*
- *Don't work in a garage with a gas-type appliance (water heater, clothes dryer)*
- *Use fuel-resistant gloves. If any fuel spills on your skin, wash it off immediately with soap and water*
- *Clean up spills immediately*
- *Do not store fuel-soaked rags where they could ignite*
- *Prior to disconnecting any fuel line, you must relieve the fuel pressure (see Section 3)*
- *Wear safety glasses*
- *Have a proper fire extinguisher on hand*

Fuel system

2   The fuel system consists of the fuel tank, electric fuel pump/fuel level sensor module (located in the fuel tank), fuel rail and fuel injectors. The fuel injection system is a multi-port system; multi-port fuel injection uses timed impulses to inject the fuel directly into the intake port of each cylinder during the intake stroke. The Powertrain Control Module (PCM) controls the injectors. The PCM monitors various engine parameters and delivers the exact amount of fuel required into the intake ports.

3   Fuel is circulated from the fuel pump to the fuel rail through fuel lines running along the underside of the vehicle. Various sections of the fuel line are either rigid metal, nylon or flexible fuel hose. The various sections of the fuel hose are connected either by quick-connect fittings or threaded metal fittings.

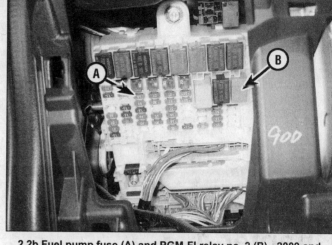

2.2a The fuel pump fuse is located in the under-dash fuse/relay box - this is a 2008 model (check the legend on the fuse box access door for the fuse location on your vehicle)

1   *Fuel pump fuse*
2   *PGM-FI relay no. 2*

2.2b Fuel pump fuse (A) and PGM-FI relay no. 2 (B) - 2009 and later models

2.9 An automotive stethoscope is used to listen to the fuel injectors in operation

Exhaust system

4   The exhaust system consists of the exhaust manifold(s), catalytic converter(s), muffler(s), tailpipe and all connecting pipes, flanges and clamps. The catalytic converters are an emission control device added to the exhaust system to reduce pollutants (see Chapter 6).

2   Troubleshooting

Fuel pump

1   The fuel pump is located inside the fuel tank. Sit inside the vehicle with the windows closed, turn the ignition key to ON (not START) and listen for the sound of the fuel pump as it's briefly activated. You will only hear the sound for a second or two, but that sound tells you that the pump is working.

Alternatively, have an assistant listen at the fuel filler cap.
2   If the pump does not come on, check the fuel pump fuse, which is located in the under-dash fuse/relay box (see illustrations). If the fuse is okay, check the wiring back to the fuel pump. If the fuse and wiring are okay, the pump might be defective. Other possibilities include a faulty PGM-FI relay no. 2, or a faulty Powertrain Control Module (PCM). If the pump runs continuously with the ignition key in the ON position, the Powertrain Control Module (PCM) is probably defective. Have the PCM checked by a professional mechanic.

Fuel injection system

Note: *The following procedure is based on the assumption that the fuel pump is working and the fuel pressure is adequate (see Section 4).*
3   Check all electrical connectors that are related to the system. Check the ground wire connections for tightness.
4   Verify that the battery is fully charged (see Chapter 5).
5   Inspect the air filter element (see Chapter 1).
6   Check all fuses (see Chapter 12).
7   Check the air induction system between the throttle body and the intake manifold for air leaks. Also inspect the condition of all vacuum hoses connected to the intake manifold and to the throttle body.
8   Remove the air intake duct from the throttle body and look for dirt, carbon, varnish, or other residue in the throttle body, particularly around the throttle plate. If it's dirty, clean it with carb cleaner, a toothbrush and a clean shop towel.
9   With the engine running, place an automotive stethoscope against each injector, one at a time, and listen for a clicking sound that indicates operation (see illustration).
Warning: *Stay clear of the drivebelt and any*

rotating or hot components.
Note: *Due to intake manifold configuration, this check might not be possible on all vehicles.*
10   If you can hear the injectors operating, but the engine is misfiring, the electrical circuits are functioning correctly, but the injectors might be dirty or clogged. Try a commercial injector cleaning product (available at auto parts stores). If cleaning the injectors doesn't help, replace the injectors.
11   If an injector is not operating (it makes no sound), disconnect the injector electrical connector and measure the resistance across the injector terminals with an ohmmeter. Compare this measurement to the other injectors. If the resistance of the non-operational injector is quite different from the other injectors, replace it.
Note: *A non-operational injector will most likely set a diagnostic trouble code (see Chapter 6).*
12   If the injector is not operating, but the resistance reading is within the range of resistance of the other injectors, the PCM or the circuit between the PCM and the injector might be faulty.

3   Fuel pressure relief procedure

Warning: *Gasoline is extremely flammable. See **Fuel system warnings** in Section 1.*
Note: *After the fuel pressure has been relieved, it's a good idea to lay a shop towel over any fuel connection to be disassembled, to absorb the residual fuel that may leak out when servicing the fuel system.*
Note: *Ensure that you have retrieved the anti-theft code from the audio system before proceeding.*
1   Remove the PGM-FI relay no. 2 from the under-dash fuse/relay box (see Section 2).

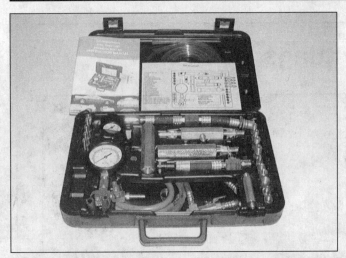

4.1a This fuel pressure testing kit contains all the necessary fittings and adapters, along with the pressure gauge, to test most automotive systems

4.1b Remove the cover and disconnect the quick-connect fitting (located at the left end of the engine, below the throttle body), then T-in an adapter and fuel pressure gauge

2   Start the engine and allow it to run until it stops. Disconnect the negative battery cable from the battery before working on the fuel system (see Chapter 5).

3   The fuel system pressure is now relieved. It is a good idea to surround any fuel line that will be disconnected with a shop rag to catch fuel that might spill out.

4   When you're finished working on the fuel system, install the PGM-FI relay back into the fuse/relay box, Connect the negative cable to the battery and perform the necessary re-learn procedures (see Chapter 5).

4   Fuel pressure - check

Warning: *Gasoline is extremely flammable. See* **Fuel system warnings** *in Section 1.*
Note: *To perform the fuel pressure test, you will need to obtain a special fuel pressure gauge and adapter set (fuel line fittings).*

1   Relieve the fuel pressure (see Section 3). Disconnect the quick-connect fuel supply line fitting from the fuel rail pipe at the left (driver's) end of the cylinder head (see illustration). You must connect a special tee adapter in the line that incorporates a fuel pressure gauge. This special tee can be purchased, or you can fabricate your own out of various fittings, hose and hose clamps (see illustration).

2   With the gauge connected and leak-tested, start the engine and allow it to idle. Note the gauge reading as soon as it stabilizes and compare it with the pressure listed in this Chapter's Specifications.

3   If the fuel pressure is out of specification, check the following:

a)   *Check for a restriction in the fuel system (kinked fuel line, plugged fuel pump inlet strainer or clogged fuel filter). If no restrictions are found, the problem could be either the fuel pump (which would require replacement of the fuel pump*

module *(see Section 7) or the fuel pressure regulator (see Section 7).*

b)   *If the fuel pressure is higher than specified, replace the fuel pressure regulator (see Section 7).*

4   Turn off the engine. Fuel pressure should not fall more than 8 psi over five minutes. If it does, the problem could be a leaky fuel injector, fuel line leak, or faulty fuel pump module.

5   Relieve the fuel system pressure (see Section 3), then disconnect the fuel pressure gauge. Wipe up any spilled gasoline.

5   Fuel lines and fittings - general information and disconnection

Warning: *Gasoline is extremely flammable. See* **Fuel system warnings** *in Section 1.*

1   Relieve the fuel pressure before servicing fuel lines or fittings (see Section 3), then disconnect the cable from the negative battery terminal (see Chapter 5) before proceeding.

2   The fuel supply line connects the fuel pump in the fuel tank to the fuel rail on the engine. The Evaporative Emission (EVAP) system lines connect the fuel tank to the EVAP canister and connect the canister to the intake manifold.

3   Whenever you're working under the vehicle, be sure to inspect all fuel and evaporative emission lines for leaks, kinks, dents and other damage. Always replace a damaged fuel or EVAP line immediately (see Chapter 6).

4   If you find signs of dirt in the lines during disassembly, disconnect all lines and blow them out with compressed air. Inspect the fuel strainer on the fuel pump pick-up unit for damage and deterioration.

Steel tubing

5   It is critical that the fuel lines be replaced with lines of equivalent type and specification.

6   Some steel fuel lines have threaded fit-

tings. When loosening these fittings, hold the stationary fitting with a wrench while turning the tube nut.

Plastic tubing

7   When replacing fuel system plastic tubing, use only original equipment replacement plastic tubing.
Caution: *When removing or installing plastic fuel line tubing, be careful not to bend or twist it too much, which can damage it. Also, plastic fuel tubing is NOT heat resistant, so keep it away from excessive heat.*

Flexible hoses

8   When replacing fuel system flexible hoses, use only original equipment replacements.

9   Don't route fuel hoses (or metal lines) within four inches of the exhaust system or within ten inches of the catalytic converter. Make sure that no rubber hoses are installed directly against the vehicle, particularly in places where there is any vibration. If allowed to touch some vibrating part of the vehicle, a hose can easily become chafed and it might start leaking. A good rule of thumb is to maintain a minimum of 1/4-inch clearance around a hose (or metal line) to prevent contact with the vehicle underbody.

Disconnecting Fuel Line Fittings

10   See chart on page 4-4.

6   Exhaust system servicing - general information

Warning: *Allow exhaust system components to cool before inspection or repair. Also, when working under the vehicle, make sure it is securely supported on jackstands.*

Disconnecting Fuel Line Fittings

Two-tab type fitting; depress both tabs with your fingers, then pull the fuel line and the fitting apart

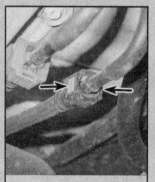

On this type of fitting, depress the two buttons on opposite sides of the fitting, then pull it off the fuel line

Threaded fuel line fitting; hold the stationary portion of the line or component (A) while loosening the tube nut (B) with a flare-nut wrench

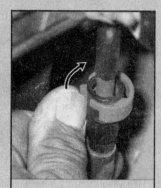

Plastic collar-type fitting; rotate the outer part of the fitting

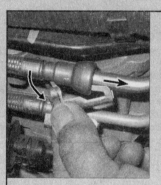

Metal collar quick-connect fitting; pull the end of the retainer off the fuel line and disengage the other end from the female side of the fitting . . .

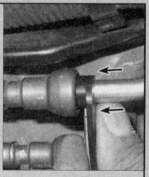

. . . insert a fuel line separator tool into the female side of the fitting, push it into the fitting and pull the fuel line off the pipe

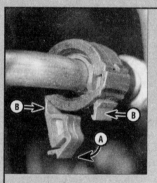

Some fittings are secured by lock tabs. Release the lock tab (A) and rotate it to the fully-opened position, squeeze the two smaller lock tabs (B) . . .

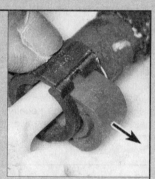

. . . then push the retainer out and pull the fuel line off the pipe

Spring-lock coupling; remove the safety cover, install a coupling release tool and close the tool around the coupling . . .

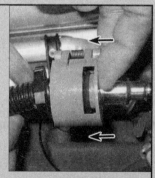

. . . push the tool into the fitting, then pull the two lines apart

Hairpin clip type fitting: push the legs of the retainer clip together, then push the clip down all the way until it stops and pull the fuel line off the pipe

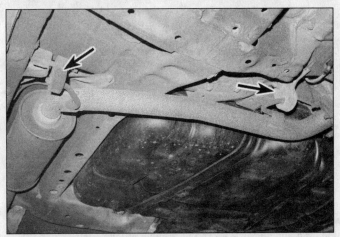

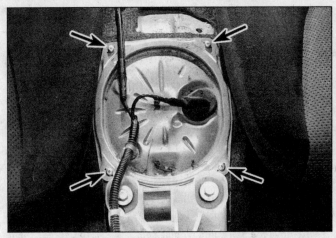

6.1 Typical exhaust system hangers. Inspect regularly and replace at the first sign of damage or deterioration

7.5 Fuel pump access cover screws

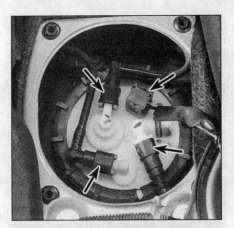

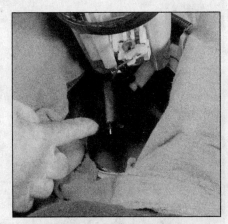

7.6 Fuel pump module electrical connector and fuel/EVAP lines

7.7 The use of a special lock ring tool (available at most auto parts stores) is the easiest way to remove the lock ring

7.8 The fuel level float arm is easily bent, so proceed carefully when lifting the fuel pump module out

1   The exhaust system consists of the exhaust manifolds, catalytic converter, muffler, tailpipe and all connecting pipes, flanges and clamps. The exhaust system is isolated from the vehicle body and from chassis components by a series of rubber hangers. Periodically inspect these hangers for cracks or other signs of deterioration, replacing them as necessary (see illustration).

2   Conduct regular inspections of the exhaust system to keep it safe and quiet. Look for any damaged or bent parts, open seams, holes, loose connections, excessive corrosion or other defects which could allow exhaust fumes to enter the vehicle. Do not repair deteriorated exhaust system components; replace them with new parts.

3   If the exhaust system components are extremely corroded, or rusted together, a cutting torch is the most convenient tool for removal. Consult a properly-equipped repair shop. If a cutting torch is not available, you can use a hacksaw, or if you have compressed air, there are special pneumatic cutting chisels that can also be used. Wear safety goggles to protect your eyes from metal chips and wear work gloves to protect your hands.

4   Here are some simple guidelines to follow when repairing the exhaust system:
a) *Work from the back to the front when removing exhaust system components.*
b) *Apply penetrating oil to the exhaust system component fasteners to make them easier to remove.*
c) *Use new gaskets, hangers and clamps.*
d) *Apply anti-seize compound to the threads of all exhaust system fasteners during reassembly.*
e) *Allow sufficient clearance between newly installed parts and all points on the underbody to avoid overheating the floor pan and possibly damaging the interior carpet and insulation. Pay particularly close attention to the catalytic converter and heat shield.*

7   Fuel pump/fuel level sensor module - removal, component replacement and installation

Warning: *Gasoline is extremely flammable. See Fuel system warnings in Section 1.*

Note: *The components of the fuel level sensor unit, fuel filter and fuel pump assembly are not replaceable individually. The entire module must be replaced if any part of it is defective.*

Removal

1   Relieve the fuel system pressure (see Section 3).
2   Disconnect the cable from the negative terminal of the battery (see Chapter 5).
3   Remove the center console (see Chapter 11).
4   Remove the bolts that attach the parking brake lever.
5   Remove the four screws that retain the access cover for the fuel pump/fuel level sending unit assembly (see illustration).
6   Disconnect the electrical connector and the quick-connect fittings from the fuel pump/fuel level sending unit (see illustration).
Note: *To remove the quick connector, hold the sides of the connector, push in the tabs, and pull out the tube.*
7   Unscrew the lock ring (see illustration).
8   Lift the fuel pump module from the fuel tank. Angle it as you lift it out so you don't bend the float arm (see illustration).

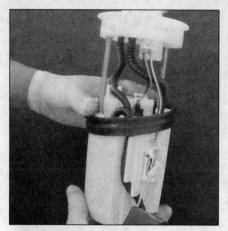

7.9 Remove the fuel pump module seal

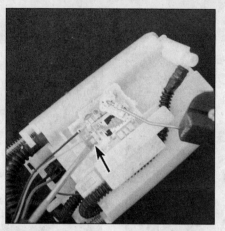

7.10 Depress the retaining tang and slide the fuel level sensor off the fuel pump module

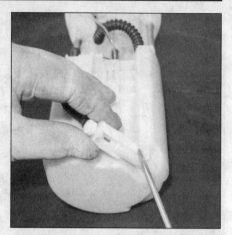

7.13 Carefully pry the suction tube off the reservoir

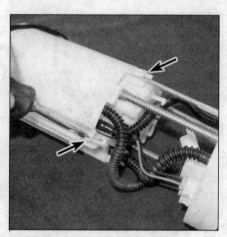

7.14a Pry up the retaining tabs...

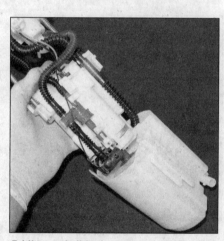

7.14b... and slide the reservoir off the fuel pump

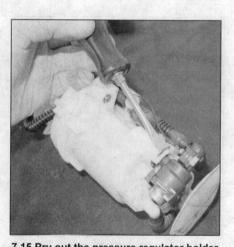

7.15 Pry out the pressure regulator holder retaining clip

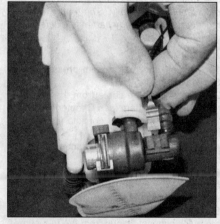

7.16 Slide the ground wire terminal from the pressure regulator holder

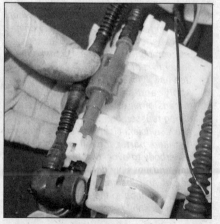

7.17 Unclip the fuel tube from the fuel pump body

9   Remove the seal from the fuel pump module (see illustration).
Note: *The seal might remain on the fuel tank.*

Component replacement
Fuel level sensor
10   Disconnect the electrical connector, then depress the retaining tang and slide it up and off the fuel pump module (see illustration).
11   Installation is the reverse of removal.

Fuel pressure regulator
12   Remove the fuel level sensor.
13   Detach the fuel suction tube from the bottom of the reservoir (see illustration).
14   Dislodge the retaining tangs and slide the reservoir off the fuel pump body (see illustrations).
15   Pry out the retaining clip from the pressure regulator holder (see illustration).
16   Detach the ground wire from the pressure regulator holder (see illustration).
17   Detach the fuel tube from the fuel pump body (see illustration).

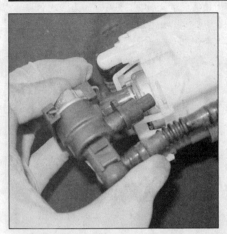

7.18 Detach the regulator holder from the fuel pump

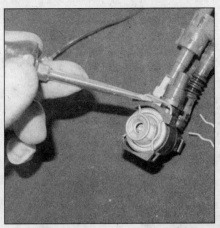

7.19a Pry out the retaining clip...

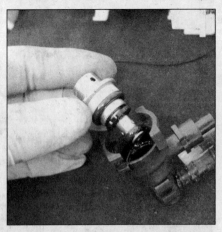

7.19b... the detach the regulator from the holder

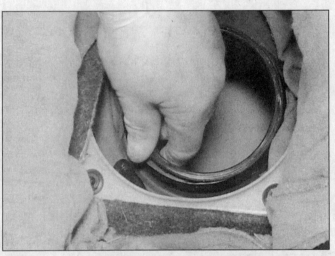

7.21 Install a new seal in the fuel tank

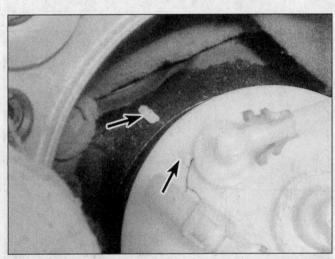

7.22 When installing the fuel pump/fuel level sensor module, align the mark on top of the module with the marks on the fuel tank

18   Pull the regulator holder from the fuel pump body (see illustration).

19   Remove the retaining clip, then pull the pressure regulator out of the holder (see illustrations).

20   Reassembly is the reverse of disassembly. Be sure to replace all O-rings with new ones, and lubricate them with clean engine oil.

Installation

21   Install a new seal in the fuel tank opening (see illustration). Make sure it seats squarely.
Caution: *Don't try to install the seal with the module; this could cause it to become pinched or distorted.*

22   Carefully lower the fuel pump module into the fuel tank, lining up the marks on the module and the fuel tank (see illustration). Make sure the module enters the seal squarely.

23   Position the lock ring over the fuel pump and tighten it securely. If you are using the special tool to do this, tighten the lock ring to the torque listed in this Chapter's Specifications.

24   Reconnect the hoses and electrical connector.

25   Reconnect the negative battery terminal, then turn to the ignition key to the On position to pressurize the fuel system. Check for leaks where the hoses connect to the fuel pump module.

26   Reinstall the access cover.

27   Reinstall the parking brake lever and center console. Verify proper parking brake operation.

8   Fuel tank - removal and installation

Warning: *Gasoline is extremely flammable. See **Fuel system warnings** in Section 1.*
Note: *The following procedure is much easier to perform if the fuel tank is empty. Drain the*

fuel into an approved fuel container using a commercially available siphoning kit or wait until the fuel tank is nearly empty, if possible. The easiest way to drain the tank is to remove the fuel pump/fuel level sensor module (see Section 7) and siphon or pump the fuel out from there. Once the tank is empty, reinstall the module (without reconnecting the lines and electrical connector) before removing the tank.
Warning: *NEVER start the siphoning action by mouth.*

1   Remove the fuel tank filler cap to relieve fuel tank pressure.

2   Relieve the fuel system pressure (see Section 3).

3   Disconnect the cable from the negative terminal of the battery (see Chapter 5).

4   Disconnect the lines and wiring from the fuel pump module at the top of the fuel tank (see Section 7).

5   Raise the vehicle and support it securely on jackstands.

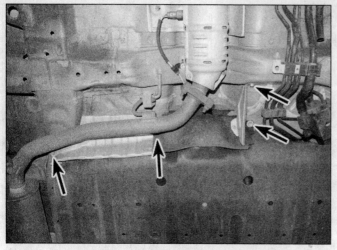

8.6 Crossmember stiffener plate bolts

8.7 Fuel tank heat shield bolts

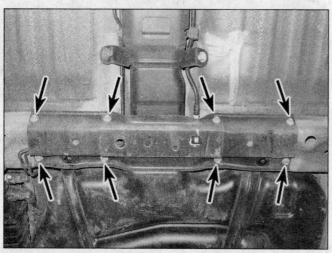

8.8 Cross-beam bolts

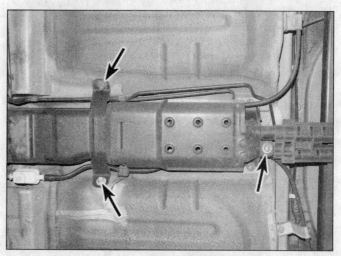

8.9 Fuel tank rear mount bracket bolts

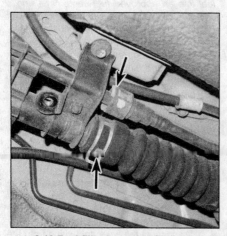

8.10 Fuel filler hose and feed line

8.11 Detach the large EVAP hose from the charcoal canister

2008 and earlier models

6   Remove the crossmember stiffener plate forward of the fuel tank (see illustration).

7   Remove the fuel tank shield (see illustration).

8   Remove the cross-beam behind the fuel tank (see illustration).

9   Remove the fuel tank mount bracket from the rear of the tank (see illustration).

10   Detach the fuel filler hose and the fuel feed line near the rear of the tank (see illustration).

11   Disconnect the EVAP hose at the left side of the tank (see illustration).

2009 and later models

12   Remove the fuel tank guard.

13   On all except on LX (automatic transmission) models, remove the fuel tank cover (see illustration).

14   On LX (automatic transmission) models, remove the splash shield from under the fuel tank.

8.13 Fuel tank cover fasteners

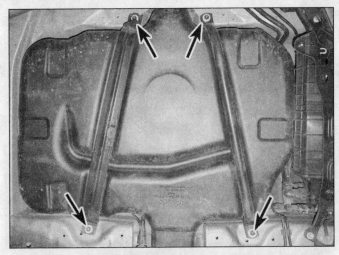

8.18 Fuel tank strap mounting bolts (2008 and earlier models shown, later models similar)

9.2 Air filter housing details (2007 and 2008 models)

1 IAT sensor
2 Throttle body clamp
3 PCV hose
4 Fresh air inlet duct
5 Mounting bolts

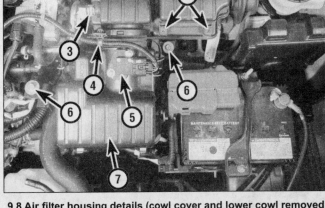

9.8 Air filter housing details (cowl cover and lower cowl removed for clarity) - 2009 and later models

1 Throttle body clamp
2 Upper filter housing chamber bolts
3 PCV hose
4 MAF/IAT sensor harness retainer
5 MAF/IAT sensor
6 Filter housing mounting bolts
7 Filter housing cover

15 Remove the front floor cross-beam and fuel tank mounting bracket.
16 Detach the fuel filler hose and the fuel feed line near the rear of the tank.
17 Disconnect the EVAP hose from the tank.

All models
18 Support the fuel tank with a floor jack and remove the fuel tank strap mounting bolts (see illustration).
Caution: *Position a piece of plywood or some thick cardboard between the jack head and the fuel tank to protect the tank.*
19 Remove the tank from the vehicle, making sure nothing is still connected.

20 Installation is the reverse of removal.
21 Reconnect the negative battery cable (see Chapter 5).

9 Air filter housing - removal and installation

2007 and 2008 models
1 Disconnect the electrical connector from the Intake Air Temperature (IAT) sensor (see Chapter 6).
2 Loosen the clamp at the throttle body (see illustration).
3 Detach the PCV fresh air hose from the

air filter housing.
4 Detach the fresh air duct from the housing.
5 Remove the two air filter housing mounting bolts.
6 Remove the air filter housing, detaching the fresh air intake duct from the left side.
7 Installation is the reverse of removal.

2009 and later models
8 Disconnect the electrical connector from the Mass Air Flow/Intake Air Temperature (MAF/IAT) sensor (see Chapter 6). Also detach the sensor's wiring harness retainer from the mount on the filter housing (see illustration).

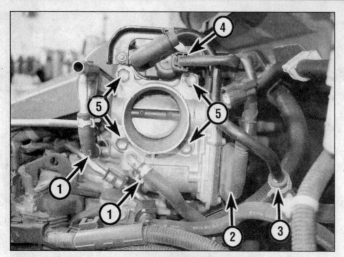

10.3 Throttle body details (2008 and earlier models shown,
later models similar)

1   Coolant hoses
2   Throttle body electrical connector
3   Power brake booster hose
4   EVAP canister purge valve electrical connector
5   Throttle body mounting bolts

11.5a Free the retaining tabs and detach the harness from the
fuel rail...

11.5b... then
disconnect the
electrical connectors
from the injectors

9   Remove the air filter housing cover and air filter element.
10   Detach the PCV fresh air hose from the housing.
11   Remove the two bolts and the upper filter housing chamber.
12   Loosen the hose clamp at the throttle body.
13   Remove the battery hold-down and reposition the battery to the side to make more working room.
14   Rotate the rear of the air filter housing towards the front of vehicle and up to remove it. While doing this, move the upper radiator hose and the breather hose near the throttle body aside as necessary.
15   Installation is the reverse of removal.

10   Throttle body - removal and installation

Warning: *The engine must be completely cool before beginning this procedure.*
Caution: *If the throttle body is removed the manufacturer recommends that a ECM/PCM idle relearn procedure is required.*
1   Disconnect the cable from the negative terminal of the battery (see Chapter 5).
2   Remove the air filter housing (see Section 9).
3   Clamp-off the coolant hoses to the throttle body, then disconnect them (see illustration). Have towels available to immediately wipe up any residual coolant that might spill.

4   Label and remove all of the remaining hoses and lines from the throttle body housing.
5   Disconnect the throttle body electrical connector and the EVAP canister purge valve electrical connector.
6   Loosen the throttle body mounting bolts a little at a time in a criss-cross pattern to prevent distortion.
7   Remove the throttle body from the intake manifold chamber.
8   Installation is the reverse of removal; use a new throttle body gasket. Reconnect the hoses and lines to their correct ports as noted during removal. Tighten the throttle body mounting bolts a little at a time in a criss-cross pattern to the torque listed in this Chapter's Specifications.
9   Reconnect the negative battery cable (see Chapter 5).

11   Fuel rail and injectors - removal and installation

Warning: *Gasoline is extremely flammable. See Fuel system warnings in Section 1.*
1   Relieve the fuel system pressure (see Section 3).
2   Disconnect the cable from the negative terminal of the battery (see Chapter 5).
3   Remove the intake manifold (see Chapter 2A).
Note: *On 2007 and 2008 models, it's only necessary to remove the plastic plenum from the intake manifold; the intake runner portion of the manifold can remain in place.*

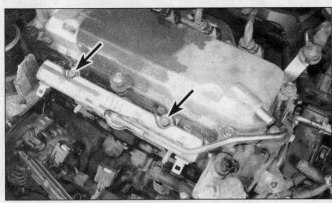

11.6 Fuel rail mounting nuts

11.7 Pull the fuel rail and injectors from the cylinder head

11.8 Fuel rail spacers

11.9a To free each injector from the fuel rail, pull off the retainer with a pair of pliers

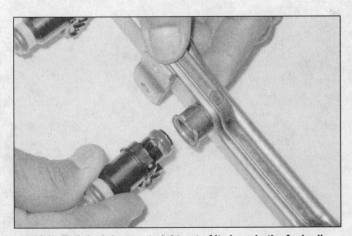

11.9b Pull the injector straight out of its bore in the fuel rail

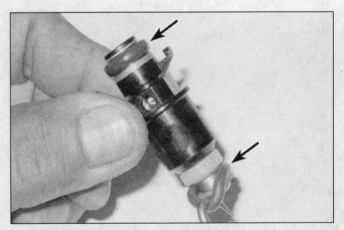

11.10 Whether you're installing new injectors or reusing the old ones, always remove the old O-rings and replace them with new ones

4   Disconnect the fuel supply line from the fuel rail (see illustration 4.1b).

5   Disconnect the electrical connector harness from the fuel injectors (see illustrations).

6   Remove the two fuel rail mounting nuts (see illustration).

7   Remove the fuel rail with the injectors attached (see illustration).

8   Be careful not to lose the spacers on the fuel rail mounting studs (see illustration).

9   Remove the fuel injector retaining clips and remove the fuel injectors from the fuel rail (see illustrations).

10   Remove and discard the fuel injector O-rings. Lubricate O-rings with clean engine oil prior to installation (see illustration).

11   Install the injectors to the fuel rail and secure them with the retaining clips.

12   Installation is the reverse of removal. Tighten the fuel rail nuts to the torque listed in this Chapter's Specifications.

13   Reconnect the negative battery cable (see Chapter 5).

Notes

Chapter 5
Engine electrical systems

Contents

Specifications

Charging voltage	13.5 to 14.5 volts

Torque specifications

Note: *One foot-pound (ft-lb) of torque is equivalent to 12 inch-pounds (in-lbs) of torque. Torque values below approximately 15 foot-pounds are expressed in inch-pounds, since most foot-pound torque wrenches are not accurate at these smaller values.*

	Ft-lbs (unless otherwise noted)	Nm
Ignition coil mounting bolts	84 in-lbs	9.5
Alternator mounting bolts	18	24
2008 and earlier models		
Upper	17	23
Lower	33	45
2009 and later models	17	23
Starter mounting bolts		
Upper	33	45
Lower	47	64

1 General information and precautions

General information

Ignition system

1   The electronic ignition system consists of the Crankshaft Position (CKP) sensor, the Camshaft Position (CMP) sensor, the Knock Sensor (KS), the Powertrain Control Module (PCM), the ignition switch, the battery, the individual ignition coils or a coil pack, and the spark plugs. For more information on the CKP, CMP and KS sensors, as well as the PCM, refer to Chapter 6.

Charging system

2   The charging system includes the alternator (with an integral voltage regulator), the Powertrain Control Module (PCM), the Body Control Module (BCM), a charge indicator light on the dash, the battery, a fuse or fusible link and the wiring connecting all of these components. The charging system supplies electrical power for the ignition system, the lights, the radio, etc. The alternator is driven by a drivebelt.

Starting system

3   The starting system consists of the battery, the ignition switch, the starter relay, the Powertrain Control Module (PCM), the Body Control Module (BCM), the Transmission Range (TR) switch, the starter motor and solenoid assembly, and the wiring connecting all of the components.

Precautions

4   Always observe the following precautions when working on the electrical system: Be extremely careful when servicing engine electrical components. They are easily damaged if checked, connected or handled improperly.

a)   *Never leave the ignition switched on for long periods of time when the engine is not running.*

b)   *Never disconnect the battery cables while the engine is running.*

c)   *Maintain correct polarity when connecting battery cables from another vehicle during jump starting (see Chapter 0, Section 7).*

d)   *Always disconnect the cable from the negative battery terminal before working on the electrical system, but read the battery disconnection procedure first (see Section 3).*

5   It's also a good idea to review the safety-related information regarding the engine electrical systems located in Chapter 0, Section 10 before beginning any operation included in this Chapter.

2 Troubleshooting

Ignition system

1   If a malfunction occurs in the ignition system, do not immediately assume that any particular part is causing the problem. First, check the following items:

a)   *Make sure that the cable clamps at the battery terminals are clean and tight.*

b)   *Test the condition of the battery (see Steps 15 through 18). If it doesn't pass all the tests, replace it.*

c)   *Check the ignition coil or coil pack connections.*

d)   *Check any relevant fuses in the engine compartment fuse and relay box (see Chapter 12). If they're burned, determine the cause and repair the circuit.*

Check

Warning: *Because of the high voltage generated by the ignition system, use extreme care when performing a procedure involving ignition components.*
Note: *The ignition system components on these vehicles are difficult to diagnose. In the event of an ignition system failure that you can't diagnose, have the vehicle tested at a dealer service department or other qualified auto repair facility.*
Note: *You'll need a spark tester for the following test. Spark testers are available at most auto supply stores.*

2   If the engine turns over but won't start, verify that there is sufficient ignition voltage to fire the spark plugs as follows.
3   Remove a coil and install the tester between the boot at the lower end of the coil and the spark plug (see illustration).
4   Crank the engine and note whether or not the tester flashes.
Caution: *Do NOT crank the engine or allow it to run for more than five seconds; running the engine for more than five seconds may set a Diagnostic Trouble Code (DTC) for a cylinder misfire.*
5   If the tester flashes during cranking, the coil is delivering sufficient voltage to the spark plug to fire it. Repeat this test for each cylinder to verify that the other coils are OK.
6   If the tester doesn't flash, remove a coil from another cylinder and swap it for the one being tested. If the tester now flashes, you know that the original coil is bad. If the tester still doesn't flash, the PCM or wiring harness is probably defective. Have the PCM checked out by a dealer service department or other qualified repair shop (testing the PCM is beyond the scope of the do-it-yourselfer because it requires expensive special tools).
7   If the tester flashes during cranking but a misfire code (related to the cylinder being tested) has been stored, the spark plug could be fouled or defective.

Charging system

8   If a malfunction occurs in the charging system, do not automatically assume the alternator is causing the problem. First check the following items:

a)   *Check the drivebelt tension and condition (see Chapter 1). Replace it if it's worn or deteriorated.*

b)   *Make sure the alternator mounting bolts are tight.*

c)   *Inspect the alternator wiring harness and the connectors at the alternator and voltage regulator. They must be in good condition, tight and have no corrosion.*

d)   *Check the fusible link (if equipped) or main fuse in the underhood fuse/relay box. If it is burned, determine the cause, repair the circuit and replace the link or fuse (the vehicle will not start and/or the accessories will not work if the fusible link or main fuse is blown).*

e)   *Start the engine and check the alternator for abnormal noises (a shrieking or squealing sound indicates a bad bearing).*

f)   *Check the battery. Make sure it's fully charged and in good condition (one bad cell in a battery can cause overcharging by the alternator).*

g)   *Disconnect the battery cables (negative first, then positive). Inspect the battery posts and the cable clamps for corrosion. Clean them thoroughly if necessary (see Chapter 1). Reconnect the cables (positive first, negative last).*

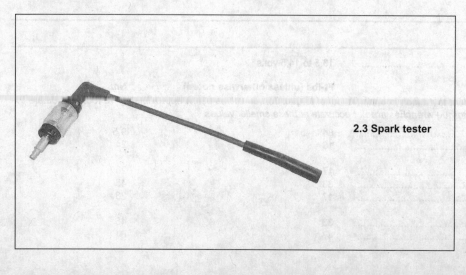

2.3 Spark tester

2.15 To test the open circuit voltage of the battery, touch the black probe of the voltmeter to the negative terminal and the red probe to the positive terminal of the battery; a fully charged battery should be at least 12.6 volts

2.17 Connect a battery load tester to the battery and check the battery condition under load following the tool manufacturer's instructions

Alternator - check

9   Use a voltmeter to check the battery voltage with the engine off. It should be at least 12.6 volts (see illustration 2.15).

10   Start the engine and check the battery voltage again. It should now be approximately 13.5 to 15 volts.

11   If the voltage reading is more or less than the specified charging voltage, the voltage regulator is probably defective, which will require replacement of the alternator (the voltage regulator is not replaceable separately). Remove the alternator and have it bench tested (most auto parts stores will do this for you).

12   The charging system (battery) light on the instrument cluster lights up when the ignition key is turned to ON, but it should go out when the engine starts.

13   If the charging system light stays on after the engine has been started, there is a problem with the charging system. Before replacing the alternator, check the battery condition, alternator belt tension and electrical cable connections.

14   If replacing the alternator doesn't restore voltage to the specified range, have the charging system tested by a dealer service department or other qualified repair shop.

Battery - check

Note: *The battery's surface charge must be removed before accurate voltage measurements can be made. Turn on the high beams for ten seconds, then turn them off and let the vehicle stand for two minutes.*

15   Check the battery state of charge. Visually inspect the indicator eye on the top of the battery (if equipped with one); if the indicator eye is black in color, charge the battery as described in Chapter 1. Next perform an open circuit voltage test using a digital voltmeter. With the engine and all accessories Off, touch the negative probe of the voltmeter to the negative terminal of the battery and the positive probe to the positive terminal of the battery (see illustration). The battery voltage should be 12.6 volts or slightly above. If the battery is less than the specified voltage, charge the battery before proceeding to the next test. Do not proceed with the battery load test unless the battery charge is correct.

16   Disconnect the negative battery cable, then the positive cable from the battery.

17   Perform a battery load test. An accurate check of the battery condition can only be performed with a load tester (see illustration). This test evaluates the ability of the battery to operate the starter and other accessories during periods of high current draw. Connect the load tester to the battery terminals. Load test the battery according to the tool manufacturer's instructions. This tool increases the load demand (current draw) on the battery.

18   Maintain the load on the battery for 15 seconds and observe that the battery voltage does not drop below 9.6 volts. If the battery condition is weak or defective, the tool will indicate this condition immediately.

Note: *Cold temperatures will cause the minimum voltage reading to drop slightly. Follow the chart given in the manufacturer's instructions to compensate for cold climates. Minimum load voltage for freezing temperatures (32 degrees F) should be approximately 9.1 volts.*

Starting system

The starter rotates, but the engine doesn't

19   Remove the starter (see Section 9). Check the overrunning clutch and bench test the starter to make sure the drive mechanism extends fully for proper engagement with the flywheel ring gear. If it doesn't, replace the starter.

20   Check the flywheel ring gear for missing teeth and other damage. With the ignition turned off, rotate the flywheel so you can check the entire ring gear.

The starter is noisy

21   If the solenoid is making a chattering noise, first check the battery (see Steps 15 through 18). If the battery is okay, check the cables and connections.

22   If you hear a grinding, crashing metallic sound when you turn the key to Start, check for loose starter mounting bolts. If they're tight, remove the starter and inspect the teeth on the starter pinion gear and flywheel ring gear. Look for missing or damaged teeth.

23   If the starter sounds fine when you first turn the key to Start, but then stops rotating the engine and emits a zinging sound, the problem is probably a defective starter drive that's not staying engaged with the ring gear. Replace the starter.

The starter rotates slowly

24   Check the battery (see Steps 15 through 18).

25   If the battery is okay, verify all connections (at the battery, the starter solenoid and motor) are clean, corrosion-free and tight. Make sure the cables aren't frayed or damaged.

26   Check that the starter mounting bolts are tight so it grounds properly. Also check the pinion gear and flywheel ring gear for evidence of a mechanical bind (galling, deformed gear teeth or other damage).

The starter does not rotate at all

27   Check the battery (see Steps 15 through 18).

28   If the battery is okay, verify all connections (at the battery, the starter solenoid and motor) are clean, corrosion-free and tight. Make sure the cables aren't frayed or damaged.

29   Check all of the fuses in the underhood fuse/relay box.

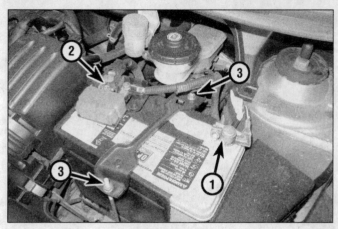

4.3 Battery details

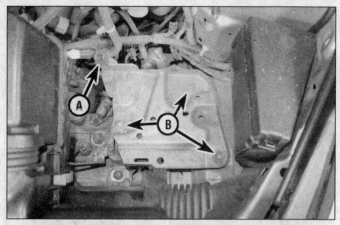

**5.2 Wiring harness retainer (A) and battery base bolts (B)
(2008 and earlier models shown)**

1   Negative terminal (disconnect first, reconnect last)
2   Positive terminal
3   Hold-down bracket nuts

30   Check that the starter mounting bolts are tight so it grounds properly.

31   Check for voltage at the starter solenoid "S" terminal when the ignition key is turned to the start position. If voltage is present, replace the starter/solenoid assembly. If no voltage is present, the problem could be the starter relay, the Transmission Range (TR) switch (see Chapter 6) or clutch start switch (see Chapter 8), or with an electrical connector somewhere in the circuit (see the wiring diagrams in Chapter 13). Also, on many modern vehicles, the Powertrain Control Module (PCM) and the Body Control Module (BCM) control the voltage signal to the starter solenoid; on such vehicles a special scan tool is required for diagnosis.

3   Battery - disconnection and reconnection

Caution: *Always disconnect the cable from the negative battery terminal FIRST and hook it up LAST or the battery may be shorted by the tool being used to loosen the cable clamps.*

1   Some systems on the vehicle require battery power to be available at all times, either to maintain continuous operation (alarm system, power door locks, etc.), or to maintain control unit memory (radio station presets, Powertrain Control Module and other control units). When the battery is disconnected, the power that maintains these systems is cut. So, before you disconnect the battery, please note that on a vehicle with power door locks, it's a wise precaution to remove the key or keyless entry fob, so that it does not get locked inside if the power door locks should engage accidentally when the battery is reconnected!

2   Devices known as "memory-savers" can be used to avoid some of these problems. Precise details vary according to the device used. The typical memory saver is plugged into the cigarette lighter and is connected to a spare battery. Then the vehicle battery can be

disconnected from the electrical system. The memory saver will provide sufficient current to maintain audio unit security codes, PCM memory, etc. and will provide power to always hot circuits such as the clock and radio memory circuits.

Warning: *Some memory savers deliver a considerable amount of current in order to keep vehicle systems operational after the main battery is disconnected. If you're using a memory saver, make sure that the circuit concerned is actually open before servicing it.*

Warning: *If you're going to work near any of the airbag system components, the battery MUST be disconnected and a memory saver must NOT be used. If a memory saver is used, power will be supplied to the airbag, which means that it could accidentally deploy and cause serious personal injury.*

Disconnection

Caution: *Make sure you have any anti-theft codes for the radio and navigation unit (if equipped) before disconnecting the battery.*

3   Install a memory saver device to avoid having to reprogram several of the vehicle's systems (see above).

Warning: *If you're working near any airbag system component, DO NOT use a memory saver.*

4   If you don't have a memory-saver device, record the radio presets.

5   To disconnect the battery for service procedures requiring power to be cut from the vehicle, loosen the cable clamp nut and disconnect the cable from the negative battery terminal. Isolate the cable end to prevent it from coming into accidental contact with the battery terminal.

Reconnection

6   Connect the positive battery cable first (if it was disconnected), followed by the negative cable.

7   After reconnecting the battery, enter the radio (and, if equipped, navigation unit) anti-

theft code. Also enter the radio presets.

*   *If a memory saver was used when the battery was disconnected, these functions won't have to be performed. Refer to your owner's manual for information on resetting the radio presets.*

4   Battery - removal and installation

1   Install a memory saver device to avoid having to reprogram several of the vehicle's systems (see Section 3).

Warning: *If you're working near any airbag system component, DO NOT use a memory saver.*

2   Disconnect the negative battery cable, then the positive battery cable, from the battery.

Warning: *Always disconnect the negative cable first and hook it up last or the battery may be shorted by the tool being used to loosen the cable clamps.*

3   Remove the battery hold-down bracket (see illustration).

4   If equipped, remove the battery cover from the battery.

5   Lift out the battery. Special battery removal and installation tools are available at auto parts stores; lifting and moving the battery is much easier if you use one.

6   Installation is the reverse of removal. Connect the positive cable first, then the negative cable (see Section 3).

5   Battery base - removal and installation

1   Remove the battery and plastic battery tray (see Section 4).

2   Disconnect the harness retainer(s), if present, from the battery base.

3   Unscrew the bolts and remove the battery base.

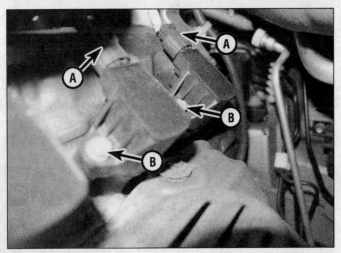

7.3a Coil electrical connector (A) and mounting bolt (B) (2007/2008 model, viewed from the left [driver's] side of the vehicle)

7.3b Coil electrical connectors (2009 and later models, viewed from the right [passenger's] side of the vehicle)

4   If the battery base or any of the surrounding area has any corrosion on it, be sure to neutralize it with baking soda and water.
5   Installation is reverse of removal.

6   Battery cables - replacement

1   When removing the cables, always disconnect the cable from the negative battery terminal first and hook it up last, or you might accidentally short out the battery with the tool you're using to loosen the cable clamps. Even if you're only replacing the cable for the positive terminal, be sure to disconnect the negative cable from the battery first.
2   Disconnect the old cables from the battery, then trace each of them to their opposite ends and disconnect them. Note the routing of each cable before disconnecting it to ensure correct installation.
3   If you are replacing any of the old cables, take them with you when buying new cables. It is vitally important that you replace the cables with identical parts.
4   Clean the threads of the solenoid or ground connection with a wire brush to remove rust and corrosion. Apply a light coat of battery terminal corrosion inhibitor or petroleum jelly to the threads to prevent future corrosion.
5   Attach the cable to the solenoid or ground connection and tighten the mounting nut/bolt securely.
6   Before connecting a new cable to the battery, make sure that it reaches the battery post without having to be stretched.
7   Connect the cable to the positive battery terminal first, then connect the ground cable to the negative battery terminal.

7   Ignition coil(s) - replacement

1   On 2008 and earlier models, disconnect the MAP sensor electrical connector (see Chapter 6) and detach the ignition coil wiring harness from its brackets.
2   On 2009 and later models, remove the wiper arms, cowl cover and lower cowl to access the ignition coils (see Chapter 11).
3   Disconnect the electrical connector(s) from the coil(s) (see illustration).
4   Remove the coil mounting bolt, then twist the coil slightly and pull it straight out.
5   Installation is the reverse of removal. Before installing the ignition coils, coat the interior of the boots with silicone dielectric compound.

8   Alternator - removal and installation

1   Disconnect the cable from the negative terminal of the battery (see Section 3).
2   Remove the drivebelt (see Chapter 1).
3   Remove the intake manifold (see Chapter 2A Section 5).
4   Disconnect the electrical connector and battery cable from the alternator (see illustration).
5   Remove the alternator mounting bolts (see illustration 8.4 and accompanying illustration) and remove the alternator from the engine.

8.4 Alternator details - rear view (2008 and earlier models shown, later models similar)

1   Electrical connector
2   Battery cable
3   Lower mounting bolt access (bolt isn't visible here)

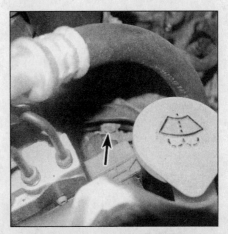

8.5 Alternator upper mounting bolt (2008 and earlier models shown, later models similar)

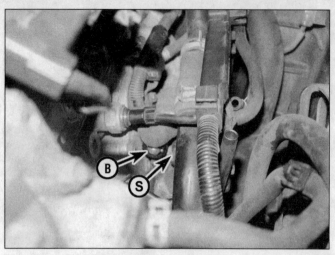

9.8 Starter electrical connections (2008 model, shown from above with the intake manifold removed)

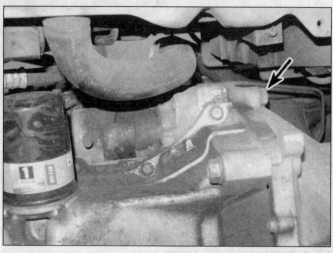

9.9 Starter lower mounting bolt (2008 and earlier models shown)

6   Installation is the reverse of removal. Tighten the alternator mounting bolts to the torque listed in this Chapter's Specifications.
7   On 2008 and earlier models, adjust the drivebelt tension (see Chapter 1).
8   Reconnect the battery (see Section 3).

9   Starter motor - removal and installation

1   Disconnect the cable from the negative terminal of the battery (see Section 3).
2   Remove the dipstick and dipstick tube from the engine.
Note: *On 2009 and later models, do this after performing Step 5.*
3   On 2008 and earlier models, raise the vehicle and support it securely on jackstands, then remove the splash shield.
4   On 2009 and later models, remove the coolant reservoir (see Chapter 3).
5   On 2009 and later models, remove the intake manifold (see Chapter 2A Section 5).
Note: *2007 and 2008 models: Although not absolutely necessary, it is helpful to remove the intake manifold for access to the electrical connectors and upper mounting bolt.*
6   Disconnect the oil pressure switch elec-

trical connector.
7   On 2008 and earlier models, detach the radiator hose holder from the starter bracket.
8   Disconnect the electrical connectors from the "S"and "B" terminals (see illustration).
9   Remove the starter mounting bolts and guide the starter out (see illustration).
10   Replace the dipstick tube O-ring with a new one before installation.
11   Installation is the reverse of removal. Tighten the starter mounting bolts to the torque listed in this Chapter's Specifications.
12   Reconnect the battery (see Section 3).

Chapter 6
Emissions and engine control systems

Contents

Specifications

Torque specifications

Note: *One foot-pound (ft-lb) of torque is equivalent to 12 inch-pounds (in-lbs) of torque. Torque values below approximately 15 ft-lbs are expressed in inch-pounds, since most foot-pound torque wrenches are not accurate at these smaller values.*

	Ft-lbs (unless otherwise indicated)	Nm
Accelerator pedal sensor mounting fasteners	113 in-lbs	13
Camshaft position sensor mounting bolt	104 in-lbs	12
Catalytic converter		
2007 and 2008 models		
Upper mounting bolts	16	22
Lower mounting nuts	24	33
2009 and later models		
Warm-up converter-to-exhaust manifold bolts	23	31
Under-floor converter-to-warm-up converter bolts	16	22
Under-floor converter-to-exhaust pipe nuts	25	33
Crankshaft position sensor mounting bolt	104 in-lbs	12
Engine Coolant Temperature (ECT) sensor	104 in-lbs	12
Knock sensor		
2007 and 2008 models	23	31
2009 and later models	24	32
Oxygen sensor	33	44
EGR valve mounting bolts		
2007 and 2008 models	17	24
2009 and later models	16	22
EGR pipe fasteners (2009 and later models)	16	22
VTEC rocker arm control valve mounting bolts	86 in-lbs	9.8
VTEC rocker arm oil pressure switch	16	22
Transmission Range (TR) switch mounting bolts	100 in-lbs	11

1   General information

1   To prevent pollution of the atmosphere from incompletely burned and evaporating gases, and to maintain good driveability and fuel economy, a number of emission control systems are incorporated. They include the:

Catalytic converter

2   A catalytic converter is an emission control device in the exhaust system that reduces certain pollutants in the exhaust gas stream. There are two types of converters: oxidation converters and reduction converters.

3   Oxidation converters contain a monolithic substrate (a ceramic honeycomb) coated with the semi-precious metals platinum and palladium. An oxidation catalyst reduces unburned hydrocarbons (HC) and carbon monoxide (CO) by adding oxygen to the exhaust stream as it passes through the substrate, which, in the presence of high temperature and the catalyst materials, converts the HC and CO to water vapor (H_2O) and carbon dioxide (CO_2).

4   Reduction converters contain a monolithic substrate coated with platinum and rhodium. A reduction catalyst reduces oxides of nitrogen (NOx) by removing oxygen, which in the presence of high temperature and the catalyst material produces nitrogen (N) and carbon dioxide (CO_2).

5   Catalytic converters that combine both types of catalysts in one assembly are known as "three-way catalysts" or TWCs. A TWC can reduce all three pollutants.

Evaporative Emissions Control (EVAP) system

6   The Evaporative Emissions Control (EVAP) system prevents fuel system vapors (which contain unburned hydrocarbons) from escaping into the atmosphere. On warm days, vapors trapped inside the fuel tank expand until the pressure reaches a certain threshold. Then the fuel vapors are routed from the fuel tank through the fuel vapor vent valve and the fuel vapor control valve to the EVAP canister, where they're stored temporarily until the next time the vehicle is operated. When the conditions are right (engine warmed up, vehicle up to speed, moderate or heavy load on the engine, etc.) the PCM opens the canister purge valve, which allows fuel vapors to be drawn from the canister into the intake manifold. Once in the intake manifold, the fuel vapors mix with incoming air before being drawn through the intake ports into the combustion chambers where they're burned up with the rest of the air/fuel mixture. The EVAP system is complex and virtually impossible to troubleshoot without the right tools and training.

Exhaust Gas Recirculation (EGR) system

7   The EGR system reduces oxides of nitrogen by recirculating exhaust gases from the exhaust manifold, through the EGR valve and intake manifold, then back to the combustion chambers, where it mixes with the incoming air/fuel mixture before being consumed. These recirculated exhaust gases dilute the incoming air/fuel mixture, which cools the combustion chambers, thereby reducing NOx emissions.

8   The EGR system consists of the Powertrain Control Module (PCM), the EGR valve, the EGR valve position sensor and various other information sensors that the PCM uses to determine when to open the EGR valve. The degree to which the EGR valve is opened is referred to as "EGR valve lift." The PCM is programmed to produce the ideal EGR valve lift for varying operating conditions. The EGR valve position sensor, which is an integral part of the EGR valve, detects the amount of EGR valve lift and sends this information to the PCM. The PCM then compares it with the appropriate EGR valve lift for the operating conditions. The PCM increases current flow to the EGR valve to increase valve lift and reduces the current to reduce the amount of lift. If EGR flow is inappropriate to the operating conditions (idle, cold engine, etc.) the PCM simply cuts the current to the EGR valve and the valve closes.

Secondary Air Injection (AIR) system

9   Some vehicles are equipped with a secondary air injection (AIR) system. The secondary air injection system is used to reduce tailpipe emissions on initial engine start-up. The system uses an electric motor/pump assembly, relay, vacuum valve/solenoid, air shut-off valve, check valves and tubing to inject fresh air directly into the exhaust manifolds. The fresh air (oxygen) reacts with the exhaust gas in the catalytic converter to reduce HC and CO levels. The air pump and solenoid are controlled by the PCM through the AIR relay. During initial start-up, the PCM energizes the AIR relay, the relay supplies battery voltage to the air pump and the vacuum valve/solenoid, engine vacuum is applied to the air shut-off valve which opens and allows air to flow through the tubing into the exhaust manifolds. The PCM will operate the air pump until closed loop operation is reached (approximately four minutes). During normal operation, the check valves prevent exhaust backflow into the system.

Powertrain Control Module (PCM)

10   The Powertrain Control Module (PCM) is the brain of the engine management system. It also controls a wide variety of other vehicle systems. In order to program the new PCM, the dealer needs the vehicle as well as the new PCM. If you're planning to replace the PCM with a new one, there is no point in trying to do so at home because you won't be able to program it yourself.

Positive Crankcase Ventilation (PCV) system

11   The Positive Crankcase Ventilation (PCV) system reduces hydrocarbon emissions by scavenging crankcase vapors, which are rich in unburned hydrocarbons. A PCV valve, or orifice, regulates the flow of gases into the intake manifold in proportion to the amount of intake vacuum available.

12   The PCV system generally consists of the fresh air inlet hose, the PCV valve or orifice and the crankcase ventilation hose (or PCV hose). The fresh air inlet hose connects the air intake duct to a pipe on the valve cover. The crankcase ventilation hose (or PCV hose) connects the PCV valve, or orifice, in the valve cover to the intake manifold.

Information sensors

13   Typical information sensors:

2   On Board Diagnosis (OBD) system

General description

1   All models are equipped with the second generation OBD-II system. This system consists of an on-board computer known as the Powertrain Control Module (PCM), and information sensors, which monitor various functions of the engine and send data to the PCM. This system incorporates a series of diagnostic monitors that detect and identify fuel injection and emissions control system faults and stores the information in the computer memory. This system also tests sensors and output actuators, diagnoses drive cycles, freezes data and clears codes.

2   The PCM is the brain of the electronically controlled fuel and emissions system. It receives data from a number of sensors and other electronic components (switches, relays, etc.). Based on the information it receives, the PCM generates output signals to control various relays, solenoids (fuel injectors) and other actuators. The PCM is specifically calibrated to optimize the emissions, fuel economy and driveability of the vehicle.

3   It isn't a good idea to attempt diagnosis or replacement of the PCM or emission control components at home while the vehicle is under warranty. Because of a federally-mandated warranty which covers the emissions system components and because any owner induced damage to the PCM, the sensors and/or the control devices may void this warranty, take the vehicle to a dealer service department if the PCM or a system component malfunctions.

Scan tool information

4   Because extracting the Diagnostic Trouble Codes (DTCs) from an engine management system is now the first step in troubleshooting many computer-controlled systems

Information Sensors

Accelerator Pedal Position (APP) sensor - as you press the accelerator pedal, the APP sensor alters its voltage signal to the PCM in proportion to the angle of the pedal, and the PCM commands a motor inside the throttle body to open or close the throttle plate accordingly

Camshaft Position (CMP) sensor - produces a signal that the PCM uses to identify the number 1 cylinder and to time the firing sequence of the fuel injectors

Crankshaft Position (CKP) sensor - produces a signal that the PCM uses to calculate engine speed and crankshaft position, which enables it to synchronize ignition timing with fuel injector timing, and to detect misfires

Engine Coolant Temperature (ECT) sensor - a thermistor (temperature-sensitive variable resistor) that sends a voltage signal to the PCM, which uses this data to determine the temperature of the engine coolant

Fuel tank pressure sensor - measures the fuel tank pressure and controls fuel tank pressure by signaling the EVAP system to purge the fuel tank vapors when the pressure becomes excessive

Intake Air Temperature (IAT) sensor - monitors the temperature of the air entering the engine and sends a signal to the PCM to determine injector pulse-width (the duration of each injector's on-time) and to adjust spark timing (to prevent spark knock)

Knock sensor - a piezoelectric crystal that oscillates in proportion to engine vibration which produces a voltage output that is monitored by the PCM. This retards the ignition timing when the oscillation exceeds a certain threshold

Manifold Absolute Pressure (MAP) sensor - monitors the pressure or vacuum inside the intake manifold. The PCM uses this data to determine engine load so that it can alter the ignition advance and fuel enrichment

Mass Air Flow (MAF) sensor - measures the amount of intake air drawn into the engine. It uses a hot-wire sensing element to measure the amount of air entering the engine

Oxygen sensors - generates a small variable voltage signal in proportion to the difference between the oxygen content in the exhaust stream and the oxygen content in the ambient air. The PCM uses this information to maintain the proper air/fuel ratio. A second oxygen sensor monitors the efficiency of the catalytic converter

Throttle Position (TP) sensor - a potentiometer that generates a voltage signal that varies in relation to the opening angle of the throttle plate inside the throttle body. Works with the PCM and other sensors to calculate injector pulse width (the duration of each injector's on-time)

Photos courtesy of Wells Manufacturing, except APP and MAF sensors.

2.4a Simple code readers are an economical way to extract trouble codes when the CHECK ENGINE light comes on

2.4b Hand-held scan tools like these can extract computer codes and also perform diagnostics

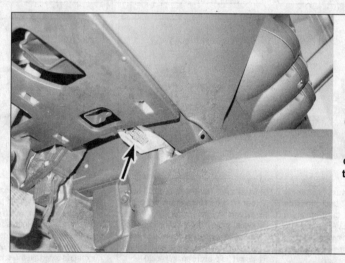

3.3 The Data Link Connector (DLC) is located under the lower edge of the dash, to the right of the steering column

and components, a code reader, at the very least, will be required (see illustration). More powerful scan tools can also perform many of the diagnostics once associated with expensive factory scan tools (see illustration). If you're planning to obtain a generic scan tool for your vehicle, make sure that it's compatible with OBD-II systems. If you don't plan to purchase a code reader or scan tool and don't have access to one, you can have the codes extracted by a dealer service department or an independent repair shop.
Note: *Some auto parts stores even provide this service.*

3   Obtaining and clearing Diagnostic Trouble Codes (DTCs)

1   All models covered by this manual are equipped with on-board diagnostics. When the PCM recognizes a malfunction in a monitored emission or engine control system, component or circuit, it turns on the Malfunction Indicator Light (MIL) on the dash. The PCM will continue to display the MIL until the problem is fixed and the Diagnostic Trouble Code (DTC) is cleared from the PCM's memory. You'll need a scan tool to access any DTCs stored in the PCM.
2   Before outputting any DTCs stored in the PCM, thoroughly inspect ALL electrical connectors and hoses. Make sure that all electrical connections are tight, clean and free of corrosion. And make sure that all hoses are correctly connected, fit tightly and are in good condition (no cracks or tears).

Accessing the DTCs
3   The Diagnostic Trouble Codes (DTCs) can only be accessed with a code reader or scan tool. Professional scan tools are expensive, but relatively inexpensive generic code readers or scan tools (see illustrations 2.4a and 2.4b) are available at most auto parts stores. Simply plug the connector of the scan tool into the diagnostic connector (see illustration). Then follow the instructions included with the scan tool to extract the DTCs.
4   Once you have outputted all of the stored DTCs, look them up on the accompanying DTC chart.
5   After troubleshooting the source of each DTC, make any necessary repairs or replace the defective component(s).

Clearing the DTCs
6   Clear the DTCs with the code reader or scan tool in accordance with the instructions provided by the tool's manufacturer.

Diagnostic Trouble Codes
7   The accompanying tables are a list of the Diagnostic Trouble Codes (DTCs) that can be accessed by a do-it-yourselfer working at home (there are many, many more DTCs available to professional mechanics with proprietary scan tools and software, but those codes cannot be accessed by a generic scan tool). If, after you have checked and repaired the connectors, wire harness and vacuum hoses (if applicable) for an emission-related system, component or circuit, the problem persists, have the vehicle checked by a dealer service department or other qualified repair shop.

OBD-II trouble codes

Code	Code identification
P0011	Intake valve timing control solenoid performance
P0031	Upstream oxygen sensor heater control circuit low voltage signal (Bank 1)
P0032	Upstream oxygen sensor heater control circuit high voltage signal (Bank 1)
P0037	Downstream oxygen sensor heater control circuit low voltage signal (Bank 1)
P0038	Downstream oxygen sensor heater control circuit high voltage signal (Bank 1)
P0043	HO2S heater control circuit low (sensor 3)
P0044	HO2S heater control circuit high (sensor 3)
P0051	Upstream oxygen sensor heater control circuit low voltage signal (Bank 2)
P0052	Upstream oxygen sensor heater control circuit high voltage signal (Bank 2)
P0057	Downstream oxygen sensor heater control circuit low voltage signal (Bank 2)
P0058	Downstream oxygen sensor heater control circuit high voltage signal (Bank 2)
P0075	Intake valve timing control solenoid circuit (Bank 1)
P0081	Intake valve timing control solenoid circuit (Bank 2)
P0101	Mass Air Flow sensor circuit range or performance fault
P0102	Mass Air Flow sensor circuit low input
P0103	Mass Air Flow sensor circuit high input
P0112	Intake Air Temperature sensor circuit low input
P0113	Intake Air Temperature sensor circuit high input
P0117	Engine Coolant Temperature sensor circuit low input
P0116	Engine coolant temperature circuit range/performance problem
P0117	Engine coolant temperature circuit, low input
P0118	Engine Coolant Temperature sensor circuit high input
P0122	Throttle Position Sensor circuit low input
P0123	Throttle Position Sensor circuit high input
P0125	Engine Coolant Temperature sensor or circuit fault
P0127	Intake Air Temperature too high
P0128	Thermostat function - engine coolant does not reach correct temperature after warm-up
P0130	Upstream oxygen sensor or circuit fault (Bank 1)
P0131	Upstream oxygen sensor lean shift monitor fault (Bank 1)
P0132	Upstream oxygen sensor rich shift monitor fault (Bank 1)

OBD-II trouble codes (continued)

Note: *Not all trouble codes apply to all models.*

Code	Code identification
P0137	Downstream oxygen sensor minimum voltage monitor fault
P0138	Downstream oxygen sensor maximum voltage monitor fault
P0139	Downstream oxygen sensor circuit slow response fault
P014C	Oxygen sensor 1 problem
P014D	Oxygen sensor 1 problem
P0143	O2 sensor circuit, low voltage (bank 1, sensor 3)
P0144	O2 sensor circuit, high voltage (bank 1, sensor 3)
P0145	O2 sensor circuit, slow response (bank 1, sensor 3)
P0146	O2 sensor circuit - no activity detected (bank 1, sensor 3)
P0150	Upstream oxygen sensor or circuit fault (Bank 2)
P0151	Upstream oxygen sensor lean shift monitor fault (Bank 2)
P0152	Upstream oxygen sensor rich shift monitor fault (Bank 2)
P0153	Upstream oxygen sensor circuit slow response fault (Bank 2)
P0154	Upstream oxygen sensor circuit high voltage fault (Bank 2)
P0157	Downstream oxygen sensor minimum voltage monitor fault
P0158	Downstream oxygen sensor maximum voltage monitor fault
P0159	Downstream oxygen sensor circuit slow response fault
P0171	Fuel injection system lean (Bank 1)
P0172	Fuel injection system rich (Bank 1)
P0174	System too lean (bank 2)
P0175	System too rich (bank 2)
P0181	Fuel Tank Temperature sensor circuit range or performance
P0182	Fuel Tank Temperature sensor circuit low input
P0183	Fuel Tank Temperature sensor circuit high input
P0196	Fuel rail pressure sensor circuit, range or performance problem
P0197	Fuel rail pressure sensor circuit, low input
P0198	Fuel rail pressure sensor circuit, high input
P0222	Throttle Position Sensor circuit low input
P0223	Throttle Position Sensor circuit high input

P0300	Multiple cylinder misfire detected
P0301	Cylinder no. 1 misfire detected
P0302	Cylinder no. 2 misfire detected
P0303	Cylinder no. 3 misfire detected
P0304	Cylinder no. 4 misfire detected
P0305	Cylinder no. 5 misfire detected
P0306	Cylinder no. 6 misfire detected
P0327	Knock Sensor circuit low input
P0328	Knock Sensor circuit high input
P0322	Crankshaft Position (CKP) sensor/engine speed (RPM) sensor - no signal
P0323	Crankshaft Position (CKP) sensor/engine speed (RPM) sensor - circuit intermittent
P0335	Crankshaft Position sensor (CKP) or circuit fault
P0340	Camshaft Position sensor or circuit fault (Bank 1)
P0345	Camshaft Position sensor or circuit fault (Bank 2)
P0420	Catalyst system defective (Bank 1)
P0430	Catalyst system defective (Bank 2)
P0441	EVAP control system incorrect purge flow
P0442	EVAP system small leak (negative pressure check)
P0443	EVAP canister purge control valve circuit fault
P0444	EVAP canister purge control valve circuit open
P0445	EVAP canister purge control valve circuit shorted
P0447	EVAP canister vent control valve circuit open
P0448	EVAP canister vent control valve remains closed under certain driving conditions
P0451	EVAP system pressure sensor or circuit fault
P0452	EVAP system pressure sensor low input voltage signal
P0453	EVAP system pressure sensor high input
P0455	EVAP system gross leak
P0456	EVAP system very small leak (negative pressure check)
P0460	Fuel level sensor or circuit fault
P0461	Fuel level sensor or circuit fault
P0462	Fuel level sensor circuit low input
P0463	Fuel level sensor circuit high input

OBD-II trouble codes (continued)

Note: *Not all trouble codes apply to all models.*

Code	Code identification
P0500	Vehicle Speed Sensor or circuit fault
P0506	Idle Air Control system signal low
P0507	Idle Air Control system signal high
P0550	Power steering pressure sensor range
P050A	Cold start control problem
P050B	Cold start control problem
P050E	Cold start control problem
P0603	PCM back-up RAM does not function properly
P0605	PCM or EEPROM fault
P0607	Control module performance
P0643	PCM detects sensor power supply low or high voltage
P0850	Park/Neutral position switch circuit fault in Drive and Park
P1148	Closed loop control fault
P1168	Oxygen sensors or circuit, bank 2, closed-loop function not available
P1211	Traction Control System (TCS), problem with ABS control unit
P1212	Traction control system communication line fault
P1217	Engine overheating
P1225	Closed throttle position learning value low
P1226	Closed throttle position learning performance fault
P1550	Battery current sensor problem
P1551	Battery current sensor problem
P1552	Battery current sensor problem
P1553	Battery current sensor problem
P1554	Battery current sensor problem
P1564	ACSD steering switch problem
P1572	ASCD brake switch or circuit fault
P1574	ASCD speed sensor signal performance fault
P1700	Automatic transmission control system problem
P1715	Input speed sensor problem

P1720	Vehicle speed sensor problem
P1800	VIAS control solenoid valve circuit performance fault
P1805	Brake switch or circuit fault
P2A00	Oxygen sensor 1
P2A03	Oxygen sensor 1
P2004	Tumble control valve problem
P2014	Tumble control valve position sensor problem
P2100	Throttle Control motor voltage signal is open or low voltage
P2103	Throttle Control motor relay voltage signal is shorted (ON)
P2101	Electric throttle control function problem
P2118	Throttle Control motor performance fault in circuit and/or throttle control motor
P2119	Throttle Control motor defective or stuck in position
P2122	Accelerator Pedal Position sensor 1 circuit low
P2123	Accelerator Pedal Position sensor 1 circuit high
P2127	Accelerator Pedal Position sensor 2 circuit low
P2128	Accelerator Pedal Position sensor 2 circuit high
P2135	Throttle Position Sensor circuit range or performance
P2138	Accelerator Pedal Position sensor or circuit range or performance
P2423	HC absorption catalyst function

4   Accelerator Pedal Position (APP) sensor - replacement

1   Disconnect the cable from the negative terminal of the battery (see Chapter 5).
2   Disconnect the electrical connector from the APP sensor/pedal assembly (see illustration).
3   Remove the APP sensor fasteners and remove the pedal/sensor assembly.
4   Installation is the reverse of removal. Tighten the sensor mounting nuts to the torque listed in this Chapter's Specifications .
5   Reconnect the battery (see Chapter 5).

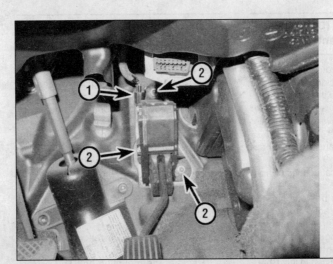

4.2 Accelerator Pedal Position (APP) sensor details

1   *Electrical connector*
2   *Mounting nuts*

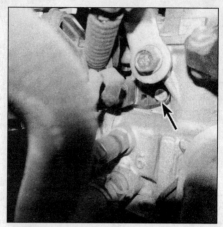

5.1a The Camshaft Position (CMP) sensor is located at the driver's end of the cylinder head, on the firewall side (2008 and earlier models shown)

5.1b CMP sensor electrical connector is accessed from below the throttle body (2009 and later models shown)

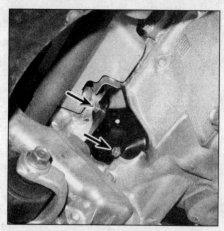

6.2 CKP sensor heat shield bolts (2009 and later models)

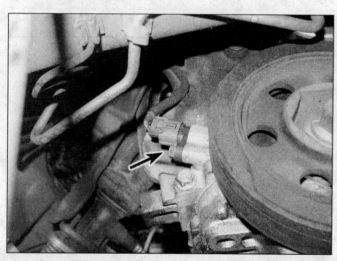

6.4a CKP sensor mounting bolt (2008 and earlier models shown)

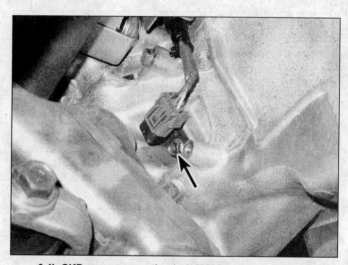

6.4b CKP sensor mounting bolt (2009 and later models)

5 Camshaft Position (CMP) sensor - replacement

1   The CMP sensor is mounted in the cylinder head on the firewall side of the engine toward the driver's side (see illustrations).
2   If you're working on a 2009 or later model, remove the cowl cover and the lower cowl (see Chapter 11).
3   Remove the air filter housing (see Chapter 4).
4   Disconnect the electrical connector from the CMP sensor.
5   Remove the mounting bolt and pull the sensor out of the cylinder head.
6   Installation is the reverse of removal. Be sure to use a new O-ring (lubricated with clean engine oil) and tighten the sensor mounting bolt to the torque listed in this Chapter's Specifications.

6 Crankshaft Position (CKP) sensor - replacement

Note: *On 2007 and 2008 models, the CKP sensor is mounted on the right end (passenger's side) of the engine, on the rear of the timing chain cover. On 2009 and later models, the CKP sensor is mounted on the rear of the cylinder block near the transaxle, on the firewall side, under a heat shield.*
1   Raise the front of the vehicle and support it securely on jackstands.
2   If you're working on a 2009 or later model, loosen the heat shield upper mounting bolt, then fully remove the lower mounting bolt and detach the heat shield (see illustration).
3   Disconnect the electrical connector from the CKP sensor.
4   Remove the mounting bolt and extract the sensor (see illustrations).
5   Installation is the reverse of the removal

procedure. Be sure to use a new O-ring (lubricated with clean engine oil) and tighten the sensor mounting bolt to the torque listed in this Chapter's Specifications.

7 Engine Coolant Temperature (ECT) sensor - replacement

Warning: *Wait until the engine has completely cooled before beginning this procedure.*
Note: *There are two ECT sensors. ECT sensor number 1 is located in the cylinder head, facing the firewall, towards the driver's side of the engine. ECT sensor number 2 is located in the right end of the lower radiator tank.*
1   Drain the coolant from engine (see Chapter 1).

ECT sensor no. 1

2   Remove the air filter housing (see Chapter 4).

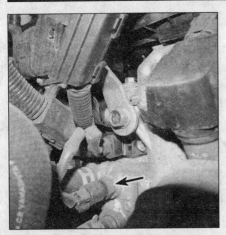

7.4 ECT sensor no. 1 is located at the left end of the cylinder head, on the rear (firewall) side

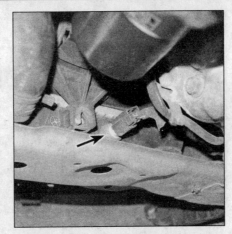

7.9 ECT sensor no. 2 is located in the radiator lower tank, at the right end

8.1a MAP sensor location (2008 and earlier models)

3   If you're working on a 2009 or later model, remove the bolt that secures the hose bracket at the left end of the cylinder head, then move the hose out of the way for access to the sensor.
4   Disconnect the electrical connector from the ECT sensor (see illustration).
5   Unscrew the sensor from the cylinder head.
6   Installation is the reverse of the removal procedure. Be sure to use a new O-ring and tighten the sensor to the torque listed in this Chapter's Specifications (see Chapter 1).
7   Refill the cooling system (see Chapter 1).

ECT sensor no. 2
8   Raise the vehicle and support it securely on jackstands.
9   Disconnect the electrical connector from the sensor (see illustration).
10   Unscrew the sensor from the radiator tank.
11   Installation is the reverse of removal. Be sure to use a new O-ring and tighten the sensor to the torque listed in this Chapter's Specifications .
12   Refill the cooling system (see Chapter 1).

8   Manifold Absolute Pressure (MAP) sensor - replacement

Note: *The MAP sensor is located on top of the intake manifold towards the driver's side of the engine.*
1   Disconnect the MAP sensor electrical connector (see illustrations).
2   Remove the MAP sensor mounting screw and remove the sensor.
3   Installation is the reverse of removal. Be sure to use a new O-ring and tighten the mounting screw securely.

8.1b MAP sensor location (2009 and later models)

9.1 IAT sensor location (2007 and 2008 models)

9   Intake Air Temperature (IAT) sensor (2007 and 2008 models) or Mass Air Flow/Intake Air Temperature (MAF/IAT) sensor (2009 and later models) - replacement

2007 and 2008 models
Note: *The IAT sensor is located on the back of the the air filter housing.*
1   Disconnect the electrical connector from the IAT sensor (see illustration).
2   Remove the IAT sensor from its grommet in the air filter housing.
3   Check the grommet for cracks or deterioration, replacing it if necessary.
4   Installation is the reverse of removal.

2009 and later models
Note: *The MAF/IAT sensor is mounted on top of the air filter housing.*
5   Disconnect the electrical connector from the MAF/IAT sensor (see illustration).

9.5 The MAF/IAT sensor is installed on the air filter housing and is retained by two screws (2009 and later models)

10.2a Depress the release tab to disconnect the electrical connector from the knock sensor (2007 and 2008 models)

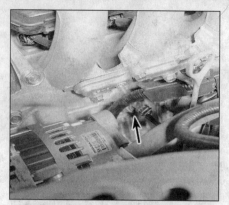

10.2b The knock sensor on 2009 and later models is accessible from below the intake manifold runners

11.4a The upstream oxygen sensor electrical connector is located on a bracket near the shift cable(s) (2007 and 2008 models)

11.4b Oxygen sensor electrical connectors, between the cylinder head and the firewall, accessible from the driver's side (2009 and later models)

1   *Upstream O2 sensor connector*
2   *Downstream O2 sensor connector*

6   Disconnect the electrical connector from the MAF/IAT sensor.
7   Remove the two mounting screws and remove the sensor from the air filter housing.
8   Inspect the MAF/IAT gasket for damage and replace it if necessary.
9   Installation is the reverse of removal. Be sure to use a new gasket and tighten the screws securely.

10 Knock sensor - replacement

Note: *The knock sensor is mounted on the front side of the engine block. On 2007 and 2008 models, it's below the intake manifold. On 2009 and later models it is accessible below the intake manifold runners for cylinders 2 and 3.*
1   On 2007 and 2008 models, remove the intake manifold to gain access to the knock sensor (see Chapter 2A).
2   Disconnect the electrical connector from the knock sensor (see illustrations).

11.5a 2008 and earlier model upstream oxygen sensor

3   Unscrew the sensor from the engine block.
4   Installation is the reverse of removal. Tighten the sensor to the torque listed in this Chapter's Specifications .

11 Oxygen sensors - replacement

Note: *Because it is installed in the exhaust system, which contracts when cool, an oxygen sensor can be very difficult to loosen when the engine is cold. Rather than risking damage to the sensor or its mounting threads, run the engine for a minute or two, then shut it off. Be careful to avoid burns during this procedure.*
1   Be very careful when servicing an oxygen sensor:
a)   *The oxygen sensor has a permanently attached pigtail and electrical connector which should not be removed from the sensor. Damage or removal of the pigtail or electrical connector can adversely affect operation of the sensor.*
b)   *Grease, dirt and other contaminants should be kept away from the electrical connector and the louvered end of the sensor.*
c)   *Do not use cleaning solvents of any kind on the oxygen sensor.*

11.5b 2009 and later model upstream oxygen sensor

d)   *Do not drop or roughly handle the sensor.*
e)   *The silicone boot must be installed in the correct position to prevent the boot from being melted and to allow the sensor to operate properly.*

Replacement

Upstream oxygen sensor

Note: *On 2007 and 2008 models, the upstream oxygen sensor (air/fuel ratio sensor) is located in the exhaust manifold just before the flange that meets the catalytic converter. On 2009 and later models the upstream oxygen sensor (air/fuel ratio sensor) is mounted on top of the warm-up catalytic converter, which is bolted to the exhaust manifold.*
2   If you're working on a 2007 or 2008 model, raise the front of the vehicle and support it securely on jackstands.
3   f you're working on a 2009 or later model, remove the cowl cover and the lower cowl (see Chapter 11).
4   Locate the upstream oxygen sensor electrical connector and disconnect it (see illustrations). Detach the sensor wiring harness from any clips.
5   Unscrew the sensor with an oxygen sensor socket if one is available (see illustrations).

11.9 Downstream oxygen sensor electrical connector (2008 and earlier models)

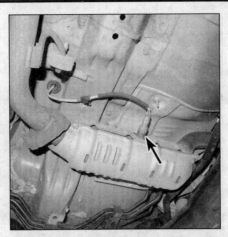

11.11a The downstream oxygen sensor is located on the catalytic converter (2008 and earlier model shown)

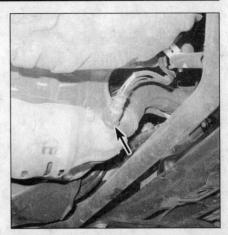

11.11b Downstream oxygen sensor (2009 and later models)

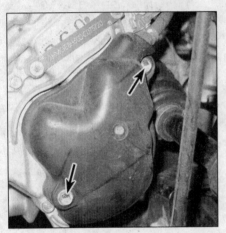

12.3 TR switch cover bolts

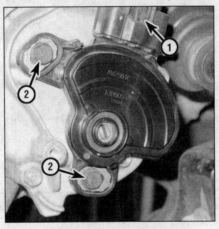

12.4 TR switch details

1   Electrical connector
2   Mounting bolts

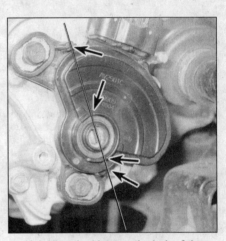

12.8 Align the slots on the hub of the switch with the cutouts on the switch body (this is the Neutral position) (2009 and later models shown; on 2007/2008 models, the slots and cutouts are angled towards the rear)

6   If you're going to reinstall the old sensor, apply anti-seize compound to the threads to ease future removal. If you're installing a new sensor, the threads will already have anti-seize on them.

7   Installation is the reverse of removal. Tighten the sensor to the torque listed in this Chapter's Specifications .

Downstream oxygen sensor

Note: *The downstream (secondary) oxygen sensor is located on the catalytic converter.*

8   Raise the vehicle and support it securely on jackstands.

9   If you're working on a 2007 or 2008 model, remove the center console (see Chapter 11), then unplug the oxygen sensor electrical connector (see illustration).

10   If you're working on a 2009 or later model, follow the sensor's wiring harness up to the electrical connector, then disconnect it (see illustration 11.4b). Also free the harness from the retaining clips

11   Unscrew the sensor (see illustrations), using an oxygen sensor socket if one is available.

12   If you're going to reinstall the old sensor, apply anti-seize compound to the threads to ease future removal. If you're installing a new sensor, the threads will already have anti-seize on them.

13   Installation is the reverse of removal. Tighten the sensor to the torque listed in this Chapter's Specifications .

12   Transmission Range (TR) switch - removal, installation and adjustment

Removal

Note: *The Transmission Range switch is mounted on the bottom of the transaxle on the driver's side.*

1   Raise the vehicle and support it securely

on jackstands.

2   Shift the transmission into the "N" or neutral position.

3   Remove the TR switch cover (see illustration).

4   Disconnect the electrical connector from the TR switch (see illustration).

5   Remove the two mounting bolts and remove the TR switch.

Installation and adjustment

6   Set the parking brake.

7   Make sure that the shift selector is in the "N" or neutral position.

8   Align the cutouts on the hub of the switch with the cutouts on the switch body, then place a 0.08 inch (2.0 mm) feeler gauge blade or equivalent (such as a drill bit) in the cutouts to hold the switch in the neutral position (see illustration).

9   Install the TR switch on the selector control shaft; make sure the feeler gauge blade or drill bit stays in position.

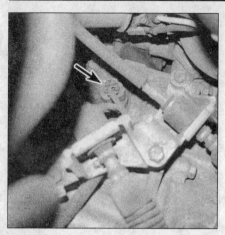

13.13 VSS location - top rear of transaxle (2008 and earlier manual transaxle models)

13.17 Input shaft speed sensor location

13.22 Output shaft speed sensor location (automatic transaxle shown)

10   While making sure the feeler gauge blade or drill bit is holding the switch in the N position, install and tighten the TR switch bolts to the torque listed in this Chapter's Specifications .

11   Verify that the engine will start only in "Park" or "Neutral." Verify that the back-up lights come on only in "Reverse." Adjust the range switch as necessary to ensure that these conditions are met.

12   Install the switch cover and tighten the bolts securely.

13   Transmission speed sensors - replacement

2007 and 2008 models

Note: *The input and output speed sensors are located on the top rear of the transaxle and are used on automatic transaxle applications only. The input shaft speed sensor is the outboard sensor, and the output shaft speed sensor is the innermost sensor. Manual transaxle models use a single Vehicle Speed Sensor and is located on the rear of the transaxle.*

Input shaft speed sensor (automatic transaxle)

1   Disconnect the negative battery cable (see Chapter 5).

2   Remove the air filter housing (see Chapter 4).

3   Remove the battery, plastic battery tray and the battery base (see Chapter 5).

4   Unbolt the transmission fluid filter bracket, then position the filter aside (don't disconnect the hoses).

5   Disconnect the electrical connector from the speed sensor.

6   Unscrew the mounting bolt and remove the input shaft speed sensor.

7   Installation is the reverse of removal. Be sure to install a new O-ring, lubricate it

with clean transmission fluid, and tighten the mounting bolt to the torque listed in this Chapter's Specifications .

Output shaft speed sensor (automatic transaxle)

8   Remove the air filter housing (see Chapter 4).

9   Disconnect the electrical connector from the output shaft speed sensor.

10   Unscrew the mounting bolt and remove the output shaft speed sensor.

11   Installation is the reverse of removal. Be sure to install a new O-ring, lubricate it with clean transmission fluid, and tighten the mounting bolt to the torque listed in this Chapter's Specifications .

Vehicle Speed Sensor (VSS) (manual transaxle)

12   Remove the air filter housing (see Chapter 4).

13   Disconnect the electrical connector from the VSS (see illustration).

14   Unscrew the mounting bolt and remove the VSS.

15   Installation is the reverse of removal. Be sure to use a new O-ring, lubricate it with clean transmission fluid, and tighten the mounting bolt to the torque listed in this Chapter's Specifications .

2009 and later models

Input shaft speed sensor (automatic transaxle)

Note: *The input shaft speed sensor is located on the rear part of the transaxle and is accessible from above.*

16   Remove the air filter housing (see Chapter 4).

17   Disconnect the sensor's electrical connector (see illustration).

18   Unscrew the mounting bolt and remove the sensor.

19   Installation is the reverse of removal.

Be sure to use a new O-ring, lubricate it with clean transmission fluid, and tighten the mounting bolt to the torque listed in this Chapter's Specifications.

Output shaft speed sensor (automatic and manual transaxles)

Note: *The output shaft speed sensor is located on the rear of the transaxle. On automatic transaxles, it is accessible from above; on manual transaxles, it is accessible from below.*

20   On automatic transaxle models, remove the air filter housing (see Chapter 4).

21   On manual transmission models, raise the vehicle and support it securely it on jackstands.

22   Disconnect the sensor's electrical connector (see illustration).

23   Unscrew the mounting bolt and remove the sensor.

24   Installation is the reverse of removal. Be sure to use a new O-ring, lubricate it with clean transmission fluid, and tighten the mounting bolt to the torque listed in this Chapter's Specifications.

14   Powertrain Control Module (PCM) - removal and installation

Note: *The Powertrain Control Module (PCM) cannot be replaced at home because the new unit must be programmed with the Vehicle Identification Number (VIN) and other data. Doing so is impossible without a factory scan tool. This procedure only shows PCM removal to gain access to other components.*

1   Disconnect the cable from the negative terminal of the battery (see Chapter 5).

2007 and 2008 models

Note: *The PCM is located under the dash on the right hand side.*

2   Remove the passenger's side under-

14.3 PCM electrical connectors

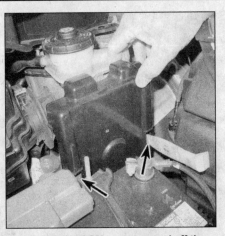

14.6 Pull the PCM cover up and off the PCM (it might be necessary to pry the sides outward slightly, working through the slots in the cover)

14.9 PCM upper mounting bolts (lower bolt not visible)

dash trim panel, the kick panel and the glove box (see Chapter 11).

3   Depress the lock tabs and disconnect the electrical connectors from the PCM (see illustration).

4   Unscrew the three mounting bolts (one on each side and one at the top) and remove the PCM from its bracket.

5   Installation is the reverse of removal.

2009 and later models

Note: *The PCM is located under the hood next to the battery.*

6   Remove the PCM cover (see illustration).

7   Remove the battery hold-down bracket and move the battery forward.

8   Loosen, but do not remove, the bolt at the bottom of the PCM.

9   Remove the two PCM upper mounting bolts, lift the PCM up, then unlatch and disconnect the electrical connectors (see illustration).

10   Installation is the reverse of removal.

---

15   Catalytic converter - replacement

Warning: *Make sure that the exhaust system is completely cooled down before proceeding. If the vehicle has just been driven, the catalytic converter can be hot enough to cause serious burns.*

Note: *Because of the Federally-mandated extended warranty which covers emission-related components such as the catalytic converter, check with a dealer service department before replacing the converter at your own expense.*

2007 and 2008 models

Note: *There is only one catalytic converter on these models, located under the vehicle.*

Note: *Spray a liberal amount of penetrating*

oil onto the threads of all fasteners to be removed.

1   Raise the vehicle and support it securely on jackstands.

2   Spray a liberal amount of penetrating oil onto the threads of all fasteners to be removed.

3   Remove the downstream oxygen sensor (see Section 11).

4   Unscrew the two bolts that fasten the catalytic converter pipe to the exhaust manifold. Retain the springs.

5   Unscrew the three nuts that fasten the catalytic converter to the exhaust pipe.

6   Remove the catalytic converter and discard the front and rear exhaust gaskets.

7   If a new converter is being installed, transfer the heat shields to the new unit.

8   Installation is the reverse of removal. Use new exhaust gaskets and self-locking nuts. Apply anti-seize compound to the threads of the fasteners and tighten them to the torque listed in this Chapter's Specifications .

2009 and later models

Note: *There are two catalytic converters. The warm-up catalytic converter is bolted to the exhaust manifold. The under-floor catalytic converter is bolted to the warm-up converter.*

Note: *Spray a liberal amount of penetrating oil onto the threads of all fasteners to be removed.*

9   Raise the vehicle and support it securely on jackstands.

Warm-up catalytic converter

10   Remove the under-floor converter-to-warm-up converter mounting bolts (see illustration), and the converter-to-mounting bracket bolt.

11   Lower the vehicle.

12   Remove the upstream oxygen sensor (see Section 11).

13   Remove the EGR pipe (see Section 17).

14   Remove the converter heat shield.

15.10 Under-floor converter-to-warm-up converter bolts

15   Unscrew the catalytic converter upper mounting bolts and remove the converter.

16   Installation is the reverse of removal. Use new gaskets and self-locking nuts. Apply anti-seize compound to the threads of the fasteners and tighten them to the torque listed in this Chapter's Specifications .

Under-floor catalytic converter

17   Remove the downstream oxygen sensor from the converter (see Section 11).

18   Remove the under-floor catalytic converter-to-warm-up converter bolts and and the converter-to-exhaust pipe nuts. Push the exhaust pipe to the rear and separate the converter from the pipes at each end.

19   If a new converter is being installed, transfer the heat shield to the new unit.

20   Installation is the reverse of removal. use new gaskets and self-locking nuts. Apply anti-seize compound to the threads of the fasteners and tighten them to the torque listed in this Chapter's Specifications .

16.1a Canister purge control solenoid valve details (2007 and 2008 models)

1   *Electrical connector*   3   *Guard mounting nuts*
2   *Hose*

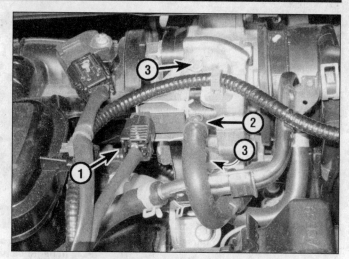

16.1b Canister purge control solenoid valve details (2009 and later models)

1   *Electrical connector*   3   *Guard mounting bolts*
2   *Hose*

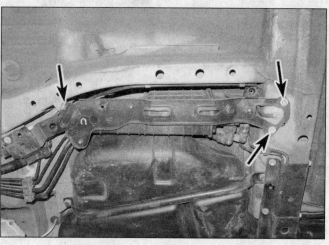

16.8 EVAP canister mounting bracket bolts

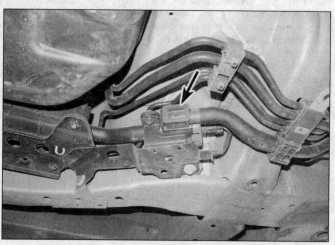

16.14 EVAP canister vent shut valve

16   Evaporative Emissions Control (EVAP) system - component replacement

Canister purge control solenoid valve

Note: *The canister purge control valve is located on the throttle body.*

1   Disconnect the hose and electrical connector from the purge valve (see illustrations).
2   On 2008 and earlier models, remove the two nuts and detach the guard, then remove the two stud bolts and detach purge valve from the throttle body.
3   On 2009 and later models, remove the two bolts and detach the valve from the throttle body.
4   Installation is the reverse of removal. Be sure to use a new O-ring and tighten the fasteners securely.

EVAP canister/Fuel Tank Pressure (FTP) sensor - replacement

Note: *The EVAP canister is located under the vehicle, next to the fuel tank on the driver's side. The FTP sensor is mounted on top of the canister.*

5   Raise the vehicle and support it securely on jackstands.
6   Remove the fuel tank cover (see Chapter 4).
7   Detach the hoses from the EVAP canister.

Note: *On some models this is easier to do after the canister mounting bracket has been unbolted and the canister lowered.*

8   Remove the canister mounting bracket bolts and remove the canister and bracket (see illustration).
9   Disconnect the electrical connectors.
10   Remove the bolts that attach the EVAP

canister to the mounting bracket.
11   Remove the hose from the FTP sensor, pull out the retainer, then remove FTP sensor from the canister.
12   Installation is the reverse of removal. Use a new O-ring when installing the FTP sensor on the canister.

EVAP canister vent shut valve

Note: *The EVAP canister vent shut valve is located directly in front of the canister.*

13   Remove the EVAP canister assembly.
14   Remove the vent shut valve hoses and electrical connector (see illustration).
15   Remove the two mounting bolts and remove the vent shut valve.
16   Carefully pry the lock tabs up and remove the cap, then pull the valve out of the valve body.
17   Installation is the reverse of removal. Be sure to use a new O-ring.

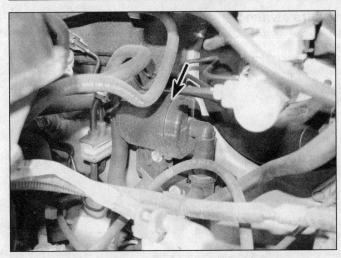

16.19 EVAP canister filter (2007 and 2008 models shown)

17.1 EGR valve electrical connector (A) and mounting bolts (B)

EVAP canister filter

Note: *The EVAP canister filter is located on the firewall (2007 and 2008 models) or on a bracket (2009 and later models), just inboard of the power brake booster.*

18   Remove the air filter housing (see Chapter 4).
19   Disconnect the hoses from the EVAP canister filter (see illustration).
20   Remove the filter mounting nut or bolt and remove the filter.
21   Installation is the reverse of removal.

17   Exhaust Gas Recirculation (EGR) - component removal and installation

Warning: *Allow exhaust system components to cool before inspection, repair or replacement.*
Note: *The EGR valve is located on the left end of the cylinder head, above the alternator.*
1   Disconnect the electrical connector from the EGR valve (see illustration).
2   Remove the two mounting bolts and remove the EGR valve.
3   Installation if the reverse of removal. Clean the mounting surfaces and install a new gasket. Tighten the EGR mounting bolts to the torque listed in this Chapter's Specifications.

EGR pipe (2009 and later models)

4   Remove the cowl cover and the lower cowl (see Chapter 11).
5   Remove the fasteners from the pipe flanges at each end of the pipe (see illustration), then detach the pipe from the catalytic converter and the cylinder head.
6   Clean the flanges and mating surfaces, then reinstall the pipe using new gaskets. Tighten the fasteners to the torque listed in this Chapter's Specifications .

7   Reinstall the lower cowl and cowl cover.

18   Positive Crankcase Ventilation (PCV) valve - replacement

1   Refer to Chapter 1, Section 27 for information on the PCV system.

19   Throttle Position (TP) sensor - replacement

1   The TP sensor on these vehicles is an integral part of the throttle body and is not serviceable separately. Refer to Chapter 4 for the throttle body replacement procedure.

20   Variable Valve Timing and Lift Electronic Control (VTEC) oil control valve/solenoid and oil pressure switch - replacement

Note: *The rocker arm oil control solenoid/ valve assembly, which controls valve timing and camshaft lift, is located on the left end (driver's side) of the cylinder head. The oil pressure switch is threaded into the valve.*
1   Disconnect the negative battery cable (see Chapter 5).
2   Remove the air filter housing (see Chapter 4).
3   If you're working on a 2009 or later model, remove the bolt and reposition the wiring harness bracket at the end of the cylinder head.

Rocker arm oil control valve/solenoid

4   Disconnect the electrical connectors from the rocker arm oil control valve solenoid and the rocker arm oil pressure switch.
5   Remove the oil control valve/solenoid

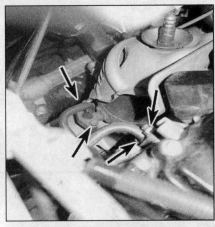

17.5 EGR pipe fasteners

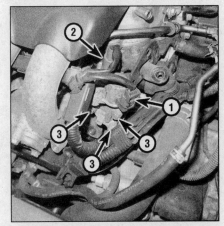

20.4 VTEC oil control valve/solenoid and oil pressure switch details (2007 and 2008 models shown)

1   *Oil control valve solenoid electrical connector*
2   *Rocker arm oil pressure switch electrical connector*
3   *Oil control valve mounting bolts*

mounting bolts and remove the assembly.

6   Installation is the reverse of removal. Use a new gasket/oil filter (small screen in gasket). Tighten the mounting bolts to the torque listed in this Chapter's Specifications.

Rocker arm oil pressure switch

7   If you're working on a 2007 or 2008 model, remove the engine cover.

8   Disconnect the electrical connector from the oil pressure switch (see illustration 20.4).

9   Unscrew the switch from the rocker arm oil control valve.

10   Installation is the reverse of removal. Be sure to use a new O-ring and tighten the switch to the torque listed in this Chapter's Specifications.

Chapter 7 Part A
Manual transaxle

Contents

Specifications

Torque specifications

Note: *One foot-pound of torque is equivalent to 12 inch-pounds of torque. Torque values below approximately 15 ft-lbs. are expressed in inch-pounds, since most foot-pound torque wrenches are not accurate at these smaller values.*

	Ft-lbs (unless otherwise indicated)	Nm
Back-up light switch	22	29
Transaxle-to-engine and engine-to-transaxle bolts	47	93
Shift lever mounting bolts	16	22
Shift cable bracket bolts	20	27

1   General information

1   The vehicles covered by this manual are equipped with either a five- speed manual transaxle or a five-speed automatic transaxle. Information on the manual transaxle is included in this Part of Chapter 7. Service procedures for the automatic transaxle are contained in Chapter 7B.
2   The manual transaxle is a compact, two-piece, lightweight aluminum alloy housing containing both the transmission and differential assemblies.
3   Because of the complexity of the transaxle and the special tools needed to work on it, internal repair procedures for the manual transaxle are beyond the scope of this manual. The information in this Chapter is devoted to removal and installation procedures.

2   Shifter assembly - removal and installation

Note: *Adjustments are not available for the shifter assembly. If the vehicle does not shift properly, check for bent brackets and verify the cables are correctly installed in the brackets and on the levers.*

1   Remove the center console and/or instrument panel components to access the shifter assembly (see Chapter 11).
Note: *If the shift knob needs to be removed, simply unscrew it from the shifter assembly.*
2   Place the shifter in Neutral.
3   To remove the right shift cable from the shifter, remove the shift cable clip from the housing and carefully pry the shift cable end from the shifter ball (see illustration). Remove the the cable from the shifter bracket (see illustration).

4   To remove the left shift cable from the shifter, remove the cotter pin and washer from the shift cable end, then rotate the shift cable housing to the left to remove from the shifter bracket (see illustrations).
5   Remove the four bolts attaching the shifter assembly to the vehicle and remove the shifter assembly (see illustration).
6   Installation is reverse of removal. Be sure to use a new cotter pin on the left shift cable.

3   Shift cables - removal and installation

Note: *Adjustments are not available for the shift cables. If the vehicle does not shift properly, check for bent brackets and verify the cables are correctly installed in the brackets and on the levers.*

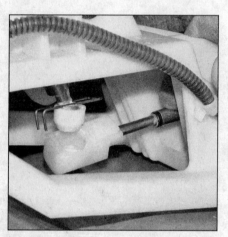
2.3a Pry apart the spring clip legs, the pull the cable off the ballstud

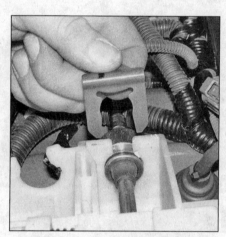
2.3b Remove the horseshoe clip and detach the cable from the shifter base

2.4a Remove the cotter pin and detach the left shift cable from its stud. . .

2.4b. . . then using a pair of pliers, rotate the cable casing out of the shifter base

2.5 Shifter assembly mounting bolts

1   Raise the vehicle and support it securely on jackstands.

2   Remove the battery and battery base (see Chapter 5).

3   Remove the air filter housing (see Chapter 4).

4   Place the shifter in Neutral.

5   Remove the spring clips or cotter pins and washers, then remove the cable retaining clips from the shift cable bracket on top of the transaxle (see illustrations).

6   Disconnect the shift cables from the shifter assembly (see Section 2).

7   Remove exhaust components as necessary (see Chapter 4) to allow access to the shift cable bracket.

8   Remove the nuts and detach the cable support bracket from the underside of the vehicle.

9   Remove the shifter and shift cables from the vehicle as an assembly from under the vehicle.

10   Installation is the reverse of removal.

Note: *When installing the shift cables, ensure the paint mark is facing up at the transaxle end.*

4   Driveaxle oil seal - replacement

1   Oil leaks can occur as a result of worn seals or O-rings. Replacement of these seals or O-rings is relatively easy, since the repairs can usually be performed without removing the transaxle from the vehicle.

2   The driveaxle oil seals are located on the sides of the transaxle, where the inner ends of the driveaxles are splined into the differential side gears. If you suspect that a driveaxle oil seal is leaking, raise the vehicle and support it securely on jackstands. If the seal is leaking, you'll see lubricant on the side of the transaxle, below the seal.

3   Remove the driveaxle or driveaxle and

intermediate shaft (if equipped) (see Chapter 8).

4   Using a screwdriver or seal removal tool, carefully pry the seal out of the transaxle bore (see illustration).

5   Using a seal driver or a large deep socket as a drift, install the new oil seal. Drive it into the bore squarely and make sure it's fully seated (see illustration). Lubricate the lip of the new seal with multi-purpose grease.

6   Install the driveaxle (or driveaxle and intermediate shaft). Be careful not to damage the lip(s) of the new seal(s). Check the transaxle lubricant level and add some, if necessary, to bring it up to the required level (see Chapter 1).

5   Transaxle mounts/roll restrictor (torque rod) - check and replacement

1   Refer to Chapter 2A Section 17 , for mount check and replacement procedures.

6   Back-up lamp switch - testing and replacement

1   Remove the air filter housing (see Chapter 4), the battery and battery base (see Chapter 5) to access the back-up lamp switch (see illustration).

2   Disconnect the electrical connector from the switch.

Testing

3   The back-up light switch should only have continuity in Reverse. It should be open (no continuity) in neutral (and all other gears) between the two terminals of the switch.

4   If continuity is not as specified, replace the switch.

3.5a Remove the cotter pin or spring slip (as applicable), then detach the shift cables and washers from the shift levers (lower cable not shown)

3.5b Shift cable horseshoe clips

4.4 Carefully pry out the driveaxle oil seal with a seal removal tool or a large screwdriver; make sure you don't damage the seal bore or the new seal may leak

4.5 Use a seal installer or a large socket to install the new seal

6.1 The back-up light switch is located on top of the transaxle

6.5 Unscrew the switch and recover the sealing washer

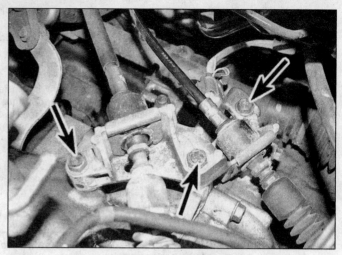

7.9 Shift cable bracket bolts

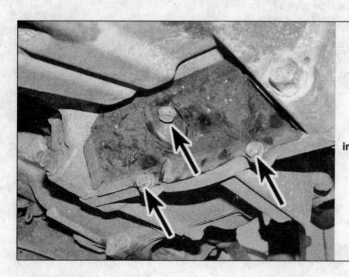

7.16 Flywheel inspection plate bolts

Replacement

5   Unscrew the switch and remove it from the transaxle (see illustration).
6   Using a NEW sealing washer, install the switch and tighten it securely.
7   The remainder of installation is the reverse of removal. Add transaxle fluid as necessary (see Chapter 1).

7   Manual transaxle - removal and installation

Removal

1   Raise the vehicle and support it securely on a hoist or jackstands.
2   Remove the engine undercover and drain the lubricant from the transaxle (see Chapter 1).
3   On 2009 and later models, remove the wiper arms and upper and lower cowl covers (see Chapter 11).
4   Remove the battery and battery tray (see

Chapter 5).
5   Remove the air filter housing (see Chapter 4).
6   On 2009 and later models, remove the air filter housing mounting bracket.
7   Remove the two bolts attaching the clutch release cylinder to the transaxle and if equipped, remove the bolt attaching the clutch line bracket to the vehicle (see Chapter 8). Position and secure the clutch release cylinder to the side using care not to bend the hard line.
8   Disconnect the back-up lamp switch connector (see Section 6).
9   Remove the three bolts securing the shift cable bracket to the transaxle (see illustration). Remove the spring clips or cotter pins and washers securing the shift cables to the shift levers and disconnect the shift cable. Position and secure the shift cables to the side.
10   On 2008 and earlier models, disconnect the Vehicle Speed Sensor (VSS) connector.
11   Attach an engine support fixture to the engine at the transaxle end. Use a bolt

threaded into the engine for the chain to attach to if a hook is not provided.
 Note: *Engine support fixtures can be obtained at most equipment rental yards and some auto parts stores.*
12   Remove the upper transaxle-to-engine bellhousing bolt under the radiator hoses.
13   On 2008 and earlier models, remove the lower starter bolt.
14   On 2009 and later models, remove the transaxle mount bracket from the transaxle (see Section 5).
15   Remove the left and right driveaxles (see Chapter 8).
16   Remove the three bolts and the flywheel inspection plate from the transaxle (see illustration).
17   On 2008 and earlier models remove the subframe from the vehicle (see Chapter 10).
18   On 2008 and earlier models, remove the front and rear transaxle mounts (see Section 5). Remove the the air filter bracket bolts accessible after removing the front mount, and remove the bracket.
19   Support the transaxle with a floor jack, preferably one equipped with a transmission adapter head. Support the transaxle with chains or straps to prevent it from falling off the jack.
20   On 2009 and later models, remove the roll restrictor (torque rod) (see Section 5). Remove the three bolts and the torque rod mounting bracket.
21   On 2008 and earlier models, remove the upper transaxle mount bracket from the transaxle (see Section 5).
22   Remove the five remining transaxle-to-engine mounting bolts. Four of the bolts are removed from the engine side, one bolt (longest) from the transaxle side. Organize the bolts so they can be installed in their original positions - there are different lengths used.
23   Check for any remaining wiring harness clips or connectors and remove from the transaxle.

24 Separate the transaxle from the engine to clear the clutch pressure plate then lower the transaxle (see illustration).
25 Remove the clutch components if necessary (see Chapter 8).

Installation

26 If removed, install the clutch components (see Chapter 8).
27 Check the condition of the dowel pins located in the engine block. If they are damaged, replace them to ensure proper transaxle alignment to the engine.
28 Raise the transaxle to installation height and slide it towards the engine, engaging the two dowel pins on the engine with the corresponding holes in the transaxle and the input shaft with the clutch plate hub splines. Do not use excessive force to install the transaxle - if the input shaft does not slide into place, readjust the angle of the transaxle so it is level and/or turn the input shaft so the splines engage properly with the clutch plate hub.
29 Install the transaxle housing-to-engine bolts and tighten them to the torque listed in this Chapter's Specifications0. Be sure the bolts are installed in the correct holes.
30 The remainder of installation is the reverse of removal. Fill the transaxle with the proper lubricant (see Chapter 8).

---

8 Manual transaxle overhaul - general information

1 Overhauling a manual transaxle is a difficult job for the do-it-yourselfer. It involves the disassembly and reassembly of many small

7.24 Move the transaxle away from the engine and lower it to the floor

parts. Numerous clearances must be precisely measured and, if necessary, changed with select fit spacers and snap-rings. As a result, if transaxle problems arise, it can be removed and installed by a competent do-it-yourselfer, but overhaul should be left to a transmission repair shop. Rebuilt transaxles may be available - check with your dealer parts department and auto parts stores. At any rate, the time and money involved in an overhaul is almost sure to exceed the cost of a rebuilt unit.
2 Nevertheless, it's not impossible for an inexperienced mechanic to rebuild a transaxle if the special tools are available and the job is done in a deliberate step-by-step manner so nothing is overlooked.
3 The tools necessary for an overhaul include internal and external snap-ring pliers, a bearing puller, a slide hammer, a set of pin punches, a dial indicator and possibly a hydraulic press. In addition, a large, sturdy workbench and a vise or transmission stand will be required.
4 During disassembly of the transaxle, make careful notes of how each piece comes off, where it fits in relation to other pieces and what holds it in place. Your notes plus the manufacturer's shop manual, which contains exploded views, will make it easier to get the transaxle back together.
5 Before taking the transaxle apart for repair, it will help if you have some idea what area of the transaxle is malfunctioning. Certain problems can be closely tied to specific areas in the transaxle, which can make component examination and replacement easier. Refer to Chapter 0, Section 11 for information regarding possible sources of trouble.

Notes

Chapter 7 Part B
Automatic transaxle

Contents

Specifications

Torque specifications

Note: *One foot-pound (ft-lb) of torque is equivalent to 12 inch-pounds (in-lbs) of torque. Torque values below approximately 15 ft-lbs are expressed in inch-pounds, since most foot-pound torque wrenches are not accurate at these smaller values.*

	Ft-lbs (unless otherwise indicated)	Nm
Driveplate-to-torque converter bolts	104 in-lbs	12
Transaxle-to-engine mounting bolts	47	64
Shifter assembly mounting bolts	16	22

1 General information

1   The vehicles covered by this manual are equipped with either a 5-speed manual transaxle or a 5-speed automatic transaxle. Information on the automatic transaxle is included in this Part of Chapter 7. Information for the manual transaxle can be found in Chapter 7A.

2   Because of the complexity of the automatic transaxle and the specialized equipment needed to service it, this Chapter contains only those procedures related to general diagnosis, adjustment, and removal and installation.

3   If the transaxle requires major repair work, it should be taken to a dealer service department or an automotive or transmission repair shop. You can, however, save money by removing and installing the transaxle yourself, even if the repair work is done by a shop.

2 Diagnosis - general

Note: *Automatic transaxle malfunctions may be caused by five general conditions: poor engine performance, improper adjustments, hydraulic malfunctions, mechanical malfunctions or malfunctions in the computer or its signal network. Diagnosis of these problems should always begin with a check of the easily repaired items: fluid level and condition (see Chapter 1), shift cable adjustment and* *throttle linkage adjustment. Next, perform a road test to determine if the problem has been corrected or if more diagnosis is necessary. If the problem persists after the preliminary tests and corrections are completed, additional diagnosis should be done by a dealer service department or transmission repair shop. Refer to Chapter 0, Section 11 for information on symptoms of transaxle problems.*

Preliminary checks

1   Drive the vehicle to warm the transaxle to normal operating temperature.

2   Check the fluid level as described in Chapter 1:

 a) *If the fluid level is unusually low, add enough fluid to bring the level within the designated area of the dipstick, then check for external leaks (see below).*

 b) *If the fluid level is abnormally high, drain off the excess, then check the drained fluid for contamination by coolant. The presence of engine coolant in the automatic transmission fluid indicates that a failure has occurred in the internal radiator walls that separate the coolant from the transmission fluid (see Chapter 3).*

 c) *If the fluid is foaming, drain it and refill the transaxle, then check for coolant in the fluid, or a high fluid level.*

3   Check for the presence of any stored diagnostic trouble codes (see Chapter 6). There are many potential transaxle-specific trouble codes that could be set, but certain engine-related problems can also affect transaxle operation.

4   Inspect the shift cable (see Section 5). Make sure that it's properly adjusted and operates smoothly.

Fluid leak diagnosis

5   Most fluid leaks are easy to locate visually. Repair usually consists of replacing a seal or gasket. If a leak is difficult to find, the following procedure may help.

6   Identify the fluid. Make sure it's transmission fluid and not engine oil or brake fluid (the fluid used in these transaxles is a light transparent red color).

7   Try to pinpoint the source of the leak. Drive the vehicle several miles, then park it over a large sheet of cardboard. After a minute or two, you should be able to locate the leak by determining the source of the fluid dripping onto the cardboard.

8   Make a careful visual inspection of the suspected component and the area immediately around it. Pay particular attention to gasket mating surfaces. A mirror is often helpful for finding leaks in areas that are hard to see.

9   If the leak still cannot be found, clean the suspected area thoroughly with a degreaser or solvent, then dry it.

10   Drive the vehicle for several miles at normal operating temperature and varying speeds. After driving the vehicle, visually inspect the suspected component again.

11   Once the leak has been located, the cause must be determined before it can be

properly repaired. If a gasket is replaced but the sealing flange is bent, the new gasket will not stop the leak. The bent flange must be straightened.

12   Before attempting to repair a leak, check to make sure that the following conditions are corrected or they may cause another leak. **Note:** *Some of the following conditions cannot be fixed without highly specialized tools and expertise. Such problems must be referred to a transmission shop or a dealer service department.*

Gasket leaks

13   Check the pan periodically. Make sure the bolts are tight, no bolts are missing, the gasket is in good condition and the pan is flat (dents in the pan may indicate damage to the valve body inside).

14   If the pan gasket is leaking, the fluid level or the fluid pressure may be too high, the vent may be plugged, the pan bolts may be too tight, the pan sealing flange may be warped, the sealing surface of the transaxle housing may be damaged, the gasket may be damaged or the transaxle casting may be cracked or porous. If sealant instead of gasket material has been used to form a seal between the pan and the transaxle housing, it may be the wrong sealant.

Seal leaks

15   If a transaxle seal is leaking, the fluid level or pressure may be too high, the vent may be plugged, the seal bore may be damaged, the seal itself may be damaged or improperly installed, the surface of the shaft protruding through the seal may be damaged or a loose bearing may be causing excessive shaft movement.

16   Make sure the dipstick tube seal is in good condition and the tube is properly seated. Periodically check the area around the speedometer gear or sensor for leakage. If transmission fluid is evident, check the O-ring for damage.

Case leaks

17   If the case itself appears to be leaking, the casting is porous and will have to be repaired or replaced.

18   Make sure the oil cooler hose fittings are tight and in good condition.

Fluid comes out vent pipe or fill hole

19   If this condition occurs, the transaxle is overfilled, there is coolant in the fluid, the case is porous, the dipstick is incorrect, the vent is plugged or the drain-back holes are plugged.

---

3   Shift knob - removal and installation

2008 and earlier models

1   Remove the two screws at the front of the shift knob (see illustration).

2   Pull up on the shift knob button, then pull the shift knob up to remove from the shifter.

3   To install, first pull up on the shift knob button, then install the shift knob on the shifter and install the two screws.

2009 and later models

4   Move the shifter to the "S" position.

5   Using a trim tool or small, flat-bladed screwdriver, carefully remove the trim from the front of the shift knob to access the fasteners.

6   Remove the two screws at the front of the shift knob and remove the shift knob by pulling up.

7   Installation is the reverse of removal.

---

4   Shifter assembly - removal and installation

Warning: *The models covered by this manual are equipped with Supplemental Restraint Systems (SRS), more commonly known as airbags. Always disable the airbag system before working in the vicinity of any airbag system components to avoid the possibility of accidental deployment of the airbags, which could cause personal injury (see Chapter 12).*

1   Place the shift lever in neutral "N" position.

2   Remove the center console (see Chapter 11).

3   Remove the nut and disconnect the shift cable from the shifter assembly pivot.

4   Rotate and disconnect the shift cable from the shifter bracket (see illustration).

5   Disconnect the shifter assembly wiring harness and electrical connectors.

6   Remove the shifter assembly mounting bolts and remove the assembly.

7   Installation is the reverse of removal. Adjust the shift cable (see Section 5).

---

5   Shift cable - replacement and adjustment

Replacement

Warning: *The models covered by this manual are equipped with Supplemental Restraint Systems (SRS), more commonly known as airbags. Always disable the airbag system before working in the vicinity of any airbag system components to avoid the possibility of accidental deployment of the airbags, which could cause personal injury (see Chapter 12).*

1   Place the shifter in Park.

2   Detach the shift cable from the shifter assembly (see Section 4).

3   Raise and support the vehicle on a hoist or jack stands.

4   Remove any exhaust or heat shields to allow access to the shift cable from under the vehicle.

5   Working from under the vehicle, remove the two nuts and shift cable bracket (see illustration). Dislodge the shift cable grommet and pull the shift cable out from under the vehicle.

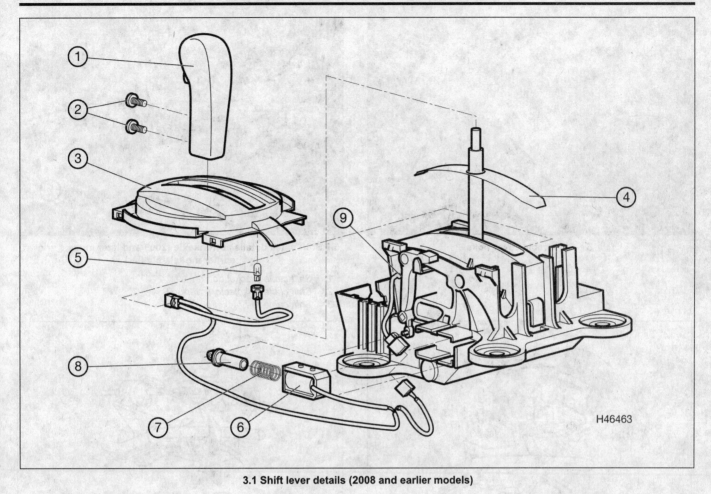

3.1 Shift lever details (2008 and earlier models)

1	Shift lever knob	4	Inner cover	7	Solenoid plunger spring
2	Knob securing screws	5	Shift indicator bulb	8	Solenoid plunger
3	Lever trim panel	6	Shift lock solenoid body	9	Park pin switch

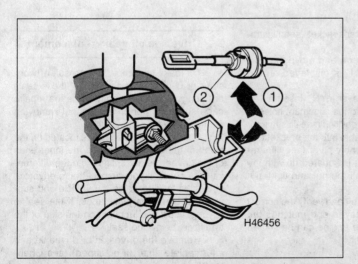

4.4 Twist the cable fitting (1) so the tab (2) is at the top, then pull the cable from the shifter bracket

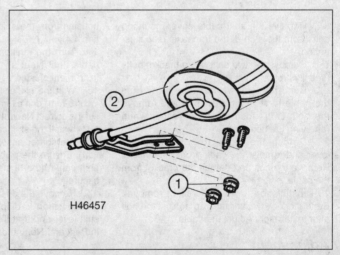

5.5 Remove the shift cable bracket nuts (1), then dislodge the grommet (2) from the floor pan

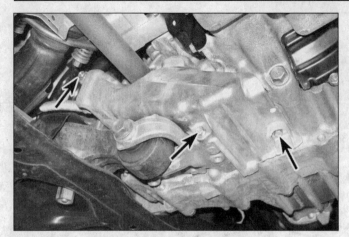

5.6 Shift cable cover bolts

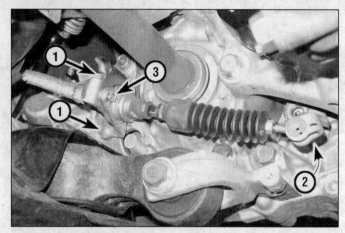

5.7 Shift cable details at transaxle (2009 and later models shown, earlier models similar)

1   Shift cable bracket bolts
2   Shift cable-to-selector lever bolt
3   Shift cable-to-bracket bolt

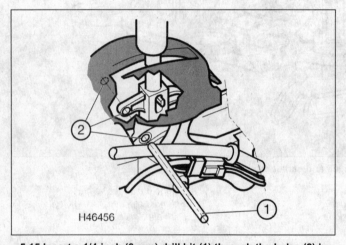

5.15 Insert a 1/4-inch (6 mm) drill bit (1) through the holes (2) in the shift lever and housing

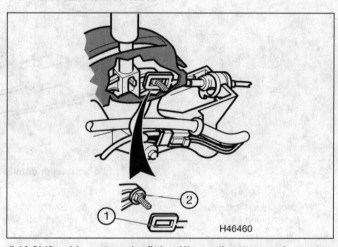

5.16 Shift cable rectangular fitting (1) must locate over the square fitting on the lever

6   Remove the shift cable cover mounting bolts from the side of the transaxle (see illustration).
7   Remove the two shift cable bracket bolts (see illustration).
8   Bend the lock washer tabs away from the cable-to-selector lever bolt and remove the bolt. Don't lose the lock washer when removing the bolt.
9   Detach the cable from the selector lever and remove the cable from the vehicle. Remove the bolt and detach the bracket from the cable.
10   Installation is the reverse of removal. Bend the lock washer tabs up against the bolt after installation. Adjust the cable.

Adjustment

11   Place the shift lever in the "N" position.
12   Remove the center console, if not already done (see Chapter 11).
13   Remove the nut and shift cable from the shifter assembly pivot. Remove the cable

housing from the shifter bracket (see illustration 4.4).
14   Turn the ignition on and move the shift cable until Neutral "N" is displayed on the instrument cluster.
15   With the shifter lever in "N", insert a 1/4-inch (6 mm) drill bit into the alignment holes to set the correct Neutral position (see illustration).
16   Install the shift cable into the bracket and onto the shifter assembly pivot (see illustration). Ensure the pivot is squared up with the shift cable hole. Install the nut and tighten it securely.
17   Remove the drill bit and verify the correct gear position is displayed and matches the shift lever and that the engine can be started in Park and Neutral only.

---

6   Transmission range switch - adjustment

1   Refer to Chapter 6 for this procedure.

7   Driveaxle oil seal - replacement

1   Oil leaks can occur as a result of worn seals or O-rings. Replacement of these seals or O-rings is relatively easy, since the repairs can usually be performed without removing the transaxle from the vehicle.
2   The driveaxle oil seals are located on the sides of the transaxle, where the inner ends of the driveaxles are splined into the differential side gears. If you suspect that a driveaxle oil seal is leaking, raise the vehicle and support it securely on jackstands. If the seal is leaking, you'll see lubricant on the side of the transaxle, below the seal.
3   Remove the driveaxle or driveaxle and intermediate shaft (if equipped) (see Chapter 8).
4   Using a screwdriver or seal removal tool, carefully pry the seal out of the transaxle bore (see illustration).
5   Using a seal driver or a large deep socket as a drift, install the new oil seal. Drive

7.4 Carefully pry out the driveaxle oil seal with a seal removal tool or a large screwdriver; make sure you don't damage the seal bore or the new seal may leak

7.5 Use a seal installer or a large socket to install the new seal

it into the bore squarely and make sure it's fully seated (see illustration) . Lubricate the lip of the new seal with multi-purpose grease.
6   Install the driveaxle (or driveaxle and intermediate shaft). Be careful not to damage the lip(s) of the new seal(s). Check the transaxle lubricant level and add some, if necessary, to bring it up to the required level (see Chapter 1).

8   Transaxle mounts/roll restrictor (torque rod) - check and replacement

1   Refer to Chapter 2A Section 17 for mount check and replacement procedures.

9   Automatic transaxle - removal and installation

Removal

2008 and earlier models
1   Remove the air filter housing (see Chapter 4) and bracket.
2   Remove the battery and battery base from the vehicle (see Chapter 5).
3   Disconnect any component connectors and harness brackets and remove the bolts securing the wiring harness to the transaxle.
4   Attach an engine support fixture to the engine at the transaxle end. Use a bolt threaded into the engine for the chain to attach to if a hook is not provided.
Note: *Engine support fixtures can be obtained at most equipment rental yards and some auto parts stores.*

5   Remove the left-side upper transaxle mount (see Chapter 2A Section 17).
6   Raise the vehicle and support it securely on a hoist or jackstands.
7   Remove the under-vehicle splash shield and drain the lubricant from the transaxle (see Chapter 1).
8   Place a drain pan under the transaxle cooler hoses and disconnect the hoses from the transaxle. Turn the hoses upwards to prevent fluid spillage.
9   Remove the shift cable cover bolts and cover and disconnect the shift cable from the transaxle (see Section 5).
10   Remove the left and right driveaxles and intermediate shaft (see Chapter 8).
11   Remove the torque converter cover, then remove the torque converter bolts (see illustrations 9.35a and 9.35b).
12   Remove the subframe (see Chapter 10).
13   Support the transaxle with a floor jack (preferable equipped with a transmission adapter). Secure the transaxle to the jack with chains or straps to prevent it from falling off the jack. Remove the engine-to-transaxle bolts. Keep them organized so they can be installed in the same positions.
14   Check for any remaining wiring harness clips or connectors and remove from the transaxle.
15   Separate the transaxle from the engine and remove it from the vehicle.
16   If necessary, remove any external transaxle components.

2009 and later models
17   Raise the vehicle and support it securely on a hoist or jackstands.
18   Disconnect the steering joint located at the base of the steering column working inside

of the drivers compartment (see Chapter 10).
19   Remove the battery and battery base from the vehicle (see Chapter 5).
20   Remove the wiper arms and upper and lower cowl covers (see Chapter 11).
21   Remove the air filter housing (see Chapter 4).
22   Remove the air filter housing bracket.
23   Disconnect any component connectors and harness brackets and remove the bolts securing the wiring harness to the transaxle.
24   Remove the two upper transaxle-to-engine bolts.
25   Raise the vehicle and support it securely on a hoist or jackstands.
26   Remove the under-vehicle splash shield and drain the lubricant from the transaxle (see Chapter 1).
27   Place a drain pan under the transaxle cooler hoses and disconnect the hoses from the transaxle. Turn the hoses upwards to prevent fluid spillage.
28   Disconnect the Electronic Power Steering (EPS) connectors from the steering gear (see Chapter 10).
29   Remove the bolt attaching the downstream (rear) oxygen sensor bracket to the steering gear (do not disconnect the harness from the bracket).
30   Remove the shift cable bolts and cover. Remove the torque rod from the vehicle (see Chapter 2A Section 17).
31   Remove the left and right driveaxles and intermediate shaft (see Chapter 7B).
32   Remove the subframe (see Chapter 10).
33   Disconnect the shift cable and bracket from the transaxle (see Section 5).
34   Remove the roll restrictor (torque rod) bracket from the transaxle (see Chapter 2A Section 17).

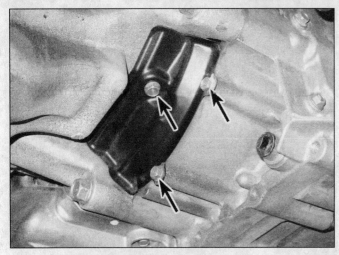

9.35a Torque converter cover bolts

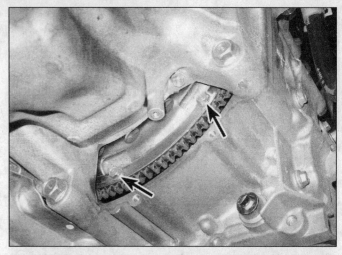

9.35b There are six driveplate-to-torque converter bolts. Turn the crankshaft pulley bolt (clockwise only) to bring them into view

35   Remove the torque converter cover, then remove the torque converter bolts (see illustrations).
36   Support the transaxle with a floor jack (preferable equipped with a transmission adapter). Secure the transaxle to the jack with chains or straps to prevent it from falling off the jack.
37   Remove the nut and bolts attaching the transaxle mount and bracket to the vehicle (see Chapter 2A Section 17).
38   Remove the three rear transaxle-to-engine bolts.
39   Remove the two lower transaxle-to-engine bolts.
40   Check for any remaining wiring harness clips or connectors and detach them from the transaxle.
41   Separate the transaxle from the engine and remove it from the vehicle.
42   If necessary, remove any external transaxle components.

Installation

Caution: *Use new O-rings and copper sealing washers during installation; DO NOT reuse*

any of these.
43   Flush the transaxle cooler and the cooler hoses and lines with solvent whenever the transaxle is removed from the vehicle. Flush the lines and fluid cooler thoroughly and make sure no solvent remains in the lines or cooler after flushing. It's a good idea to repeat the flushing procedure with clean automatic transmission fluid to ensure that no solvent remains in the lines or cooler.
44   Check the condition of the dowel pins located in the engine block. If they are damaged, replace them to ensure proper transaxle alignment to the engine.
45   Prior to installation, make sure that the torque converter hub is securely engaged in the pump.
46   Using the jack, raise and maneuver the transaxle to the rear of the engine.
47   Rotate the torque converter to line up the bolt holes with those in the driveplate.
48   Move the transaxle forward carefully until the dowel pins and the torque converter are engaged.
49   Install and the transaxle-to-engine bolts and tighten them to the torque values listed in

this Chapter's Specifications.
50   Install the torque converter bolts and tighten them to the torque listed in this Chapter's Specifications.
Note: *Install all of the bolts before tightening any of them.*
51   The remainder of installation is the reverse of removal.
52   Refill the transaxle with fluid to the specified level (see Chapter 1).
Note: *The transaxle may require more fluid than in a normal fluid and filter change, since the torque converter may be empty (the converter is not drained during a fluid change).*
53   Start the engine, set the parking brake and shift the transaxle through all gears three times. Make sure the shift cable is working properly (see Section 5).
54   Allow the engine to reach its proper operating temperature with the transaxle in Park or Neutral, then turn it off and check the fluid level.
55   Road test the vehicle and check for fluid leaks.

Chapter 8
Driveline

Contents

Specifications

Clutch
Clutch fluid type .... See Chapter 1

Driveaxles
Driveaxle length
2008 and earlier models
Manual transaxle
Left .... 19.72 to 19.92 inches 501 to 506 mm
Right .... 30.98 to 31.18 inches 787 to 792 mm
Automatic transaxle
Left .... 19.92 to 20.12 inches 506 to 511 mm
Right .... 19.02 to 19.21 inches 483 to 488 mm
2009 and later models
Manual transaxle
Left .... 20.79 to 20.98 inches 528 to 533 mm
Right .... 30.83 to 31.02 inches 783 to 788 mm
Automatic transaxle
Left .... 20.79 to 20.98 inches 528 to 533 mm
Right .... 19.02 to 19.21 inches 483 to 488 mm

Torque specifications

Note: *One foot-pound of torque is equivalent to 12 inch-pounds of torque. Torque values below approximately 15-ft-lbs. are expressed in inch-pounds, since most foot-pound torque wrenches are not accurate at these smaller values.*

	Ft-lbs (unless otherwise indicated)	Nm
Clutch master cylinder mounting nuts	150 In-lbs	17
Clutch release cylinder mounting bolts	16	22
Clutch damper bracket bolts	16	22
Clutch hose-to-damper banjo bolt	22	29
Clutch pressure plate-to-flywheel bolts	19	26
Flywheel-to-crankshaft bolts	See Chapter 2A	
Intermediate shaft support bearing bolts	29	39
Driveaxle/hub nut	133	181

1   General information

1   The information in this Chapter deals with the components from the rear of the engine to the front wheels, except for the transaxle, which is dealt with in Chapters 7A and 7B. For the purposes of this Chapter, these components are grouped into two categories: clutch and driveaxles. Separate Sections within this Chapter offer general descriptions and checking procedures for both groups.

2   Since nearly all the procedures covered in this Chapter involve working under the vehicle, make sure it's securely supported on sturdy jackstands or a hoist where the vehicle can be easily raised and lowered.

2   Clutch - description

1   All vehicles with a manual transaxle use a single dry plate, diaphragm spring type clutch. The clutch disc has a splined hub which allows it to slide along the splines of the transaxle input shaft. The clutch and pressure plate are held in contact by spring pressure exerted by the diaphragm in the pressure plate.

2   The clutch release system is hydraulically operated. The release system consists of the clutch pedal, the clutch master cylinder, the clutch concentric slave (release) cylinder and bearing and the hydraulic line and clutch damper between the master cylinder and release cylinder.

3   When force is applied to the clutch pedal to release the clutch, the clutch master cylinder transmits this movement to the clutch release cylinder and bearing. As the bearing moves, it pushes against the fingers of the diaphragm spring of the pressure plate assembly, which in turn releases the clutch plate.

4   Terminology can be a problem regarding the clutch components because common names have in some cases changed from that used by the manufacturer. For example, the clutch release cylinder is sometimes referred to as a slave cylinder, the driven plate is also called the clutch plate or disc and the pressure plate assembly is also known as the clutch cover.

3   Clutch master cylinder - removal and installation

Caution: *Brake fluid will damage paint. Use care not to spill brake fluid on painted surfaces.*

1   Remove the battery (see Chapter 5).

2   Remove the brake fluid from the clutch master cylinder reservoir.

3   Place rags under the master cylinder to catch spillage.

4   Remove the driver's-side under-dash panel.

Removal

2008 and earlier models

5   Remove the air filter housing (see Chapter 5).

6   Squeeze the clamp and remove the reservoir hose from the master cylinder. Using needle-nosed pliers, pull out the clutch line retaining clip (see illustration).

7   Remove the clutch line fitting from the master cylinder. Plug the end of the clutch line to prevent debris from entering the line.

8   Working under the driver's side of the instrument panel, remove the spring clip and clevis pin and disconnect the clutch master cylinder pushrod from the pedal (see illustration).

9   Remove the two nuts retaining the clutch master cylinder to the firewall (see illustration).

10   Remove the clutch master cylinder from the vehicle.

2009 and later models

11   Working under the driver side of the instrument panel, remove the spring clip and clevis pin and disconnect the clutch master cylinder pushrod from the pedal.

12   Remove the two nuts retaining the clutch master cylinder to the firewall.

13   Remove the wiper blades and upper and lower cowl cover (see Chapter 4).

14   Remove the air filter housing assembly (see Chapter 4).

15   Remove the two bolts attaching the clutch line bracket to the vehicle.

16   Squeeze the clamp and remove the reservoir hose from the master cylinder.

17   Using a flare-nut wrench, remove the clutch line fitting from the master cylinder while holding the clutch line connector with a wrench. Plug the end of the clutch line to prevent debris from entering the line.

18   Remove the clutch master cylinder from the vehicle.

19   If necessary, using needle-nosed pliers, carefully pull out the clutch line retaining clip and clutch line connector from the master cylinder.

Installation

20   On 2008 and earlier models, before installing the new master cylinder, ensure a new O-ring is used for the clutch line fitting. If the fitting connector on 2009 and later models was removed from the master cylinder, also be sure to replace the O-ring.

21   Installation is the reverse of removal. Apply grease to the brake pedal clevis pin.

22   Fill the clutch master cylinder reservoir with brake fluid conforming to DOT 3 specifications and bleed the clutch system (see Section 6).

23   Check the interlock and pedal position switch adjustment (see Section 7).

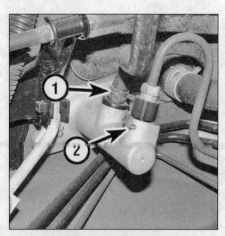

3.6 Clutch master cylinder details

1   *Fluid feed hose from reservoir*
2   *Clutch line retaining clip (pull out from opposite side, or tap out with a hammer and small punch)*

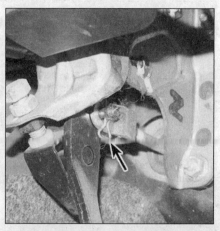

3.8 Remove the clip from the pushrod clevis pin, then remove the pin

3.9 Clutch master cylinder retaining nuts

4 Clutch release cylinder - removal and installation

Caution: *Brake fluid will damage paint. Use care not to spill brake fluid on painted surfaces.*
1   Remove the battery and battery tray (see Chapter 5).
2   Remove the air filter housing (see Chapter 4).
3   Remove the two bolts and detach the release cylinder from the transaxle (see illustration). On 2009 and later models, remove the bolt securing the clutch line bracket to the vehicle.
4   Use a flare-nut wrench to disconnect the clutch line from the release cylinder while holding the clutch line connector with a wrench.
5   On 2008 and earlier models, if the clutch line connector was removed, be sure to install a new O-ring.
Note: *The clutch line connector can be removed from the cylinder body by driving out the two roll pins with a small punch.*
6   Installation is the reverse of removal.
7   Fill the clutch master cylinder reservoir with brake fluid (conforming to DOT 3 specifications) and bleed the clutch hydraulic system (see Section 6).

5 Clutch damper (2008 and earlier models) - removal and installation

Note: *On 2009 and later models, the damper is part of the clutch master cylinder (see Section 3).*
Caution: *Brake fluid will damage paint. Use care not to spill brake fluid on painted surfaces.*
1   Place rags under the damper to catch spillage.
2   Remove the battery and battery tray (see

Chapter 5).
3   Remove the air filter housing (see Chapter 4).
4   Remove the banjo bolt for the clutch hose and disconnect the clutch line from the damper (see illustration).
5   Remove the two mounting bolts and detach the damper from the bracket.
6   Before installing the new damper, ensure new sealing washers are used for the clutch hose banjo fitting.
7   The remainder of the installation is the reverse of removal. Tighten the banjo bolt to the torque listed in this Chapter's Specifications.
8   Fill the clutch master cylinder with brake fluid (conforming to DOT 3 specifications) and bleed the clutch hydraulic system (see Section 6).

6 Clutch hydraulic system - bleeding

Caution: *Brake fluid will damage paint. Use care not to spill brake fluid on painted surfaces.*
1   The hydraulic system should be bled of all air whenever any part of the system has been removed, or if the fluid level has been allowed to fall so low that air has been drawn into the master cylinder. The procedure is similar to bleeding a brake system.
2   Fill the master cylinder with new brake fluid conforming to DOT 3 specifications.
Caution: *Do not re-use any of the fluid coming from the system during the bleeding operation or use fluid which has been inside an open container for an extended period of time.*
3   Remove the air filter housing (see Chapter 4 Section 9).
4   Locate the clutch release cylinder bleeder valve (see illustration 4.3). Remove the dust cap that fits over the bleeder valve and push a length of clear plastic hose over the valve. Place the other end of the hose

into a clear container with about two inches of DOT 3 brake fluid in it. The hose end must be submerged in the fluid.
5   Loosen the clutch release cylinder bleeder valve.
6   Have an assistant slowly push the clutch pedal in and hold it there. Check for the presence of air bubbles in the clutch fluid.
7   Tighten the clutch release cylinder bleeder valve.
8   Have your assistant slowly release the clutch pedal.
9   Loosen the clutch release cylinder bleeder screw and repeat Steps 5 through 8 until there are no more air bubbles visible in the fluid.
10   Disconnect the plastic hose.
11   Add fluid to the reservoir as necessary (see Chapter 1).

7 Clutch interlock and pedal position switches - replacement and adjustment

Note: *The interlock switch allows the engine to start only when the clutch pedal is depressed. The clutch pedal position switch turns off the cruise control when the clutch pedal is depressed. On vehicles without cruise control, an adjustment bolt is used in place of the pedal position switch.*

Replacement
Note: *Both switches are located at the top of the clutch pedal. The interlock switch is mounted higher up no the clutch pedal bracket; the pedal position switch is mounted lower on the bracket.*
1   Disconnect the wiring from the switch to be replaced.
2   Loosen and remove the locknut and remove the switch.
3   Installation is the reverse of removal.
4   Adjust the switch.

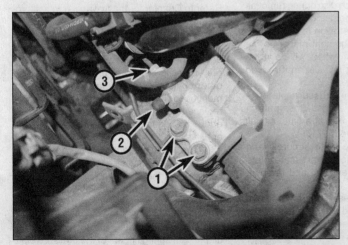

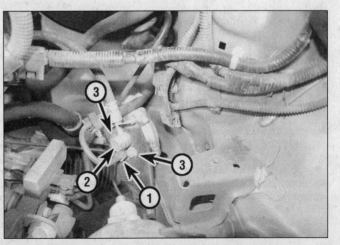

4.3 Clutch release cylinder details (2008 and earlier model shown, later models similar)

1   Mounting bolts   *3   Hydraulic line fitting*
2   Bleeder screw

5.4 Clutch damper details (2008 and earlier models)

1   Hydraulic line fitting   *3   Damper mounting bolts*
2   Banjo bolt

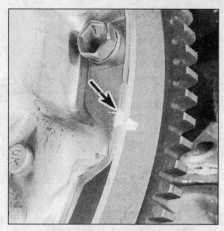

8.4 Mark the relationship of the pressure plate to the flywheel (if you're going to re-use the same pressure plate)

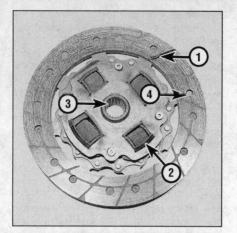

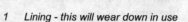

8.12 Examine the clutch disc for evidence of excessive wear, such as burned friction material, loose rivets, worn hub splines and distorted damper cushions or springs

1　Lining - this will wear down in use
2　Springs or dampers - check for cracking and deformation
3　Splined hub - the splines must not be worn and should slide smoothly on the transaxle input shaft splines
4　Rivets - these secure the lining and will damage the flywheel or pressure plate if allowed to contact the surfaces

8.15a Examine the pressure plate friction surface for score marks, cracks and evidence of overheating (blue spots)

Adjustment

5　Disconnect the electrical connector, loosen the locknut and turn the switch to adjust it.

6　Clutch pedal position switch: With the pedal RELEASED, install the switch so that the plunger just contacts the clutch pedal. screw in an additional 3/4 turn and secure the locknut.

7　Clutch interlock switch: With the pedal DEPRESSED approximately 2-1/2 inches (2008 and earlier models) or 1/2-inch (2009 and later models) from the floor, adjust the interlock switch to allow the vehicle to start with the clutch pedal in this position and tighten the locknut.

8　Reconnect the electrical connector.

8　Clutch components - removal, inspection and installation

Warning: Dust produced by clutch wear and deposited on clutch components is hazardous to your health. DO NOT blow it out with compressed air and DO NOT inhale it. DO NOT use gasoline or petroleum-based solvents to remove the dust. Brake system cleaner should be used to flush the dust into a drain pan. After the clutch components are wiped clean with a rag, dispose of the contaminated rags and cleaner in a labeled, covered container.

Removal

1　Access to the clutch components is normally accomplished by removing the transaxle. If the engine is being removed for major overhaul, then the opportunity should always be taken to check the clutch for wear and replace worn components as necessary. However, the relatively low cost of the clutch components compared to the time and labor involved in gaining access to them warrants their replacement any time the engine or transaxle is removed, unless they are new or in near-perfect condition. This includes the release cylinder.

2　Remove the transaxle (see Chapter 7A).

3　To support the clutch disc during removal, install a clutch alignment tool through the clutch disc hub (see illustration 8.16).

4　Scribe or paint alignment marks so the pressure plate and the flywheel will be in the same alignment during installation if reused (see illustration).

5　Slowly loosen the pressure plate-to-flywheel bolts. Work in a criss-cross pattern and loosen each bolt a little at a time until all spring pressure is relieved.

6　Hold the pressure plate securely and remove the bolts. Slide the pressure plate over the clutch alignment tool and remove. Remove the clutch disc.

7　To replace the release bearing, remove the release fork boot and pinch the release for retaining spring together using needle-nose pliers.

8　Pull the release fork from the transaxle through the boot opening and replace the release bearing.

9　When installing the release bearing, use hi-temp grease on all pivot points for the bearing and fork.

Inspection

10　Ordinarily, when a problem occurs in the clutch, it can be attributed to wear of the clutch driven plate assembly (clutch disc). However, all components should be inspected at this time.

11　Inspect the flywheel for cracks, heat checking, score marks and other damage. If the imperfections are slight, a machine shop can resurface it to make it flat and smooth. Refer to Chapter for the flywheel removal procedure.

12　Inspect the lining on the clutch disc. There should be at least 1/16-inch of lining above the rivet heads. Check for loose rivets, distortion, cracks, broken springs and other obvious damage (see illustration). As mentioned above, ordinarily the clutch disc is replaced as a matter of course, so if in doubt about the condition, replace it with a new one.

13　The release bearing should be replaced along with the clutch disc (see Section 4).

14　Inspect the pilot bearing using your finger. The bearing should turn smoothly and quietly and fit securely into the end of the crankshaft.

15　Check the machined surface and the diaphragm spring fingers of the pressure plate (see illustrations). If the surface is grooved or otherwise damaged, replace the pressure plate assembly. Also check for obvious dam-

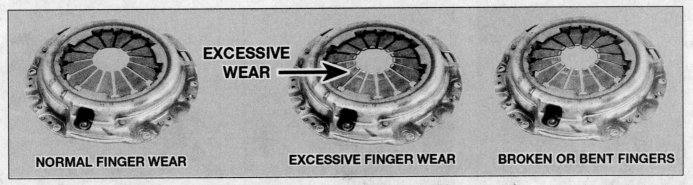

8.15b Replace the pressure plate if any of these conditions are noted

NORMAL FINGER WEAR   EXCESSIVE FINGER WEAR   BROKEN OR BENT FINGERS

EXCESSIVE WEAR

8.16 Center the clutch disc in the pressure plate with a clutch alignment tool, then tighten the pressure plate-to-flywheel bolts

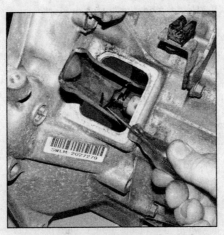

9.4a Use a screwdriver to release the spring from the ballstud. . .

9.4b. . . and remove the release fork with the bearing

age, distortion, cracking, etc. Light glazing can be removed with emery cloth or sandpaper. If a new pressure plate is indicated, new or factory rebuilt units are available.

Installation

16   Carefully wipe the flywheel and pressure plate machined surfaces clean. It's important that no oil or grease is on these surfaces or the lining of the clutch disc. Handle these parts only with clean hands. Apply hi-temp grease to the pilot bearing. Position the clutch disc and pressure plate with the clutch held in place with an alignment tool (see illustration). Make sure it's installed properly (most replacement clutch plates will be marked "flywheel side" or something similar - if not marked, install the clutch disc with the damper springs or cushion toward the transaxle).

17   Tighten the pressure plate-to-flywheel bolts only finger tight, working around the pressure plate in a criss-cross pattern.

18   Center the clutch disc by ensuring the alignment tool is through the splined hub and into the recess in the crankshaft. Wiggle the tool up, down or side-to-side as needed to bottom the tool. Tighten the pressure plate-to-

flywheel bolts a little at a time, working in a criss-cross pattern to prevent distortion of the cover. After all of the bolts are snug, tighten them in two steps to the torque listed in this Chapter's Specifications.

19   Remove the clutch alignment tool.

Note: *If the clutch alignment tool slides out of the clutch disc splines easily, it is properly aligned. If the clutch alignment tool is stuck and cannot be removed or must be forced to remove, loosen the pressure plate and align the clutch again.*

20   Install the transaxle and all components removed previously, tightening all fasteners to the proper torque specifications.

9   Clutch release bearing and fork - removal, inspection and installation

Removal

1   Unbolt the clutch release cylinder (see Section 4), but don't disconnect the hydraulic line. Support the release cylinder out of the

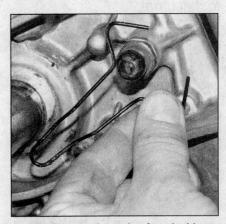

9.4c Remove the spring from inside the bellhousing

way with a piece of wire.

2   Remove the transaxle (see Chapter 7A).

3   Remove the release fork dust boot.

4   Release the spring from the ballstud, then pull the release fork out from the bellhousing. Recover the spring (see illustrations).

9.5 Slide the release bearing off the fork

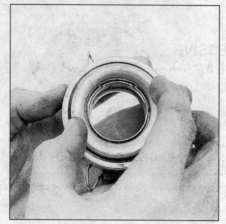

9.6 Hold the bearing by the outer race and
rotate the inner race while
applying pressure

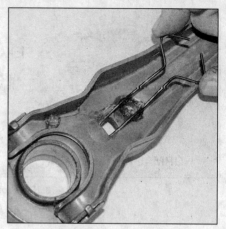

9.10 Installing the spring to the
release fork

5   Slide the release bearing off the end of the fork (see illustration).

Inspection
6   Hold the bearing by the outer race and rotate the inner race while applying pressure (see illustration). if the bearing doesn't turn smoothly, or if it's noisy replace it.
7   Wipe the bearing with a clean rag and inspect it for damage, wear and cracks. It's common practice to replace the bearing whenever a clutch is changed, to decrease the possibility of a bearing failure in the future.
Caution: *Don't immerse the bearing in solvent - it is sealed for life and to do so would ruin it.*
8   Check the release lever for cracks and bends.

Installation
9   Fill the inner groove of the release bearing with high-temperature grease. Lubricate the release fork ball socket, fork ends and release cylinder socket with the same grease.
10   Attach the release bearing to the release fork. Slide the curved end of the spring

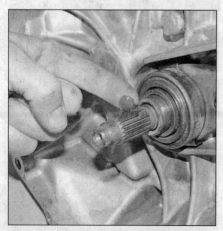

9.12 Lightly grease the shaft splines and
the release bearing guide

through the hole in the fork, then squeeze the ends together and attach it to the inside of the fork (see illustration).
11   Slide the release bearing onto the transaxle input shaft bearing retainer while passing the end of the fork through the opening in the bellhousing. Push the fork onto the ballstud until the spring clicks over the ball.
12   Apply a light coat of grease to the transaxle input shaft splines and release bearing guide (see illustration). Also apply a little grease to the face of the release bearing where it contacts the pressure plate diaphragm spring fingers.
13   The remainder of installation is the reverse of the removal procedure.

10   Pilot bearing - replacement

1   The pilot bearing is located in the end of the crankshaft and supports the end of the transaxle input shaft. Whenever the transaxle is removed, the pilot bearing should be checked for wear.
2   Remove the tranasaxle (see Chapter 7A).
3   The pilot bearing can be accessed through the center of the flywheel. Turn the bearing with your finger and check it for roughness, excess play, or any other sign of wear.
4   The bearing is press-fitted into the crankshaft - a slide hammer with a puller attachment will be required.
5   The new bearing should be lightly oiled, then tapped into the bore to the shoulder inside the crankshaft, using a bearing driver or a socket with a diameter slightly smaller than that of the bearing outer race.
6   Reinstall the transaxle (see Chapter 7A).

11   Driveaxles - general information

1   Power is transmitted from the transaxle to the wheels through a pair of driveaxles.

The inner end of each driveaxle is splined into the differential side gears. The outer ends of the driveaxles are splined to the wheel hubs and locked in place by a large nut.
2   The inner ends of the driveaxle are equipped with tripod-type constant velocity joints which are capable of both angular and axial motion.
3   The outer CV joints are the ball-and-cage type.
4   The boots should be inspected periodically for damage and leaking lubricant. Torn CV joint boots must be replaced as soon as possible or the joints can be damaged. Boot replacement involves removal of the driveaxle (see Section). The most common symptom of worn or damaged CV joints, besides lubricant leaks, is a clicking noise in turns, a clunk when accelerating after coasting and vibration at highway speeds. To check for wear in the CV joints and driveaxle shafts, grasp each axle (one at a time) and rotate it in both directions while holding the CV joint housings, feeling for play indicating worn splines or sloppy CV joints.

12   Driveaxles and intermediate shaft - removal and installation

Note: *On automatic transaxle models, an intermediate shaft and support bearing is used on the right (passenger's) side.*

Driveaxles
Removal
1   Loosen the front wheel lug nuts, raise the vehicle and support it securely on jackstands. Remove the wheel.
Note: *As an alternative you can leave the vehicle on the ground, remove the hubcap or center cap, then unstake and loosen the driveaxle nut (see the next Step).*
2   Unstake the driveaxle/hub nut (see illustration).

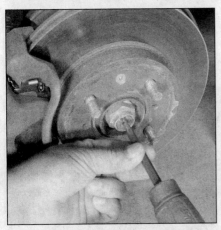

12.2 Use a punch or narrow chisel to unstake the driveaxle/hub nut from the slot in the driveaxle before attempting to unscrew the nut

12.3 To prevent the hub from turning while you're loosening the nut, wedge a prybar between two of the wheel studs

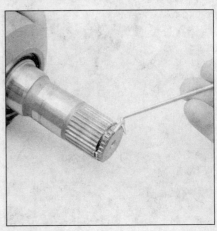

12.13a Pry the old retaining clip from the driveaxle with a small screwdriver or pick

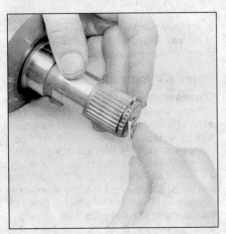

12.13b To install the new retaining clip, start one end in the groove and work the clip over the shaft end

12.17a A punch can be inserted into a brake disc cooling vane and rested against the brake caliper while tightening the driveaxle nut

12.17b Once tightened to the specified torque, stake the collar of the nut into the groove in the driveaxle

3   Unscrew the nut. To prevent the hub from turning, have an assistant apply the brakes firmly, or insert a punch into one of the cooling vanes in the brake disc and let it rest against the brake caliper. Alternatively, a long prybar can be braced across two of the wheel studs and rested on the ground (see illustration).

4   Remove the under-vehicle splash shield.

5   Drain the transaxle fluid (see Chapter 1). **Note:** *This won't be necessary if you are only removing the right side driveaxle.*

6   Detach the control arm from the steering knuckle (see Chapter 10).

7   Push the driveaxle out of the hub while pulling outward on the steering knuckle and hub assembly. If the driveaxle splines are frozen, free them by tapping the end of the drive-axle with a soft-faced hammer or a hammer and a brass punch, or use a puller to push the driveaxle from the hub.

8   Place a drain pan underneath the transaxle to catch any lubricant that may spill

out when the driveaxles are removed.

9   On manual transaxle vehicles, remove the right (passenger side) driveaxle heat shield bolts and heat shield.

10   For the left (driver's side) driveaxle, or the right driveaxle on manual transaxle models, use a prybar to carefully pry the inner CV joint out of the transaxle, then remove the driveaxle.

11   For the right (passenger side) driveaxle on models with an automatic transaxle, use a drift and a hammer to release the right drive-axle inner CV from the intermediate shaft.

12   Install a new driveaxle oil seal in the transaxle case, if necessary (see Chapter 7A or 7B).

Installation

13   If reusing the old driveaxle, install a new retaining clip on the axle end (or on the inter-mediate shaft, as applicable) before installation (see illustrations).

14   The remainder of installation is the reverse of the removal procedure, noting the following points:

15   When installing the driveaxle, push the driveaxle in sharply to seat the retaining ring on the inner CV joint into its groove in the dif-ferential side gear or onto the intermediate shaft. To ease insertion and seating of the retaining ring, position the gap in the ring at the bottom.

16   Reconnect the control arm to the steer-ing knuckle as described in Chapter 10.

17   Install a new driveaxle/hub nut. Tighten the nut to the torque listed in this Chapter's Specifications , then stake the collar of the nut into the groove in the driveaxle (see illustra-tions).

18   Refill the transaxle with the proper lubri-cant (see Chapter 1).

19   Install the wheel and lug nuts, lower the vehicle and tighten the lug nuts to the torque listed in the Chapter 1 Specifications.

12.21 Shift cable cover bolts

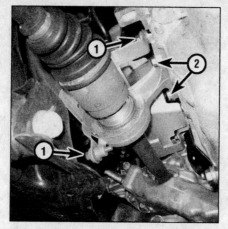

12.22 Intermediate shaft details

1   *Heat shield bolts (2009 and later models only; third bolt not visible)*
2   *Support bearing bracket bolts (third bolt not visible)*

13.3 Cut off the boot clamps and discard them - don't try to re-use old clamps

Intermediate shaft

20 Remove the right-side driveaxle (see above), then drain the transaxle fluid (see Chapter 1).
21 Remove the shift cable cover (see illustration).
22 If you're working on a 2009 or later model, remove the heat shield (see illustration).
23 Slide the intermediate shaft straight out of the transaxle, taking care not to damage the transaxle oil seal.
24 If necessary, replace the oil seal (see Chapter 7B).
25 If the support bearing is in need of replacement, take the shaft to an automotive machine shop to have the old bearing pressed out and a new one pressed in.
26 Install a new retaining clip on the end of the shaft (see illustrations 12.14a and 12.14b).
27 Install the shaft by reversing the removal

procedure. Tighten the support bearing bracket bolts to the torque listed in the Chapter 7B Specifications.
28 Install the wheel and lug nuts, then lower the vehicle and tighten the lug nuts to the torque listed in the Chapter 1 Specifcations 0.
29 Refill the transaxle with the proper fluid (see Chapter 1).

13 Driveaxle boot - replacement

Note: *If the CV joints are worn, indicating the need for an overhaul (usually due to torn boots), explore all options before beginning the job. Complete rebuilt driveaxles are available on an exchange basis, which eliminates much time and work. If you decide to rebuild a CV joint, check on the cost and availability of parts before disassembling the driveaxle.*

1   Remove the driveaxle from the vehicle (see Section 12).

2   Mount the driveaxle in a vise. The jaws of the vise should be lined with wood or rags to prevent damage to the driveaxle.

Inner CV joint and boot
Disassembly

3   If you have any doubts about the condition of the outer boot this would be a good time to replace it as well. Cut off both boot clamps and slide the boot towards the center of the driveaxle (see illustration).
4   Make alignment marks on the outer race and the tri-pot bearing assembly so they can be returned to their original position, then slide the outer race off the tri-pot bearing assembly.
5   Remove the snap-ring from the end of the axleshaft.
6   Secure the bearing rollers with tape, then remove the tri-pot bearing assembly from the axleshaft with a brass drift and a hammer (see illustration). Remove the tape, but don't let the rollers fall off and get mixed up.
7   Slide the old boot off the driveaxle and discard it.

Inspection
8   Clean the old grease from the outer race and the tri-pot bearing assembly. Carefully disassemble each section of the tri-pot assembly, one at a time so as not to mix up the parts, and clean the needle bearings with solvent.
9   Inspect the rollers, tri-pot, bearings and outer race for scoring, pitting or other signs of abnormal wear, which will warrant the replacement of the inner CV joint.

Reassembly
10 Wrap the splines of the axleshaft with tape to avoid damaging the new boot, then slide the boot onto the axleshaft (see illustration). Remove the tape.
11 Slide the tri-pot assembly onto the axleshaft.

13.6 Secure the bearing rollers with tape and drive the tri-pot off the shaft with a hammer and brass drift, then remove the stop-ring

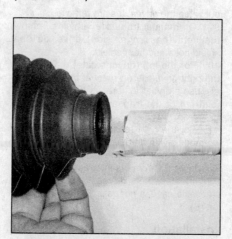

13.10 Wrap the splined area of the axleshaft with tape to prevent damage to the boot when installing it

13.12 Install the tri-pot assembly on the axleshaft, then install the snap-ring

13.13 Use plenty of CV joint grease to hold the needle bearings in place when you install the roller assemblies on the tri-pot, and make sure you put each roller in its original position

12   Install the outer snap-ring (see illustration).

13   Apply a coat of CV joint grease to the inner bearing surfaces to hold the needle bearings in place when reassembling the tri-pot assembly (see illustration). Make sure each roller is installed on the same post as before.

14   Pack the outer race with half of the grease furnished with the new boot and place the remainder in the boot. Install the outer race (see illustration). Make sure the marks you made on the tri-pot assembly and the outer race are aligned.

15   Seat the boot in the grooves in the outer race and the axleshaft, then adjust the driveaxle to the length listed in this Chapter's Specifications (see illustration).

16   With the shaft set to the proper length, equalize the pressure in the boot by inserting a blunt screwdriver between the boot and the outer race (see illustration). Don't damage the boot with the tool.

13.14 Pack the outer race with grease and slide it over the tri-pot assembly - make sure the match marks on the outer race and tri-pot line up

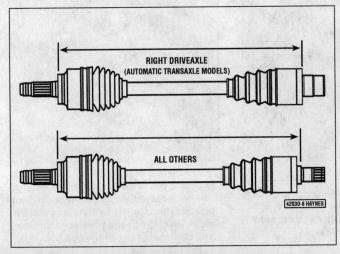

13.15 Measure the length of the driveaxle from the indicated points

13.16 Equalize the pressure inside the boot by inserting a small, dull screwdriver between the boot and the outer race

17   Install and tighten the new boot clamps (see illustrations).
18   Install the driveaxle assembly (see Section 12).

Outer CV joint and boot (front driveaxle)

Disassembly

19   Following Steps 3 through 7, remove the inner CV joint from the driveaxle and disassemble it.
20   If the driveaxle is equipped with a dynamic damper, scribe or paint a location mark on the axleshaft along the outer edge of the damper (the side facing the outer CV joint), cut the retaining clamp and slide the damper off.
Note: *If you're planning to replace the axleshaft and outer CV joint assembly, measure the distance between the inner CV joint boot and the dynamic damper so the damper can be placed in the proper position on the new driveaxle.*
21   Cut the boot clamps from the outer CV joint. Slide the boot off the shaft.

Inspection

22   Thoroughly wash the inner and outer CV joints in clean solvent and blow them dry with compressed air, if available
Warning: *Wear eye protection when using compressed air.*
23   Bend the outer CV joint housing at an angle to the axleshaft to expose the bearings, inner race and cage (see illustration). Inspect the bearing surfaces for signs of wear. If the bearings are damaged or worn, replace the driveaxle.

Reassembly

24   Slide the new outer boot onto the axle-shaft. It's a good idea to wrap tape around the splines of the shaft to prevent damage to the boot (see illustration 13.10). When the boot is in position, add the specified amount of grease (included in the boot replacement kit) to the outer joint and the boot (pack the joint with as much grease as it will hold and put the rest into the boot). Slide the boot on the rest of the way and install the new clamps (see illustrations 13.17a through 13.17e).
25   Slide the dynamic damper, if equipped, onto the shaft. Make sure its outer edge is aligned with the previously applied mark. Install a new retaining clamp.
Note: *If you're using a new axleshaft and outer CV joint assembly, install the damper on the shaft to the distance from the inner CV joint boot measured in Step 20.*
26   Clean and reassemble the inner CV joint by following Steps 8 through 17, then install the driveaxle as outlined in Section 12.

13.17a To install fold-over type clamps, bend the tang down. . .

13.17b. . . and flatten the tabs to hold it in place

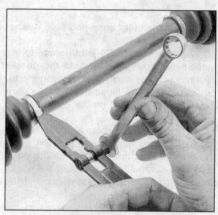

13.17c You'll need a special tightening tool to install band type boot clamps. Install the band with its end pointing in the direction of axle rotation and tighten it securely. . .

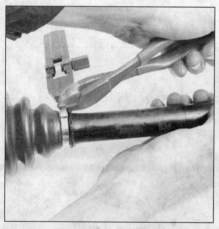

13.17d. . . bend back the end of the clamp, cut off the excess, then place a dimple in the center of the folded-over portion with a hammer and center punch

13.17e If you're installing crimp-type boot clamps, you'll need a pair of special crimping pliers (available at most auto parts stores)

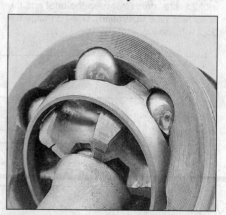

13.23 After the old grease has been rinsed away and the solvent has been blown out with compressed air, rotate the outer joint assembly through its full range of motion and inspect the bearing surfaces for wear and damage - if any of the ball bearings, the race or the cage look damaged, replace the driveaxle and outer joint assembly

Chapter 9
Brakes

Contents

Specifications

General
Brake fluid type.. See Chapter 1

Disc brakes
Minimum pad thickness	See Chapter 1
Brake disc minimum thickness	Cast into disc
Maximum disc runout	0.0014 inch
Maximum disc thickness variation	0.0008 inch

Drum brakes
Minimum shoe lining thickness	See Chapter 1
Maximum drum diameter	Cast into drum

Power brake booster
Booster-to-clevis hole center dimension	4.6 inches

Brake pedal dimensions
Free height from steel floor to top of pedal pad
2008 and earlier models	
Automatic transaxle	5 11/16 inches
Manual transaxle	5 9/16 inches
2009 and later models	
Automatic transaxle	5.8 inches
Manual transaxle	5.2 inches

Parking brake
Parking brake adjustment
2008 and earlier models	6 to 8 clicks
2009 and later models	5 to 7 clicks

Brake light and cruise control cancel switches
Clearance between pedal lever and threaded end of switch	0.03 to 0.08 inch

Torque specifications
Ft-lbs (unless otherwise indicated)

Note: *One foot-pound (ft-lb) of torque is equivalent to 12 inch-pounds (in-lbs) of torque. Torque values below approximately 15 foot-pounds are expressed in inch-pounds, since most foot-pound torque wrenches are not accurate at these smaller values.*

Brake caliper	
Caliper mounting bolts	17
Caliper mounting bracket bolts	79
Brake hose-to-caliper banjo bolt	25
Master cylinder-to-brake booster retaining nuts	11
Power brake booster mounting nuts	108 in-lbs

1   General information

General

1   The vehicles covered by this manual are equipped with hydraulically operated front and rear brake systems. The front brakes are disc-type and the rear brakes are either disc or drum type. Both are self-adjusting.

Hydraulic system

2   The hydraulic system consists of two separate circuits. The master cylinder has separate reservoirs for the two circuits, and, in the event of a leak or failure in one hydraulic circuit, the other circuit will remain operative and a warning indicator will light up on the instrument panel when a substantial amount of brake fluid is lost, showing that a failure has occurred.

Power brake booster

3   The power brake booster uses engine manifold vacuum to provide assistance to the brakes. It is mounted on the firewall in the engine compartment, directly behind the master cylinder.

Parking brake

4   Control cables are routed to the rear brake backing plates, where they actuate the drum brake shoes.

Service

5   After completing any operation involving disassembly of any part of the brake system, always test drive the vehicle to check for proper braking performance before resuming normal driving. When testing the brakes, perform the tests on a clean, dry, flat surface. Conditions other than these can lead to inaccurate test results.

6   Test the brakes at various speeds with both light and heavy pedal pressure. The vehicle should stop evenly without pulling to one side or the other. Under hard braking, the ABS system may engage, resulting in brake pedal pulsation. This is considered normal operation.

7   Tires, vehicle load and wheel alignment are factors which also affect braking performance.

Precautions

8   There are some general cautions and warnings involving the brake system on this vehicle:

a) *Use only brake fluid conforming to DOT 3 specifications.*

b) *The brake pads and linings contain fibers which are hazardous to your health if inhaled. Whenever you work on brake system components, clean all parts with brake system cleaner. Do not allow the fine dust to become airborne. Also, wear an approved filtering mask.*

c) *Safety should be paramount whenever any servicing of the brake components is performed. Do not use parts or fasteners which are not in perfect condition, and be sure that all clearances and torque specifications are adhered to. If you are at all unsure about a certain procedure, seek professional advice. Upon completion of any brake system work, test the brakes carefully in a controlled area before putting the vehicle into normal service. If a problem is suspected in the brake system, don't drive the vehicle until it's fixed.*

d) *Used brake fluid is considered a hazardous waste and it must be disposed of in accordance with federal, state and local laws. DO NOT pour it down the sink, into septic tanks or storm drains, or on the ground.*

e) *Clean up any spilled brake fluid immediately and then wash the area with large amounts of water. This is especially true for any finished or painted surfaces.*

2   Troubleshooting

PROBABLE CAUSE	CORRECTIVE ACTION

No brakes - pedal travels to floor

PROBABLE CAUSE	CORRECTIVE ACTION
1 Low fluid level	1 and 2 Low fluid level and air in the system are symptoms of another problem a leak somewhere in the hydraulic system. Locate and repair the leak
2 Air in system	1 and 2 Low fluid level and air in the system are symptoms of another problem a leak somewhere in the hydraulic system. Locate and repair the leak
3 Defective seals in master cylinder	3 Replace master cylinder
4 Fluid overheated and vaporized due to heavy braking	4 Bleed hydraulic system (temporary fix). Replace brake fluid (proper fix)

Brake pedal slowly travels to floor under braking or at a stop

PROBABLE CAUSE	CORRECTIVE ACTION
1 Defective seals in master cylinder	1 Replace master cylinder
2 Leak in a hose, line, caliper or wheel cylinder	2 Locate and repair leak
3 Air in hydraulic system	3 Bleed the system, inspect system for a leak

Brake pedal feels spongy when depressed

PROBABLE CAUSE	CORRECTIVE ACTION
1 Air in hydraulic system	1 Bleed the system, inspect system for a leak
2 Master cylinder or power booster loose	2 Tighten fasteners
3 Brake fluid overheated (beginning to boil)	3 Bleed the system (temporary fix). Replace the brake fluid (proper fix)
4 Deteriorated brake hoses (ballooning under pressure)	4 Inspect hoses, replace as necessary (it's a good idea to replace all of them if one hose shows signs of deterioration)

PROBABLE CAUSE

CORRECTIVE ACTION

Brake pedal feels hard when depressed and/or excessive effort required to stop vehicle

1 Power booster faulty	1 Replace booster
2 Engine not producing sufficient vacuum, or hose to booster clogged, collapsed or cracked	2 Check vacuum to booster with a vacuum gauge. Replace hose if cracked or clogged, repair engine if vacuum is extremely low
3 Brake linings contaminated by grease or brake fluid	3 Locate and repair source of contamination, replace brake pads or shoes
4 Brake linings glazed	4 Replace brake pads or shoes, check discs and drums for glazing, service as necessary
5 Caliper piston(s) or wheel cylinder(s) binding or frozen	5 Replace calipers or wheel cylinders
6 Brakes wet	6 Apply pedal to boil-off water (this should only be a momentary problem)
7 Kinked, clogged or internally split brake hose or line	7 Inspect lines and hoses, replace as necessary

Excessive brake pedal travel (but will pump up)

1 Drum brakes out of adjustment	1 Adjust brakes
2 Air in hydraulic system	2 Bleed system, inspect system for a leak

Excessive brake pedal travel (but will not pump up)

1 Master cylinder pushrod misadjusted	1 Adjust pushrod
2 Master cylinder seals defective	2 Replace master cylinder
3 Brake linings worn out	3 Inspect brakes, replace pads and/or shoes
4 Hydraulic system leak	4 Locate and repair leak

Brake pedal doesn't return

1 Brake pedal binding	1 Inspect pivot bushing and pushrod, repair or lubricate
2 Defective master cylinder	2 Replace master cylinder

Brake pedal pulsates during brake application

1 Brake drums out-of-round	1 Have drums machined by an automotive machine shop
2 Excessive brake disc runout or disc surfaces out-of-parallel	2 Have discs machined by an automotive machine shop
3 Loose or worn wheel bearings	3 Adjust or replace wheel bearings
4 Loose lug nuts	4 Tighten lug nuts

Brakes slow to release

1 Malfunctioning power booster	1 Replace booster
2 Pedal linkage binding	2 Inspect pedal pivot bushing and pushrod, repair/lubricate
3 Malfunctioning proportioning valve	3 Replace proportioning valve
4 Sticking caliper or wheel cylinder	4 Repair or replace calipers or wheel cylinders
5 Kinked or internally split brake hose	5 Locate and replace faulty brake hose

Brakes grab (one or more wheels)

1 Grease or brake fluid on brake lining	1 Locate and repair cause of contamination, replace lining
2 Brake lining glazed	2 Replace lining, deglaze disc or drum

Troubleshooting (continued)

PROBABLE CAUSE	CORRECTIVE ACTION

Vehicle pulls to one side during braking

PROBABLE CAUSE	CORRECTIVE ACTION
1 Grease or brake fluid on brake lining	1 Locate and repair cause of contamination, replace lining
2 Brake lining glazed	2 Deglaze or replace lining, deglaze disc or drum
3 Restricted brake line or hose	3 Repair line or replace hose
4 Tire pressures incorrect	4 Adjust tire pressures
5 Caliper or wheel cylinder sticking	5 Repair or replace calipers or wheel cylinders
6 Wheels out of alignment	6 Have wheels aligned
7 Weak suspension spring	7 Replace springs
8 Weak or broken shock absorber	8 Replace shock absorbers

Brakes drag (indicated by sluggish engine performance or wheels being very hot after driving)

PROBABLE CAUSE	CORRECTIVE ACTION
1 Brake pedal pushrod incorrectly adjusted	1 Adjust pushrod
2 Master cylinder pushrod (between booster and master cylinder)	2 Adjust pushrod incorrectly adjusted
3 Obstructed compensating port in master cylinder	3 Replace master cylinder
4 Master cylinder piston seized in bore	4 Replace master cylinder
5 Contaminated fluid causing swollen seals throughout system	5 Flush system, replace all hydraulic components
6 Clogged brake lines or internally split brake hose(s)	6 Flush hydraulic system, replace defective hose(s)
7 Sticking caliper(s) or wheel cylinder(s)	7 Replace calipers or wheel cylinders
8 Parking brake not releasing	8 Inspect parking brake linkage and parking brake mechanism, repair as required
9 Improper shoe-to-drum clearance	9 Adjust brake shoes
10 Faulty proportioning valve	10 Replace proportioning valve

Brakes fade (due to excessive heat)

PROBABLE CAUSE	CORRECTIVE ACTION
1 Brake linings excessively worn or glazed	1 Deglaze or replace brake pads and/or shoes
2 Excessive use of brakes down hills)	2 Downshift into a lower gear, maintain a constant slower speed (going
3 Vehicle overloaded	3 Reduce load
4 Brake drums or discs worn too thin required	4 Measure drum diameter and disc thickness, replace drums or discs as
5 Contaminated brake fluid	5 Flush system, replace fluid
6 Brakes drag	6 Repair cause of dragging brakes
7 Driver resting left foot on brake pedal	7 Don't ride the brakes

Brakes noisy (high-pitched squeal)

PROBABLE CAUSE	CORRECTIVE ACTION
1 Glazed lining	1 Deglaze or replace lining
2 Contaminated lining (brake fluid, grease, etc.)	2 Repair source of contamination, replace linings
3 Weak or broken brake shoe hold-down or return spring	3 Replace springs
4 Rivets securing lining to shoe or backing plate loose	4 Replace shoes or pads
5 Excessive dust buildup on brake linings	5 Wash brakes off with brake system cleaner
6 Brake drums worn too thin	6 Measure diameter of drums, replace if necessary
7 Wear indicator on disc brake pads contacting disc	7 Replace brake pads
8 Anti-squeal shims missing or installed improperly	8 Install shims correctly

PROBABLE CAUSE	CORRECTIVE ACTION

Brakes noisy (scraping sound)

1 Brake pads or shoes worn out; rivets, backing plate or brake	1 Replace linings, have discs and/or drums machined (or replace) shoe metal contacting disc or drum

Brakes chatter

1 Worn brake lining	1 Inspect brakes, replace shoes or pads as necessary
2 Glazed or scored discs or drums	2 Deglaze discs or drums with sandpaper (if glazing is severe, machining will be required)
3 Drums or discs heat checked	3 Check discs and/or drums for hard spots, heat checking, etc. Have discs/drums machined or replace them
4 Disc runout or drum out-of-round excessive	4 Measure disc runout and/or drum out-of-round, have discs or drums machined or replace them
5 Loose or worn wheel bearings	5 Adjust or replace wheel bearings
6 Loose or bent brake backing plate (drum brakes)	6 Tighten or replace backing plate
7 Grooves worn in discs or drums	7 Have discs or drums machined, if within limits (if not, replace them)
8 Brake linings contaminated (brake fluid, grease, etc.)	8 Locate and repair source of contamination, replace pads or shoes
9 Excessive dust buildup on linings	9 Wash brakes with brake system cleaner
10 Surface finish on discs or drums too rough after machining	10 Have discs or drums properly machined (especially on vehicles with sliding calipers)
11 Brake pads or shoes glazed	11 Deglaze or replace brake pads or shoes

Brake pads or shoes click

1 Shoe support pads on brake backing plate grooved or	1 Replace brake backing plate excessively worn
2 Brake pads loose in caliper	2 Loose pad retainers or anti-rattle clips
3 Also see items listed under Brakes chatter	

Brakes make groaning noise at end of stop

1 Brake pads and/or shoes worn out	1 Replace pads and/or shoes
2 Brake linings contaminated (brake fluid, grease, etc.)	2 Locate and repair cause of contamination, replace brake pads or shoes
3 Brake linings glazed	3 Deglaze or replace brake pads or shoes
4 Excessive dust buildup on linings	4 Wash brakes with brake system cleaner
5 Scored or heat-checked discs or drums	5 Inspect discs/drums, have machined if within limits (if not, replace discs or drums)
6 Broken or missing brake shoe attaching hardware	6 Inspect drum brakes, replace missing hardware

Rear brakes lock up under light brake application

1 Tire pressures too high	1 Adjust tire pressures
2 Tires excessively worn	2 Replace tires
3 Defective proportioning valve	3 Replace proportioning valve

Brake warning light on instrument panel comes on (or stays on)

1 Low fluid level in master cylinder reservoir (reservoirs with fluid level sensor)	1 Add fluid, inspect system for leak, check the thickness of the brake pads and shoes
2 Failure in one half of the hydraulic system	2 Inspect hydraulic system for a leak
3 Piston in pressure differential warning valve not centered soon as the light goes out)	3 Center piston by bleeding one circuit or the other (close bleeder valve as

Troubleshooting (continued)

PROBABLE CAUSE   CORRECTIVE ACTION

Brake warning light on instrument panel comes on (or stays on) (continued)

4 Defective pressure differential valve or warning switch	4 Replace valve or switch
5 Air in the hydraulic system	5 Bleed the system, check for leaks
6 Brake pads worn out (vehicles with electric wear sensors - small	6 Replace brake pads (and sensors) probes that fit into the brake pads and ground out on the disc when the pads get thin)

Brakes do not self adjust

Disc brakes

1 Defective caliper piston seals	1 Replace calipers. Also, possible contaminated fluid causing soft or swollen seals (flush system and fill with new fluid if in doubt)
2 Corroded caliper piston(s)	2 Same as above

Drum brakes

1 Adjuster screw frozen	1 Remove adjuster, disassemble, clean and lubricate with high-temperature grease
2 Adjuster lever does not contact star wheel or is binding	2 Inspect drum brakes, assemble correctly or clean or replace parts as required
3 Adjusters mixed up (installed on wrong wheels after brake job)	3 Reassemble correctly
4 Adjuster cable broken or installed incorrectly (cable-type adjusters)	4 Install new cable or assemble correctly

Rapid brake lining wear

1 Driver resting left foot on brake pedal	1 Don't ride the brakes
2 Surface finish on discs or drums too rough	2 Have discs or drums properly machined
3 Also see Brakes drag	

3 Anti-lock Brake System (ABS) - general information

1   The Anti-lock Brake System (ABS) is designed to maintain vehicle steerability, directional stability and optimum deceleration under severe braking conditions and on most road surfaces. It does so by monitoring the rotational speed of each wheel and controlling the brake line pressure to each wheel during braking. This prevents the wheels from locking up.

Components
Actuator assembly
2   The actuator assembly consists of an electric hydraulic pump and a pair of solenoid valves for each wheel. It's located at the right rear corner of the engine compartment (see illustration). The electric pump provides hydraulic pressure to charge the reservoirs in the actuator, which supplies pressure to the

3.2 ABS actuator

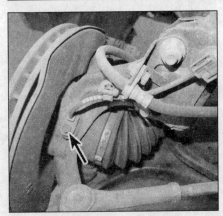

3.3a Location of the front wheel speed sensor

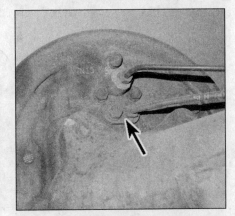

3.3b Location of the rear wheel speed sensor

4.5 Use a C-clamp to depress the piston into the caliper before removing the caliper and pads

braking system during ABS operation. The solenoid valves modulate brake line pressure during ABS operation. The body contains four valves - one for each wheel. The pump, the reservoirs and the solenoid valves are all housed in the actuator assembly.

Speed sensors

3   The speed sensors, which are located at each wheel, generate a sine wave current when the sensor rotors are turning (see illustrations). This analog voltage signal is monitored by the ABS control unit, which converts it to a digital signal from which it can determine wheel rotational speed.

ABS computer

4   The ABS control unit is the brain of the ABS system. The function of the control unit is to monitor and process information received from the wheel speed sensors to control the hydraulic line pressure, avoiding wheel lock up. The control unit also monitors the system for malfunctions, even when the ABS system is inactive during normal driving conditions.
5   Each time you start the engine, the system turns on the ABS warning light on the

instrument cluster for about a second. As soon as the engine is running, the light should go off. The system then performs a self-test the first time the vehicle speed exceeds four mph. You may hear a mechanical noise during the test; this is normal. If the system detects a problem, the ABS light will come on and remain on. A diagnostic code will also be stored in the control unit, which indicates the problem area or component.

4   Disc brake pads - replacement

Warning: *Disc brake pads must be replaced on both front wheels at the same time - never replace the pads on only one wheel. Also, the dust created by the brake system is harmful to your health. Never blow it out with compressed air and don't inhale any of it. An approved filtering mask should be worn when working on the brakes. Do not, under any circumstances, use petroleum-based solvents to clean brake parts. Use brake system cleaner only!*
1   Remove the cap from the brake fluid reservoir.
2   Loosen the front wheel lug nuts, raise

the front of the vehicle and support it securely on jackstands. Block the wheels at the opposite end.
3   Remove the wheels. Work on one brake assembly at a time, using the assembled brake for reference if necessary.
4   Inspect the brake disc carefully (see Section 6). If machining is necessary, follow the information in that Section to remove the disc.
5   Push the piston back into its bore to provide room for the new brake pads. A C-clamp can be used to accomplish this (see illustration). As the piston is depressed to the bottom of the caliper bore, the fluid in the master cylinder will rise. Make sure that it doesn't overflow. If necessary, siphon off some of the fluid.
6   Follow the accompanying photos (see illustrations) for the front or rear pad replacement procedure. Be sure to stay in order and read the caption under each illustration.
Note: *The illustrations show a front brake job, but the rear is almost identical.*
Note: *If the caliper won't fit over the pads, use a C-clamp to push the piston into the caliper a little farther*

4.6a Before disassembling the brake, wash it thoroughly with brake system cleaner and allow it to dry - position a drain pan under the brake to catch the residue - DO NOT use compressed air to blow off brake dust!

4.6b Remove the caliper lower mounting bolt (A); don't remove the brake hose banjo bolt (B) unless the caliper or hose requires service. . .

4.6c. . . then pivot the caliper up and secure it in that position with a piece of wire

4.6d Remove the inner brake pad

4.6e Remove the outer brake pad

4.6f Remove the lower pad retainer

4.6g Remove the upper pad retainer

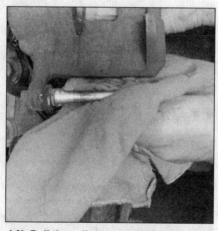

4.6h Pull the caliper upper slide pin out of the mounting bracket and clean it. . .

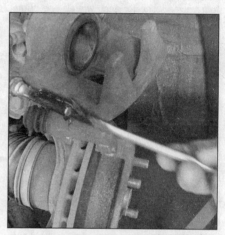

4.6i. . . then lubricate it with high-temperature brake grease

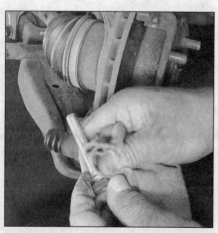

4.6j Also remove the lower slide pin and clean it. . .

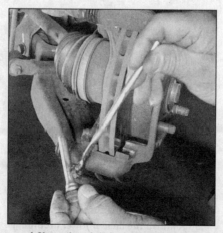

4.6k. . . then lubricate it with high-temperature brake grease and reinstall it

4.6l Install the lower. . .

4.6m. . . and upper pad retainers

4.6n Install the inner brake pad and shim, making sure the wear indicator is positioned correctly

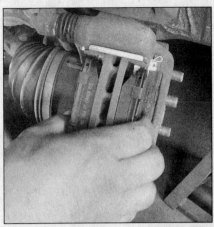

4.6o Install the outer brake pad. Note how the wear indicator and spring are oriented

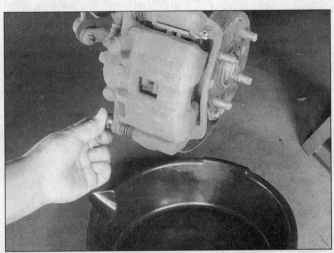

4.6p Swing the caliper down, install the caliper mounting bolt and tighten it to the torque listed in this Chapter's Specifications.

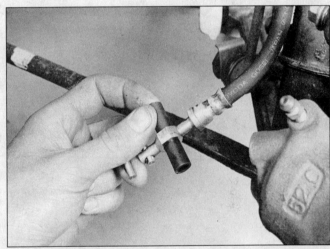

5.2 Using a piece of rubber hose of the appropriate size, plug the brake line

7   When reinstalling the caliper, tighten the mounting bolts to the torque listed in this Chapter's Specifications. Tighten the wheel lug nuts to the torque listed in the Chapter 1 Specifications.

8   After the job has been completed, firmly depress the brake pedal a few times to bring the pads into contact with the disc. Check the level of the brake fluid, adding some if necessary. Check the operation of the brakes carefully before placing the vehicle into normal service.

---

5   Disc brake caliper - removal and installation

Warning: *The dust created by the brake system is harmful to your health. Never blow it out with compressed air and don't inhale any of*

it. An approved filtering mask should be worn when working on the brakes. Do not, under any circumstances, use petroleum-based solvents to clean brake parts. Use brake system cleaner only!

Note: *If replacement is indicated (usually because of fluid leakage), it is recommended that the calipers be replaced, not overhauled. New and factory rebuilt units are available on an exchange basis, which makes this job quite easy. Always replace the calipers in pairs - never replace just one of them.*

Removal

1   Loosen the front wheel lug nuts, raise the front of the vehicle and place it securely on jackstands. Block the wheels at the opposite end. Remove the front wheel.

2   Remove the banjo bolt (see illustration 4.6b). Disconnect the brake hose from the caliper and discard the sealing washers (new

ones should be used on installation). Plug the brake hose to keep contaminants out of the brake system and to prevent losing any more brake fluid than is necessary (see illustration).

3   Remove the caliper mounting bolts and lift the caliper from its bracket.

Note: *See Section 4 for additional information (it's part of brake pad replacement).*

Installation

4   Installation is the reverse of removal. Tighten the caliper mounting bolt to the torque listed in this Chapter's Specifications and the wheel lug nuts to the torque in the Chapter 1 Specifications. Use new sealing washers for the brake hose-to-caliper banjo bolt.

5   Bleed the brake system (see Section 11). Make sure there are no leaks from the hose connections. Test the brakes carefully before returning the vehicle to normal service.

6   Brake disc - inspection, removal and installation

Inspection

1   Loosen the wheel lug nuts, raise the vehicle and support it securely on jackstands. Remove the wheel and install the lug nuts to hold the disc in place.

Note: *If the lug nuts don't contact the disc when screwed on all the way, install washers under them.*

2   Remove the brake caliper (see Section 5). It isn't necessary to disconnect the brake hose. After removing the caliper bolts, suspend the caliper out of the way with a piece of wire.

3   Visually inspect the disc surface for score marks and other damage. Light scratches and shallow grooves are normal after use and may not always be detrimental to brake operation, but deep scoring - over 0.039-inch (1.0 mm) - requires disc removal and refinishing by an automotive machine shop. Be sure to check both sides of the disc (see illustration). If pulsating has been noticed during application of the brakes, suspect disc runout.

4   To check disc runout, place a dial indicator at a point about 1/2-inch from the outer edge of the disc (see illustration). Set the indicator to zero and turn the disc. The indicator reading should not exceed the specified allowable runout limit. If it does, the disc should be refinished by an automotive machine shop.

Note: *When replacing the brake pads, it's a good idea to resurface the discs regardless of the dial indicator reading, as this will impart a smooth finish and ensure a perfectly flat surface, eliminating any brake pedal pulsation or other undesirable symptoms related to questionable discs. At the very least, if you elect not to have the discs resurfaced, remove the glaze from the surface with emery cloth using a swirling motion (see illustrations).*

5   It's absolutely critical that the disc not be machined to a thickness under the specified minimum allowable disc refinish thickness. The minimum wear (or discard) thickness is cast into the disc. The disc thickness can be checked with a micrometer (see illustration).

Removal

6   Remove the two caliper mounting bracket bolts (see illustration) and detach the caliper mounting bracket.

7   Remove the lug nuts which you installed to hold the disc in place and remove the disc from the hub.

Installation

8   Place the disc in position over the threaded studs.

9   Install the caliper mounting bracket over the disc and tighten the bolts to the torque listed in this Chapter's Specifications.

10   Install the caliper and tighten the bolts to the torque listed in this Chapter's Specifications0.

11   Install the wheel, then lower the vehicle to the ground. Tighten the lug nuts to the torque listed in the Chapter 1 Specifications.

6.3 The brake pads on this vehicle were obviously neglected, as they wore down completely and cut deep grooves into the disc - wear this severe means the disc must be replaced

6.4a To check disc runout, mount a dial indicator as shown and rotate the disc

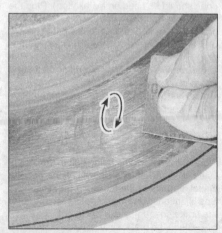

6.4b Using a swirling motion, remove the glaze from the disc surface with sandpaper or emery cloth

6.5 Use a micrometer to measure disc thickness

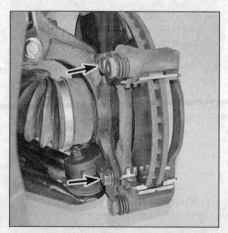

6.6 To remove the caliper mounting bracket, remove these bolts

Depress the brake pedal a few times to bring the brake pads into contact with the disc. Bleeding won't be necessary unless the brake hose was disconnected from the caliper. Check the operation of the brakes carefully before driving the vehicle.

7   Drum brake shoes - replacement

Warning: *Drum brake shoes must be replaced on both wheels at the same time - never replace the shoes on only one wheel. Also, the dust created by the brake system is harmful to your health. Never blow it out with compressed air and don't inhale any of it. An approved filtering mask should be worn when working on the brakes. Do not, under any circumstances, use petroleum-based solvents to clean brake parts. Use brake system cleaner only!*
Caution: *Whenever the brake shoes are replaced, the return and hold-down springs should also be replaced. Due to the continuous*

heating/cooling cycle the springs are subjected to, they lose tension over a period of time and may allow the shoes to drag on the drum and wear at a much faster rate than normal.

1   Loosen the wheel lug nuts, raise the rear of the vehicle and support it securely on jackstands. Block the front wheels to keep the vehicle from rolling. Remove the wheels.
2   Release the parking brake and remove the brake drums. If the brake drum is difficult to remove, remove the access plug from the backing plate, insert a small screwdriver through the hole, lift the adjuster lever off the adjusting wheel and turn the wheel with another screwdriver to back off the brake shoes (see illustrations). The drum should now come off.
3   All four rear brake shoes must be replaced at the same time, but to avoid mixing up parts, work on only one brake assembly at a time (see illustration).
4   Before disassembling anything, wash off the brake assembly with brake system cleaner

(see illustration). Follow the accompanying illustrations for the brake shoe replacement procedures (see illustrations). Be sure to stay in order and read the caption under each illustration.
5   Before reinstalling the drum, it should be checked for cracks, score marks, deep scratches and hard spots, which will appear as small discolored areas. If the hard spots cannot be removed with fine emery cloth or if any of the other conditions listed above exist, the drum must be taken to an automotive machine shop to have it resurfaced.
Caution: *Professionals recommend resurfacing the drums each time a brake job is done. Resurfacing will eliminate the possibility of out-of-round drums. If the drums are worn so much that they can't be resurfaced without exceeding the maximum allowable diameter, which is stamped into the drum, then new ones will be required. At the very least, if you elect not to have the drums resurfaced, remove the glaze from the surface with emery cloth using a swirling motion.*

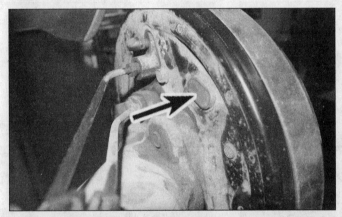

7.2a If the brake drums are hanging up on the brake shoes because of excessive wear, remove the access plug from the brake drum, insert a hooked tool and a small screwdriver (or a brake adjuster tool) and retract the shoes

7.2b Lift the adjuster lever off the adjuster wheel and rotate the adjuster wheel until the shoes are retracted sufficiently to allow drum removal (brake drum removed for clarity)

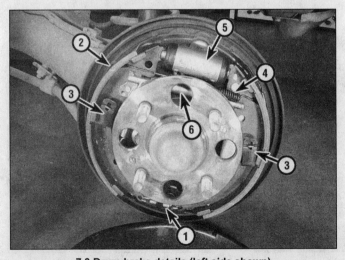

7.3 Drum brake details (left side shown)

1	Lower return spring	4	Adjuster spring
2	Leading shoe	5	Wheel cylinder
3	Hold-down spring	6	Adjuster

7.4a Before disassembling the brake, wash it thoroughly with brake system cleaner and allow it to dry - position a drain pan under the brake to catch the residue - DO NOT use compressed air to blow the brake dust off!

7.4b Remove the upper spring

7.4c Remove the hold-down spring from
the leading shoe

7.4d Unhook the lower return spring from
the leading shoe

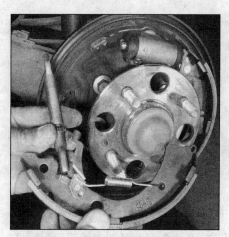

7.4e Remove the adjuster lever and
leading shoe

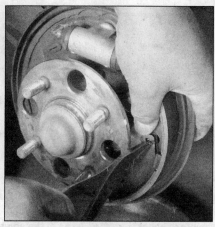

7.4f Remove the hold-down spring from
the trailing shoe

7.4g Remove the trailing shoe from the
backing plate. . .

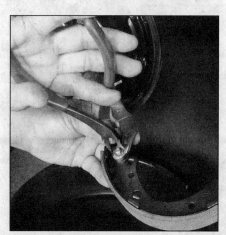

7.4h. . . then remove the retaining clip and
detach the parking brake lever from
the shoe

7.4i Clean the backing plate, then apply a
thin film of high-temperature brake grease
to the brake shoe contact areas

7.4j Connect the parking brake lever to the
new trailing shoe and secure it with a new
retaining clip

7.4k Place the trailing shoe against the backing plate and install the hold-down spring

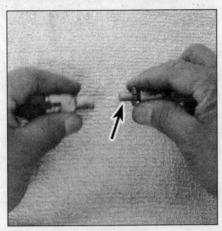

7.4l Clean and lubricate . . .

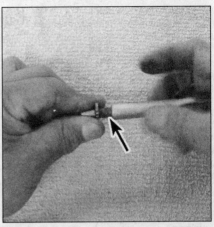

7.4m. . . the moving parts of the adjuster

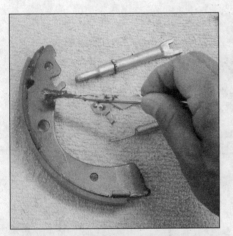

7.4n On the leading shoe, lubricate the contact point of the adjuster lever. . .

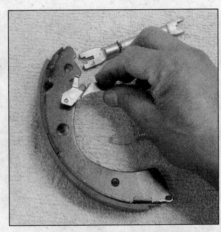

7.4o. . . then install the lever

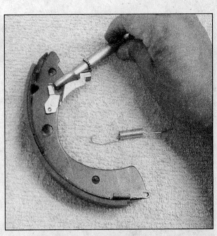

7.4p Install the adjuster onto the leading shoe. . .

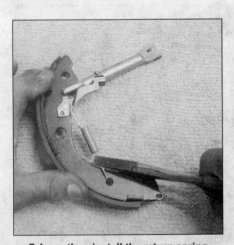

7.4q. . . then install the return spring

7.4r Attach the lower return spring to the bottom of each shoe. . .

7.4s. . . then insert the adjuster into the trailing shoe, making sure it properly engages the notch

6   Install the brake drum.

7   To make a preliminary adjustment of the brake, turn the adjuster star wheel until the brakes just begin to drag on the drum as it is turned, then back-off the star wheel until no dragging can be heard when you rotate the drum. Depress the brake pedal firmly several times, then rotate the drum to ensure that the brakes are not dragging. If they are, back off the star wheel a little more.

8   Mount the wheel, install the lug nuts, then lower the vehicle. Tighten the wheel lug nuts to the torque listed in the Chapter 1 Specifications.

9   Make a number of forward and reverse stops and operate the parking brake to adjust the brakes until satisfactory pedal action is obtained.

10   Check the operation of the brakes carefully before driving the vehicle.

8   Wheel cylinder - removal and installation

Note: *If replacement is warranted (usually because of fluid leakage or sticky operation) explore all options before beginning the job. New wheel cylinders are available, which makes this job quite easy. Never replace only one wheel cylinder. Always replace both of them at the same time.*

Removal

1   Remove the rear brake shoes (see Section 7).

2   Using a flare-nut wrench (if available), disconnect the brake line fitting from the wheel cylinder (see illustration). Plug the end of the brake line to prevent fluid loss and contamination.

3   Remove the two bolts securing the wheel cylinder to the backing plate and remove the wheel cylinder.

Installation

4   Installation is the reverse of removal. Tighten the wheel cylinder mounting bolts and line fitting securely.

5   Install the brake shoes and brake drum (see Section 7).

6   Bleed the brakes (see Section 11). Carefully test the brakes before resuming normal operation.

9   Master cylinder - removal and installation

Removal

1   Turn ignition switch to OFF and remove the battery (see Chapter 5).

2   Lift and remove the cowl cover between the wiper arm pivots (see illustration).

3   Manual transmission models: Remove

7.4t Secure the leading shoe with the hold-down spring

7.4u Install the upper spring

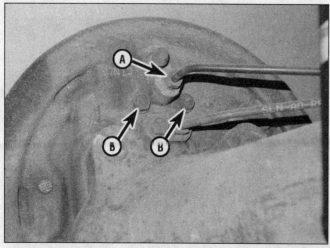

8.2 To detach the wheel cylinder from the brake backing plate, disconnect the brake line fitting (A), then remove the wheel cylinder bolts (B)

9.2 Lift the cover off the cowl

the bolt from the clutch hydraulic reservoir bracket and position the reservoir to the side (see illustration 9.6). DO NOT disconnect the hydraulic line from the clutch reservoir.

4   Remove the master cylinder reservoir cap and use a syringe (a turkey baster works good) to remove as much brake fluid as possible from the reservoir.

Warning: *If a turkey baster is used, it must never again be used in food preparation.*

Caution: *Brake fluid will damage paint. Cover all body panels and be careful not to spill any fluid during this proceedure.*

5   Unplug the electrical connector for the fluid level warning switch (see illustrations).

6   On 2009 and later models, squeeze the clamp and remove the reservoir hose from the master cylinder.

7   Place rags under the fittings and prepare caps or plastic bags to cover the ends of the lines once they're disconnected. Loosen the fittings at the ends of the brake lines where they enter the master cylinder. To prevent rounding off the flats, use a flare-nut wrench, which wraps around the fitting hex.

8   Pull the brake lines away from the master cylinder and plug the ends to prevent contamination.

9   Remove the nuts and washers attaching the master cylinder to the power booster. Pull the master cylinder off the studs to remove it. Again, be careful not to spill any remaining fluid as this is done.

10   Remove and discard the rod seal from the master cylinder.

Installation

11   Bench bleed the new master cylinder before installing it. Mount the master cylinder in a vise, with the jaws of the vise clamping on the mounting flange.

12   Attach a pair of master cylinder bleeder tubes to the outlet ports of the master cylinder (see illustration).

13   Fill the reservoir with brake fluid of the recommended type (see Chapter 1).

14   Slowly push the pistons into the master cylinder (a large Phillips screwdriver can be used for this) - air will be expelled from the pressure chambers and into the reservoir. Because the tubes are submerged in fluid, air can't be drawn back into the master cylinder when you release the pistons. Repeat the procedure until no more air bubbles are present.

15   Remove the bleed tubes, one at a time, and install plugs in the open ports to prevent fluid leakage and air from entering. Install the reservoir cap.

16   Install a new on the end of the master cylinder and coat it with silicone grease. The grooved side of the seal faces towards the master cylinder. Also coat the bore of the power brake booster.

17   Install the master cylinder over the studs on the power brake booster and tighten the nuts only finger-tight at this time.

18   Thread the brake line fittings into the master cylinder. Since the master cylinder is still a bit loose, it can be moved slightly so the fittings thread in easily. Don't strip the threads as the fittings are tightened.

19   Tighten the mounting nuts to the torque listed in this Chapter's Specifications0. Tighten the brake line fittings securely.

20   Fill the master cylinder reservoir with fluid, then bleed the lines at the master cylinder, followed by bleeding the remainder of the brake system (see Section 11). To bleed the lines at the master cylinder, have an assistant depress the brake pedal and hold it down. Loosen the fitting to allow air and fluid to escape (see illustration). Tighten the fitting, then allow your assistant to return the pedal to its rest position. Repeat this procedure on

both fittings until the fluid is free of air bubbles, then bleed the rest of the system. Check the operation of the brake system carefully before driving the vehicle.

Warning: *If you do not have a firm brake pedal at the end of the bleeding procedure, or have any doubts as to the effectiveness of the brake system, DO NOT drive the vehicle. Have it towed to a dealer service department or other qualified repair shop for diagnosis.*

21   Check and adjust the brake pedal height and freeplay.

22   Reconnect the battery and perform the necessary re-learn procedures (see Chapter 1).

9.5a Master cylinder details (2008 and earlier models)

1   *Electrical connector*
2   *Fluid lines*
3   *Mounting nuts*
4   *Clutch master cylinder hydraulic reservoir bracket (manual transaxle models)*

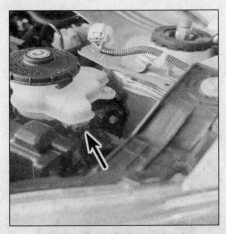

9.5b Master cylinder reservoir electrical connector (20009 and later model)

9.12 The best way to bleed the master cylinder before installing it is with a pair of bleeder tubes

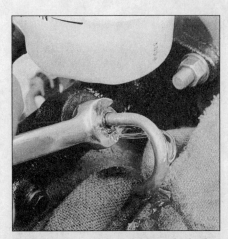

9.20 Have an assistant depress the brake pedal and hold it down, then loosen the fitting nut, allowing the air and fluid to escape; repeat this procedure on both fittings until the fluid is clear of air bubbles

10 Brake hoses and lines - inspection and replacement

Inspection

1   About every six months, with the vehicle raised and supported securely on jackstands, the flexible hoses which connect the steel brake lines with the front and rear brake assemblies should be inspected for cracks, chafing of the outer cover, leaks, blisters and other damage. These are important and vulnerable parts of the brake system and inspection should be complete. A light and mirror will be helpful for a thorough check. If a hose exhibits any of the above conditions, replace it with a new one.

Replacement

Brake hoses

2   Loosen the wheel lug nuts, raise the vehicle and support it securely on jackstands. Remove the wheel.

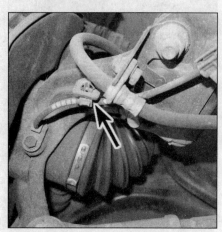

10.4 Carefully pry off the retaining clip (2008 and earlier models)

3   Have a drip pan and some rags ready to contain the brake fluid and control any spills.
Caution: *Brake fluid will damage paint. Be sure to keep it off painted surfaces and don't touch any body panels with brake fluid on your hands.*

Front brake hoses

4   On 2008 and earlier models, release the retaining clip holding the wheel speed sensor connector to the brake hose mounting bracket. Do not disconnect the electrical connector (see illustration).
5   Use a flare nut wrench to disconnect the brake line from the brake hose joint (see illustrations).
6   On 2008 and earlier models, remove the bolts holding the brake hose bracket to the body.
7   Remove the bolt from the banjo fitting on the caliper and remove the brake hose.
8   Installation is the reverse of removal. Use new sealing washers on the banjo fitting and ensure there are no twists or kinks in the brake hose.
9   Proceed to Step 15.

Rear brake hoses

10   At the frame bracket, use a flare nut wrench to disconnect the brake hose from the brake line.
11   Use pliers to remove the retaining clip from the brake hose. Discard the retaining clip.
12   Disconnect the hose and retainers from the lower bracket in the same manner.
13   Installation is the reverse of removal. Use new retaining clips and ensure there are no twists or kinks in the brake hose.
14   Start the threads by hand, install the new retaining clip, then tighten the fitting to the torque listed in this Chapter's Specifications. A soft hammer can be used to seat the retaining clips into the bracket.

Front and rear brake hoses

15   Bleed the brakes at the wheel(s) you've been working on.
16   Install the wheel and lug nuts, lower the vehicle and tighten the lug nuts to the torque listed in the Chapter 1 Specifications.
17   Check the brake system operation before placing the vehicle in normal service.

Metal brake lines

18   When replacing brake lines, be sure to use the correct parts. Don't use copper tubing for any brake system components. Purchase steel brake lines from a dealer or auto parts store.
19   Prefabricated brake line, with the tube ends already flared and fittings installed, is available at auto parts stores and dealer parts departments.
20   When installing the new line, make sure it's securely supported in the brackets and has plenty of clearance between moving or hot components.
21   After installation, check the master cylinder fluid level and add fluid as necessary. Bleed the brake system (see Section 11) and test the brakes carefully before driving the vehicle in traffic.

11 Brake hydraulic system - bleeding

Warning: *Wear eye protection when bleeding the brake system. If the fluid comes in contact with your eyes, immediately rinse them with water and seek medical attention.*
Note: *Bleeding the hydraulic system is necessary to remove any air that manages to find its way into the system when it's been opened during removal and installation of a hose, line, caliper or master cylinder.*

10.5a Use a flare nut wrench (2008 and earlier models). . .

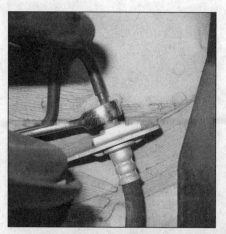

10.5b Loosen the threaded fitting on the brake line (use a flare-nut wrench to protect the corners of the nut). . .

10.5c. . . then remove the U-clip (2009 and later models)

1   You'll probably have to bleed the system at all four brakes if air has entered it due to low fluid level, or if the brake lines have been disconnected at the master cylinder.

2   If a brake line was disconnected only at a wheel, then only that caliper or wheel cylinder must be bled.

3   If a brake line is disconnected at a fitting located between the master cylinder and any of the brakes, that part of the system served by the disconnected line must be bled.

4   Remove any residual vacuum from the brake power booster by applying the brake several times with the engine off.

5   Remove the master cylinder reservoir cover and fill the reservoir with brake fluid. Reinstall the cover. Check the fluid level often during the bleeding operation and add fluid as necessary to prevent the fluid level from falling low enough to allow air bubbles into the master cylinder.

Caution: *Turn the ignition switch off and disconnect the electrical connectors for the ABS actuator or detach the battery ground cable.*

6   Have an assistant on hand, as well as a supply of new brake fluid, a clear plastic container partially filled with clean brake fluid, a length of 3/16-inch plastic, rubber or vinyl tubing to fit over the bleeder valve and a wrench to open and close the bleeder valve.

7   Beginning at the left front wheel, loosen the bleeder valve slightly, then tighten it to a point where it's snug but can still be loosened quickly and easily.

8   Place one end of the tubing over the bleeder valve and submerge the other end in brake fluid in the container (see illustration).

9   Have the assistant pump the brakes slowly a few times to get pressure in the system, then hold the pedal down firmly.

10   While the pedal is held down, open the bleeder valve just enough to allow a flow of fluid to leave the valve. Watch for air bubbles to exit the submerged end of the tube. When the fluid flow slows after a couple of seconds, close the valve and have your assistant release the pedal.

11   Repeat Steps 9 and 10 until no more air is seen leaving the tube, then tighten the bleeder valve and proceed to the right front wheel, the right rear wheel and the left rear wheel, in that order, and perform the same procedure. Check the fluid in the master cylinder reservoir frequently.

12   Never use old brake fluid. It contains moisture which will deteriorate the brake system components and could cause the fluid to boil, which could render the brake system inoperative.

13   Refill the master cylinder with fluid at the end of the operation. On models with ABS, reconnect the electrical connectors to the ABS actuator, or reconnect the battery.

14   Check the operation of the brakes. The pedal should feel solid when depressed, with no sponginess. If necessary, repeat the entire process.

Warning: *Do not operate the vehicle if you're in doubt about the effectiveness of the brake system.*

12   Power brake booster - check, replacement and adjustment

Check

Operating check

1   Depress the brake pedal several times with the engine off and make sure there's no change in the pedal reserve distance.

2   Depress the pedal and start the engine. If the pedal goes down slightly, operation is normal.

Airtightness check

3   Start the engine and turn it off after one or two minutes. Depress the brake pedal slowly several times. If the pedal depresses less each time, the booster is airtight.

4   Depress the brake pedal while the engine is running, then stop the engine with the pedal depressed. If there's no change in the pedal reserve travel after holding the pedal for 30 seconds, the booster is airtight.

Replacement

Note: *Power brake booster units shouldn't be disassembled. They require special tools not normally found in most automotive repair stations or shops. They're fairly complex and, because of their critical relationship to brake performance, should be replaced with a new or rebuilt one.*

5   Remove the master cylinder (see Chapter 5).

6   Release the clamp and disconnect the vacuum hose from the brake booster.

7   Unclip the brake lines from the retainer on the firewall.

8   Remove the bolts securing the filter canister and remove the canister.

9   On 2008 and earlier models, working under the dash, remove the instrument panel brace (see illustration).

10   Pull out the safety clip, then remove the clevis pin to detach it from the brake pedal (see illustration).

11   Remove the four mounting nuts securing the booster to the firewall (see illustration 12.10), then remove the booster from the engine compartment.

12   On 2008 and earlier models, before installing the new booster, measure the booster input rod length and adjust it if necessary.

13   Installation is the reverse of removal. Use a new gasket between the booster and the firewall.

11.8 When bleeding the brakes, a hose is connected to the bleed screw at the caliper or wheel cylinder and then submerged in brake fluid - air will be seen as bubbles in the tube and container (all air must be expelled before moving to the next wheel)

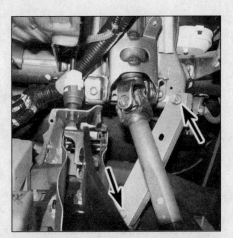

12.9 Remove the fasteners securing the instrument panel brace

12.10 Clevis pin safety clip (A), clevis pin (B) and bottom mounting nuts (C)

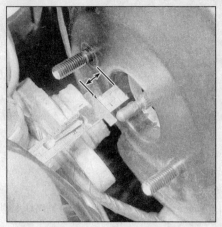

12.14 Measure the distance between the power brake booster and the hole in the clevis and compare your measurement to the dimension listed in this Chapter's Specifications; if necessary, adjust the clevis before installing the power brake booster

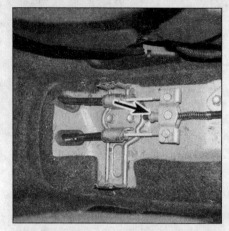

13.5 The parking brake adjustment nut is accessed through a hole in the lever trim

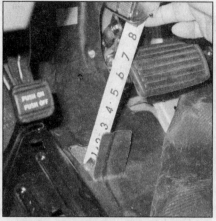

14.2 With the brake pedal fully released (up), from the middle of the pedal on the left side, measure the distance from the bottom edge of the pedal pad to the floor

Adjustment (2008 and earlier models)

14   Measure the distance between the power brake booster and the hole in the input rod clevis (see illustration) and compare it to the dimension listed in this Chapter's Specifications0. If necessary, loosen the adjusting nut and turn the clevis in or out to the specified length, then install the booster, connect the clevis to the brake pedal, and tighten the nut securely.

13 Parking brake - check and adjustment

Check

1   The parking brake lever, when properly adjusted, should travel the correct number of clicks when a 45 pound force is applied - see this Chapter's Specifications.
2   If the parking brake lever travels less than the specified minimum number of clicks, it might not be releasing completely and the shoes could even be dragging against the drum. If it moves more than the specified maximum number of clicks, the parking brake may not hold adequately on an incline, allowing the car to roll.

Adjustment

3   Loosen the rear wheel lug nuts. Raise the vehicle and support it securely on jackstands. Remove the rear wheels.
4   Remove the center console (see Chapter 11).
5   Release the parking brake lever and loosen the adjusting nut on the cable equalizer (see illustration).
6   Install the lug nuts snugly to each rear brake drum or disc to support it against the

hub flange.
7   Depress and release the brake pedal several times then pull up on the parking brake lever one click.
8   Tighten the cable adjusting nut until the parking brakes just barely drag when you or an assistant rotate the rear wheels.
9   Release the parking brake lever and confirm that the parking brakes do not drag when the rear wheels are rotated. Adjust again if necessary.
10   The parking brakes should be fully applied when the parking brake lever is pulled up completely.
11   Install the rear wheels, lower the vehicle

![Diagram of brake pedal with labeled points A, B, C] 92095-9-13.1 HAYNES

14.3 Brake pedal height measuring and adjustment:

A   *Pushrod/clevis locknut*
B   *Brake power booster push rod (turn this rod to raise or lower the pedal)*
C   *Pedal height measurement points*

and replace the center console.
12   Check the parking brake for proper operation and adjustment before placing the vehicle in normal service.
13   Remove the rubber adjuster hole plugs from the brake drums.
14   Turn the star wheel until it locks the drum or disc, then back it off five or six notches.
15   Turn the drum and make sure there is no drag. Readjust it if necessary to obtain a close adjustment with zero drag. Reinstall the hole plugs.
16   Tighten the adjusting nut (see Step 4 or 5) so you get the proper number of clicks when you apply a 45 pound force to the lever.
17   Release the parking brake and turn the rear drums again to verify that there is no drag. If drag exists, go over the adjustment procedure until it's correct.
18   Reinstall the wheels, lower the vehicle and tighten the lug nuts to the torque listed in the Chapter 1 Specifications.

14 Brake pedal - adjustment

Note: *The brake pedal height and freeplay are not adjustable on all models but can be inspected to rule out damage or wear to any of the related components.*
1   Remove the brake pedal position (BPP) switch (see Section).
2   Pull the carpet back and find the insulator cutout, then with the brake pedal fully released (up), measure the distance from the brake pedal pad to the floor (see illustration).
3   The height should be within the Specifications listed at the beginning of this Chapter. If it is not, inspect the brake pedal arm and linkage for wear and damage. On models that are adjustable, perform a pedal adjustment by loosening the locknut on the pushrod and then turning the pushrod with a pair of pliers to raise of lower the pedal (see illustration).

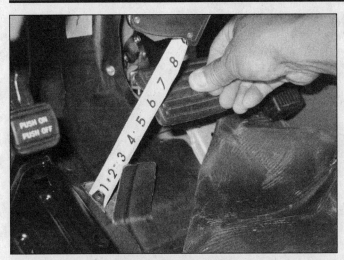

14.5 To measure brake pedal freeplay, lightly press down on the pedal and measure the distance that it moves freely before resistance is felt

15.3 BPP switch details:

1   *Threaded barrel section*
2   *Rubber pad*
3   *Clearance between switch and rubber pad on the brake pedal arm*
4   *Switch mount*

4   Install the BPP switch and check the brake pedal freeplay.

5   Press down lightly on the brake pedal to measure the freeplay (see illustration). This distance should be very small and within the Specifications listed at the beginning of this Chapter. If it isn't, check the brake booster pushrod clevis, lock pin and the hole in the brake pedal arm for excessive wear. Also make sure the BPP switch is properly installed (see Section 15).

15   Brake Pedal Position (BPP) switch - replacement

1   Disconnect the electrical connector from the brake pedal position (BPP) switch (see illustration 12.3).

2   Rotate the switch counterclockwise until it unlocks from its mount. With the switch loose, it can be pulled straight out.

3   To install the switch, insert it into its mount until the switch's plunger is compressed and the threaded barrel section of the switch is against the rubber pad on the brake pedal arm. Lightly lift up on the brake pedal to make sure it's fully released (up). Rotate the switch 45-degrees clockwise to lock it into place. With the switch secured in place, the proper gap between the switch and the pedal arm is automatically set (see illustration). Note: Make certain that the brake pedal arm is fully released (up) while installing the BPP switch.

4   Plug the electrical connector into the switch.

5   Confirm proper operation of the brake lights when the pedal is depressed and released. If necessary, adjust the switch again until the proper adjustment is achieved.

Note

Chapter 10
Suspension and steering

Contents

Specifications

Torque specifications

Note: *One foot-pound (ft-lb) of torque is equivalent to 12 inch-pounds (in-lbs) of torque. Torque values below approximately 15-ft-lbs. are expressed in inch-pounds, since most foot-pound torque wrenches are not accurate at these smaller values.*

Front suspension

	Ft-lbs (unless otherwise indicated)	Nm
Strut/coil spring assembly		
Strut upper mounting nut	33	44
Strut piston rod nut	25	34
Strut-to-knuckle bolt/nuts*		
2007 and 2008 models	76	103
2009 and later models	66	90
Stabilizer bar		
Stabilizer bushing clamp bolts		
2007 and 2008 models	25	34
2009 and later models	16	21
Stabilizer bar link nuts*		
Upper	22	29
Lower	28	38
Control arm		
Front pivot bolt*		
2007 and 2008 models	51	69
2009 and later models	69	93
Rear bushing bracket bolts*	69	93
Balljoint-to-steering knuckle nut*		
2007 and 2008 models	36 to 43	49 to 59
2009 and later models	47 to 55	64 to 74
Subframe bolts*	69	93
Wheel lug nuts	See Chapter 1	

Replace fastener whenever removed.

Torque specifications	Ft-lbs (unless otherwise indicated)	Nm

Note: *One foot-pound (ft-lb) of torque is equivalent to 12 inch-pounds (in-lbs) of torque. Torque values below approximately 15-ft-lbs. are expressed in inch-pounds, since most foot-pound torque wrenches are not accurate at these smaller values.*

Rear suspension

Shock absorber		
Upper mounting nut*	22	29
Lower mounting bolt*	40	54
Rear axle beam pivot bolt*	69	93
Hub/bearing nut*	134	181
Brake backing plate/spindle bolts*	61	83

Steering

Airbag module bolts*		
2007 and 2008 models	86 in-lbs	9.8
2009 and later models	84 in-lbs	9.4
Steering gear		
2007 and 2008 models		
Right-side mounting bracket bolts (10 mm)	33	44
Left-side mounting bolt	38	52
Rear stiffener plate bolts*		
Short bolt (right side)	36	49
Long bolt (left side)	38	52
Short bolt (left side)	36	49
2009 and later models		
Steering gear-to-crossmember bolts*	44	60
Stiffener plate bolts (short)	43	59
Steering wheel bolt	29	39
Steering column		
Steering column shaft U-joint pinch bolt(s)	21	28
Upper mounting nuts	113 in-lbs	13
Lower mounting bolts	16	22
Tie-rod end-to-steering knuckle nuts		
2007 and 2008 models	36 to 43	49 to 59
2009 and later models	47 to 55	64 to 74
Wheel lug nuts	See Chapter 1	

Replace fastener whenever removed.

Front suspension components

1	Strut/coil spring assembly	4	Control arm	6	Steering knuckle
2	Steering gear boot	5	Tie-rod end	7	Balljoint
3	Stabilizer bar				

Typical rear suspension components

1 Shock absorber
2 Coil spring

3 Rear axle beam

1 General information

1   The front suspension system (see illustration) is a strut/coil spring design. The upper end of each strut is attached to the vehicle body. The lower end of the strut is connected to the upper end of the steering knuckle. The steering knuckle is attached to a balljoint mounted on the outer end of the control arm. The balljoint is an integral part of the control arm; if the balljoint is worn, the control arm must be replaced. A stabilizer bar is used on all models. The bar is attached to the subframe with a pair of clamps and to the struts with link rods.

2   The rear suspension system (see illustration) uses separate shock absorbers and coil springs, The upper ends of the shocks are attached to the vehicle body and their lower ends are attached to the rear suspension beam. The coil springs are positioned between the rear suspension beam and the vehicle body.

3   The rack-and-pinion steering gear is bolted to the subframe. The steering gear actuates the tie-rods, which are attached to the steering knuckles. The inner ends of the tie-rods are protected by rubber boots which should be inspected periodically for secure attachment, tears and leaking lubricant (which would indicate failed rack seals).

4   The power assist system consists of an electric motor system, which should be checked on a periodic basis.

5   The steering wheel operates the steering shaft, which actuates the steering gear through universal joints. Looseness in the steering can be caused by wear in the steering shaft universal joints, the steering gear, or the tie-rod ends, as well as loose retaining bolts.

6   Frequently, when working on the suspension or steering system components, you may come across fasteners which seem impossible to loosen. These fasteners on the under side of the vehicle are continually subjected to water, road grime, mud, etc., and can become rusted or frozen, making them extremely difficult to remove. In order to unscrew these stubborn fasteners without damaging them (or other components), be sure to use lots of penetrating oil and allow it to soak in for a while. Using a wire brush to clean exposed threads will also ease removal of the nut or bolt and prevent damage to the threads. Sometimes a sharp blow with a hammer and punch will break the bond between a nut and bolt threads, but care must be taken to prevent the punch from slipping off the fastener and ruining the threads. Heating the stuck fastener and surrounding area with a torch sometimes helps too, but isn't recommended because of the obvious dangers associated with fire. Long breaker bars and extension, or cheater, pipes will increase leverage, but never use an extension pipe on a ratchet - the ratcheting mechanism could be damaged. Sometimes tightening the nut or bolt first will help to break it loose. Fasteners that require drastic measures to remove should always be replaced with new ones.

7   Since most of the procedures dealt with in this Chapter involve jacking up the vehicle and working underneath it, a good pair of jackstands will be needed. A hydraulic floor jack is the preferred type of jack to lift the vehicle, and it can also be used to support certain components during various operations.

Warning: *Never, under any circumstances, rely on a jack to support the vehicle while working on it. Whenever any of the suspension or steering fasteners are loosened or removed they must be inspected and, if necessary, replaced with new ones of the same part number or of original equipment quality and design. Torque specifications must be followed for proper reassembly and component retention. Never attempt to heat or straighten any suspension or steering components. Instead, replace any bent or damaged part with a new one.*

2 Strut/coil spring assembly (front) - removal, inspection and installation

Removal

1   If you're working on a 2009 or later model, remove the cowl cover and lower cowl (see Chapter 11).

2   Loosen the front wheel lug nuts, raise the front of the vehicle and support it securely on jackstands. Remove the wheels.

3   Disconnect the wheel speed sensor wiring harness and the brake hose from the strut (see illustration).

4   Remove the wheel speed sensor from the steering knuckle.

5   Disconnect the stabilizer bar link from the strut (see illustration).

6   Remove the strut-to-knuckle nuts and knock the bolts out with a hammer and punch.

7   Separate the strut from the steering knuckle.

Caution: *Don't allow the steering knuckle to fall too far outward - the driveaxle inner CV joint could become overextended.*

8   Using an Allen wrench, hold the strut piston rod from turning and remove the strut upper mounting nut and washer (see illustration).

9   Remove the damper mounting base and remove the strut/spring assembly from the vehicle.

Inspection

10   Check the strut body for leaking fluid, dents, cracks and other obvious damage which would warrant repair or replacement.

11   Check the coil spring for chips or cracks in the spring coating (this will cause premature spring failure due to corrosion). Inspect the spring seat for cuts, hardness and general deterioration.

12   If any undesirable conditions exist, proceed to the strut disassembly procedure (see Section 3).

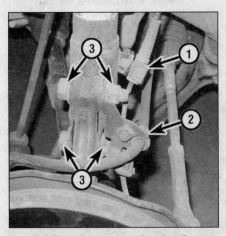

2.3 Strut lower mounting details

1   Wheel speed sensor harness retainer
2   Brake hose retaining bracket
3   Strut-to-steering knuckle nuts/bolts

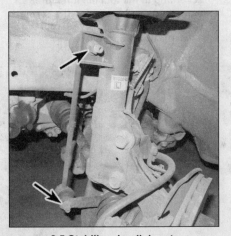

2.5 Stabilizer bar link nuts

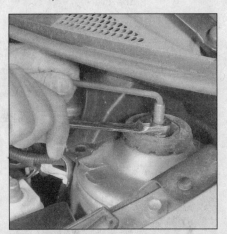

2.8 Hold the piston rod with an Allen wrench while loosening the strut mounting nut

Installation

13   Place the strut mounting cushion onto the strut and guide the unit into place.

14   Install the strut mounting base, washer and upper mounting nut.

15   Install new strut-to-knuckle bolts and nuts.

16   Raise the front suspension with a jack to load the strut with the vehicle weight, then tighten the strut-to-knuckle bolts and nuts to the torque listed in this Chapter's Specifications.

17   Connect the stabilizer bar link to the strut and tighten the nut to the torque listed in this Chapter's Specifications.

18   Hold the strut piston rod with an Allen wrench and tighten the strut upper mounting nut to the torque listed in this Chapter's Specifications.

19   If you're working on a 2009 or later model, install the lower cowl and cowl cover (see Chapter 11).

20   Install the wheel and lug nuts, then lower the vehicle and tighten the lug nuts to the torque listed in this Chapter's Specifications.

21   Have the front end alignment checked and, if necessary, adjusted.

3   Strut/coil spring assembly (front) - component replacement

Warning: *Always replace the struts or coil springs in pairs - never replace just one of them.*

1   If the struts or coil springs exhibit signs of wear (leaking fluid, loss of damping capability, chipped, sagging or cracked coil springs) explore all options before beginning any work. The strut/shock absorber assemblies are not serviceable and must be replaced if a problem develops. However, strut assemblies complete with springs may be available on an exchange basis, which eliminates much time and work. Whichever route you choose to take, check on the cost and availability of parts before disassembling your vehicle.

Warning: *Disassembling a strut is a potentially dangerous undertaking and utmost attention must be directed to the job, or serious injury may result. Use only a high-quality spring compressor and carefully follow the manufacturer's instructions furnished with the tool. After removing the coil spring from the strut assembly, set it aside in a safe, isolated area.*

Disassembly

2   Remove the strut and spring assembly (see Section 2), then remove the mounting base from the strut (see illustration).

3   Following the tool manufacturer's instructions, install the spring compressor (which can be obtained at most auto parts stores or equipment yards on a daily rental basis) on the spring and compress it sufficiently to relieve all pressure from the upper spring seat (see illustration). This can be verified by wiggling the spring.

4   Remove the piston rod nut (see illustration).

5   Remove the strut bearing (see illustration). Inspect the bearing for smooth operation. If it does not turn smoothly, replace it.

6   Lift the spring seat and upper insulator from the piston rod. Check the rubber spring seat for cracking and hardness, replacing it if necessary.

7   Carefully lift the compressed spring from the assembly (see illustration) and set it in a safe place.

Warning: *Carry the spring carefully and never place any part of your body near the end of the spring!*

3.2 Remove the mounting base from the strut

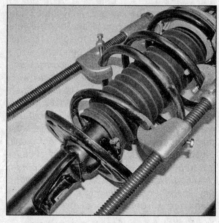

3.3 Install the spring compressor according to the tool manufacturer's instructions and compress the spring until all pressure is relieved from the upper spring seat

3.4 Hold the piston rod with an Allen wrench, then unscrew the nut

3.5 Remove the strut bearing

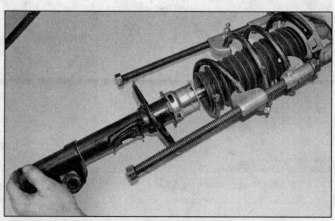

3.7 Remove the compressed spring assembly, upper seat and boot

8   Slide the dust boot off the piston rod.
9   Check the lower insulator (if equipped) for wear, cracking and hardness and replace it if necessary.

Reassembly

10   If the lower insulator is being replaced, set it into position with the dropped portion seated in the lowest part of the seat. Extend the damper rod to its full length and install the dust boot.
11   Place the coil spring onto the lower insulator, with the end of the spring resting in the lowest part of the insulator (see illustration).
12   Install the upper insulator and the spring seat.
13   Install the upper spring seat and the strut bearing.
14   Install the strut piston rod nut and tighten it to the torque listed in this Chapter's Specifications.
15   Remove the spring compressors.
16   Install the mounting base on the strut, then install the strut/coil spring assembly (see Section 2).

4   Stabilizer bar (front) - removal and installation

1   Loosen the front wheel lug nuts, raise the front of the vehicle, support it securely on jackstands and remove the wheels.
2   Detach the stabilizer bar links from the bar (see illustration 2.5).
3   Remove the front subframe (see Section 13).
4   If you're working on a 2009 or later model, remove the steering gear (see Section 17).
5   Remove the bushing clamps.
6   Remove the stabilizer bar and bushings from the subframe (see illustration).
7   Inspect the clamp bushings and the link bushings. If they're cracked or deteriorated, replace them.
Note: *When installing new bushings, the slit in the bushing must face the rear of the vehicle. Install the clamps in their original positions.*
8   Installation is the reverse of removal. Align the paint marks on the bar with the bushings. Tighten all suspension and steering fasteners to the torque values listed in this

Chapter's Specifications0. Tighten the wheel lug nuts to the torque listed in the Chapter 1 Specifications.
Note: *On 2007 and 2008 models, if both links were also removed from the struts, be sure to install them on the proper side; the left-side link has a yellow paint mark and the right-side link has a white paint mark.*

5   Control arm - removal, inspection and installation

Removal

1   Loosen the front wheel lug nuts, raise the front of the vehicle, support it securely on jackstands and remove the wheel.
2   On models where it would interfere, remove the under-vehicle splash shield.
3   Remove the lock pin from the balljoint castle nut (see illustration), then unscrew the nut a few turns (but don't remove it).
4   Using a balljoint separator, separate the control arm balljoint from the steering knuckle (see illustration). Remove the castle nut.

3.11 When installing the spring, make sure the end fits into the recessed portion of the lower seat

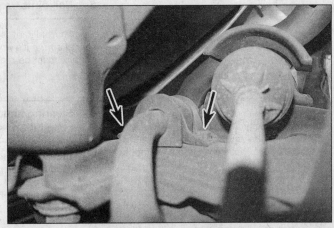

4.6 Stabilizer bar bushing bolts

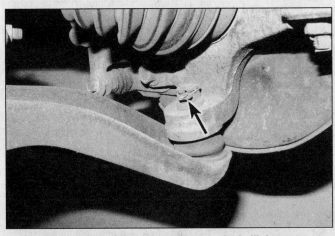

5.3 Remove the lock pin and loosen the balljoint nut

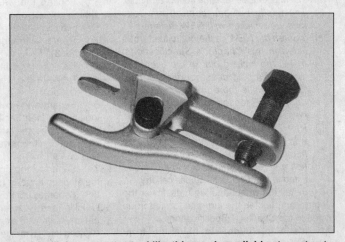

5.4 A balljoint separator tool like this one is available at most auto parts stores and will not damage the balljoint boot when used correctly

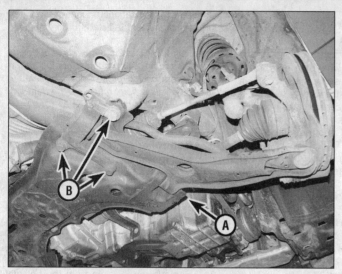

5.5a Control arm pivot bolt (A) and rear bushing bolts (B) (2007 and 2008 models)

5.5b Control arm pivot bolt (A) and rear bushing bolts (B) (2009 and later models)

5   Remove the control arm fasteners and remove the arm from the subframe (see illustrations).

Inspection

6   Inspect the front and rear bushings for cracks and tears. If either bushing is damaged or worn, replace the control arm; the bushings are not replaceable.
7   Inpspect the balljoint for looseness. If it's worn out, the control arm must be replaced.
8   Inspect the control arm for straightness. If it's bent, replace it. Do not attempt to straighten a bent control arm.

Installation

9   Installation is the reverse of removal, noting the following:
a) Degrease/clean the threads and taper on the balljoint, the mating surface on the steering knuckle, and the control arm hole.
b) The castle nut and control arm bolts must be replaced with NEW fasteners.
c) Tighten the NEW castle nut to the torque listed in this Chapter's Specifications. Install the locking pin. In the event the locking pin hole does not align, tighten the nut a little more until the hole lines up. NEVER loosen the nut to align the hole.
d) Raise the outer end of the control arm with a floor jack to simulate normal ride height, then tighten the control arm pivot bolt and rear bushing bolts to the torque listed in this Chapter's Specifications.
10   Install the wheel and lug nuts, lower the vehicle and tighten the lug nuts to the torque listed in the Chapter 1 Specifications.
11   It's a good idea to have the front wheel alignment checked and, if necessary, adjusted.

6   Balljoints - replacement

1   The balljoint is an integral part of the control arm. If it's worn or damaged, the control arm must be replaced (see Section Section 5).

7   Steering knuckle - removal and installation

Warning: Dust created by the brake system is harmful to your health. Never blow it out with compressed air and don't inhale any of it. Do not, under any circumstances, use petroleum-based solvents to clean brake parts. Use brake system cleaner only.

Removal

1   Loosen the wheel lug nuts, raise the vehicle and support it securely on jackstands. Remove the wheel.
2   Remove the driveaxle/hub nut (see Chapter 8).
3   Remove the brake disc (see Chapter 9).
4   Remove the wheel speed sensor from the knuckle.
5   Separate the tie-rod end from the steering knuckle (see Section 15).
6   Remove the strut-to-steering knuckle nuts, but don't remove the bolts yet (see Section 2).
7   Separate the control arm balljoint from the steering knuckle (see Section 5).
8   Separate the driveaxle from the steering knuckle (see Chapter 8). Support the end of the driveaxle with a length of wire so the inner CV joint isn't overextended.
9   Remove the strut-to-knuckle bolts and separate the knuckle from the strut.

10   Remove the hub-to-steering knuckle bolts, then detach the two components and remove the brake disc splash shield.

Installation

11   Assemble the hub, knuckle and splash shield. Tighten the bolts to the torque listed in this Chapter's Specifications.
12   Lubricate the splines of the driveaxle with multi-purpose grease. Guide the knuckle and hub assembly into position, inserting the driveaxle into the hub.
13   Push the knuckle into the strut flange and install the bolts and nuts, but don't tighten them yet.
14   Attach the control arm balljoint to the steering knuckle (see Section 5).
15   Attach the tie-rod end to the steering knuckle arm (see Section 15). Tighten the tie-rod end nut and the strut-to-knuckle nuts to the torque listed in Chapter 1 Specifications. Install a new cotter pin through the tie-rod end ballstud.
16   Place the brake disc on the hub, lining up the marks made in Step 4, then install the caliper (see Chapter 9).
17   Install the driveaxle/hub nut and tighten it to the torque listed in the Chapter 8 Specifications.
18   Install the wheel and lug nuts. Lower the vehicle and tighten the lug nuts to the torque listed in the Chapter 1 Specifications.

8   Hub and bearing assembly - removal and installation

Front

1   The wheel hub and bearing assembly is part of the steering knuckle and removal of the bearing involves specific tools not read-

8.4 Use a chisel to knock the hub cap loose from the hub

8.5 Use a punch or narrow chisel to unstake the hub nut from the slot in the spindle before attempting to unscrew the nut

8.8 Stake the new nut into the slot in the spindle

ily available to the DIY mechanic. It is highly advised that the steering knuckle be removed (see Section 7) and taken to a automotive repair shop or automotive machine shop if a new bearing is needed.

Rear

2   Loosen the rear wheel lug nuts. Raise the rear of the vehicle and support it securely on jackstands. Remove the wheel.
3   Remove the brake drum (see Chapter 9).
4   Remove the cap from the hub (see illustration).
5   Unstake the hub nut, then unscrew it (see illustration).
6   Silde the hub and bearing asssembly off the spindle.
7   If it's necessary to remove the spindle, see Section 9.
8   Installation is the reverse of the removal procedure. Use a NEW nut. Before installing the nut, lubricate the seating flange of the nut with clean engine oil. Install the nut and tighten it to the torque listed in this Chapter's Specifications , then stake the collar of the nut into the slot in the spindle (see illustration).
9   Install a new hub cap.
10   Install the wheel and tighten the lug nuts and lower the vehicle. Tighten the lug nuts to the torque listed in the Chapter 1 Specifications.

9   Rear axle beam - removal and installation

1   Loosen the rear wheel lug nuts. Raise the vehicle and support it securely on jackstands.
2   Remove the brake drum (see Chapter 9).
3   Unscrew the brake line fitting from the wheel cylinder (see Chapter 9).
4   Remove the parking brake cable and brake line brackets from the rear axle.
5   Remove the brake and backing plate

assembies from the spindles by removing the four flange bolts from each side.
Warning: *DO NOT use compressed air to blow the brake dust from the drum or brake assembly. Use brake system cleaner only.*
6   Remove the wheel speed sensors and detach the harness clips from the axle beam, but don't disconnect the electrical connectors (see Chapter 9).
7   Remove the spindles from the axle beam.
8   Detach the brake line from the brake hose and detach the brake hose from the suspension/axle beam by removing the spring steel clip.
9   Remove the brake line clip and the wheel sensor clip from the axle beam.
10   If you're working on a 2007 or 2008 model, remove the exhaust pipe and the fuel filler pipe.
11   Place a floor jack under the coil spring pocket on each side of the axle, then remove the shock absorber lower mounting bolts (see Section 11).
12   Remove the rear coil springs (see Section 10), then move the floor jacks under the forward (straight) part of the axle beam.
13   Remove the axle beam pivot bolts (see illustration). Discard the bolts and obtain new ones.
14   Lower the jacks slowly and remove the axle beam.
15   Installation is the reverse of removal. Note the following steps.

a)   Install the rear suspension components and tighten the bolts finger tight. Be sure to use NEW axle pivot bolts and shock absorber lower mounting bolts.
b)   Once all the rear suspension components are installed, position the floor jacks under the coil spring pockets and raise the suspension to simulate normal ride height, then tighten the shock absorber mounting bolts and the axle beam pivot bolts to the torque listed in this Chapter's Specifications.

c)   Fill the brake system with new fluid and bleed the brakes (see Chapter 9)
d)   Install the wheels and lug nuts, then lower the vehicle and tighten the lug nuts to the torque listed in the Chapter 1 Specifications.

10   Coil springs (rear) - removal and installation

Warning: *Always replace the coil springs in pairs - never replace just one of them.*
1   Loosen the rear wheel lug nuts, raise the rear of the vehicle, support it securely on jackstands and remove the wheels.
2   Position a floor jack under each coil spring seat portion of the rear suspension beam, then raise the jacks slightly.
3   Remove both shock absorber lower mounting bolts (see Section 11).
4   On 2009 and later models, remove the wheel speed sensor and wire harness retainer from both sides of the axle beam.
5   Carefully lower the floor jacks until the coil springs are fully extended.

9.13 Rear axle beam pivot bolt

11.3 Hold the shock absorber piston rod with an Allen wrench while loosening the upper mounting nut

11.4 Shock absorber lower mounting bolt

11.5a The lower mounting cushion is installed on the piston rod with the conical side facing down (toward the shock absorber)

6   Remove the coil spring, the rubber mount and the rubber seat.

7   Installation is the reverse of removal, noting the following points:

a) *Replace rubber components if they are deteriorated.*

b) *Replace the shock absorber lower mounting bolts with new ones.*

c) *Raise the trailing arm portions of the rear axle with the floor jacks until each side is at normal ride height, then tighten the shock absorber lower mounting bolts to the torque listed in this Chapter's Specifications.*

d) *Install the wheels and lug nuts. Lower the vehicle and tighten the lug nuts to the torque listed in the Chapter 1 Specifications.*

11   Shock absorbers (rear) - removal and installation

Warning: *Always replace the shock absorbers in pairs - never replace just one of them.*

1   Loosen the rear wheel lug nuts. Raise the rear of the vehicle and support it securely on jackstands. Block the front wheels to prevent the vehicle from rolling. Remove the wheel.

2   Support the rear axle beam with a floor jack placed under the coil spring pocket.

Warning: *The jack must remain in this position until the shock absorber is reinstalled.*

3   Remove the access panel in the luggage compartment and unscrew the shock absorber upper mounting nut (see illustration). Remove the washer and mounting cushion.

4   Unscrew the shock absorber lower mounting bolt and nut and remove the shock absorber (see illustration).

5   Installation is the reverse of removal. Be sure the mounting cushions and upper washer are properly installed on the piston rod (see illustrations), then tighten the NEW upper mounting nut to the torque listed in this

Chapter's Specifications.

6   Raise the floor jack to simulate normal ride height, then tighten the NEW lower mounting bolt to the torque listed in this Chapter's Specifications.

7   Install the wheel and lug nuts. Lower the vehicle and tighten the lug nuts to the torque listed in the Chapter 1 Specifications.

12   Steering column - removal and installation

Warning: *The models covered by this manual are equipped with Supplemental Restraint Systems (SRS), more commonly known as airbags. Always disarm the airbag system before working in the vicinity of any airbag system component to avoid the possibility of accidental deployment of the airbag, which could cause personal injury (see Chapter 12). Do not use a memory saving device to preserve the PCM's memory when working on or near airbag system components.*

Note: *Before you begin, ensure you have the anti-theft code for the audio system. If you don't, the audio system/navigation will not function upon installation.*

1   Disconnect the cable from the negative terminal of the battery (see Chapter 5).

2   Set the wheels in the straight ahead position.

Note: *On 2009 and later models, tilt the steering all the way up and push it all the way in.*

3   Remove the steering wheel (see Section).

4   Remove the under-dash panel.

5   Remove the cover from the U-joint at the bottom of the steering column shaft (see illustration).

Note: *On 2009 and later models, hold the lower shaft on the column with a a length of wire or suitable fastener between the lower U-joint yoke and the upper shaft to prevent the slide shaft from pulling out.*

Note: *On 2009 and later models models, release the locking lever and slide it all the way out and tighten the lock lever.*

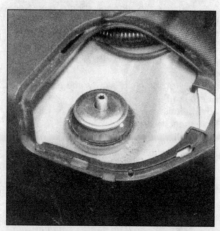

11.5b The upper mounting cushion is installed with the conical side facing up, and the washer is installed with the concave side against the cushion

12.5 Remove the plastic retainers and take off the steering column U-joint cover

12.9 On 2007 and 2008 models, remove both pinch bolts from the U-joint at the bottom of the steering column (on 2009 and later models there's only one)

12.10a Steering column mounting bolts...

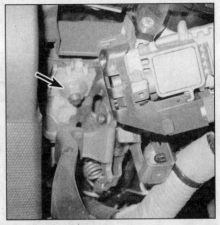

12.10b... and nuts (other nut not visible in this photo) (2007 and 2008 model shown)

6   Remove the steering column covers (see Chapter 11).

7   Disconnect the electrical connectors from the combination switch and the airbag clockspring.

8   Remove the combination switch, disconnect the ignition switch electrical connectors and detach the harness clips.

9   Mark the U-joint to the steering column shaft (2007 and 2008 models) and to the steering gear pinion shaft, then remove the U-joint pinch bolt(s) and disconnect the U-joint from the steering gear pinion shaft (see illustration).

10   Remove the column mounting bolts (lower) and nuts (upper) (see illustrations).

11   Guide the column out from the instrument panel.

12   Remove the plastic center installation guide (if equipped) from the steering gear pinion shaft or the steering column U-joint and discard it. This part will not be re-used as it was for factory installation purposes only.

13   Installation is the reverse of removal. Refer to Section for airbag clockspring and steering wheel installation.

14   Reconnect the battery (see Chapter 5).

---

13   Subframe (front) - removal and installation

Warning: *The models covered by this manual are equipped with Supplemental Restraint Systems (SRS), more commonly known as airbags. Always disarm the airbag system before working in the vicinity of any airbag system component to avoid the possibility of accidental deployment of the airbag, which could cause personal injury (see Chapter 12). Do not use a memory saving device to preserve the PCM's memory when working on or near airbag system components.*

1   If you're working on a 2009 or later model, remove the cowl cover and lower cowl (see Chapter 11).

2   Remove the air filter housing (see Chapter 4).

3   Disconnect the cable from the negative terminal of the battery (see Chapter 5).

4   Secure the steering wheel from turning using a steering wheel holder, or by threading the seat belt through the steering wheel and connecting it to its latch. Alternatively, remove the steering wheel (see Section 14).

Warning: *If this is not done and the steering wheel is allowed to turn, the airbag clockspring could be damaged, which would render the driver's airbag inoperative in the event of a collision.*

5   Support the engine from above with an engine support fixture. If no lifting brackets are present on the engine/transaxle, aftermarket hangers are available that can be attached to threaded holes on either end of the engine/transaxle.

Note: *Engine support fixtures are available at most auto parts stores and equipment rental yards.*

Note: *The objective of using a support fixture is to prevent the engine/transaxle assembly from tilting forward or backward (the engine/transaxle will still be attached to the chassis*

via the engine mount at the right end and the transaxle mount at the left end).

6   Loosen the front wheel lug nuts. Raise the front of the vehicle and support it securely on jackstands, then remove the wheels.

7   Remove the under-vehicle splash shield, then mark the relation of the subframe to the chassis at each corner.

8   Disconnect the stabilizer bar links from the stabilizer bar (see Section 4).

9   Disconnect the tie-rod ends from the steering knuckles (see Section 15).

10   Disconnect the control arm balljoints from the steering knuckles (see Section 5).

11   Disconnect the U-joint at the bottom of the steering column shaft from the steering gear pinion shaft (see Section 12).

12   On 2009 and later models, unbolt the downstream oxygen sensor harness bracket from the steering gear. Also remove the front crossmember brace.

13   Disconnect the front (on models so equipped) and rear (roll restrictor) engine mounts from the subframe.

14   Disconnect the power steering gear electrical connectors (see illustration).

15   Support the subframe with a floor jack,

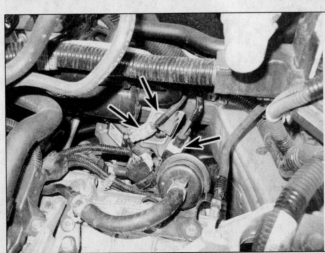

13.14 Steering gear electrical connectors (2009 and later models shown)

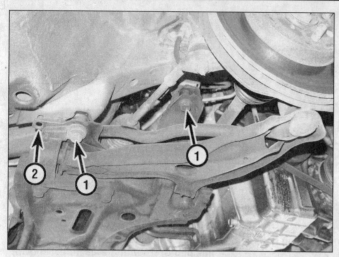

13.15a Subframe mounting details - 2007 and 2008 models

1 Subframe mounting bolts   2 Alignment hole

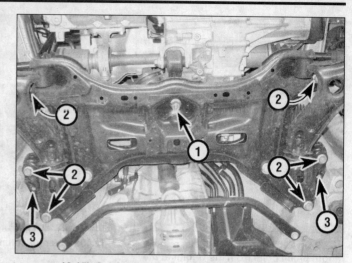

13.15b Subframe details - 2009 and later models

1 Roll restrictor bracket nut   3 Alignment hole
   Subframe mounting bolts

then remove the subframe mounting bolts (see illustrations). Discard the bolts and obtain new ones for installation.

16 Make sure nothing is still connected between the subframe and the chassis, then lower the subframe with the jack.

17 Installation is the reverse of removal. Insert long drift punches through the alignment holes to align the subframe with the previously-made marks on the chassis, then tighten the NEW mounting bolts a little at a time, in a criss-cross pattern, to the torque listed in this Chapter's Specifications.

18 Install the wheels and lug nuts. Lower the vehicle and tighten the lug nuts to the torque listed in the Chapter 1 Specifications.

19 Reconnect the battery (see Chapter 5).

20 Have the front wheel alignment checked and, if necessary, adjusted.

14 Steering wheel - removal and installation

Warning: *These models are equipped with a Supplemental Restraint System (SRS), more commonly known as airbags. Always disable the airbag system before working in the vicinity of any airbag system component to avoid the possibility of accidental deployment of the airbag(s), which could cause personal injury (see Chapter 12).*

Warning: *Do not use a memory saving device to preserve the PCM or radio memory when working on or near airbag system components.*

Removal

1 Make sure the front wheels are pointed straight ahead, then disconnect the cable from the negative terminal of the battery (see Chapter 5). Wait at least three minutes before proceeding.

2 Remove the airbag connector access panel from the bottom of the steering wheel (see illustration).

3 Unplug the airbag module connector (see illustration).

4 On each side of the steering wheel, remove the fasteners retaining the airbag module to the steering wheel (see illustration).

5 Disconnect the horn electrical connector (see illustration).

6 Pull off the airbag module, then carefully set it in a safe location.

Warning: *Carry the airbag module with the trim side facing away from you, and set the*

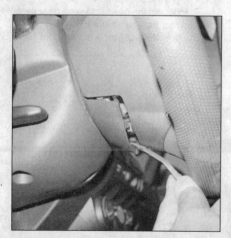

14.2 Remove the panel from the underside of the steering wheel

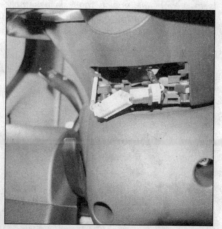

14.3 Disconnect the electrical connector for the airbag module

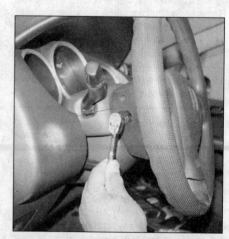

14.4 Remove the airbag fasteners on each side of the steering wheel

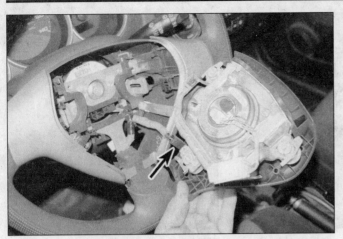

14.5 Disconnect the horn electrical connector

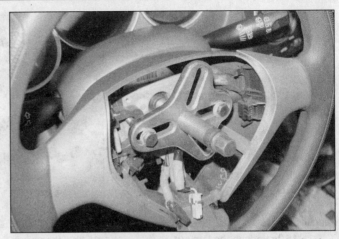

14.8a Use a steering wheel puller to break the steering wheel loose from the shaft splines...

steering wheel/airbag module down with the trim side facing up. Don't place anything on top of the airbag module.

7   Loosen the steering wheel retaining bolt until about 1/4-inch of threads are showing between the bolt head and the steering wheel.

8   Dislodge the steering wheel from the shaft using a steering wheel puller (see illustration). The puller screw must be contacting the steering wheel bolt. Once the steering wheel has been released from the shaft, remove the puller and retaining bolt, make a mark indicating the relationship of the steering wheel hub to the steering shaft, then pull the steering wheel off the shaft (see illustration).

Caution: *Don't thread the bolts of the puller into the steering wheel more than five turns, as they could contact the airbag clockspring and damage it.*

Caution: *While the steering wheel is removed, DO NOT turn the steering shaft.*

9   If it is necessary to remove the clockspring, remove the steering column covers (see Chapter 11).

10   Unplug the clockspring electrical connec-

tors, then release the locking tabs and detach it from the column.

Note: *There are two locking tabs located on the back side of the clockspring - one at the top and one at the bottom.*

Installation

11   With the front wheels pointed straight ahead, make sure that the airbag clockspring is centered with the arrow on the clockspring pointing up. This shouldn't be a problem as long as you have not turned the steering shaft while the wheel was removed. If for some reason the shaft was turned, center the clockspring by turning the clockspring clockwise until it stops (don't apply too much force), then rotate the clockspring counterclockwise about 2-1/2 to 3 turns until the arrow on the clockspring points straight up (see illustration).

12   Be sure to align the index mark on the steering wheel hub with the mark on the shaft when you slip the wheel onto the shaft. Make sure the turn signal canceling cam tabs are positioned at 12 and 6 o'clock, the locating pins on the clockspring engage the holes in

the backside of the steering wheel, and the notches in the steering wheel hub engage the tabs on the turn signal canceling cam (see illustration). Install a NEW steering wheel bolt and tighten it to the torque listed in this Chapter's Specifications.

14.8b... then remove the bolt and mark the relationship of the steering wheel to the shaft

14.11 When the clockspring windings are properly centered, the arrow on the face of the clockspring will be pointing straight up

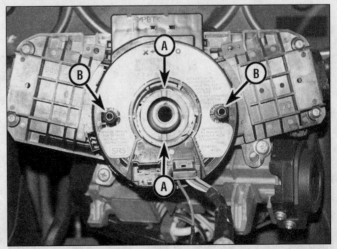

14.12 The turn signal canceling cam tabs (A) and the locating pins (B) on the clockspring must engage with their corresponding notches and holes on the steering wheel

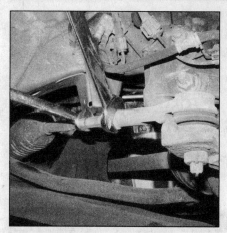

15.2a Loosen the jam nut...

15.2b... then mark the position of the tie-rod end on the threaded part of the tie-rod

15.3 Loosen (but don't remove) the tie-rod end nut, then use a puller to detach the tie-rod end

13   Connect the horn electrical connector.
14   Reattach the airbag module using NEW fasteners and tighten them to the torque listed in this Chapter's Specifications.
15   Plug in the electrical connector for the airbag module.
16   Reconnect the negative battery cable (see Chapter 5).

15   Tie-rod ends - removal and installation

Removal

1   Loosen the front wheel lug nuts. Raise the front of the vehicle, support it securely on jackstands, then remove the front wheel.
2   Loosen the jam nut enough to mark the position of the tie-rod end in relation to the threads (see illustrations).
3   Remove the cotter pin (2007 and 2008 models) or lock pin (2009 and later models)

and loosen, but don't remove, the nut on the tie-rod end ballstud, then disconnect the tie-rod end from the steering knuckle arm with a puller (see illustration).
4   Remove the nut and separate the tie-rod end from the steering knuckle.
5   Unscrew the tie-rod end from the tie-rod.

Installation

6   Thread the tie-rod end on to the marked position and insert the tie-rod end stud into the steering knuckle arm. Tighten the jam nut securely.
7   Install the tie-rod end-to-steering knuckle nut and tighten it to the torque listed in this Chapter's Specifications. Install the lock pin (2009 and later models) or a NEW cotter pin (2007 and 2008 models).
Warning: *In the event the cotter pin/lock pin hole does not align, tighten the nut a little more until the hole lines up. NEVER loosen the nut to align the hole.*
8   Install the wheel and lug nuts. Lower the

vehicle and tighten the lug nuts to the torque listed in the Chapter 1 Specifications.
9   Have the wheel alignment checked and, if necessary, adjusted.

16   Steering gear boots - replacement

1   Loosen the lug nuts, raise the vehicle and support it securely on jackstands. Remove the wheel.
2   Remove the tie-rod end and jam nut (see Section 15).
3   Remove the outer steering gear boot clamp (see illustration) with a pair of pliers. Cut off the inner boot clamp (see illustration) with a pair of diagonal cutters. Slide the boot off.
4   Before installing the new boot, wrap the threads on the end of the tie-rod with a layer of tape so the small end of the new boot isn't damaged.

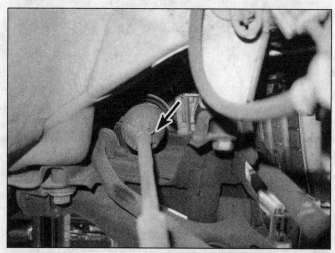

16.3a The outer end of the boot is secured by a spring clamp that can be slid off by pinching the ends together

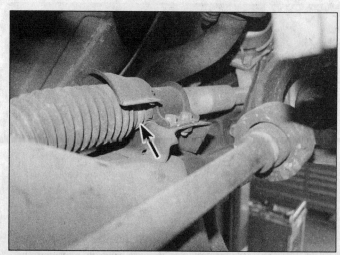

16.3b The inner end of the boot is retained by a clamp that must be cut off and discarded

5   Slide the new boot into position on the steering gear until it seats in the groove in the tie-rod and install new clamps.
6   Remove the tape and install the tie-rod end (see Section 15).
7   Install the wheel and lug nuts. Lower the vehicle and tighten the lug nuts to the torque listed in the Chapter 1 Specifications.
8   Have the wheel alignment checked and, if necessary, adjusted.

17   Steering gear - removal and installation

Warning: *The models covered by this manual are equipped with Supplemental Restraint Systems (SRS), more commonly known as airbags. Always disarm the airbag system before working in the vicinity of any airbag system component to avoid the possibility of accidental deployment of the airbag, which could cause personal injury (see Chapter 12). Do not use a memory saving device to preserve the PCM's memory when working on or near airbag system components.*
1   Remove the subframe (see Section 13).
2   On 2007 and 2008 models, remove the flange bolts, stiffener plate, gearbox mounting bracket, and the mounting cushion.
3   On 2009 and later models, remove the stiffener plate bolts and the steering gear-to-subframe bolts.
4   Remove the steering gear from the subframe.
5   Installation is the reverse of the removal procedure. Replace any deteriorated rubber parts with new ones. On 2007 and 2008 models, install the mounting cushion and ensure the tab is aligned with the paint mark on the steering gear. Tighten all fasteners to the torque values listed in this Chapter's Specifications.

18   Wheels and tires - general information

1   All vehicles covered by this manual are equipped with metric-sized steel belted radial tires (see illustration). Use of other size or type of tires may affect the ride and handling of the vehicle. Don't mix different types of tires, such as radials and bias belted, on the same vehicle as handling may be seriously affected. It's recommended that tires be replaced in pairs on the same axle, but if only one tire is being replaced, be sure it's the same size, structure and tread design as the other.
2   Because tire pressure has a substantial effect on handling and wear, the pressure on all tires should be checked at least once a month or before any extended trips (see Chapter 1).
3   Wheels must be replaced if they are bent, dented, leak air, have elongated bolt holes, are heavily rusted, out of vertical symmetry or if the lug nuts won't stay tight. Wheel

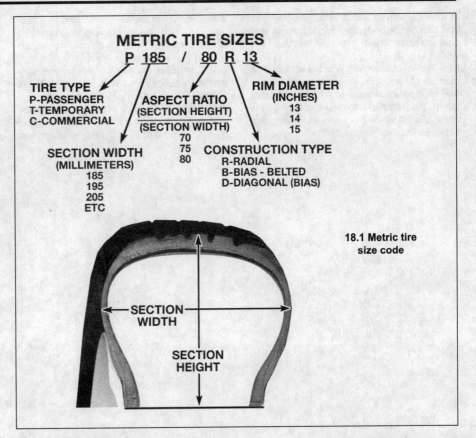

18.1 Metric tire size code

repairs that use welding or peening are not recommended.
4   Tire and wheel balance is important in the overall handling, braking and performance of the vehicle. Unbalanced wheels can adversely affect handling and ride characteristics as well as tire life. Whenever a tire is installed on a wheel, the tire and wheel should be balanced by a shop with the proper equipment.

19   Wheel alignment - general information

1   A wheel alignment refers to the adjustments made to the wheels so they are in proper angular relationship to the suspension and the ground. Wheels that are out of proper alignment not only affect vehicle control, but also increase tire wear. The front end angles normally measured are camber, caster and toe-in (see illustration). Camber and caster are preset at the factory on the vehicles covered by this manual; toe-in is the only adjustable angle on these vehicles (however, camber and caster are usually measured to check for bent or worn suspension parts). Toe-in and camber are both adjustable at the rear.
2   Getting the proper wheel alignment is an exacting process, one in which complicated and expensive machines are necessary to perform the job properly. Because of this, you should have a technician with the proper equipment perform these tasks. We will, however, use this space to give you a basic idea

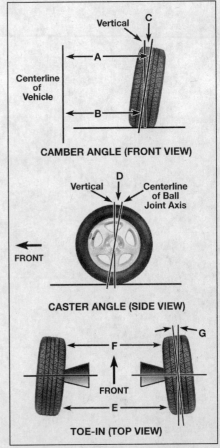

19.1 Camber, caster and toe-in angles

of what is involved with a wheel alignment so you can better understand the process and deal intelligently with the shop that does the work.

3   Toe-in is the turning in of the wheels. The purpose of a toe specification is to ensure parallel rolling of the wheels. In a vehicle with zero toe-in, the distance between the front edges of the wheels will be the same as the distance between the rear edges of the wheels. The actual amount of toe-in is normally only a fraction of an inch. Incorrect toe-in will cause the tires to wear improperly by making them scrub against the road surface.

4   Camber is the tilting of the wheels from vertical when viewed from one end of the vehicle. When the wheels tilt out at the top, the camber is said to be positive (+). When the wheels tilt in at the top the camber is negative (-). The amount of tilt is measured in degrees from vertical and this measurement is called the camber angle. This angle affects the amount of tire tread which contacts the road and compensates for changes in the suspension geometry when the vehicle is cornering or traveling over an undulating surface.

5   Caster is the tilting of the front steering axis from the vertical. A tilt toward the rear is positive caster and a tilt toward the front is negative caster.

Chapter 11
Body

Contents

1 General information

Warning: *The models covered by this manual are equipped with Supplemental Restraint Systems (SRS), more commonly known as airbags. Always disable the airbag system before working in the vicinity of any airbag system components to avoid the possibility of accidental deployment of the airbags, which could cause personal injury (see Chapter 12).*

1   Certain body components are particularly vulnerable to accident damage and can be unbolted and repaired or replaced. Among these parts are the hood, doors, tailgate, liftgate, bumpers and front fenders.

2   Only general body maintenance practices and body panel repair procedures within the scope of the do-it-yourselfer are included in this Chapter.

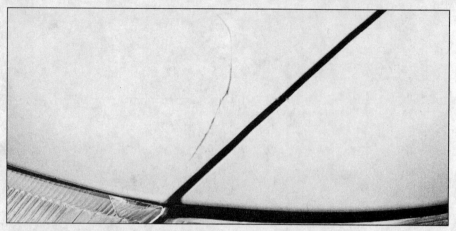

Make sure the damaged area is perfectly clean and rust free. If the touch-up kit has a wire brush, use it to clean the scratch or chip. Or use fine steel wool wrapped around the end of a pencil. Clean the scratched or chipped surface only, not the good paint surrounding it. Rinse the area with water and allow it to dry thoroughly

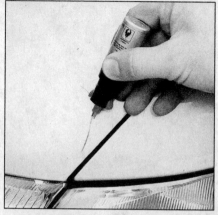

Thoroughly mix the paint, then apply a small amount with the touch-up kit brush or a very fine artist's brush. Brush in one direction as you fill the scratch area. Do not build up the paint higher than the surrounding paint

2   Repairing minor paint scratches

1   No matter how hard you try to keep your vehicle looking like new, it will inevitably be scratched, chipped or dented at some point. If the metal is actually dented, seek the advice of a professional. But you can fix minor scratches and chips yourself. Buy a touch-up paint kit from a dealer service department or an auto parts store. To ensure that you get the right color, you'll need to have the specific make, model and year of your vehicle and, ideally, the paint code, which is located on a special metal plate under the hood or in the door jamb.

3   Body repair - minor damage

Plastic body panels

1   The following repair procedures are for minor scratches and gouges. Repair of more serious damage should be left to a dealer service department or qualified auto body shop. Below is a list of the equipment and materials necessary to perform the following repair procedures on plastic body panels.

   Wax, grease and silicone removing solvent
   Cloth-backed body tape
   Sanding discs
   Drill motor with three-inch disc holder
   Hand sanding block
   Rubber squeegees
   Sandpaper
   Non-porous mixing palette
   Wood paddle or putty knife
   Wood paddle or putty knife
   Curved-tooth body file
   Flexible parts repair material

Flexible panels (bumper trim)

2   Remove the damaged panel, if necessary or desirable. In most cases, repairs can be carried out with the panel installed.

3   Clean the area(s) to be repaired with a

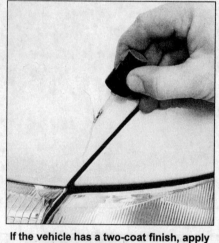

If the vehicle has a two-coat finish, apply the clear coat after the color coat has dried

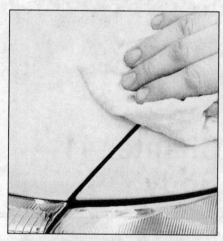

Wait a few days for the paint to dry thoroughly, then rub out the repainted area with a polishing compound to blend the new paint with the surrounding area. When you're happy with your work, wash and polish the area

wax, grease and silicone removing solvent applied with a water-dampened cloth.

4   If the damage is structural, that is, if it extends through the panel, clean the backside of the panel area to be repaired as well. Wipe dry.

5   Sand the rear surface about 1-1/2 inches beyond the break.

6   Cut two pieces of fiberglass cloth large enough to overlap the break by about 1-1/2 inches. Cut only to the required length.

7   Mix the adhesive from the repair kit according to the instructions included with the kit, and apply a layer of the mixture approximately 1/8-inch thick on the backside of the panel. Overlap the break by at least 1-1/2 inches.

8   Apply one piece of fiberglass cloth to the adhesive and cover the cloth with additional adhesive. Apply a second piece of fiberglass cloth to the adhesive and immediately cover the cloth with additional adhesive in sufficient quantity to fill the weave.

9   Allow the repair to cure for 20 to 30 min-

utes at 60-degrees to 80-degrees F.

10   If necessary, trim the excess repair material at the edge.

11   Remove all of the paint film over and around the area(s) to be repaired. The repair material should not overlap the painted surface.

12   With a drill motor and a sanding disc (or a rotary file), cut a V along the break line approximately 1/2-inch wide. Remove all dust and loose particles from the repair area.

13   Mix and apply the repair material. Apply a light coat first over the damaged area; then continue applying material until it reaches a level slightly higher than the surrounding finish.

14   Cure the mixture for 20 to 30 minutes at 60-degrees to 80-degrees F.

15   Roughly establish the contour of the area being repaired with a body file. If low areas or

pits remain, mix and apply additional adhesive.

16 Block sand the damaged area with sandpaper to establish the actual contour of the surrounding surface.

17 If desired, the repaired area can be temporarily protected with several light coats of primer. Because of the special paints and techniques required for flexible body panels, it is recommended that the vehicle be taken to a paint shop for completion of the body repair.

Steel body panels

Repairing simple dents

18 When repairing dents, the first job is to pull the dent out until the affected area is as close as possible to its original shape. There is no point in trying to restore the original shape completely as the metal in the damaged area will have stretched on impact and cannot be restored to its original contours. It is better to bring the level of the dent up to a point that is about 1/8-inch below the level of the surrounding metal. In cases where the dent is very shallow, it is not worth trying to pull it out at all.

19 If the backside of the dent is accessible, it can be hammered out gently from behind using a soft-face hammer. While doing this, hold a block of wood firmly against the opposite side of the metal to absorb the hammer blows and prevent the metal from being stretched.

22 If the dent is in a section of the body which has double layers, or some other factor makes it inaccessible from behind, a different technique is required. Drill several small holes through the metal inside the damaged area, particularly in the deeper sections. Screw long, self-tapping screws into the holes just enough for them to get a good grip in the metal. Now pulling on the protruding heads of the screws with locking pliers can pull out the dent.

23 The next stage of repair is the removal of paint from the damaged area and from an inch or so of the surrounding metal. This is easily done with a wire brush or sanding disk in a drill motor, although it can be done just as effectively by hand with sandpaper. To complete the preparation for filling, score the surface of the bare metal with a screwdriver or the tang of a file or drill small holes in the affected area. This will provide a good grip for the filler material. To complete the repair, see the Section on filling and painting.

Repair of rust holes or gashes

24 Remove all paint from the affected area and from an inch or so of the surrounding metal using a sanding disk or wire brush mounted in a drill motor. If these are not available, a few sheets of sandpaper will do the job just as effectively.

25 With the paint removed, you will be able to determine the severity of the corrosion and decide whether to replace the whole panel, if possible, or repair the affected area. New body panels are not as expensive as most people think and it is often quicker to install a new panel than to repair large areas of rust.

26 Remove all trim pieces from the affected area except those which will act as a guide to the original shape of the damaged body, such as headlight shells, etc. Using metal snips or a hacksaw blade, remove all loose metal and any other metal that is badly affected by rust. Hammer the edges of the hole in to create a slight depression for the filler material.

27 Wire-brush the affected area to remove the powdery rust from the surface of the metal. If the back of the rusted area is accessible, treat it with rust inhibiting paint.

28 Before filling is done, block the hole in some way. This can be done with sheet metal riveted or screwed into place, or by stuffing the hole with wire mesh.

29 Once the hole is blocked off, the affected area can be filled and painted. See the following subsection on filling and painting.

Filling and painting

30 Many types of body fillers are available, but generally speaking, body repair kits which contain filler paste and a tube of resin hardener are best for this type of repair work. A wide, flexible plastic or nylon applicator will be necessary for imparting a smooth and contoured finish to the surface of the filler material. Mix up a small amount of filler on a clean piece of wood or cardboard (use the hardener sparingly). Follow the manufacturer's instructions on the package, otherwise the filler will set incorrectly.

31 Using the applicator, apply the filler paste to the prepared area. Draw the applicator across the surface of the filler to achieve the desired contour and to level the filler surface. As soon as a contour that approximates the original one is achieved, stop working the paste. If you continue, the paste will begin to stick to the applicator. Continue to add thin layers of paste at 20-minute intervals until the level of the filler is just above the surrounding metal.

32 Once the filler has hardened, the excess can be removed with a body file. From then on, progressively finer grades of sandpaper should be used, starting with a 180-grit paper and finishing with 600-grit wet-or-dry paper. Always wrap the sandpaper around a flat rubber or wooden block, otherwise the surface of the filler will not be completely flat. During the sanding of the filler surface, the wet-or-dry paper should be periodically rinsed in water. This will ensure that a very smooth finish is produced in the final stage.

33 At this point, the repair area should be surrounded by a ring of bare metal, which in turn should be encircled by the finely feathered edge of good paint. Rinse the repair area with clean water until all of the dust produced by the sanding operation is gone.

34 Spray the entire area with a light coat of primer. This will reveal any imperfections in the surface of the filler. Repair the imperfections with fresh filler paste or glaze filler and once more smooth the surface with sandpaper. Repeat this spray-and-repair procedure until you are satisfied that the surface of the filler and the feathered edge of the paint are perfect. Rinse the area with clean water and allow it to dry completely.

35 The repair area is now ready for painting. Spray painting must be carried out in a warm, dry, windless and dust free atmosphere. These conditions can be created if you have access to a large indoor work area, but if you are forced to work in the open, you will have to pick the day very carefully. If you are working indoors, dousing the floor in the work area with water will help settle the dust that would otherwise be in the air. If the repair area is confined to one body panel, mask off the surrounding panels. This will help minimize the effects of a slight mismatch in paint color. Trim pieces such as chrome strips, door handles, etc., will also need to be masked off or removed. Use masking tape and several thickness of newspaper for the masking operations.

36 Before spraying, shake the paint can thoroughly, then spray a test area until the spray painting technique is mastered. Cover the repair area with a thick coat of primer. The thickness should be built up using several thin layers of primer rather than one thick one. Using 600-grit wet-or-dry sandpaper, rub down the surface of the primer until it is very smooth. While doing this, the work area should be thoroughly rinsed with water and the wet-or-dry sandpaper periodically rinsed as well. Allow the primer to dry before spraying additional coats.

37 Spray on the top coat, again building up the thickness by using several thin layers of paint. Begin spraying in the center of the repair area and then, using a circular motion, work out until the whole repair area and about two inches of the surrounding original paint is covered. Remove all masking material 10 to 15 minutes after spraying on the final coat of paint. Allow the new paint at least two weeks to harden, then use a very fine rubbing compound to blend the edges of the new paint into the existing paint. Finally, apply a coat of wax

4 Body repair - major damage

1 Major damage must be repaired by an auto body shop specifically equipped to perform body and frame repairs. These shops have the specialized equipment required to do the job properly.

2 If the damage is extensive, the frame must be checked for proper alignment or the vehicle's handling characteristics may be adversely affected and other components may wear at an accelerated rate.

3 Due to the fact that all of the major body components (hood, fenders, etc.) are separate and replaceable units, any seriously damaged components should be replaced rather than repaired. Sometimes the components can be found in a wrecking yard that specializes in used vehicle components, often at considerable savings over the cost of new parts.

These photos illustrate a method of repairing simple dents. They are intended to supplement *Body repair - minor damage* in this Chapter and should not be used as the sole instructions for body repair on these vehicles.

1 If you can't access the backside of the body panel to hammer out the dent, pull it out with a slide-hammer-type dent puller. Tap with a hammer near the edge of the dent to help 'pop' the metal back to its original shape, about 1/8-inch below the surface of the surrounding metal

2 Using coarse-grit sandpaper, remove the paint down to the bare metal. Clean the repair area with wax/silicone remover.

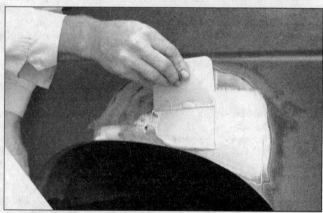

3 Following label instructions, mix up a batch of plastic filler and hardener, then quickly press it into the metal with a plastic applicator. Work the filler until it matches the original contour and is slightly above the surrounding metal

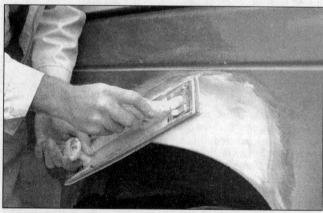

4 Let the filler harden until you can just dent it with your fingernail. File, then sand the filler down until it's smooth and even. Work down to finer grits of sandpaper - always using a board or block - ending up with 360 or 400 grit

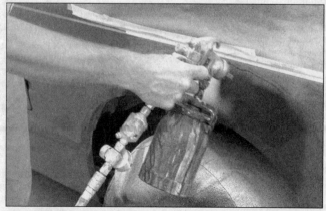

5 When the area is smooth to the touch, clean the area and mask around it. Apply several layers of primer to the area. A professional-type spray gun is being used here, but aerosol spray primer works fine

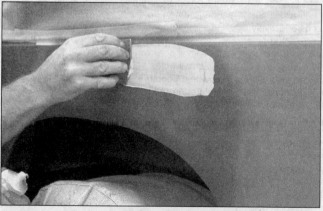

6 Fill imperfections or scratches with glazing compound. Sand with 360 or 400-grit and re-spray. Finish sand the primer with 600 grit, clean thoroughly, then apply the finish coat. Don't attempt to rub out or wax the repair area until the paint has dried completely (at least two weeks)

5 Fastener and trim removal

1 There is a variety of plastic fasteners used to hold trim panels, splash shields and other parts in place in addition to typical screws, nuts and bolts. Once you are familiar with them, they can usually be removed without too much difficulty.

2 The proper tools and approach can prevent added time and expense to a project by minimizing the number of broken fasteners and/or parts.

3 The following illustration shows various types of fasteners that are typically used on most vehicles and how to remove and install them (see illustration). Replacement fasteners are commonly found at most auto parts stores, if necessary.

4 Trim panels are typically made of plastic and their flexibility can help during removal. The key to their removal is to use a tool to pry the panel near its retainers to release it without damaging surrounding areas or breaking-off any retainers. The retainers will usually snap out of their designated slot or hole after force is applied to them. Stiff plastic tools designed for prying on trim panels are available at most auto parts stores (see illustration). Tools that are tapered and wrapped in protective tape, such as a screwdriver or small pry tool, are also very effective when used with care.

6 Upholstery, carpets and vinyl trim - maintenance

Upholstery and carpets

1 Every three months remove the floormats and clean the interior of the vehicle (more frequently if necessary). Use a stiff whiskbroom to brush the carpeting and loosen dirt and dust, then vacuum the upholstery and carpets thoroughly, especially along seams and crevices.

2 Dirt and stains can be removed from carpeting with basic household or automotive carpet shampoos available in spray cans. Follow the directions and vacuum again, then use a stiff brush to bring back the nap of the carpet.

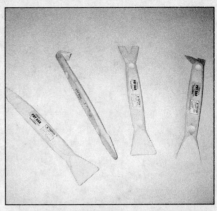

5.4 These small plastic pry tools are ideal for prying off trim panels

Fasteners

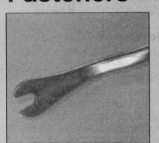

This tool is designed to remove special fasteners. A small pry tool used for removing nails will also work well in place of this tool

A Phillips head screwdriver can be used to release the center portion, but light pressure must be used because the plastic is easily damaged. Once the center is up, the fastener can easily be pried from its hole

Here is a view with the center portion fully released. Install the fastener as shown, then press the center in to set it

This fastener is used for exterior panels and shields. The center portion must be pried up to release the fastener. Install the fastener with the center up, then press the center in to set it

This type of fastener is used commonly for interior panels. Use a small blunt tool to press the small pin at the center in to release it . . .

. . . the pin will stay with the fastener in the released position

Reset the fastener for installation by moving the pin out. Install the fastener, then press the pin flush with the fastener to set it

This fastener is used for exterior and interior panels. It has no moving parts. Simply pry the fastener from its hole like the claw of a hammer removes a nail. Without a tool that can get under the top of the fastener, it can be very difficult to remove

9.2 Before removing the hood, draw a mark around the hinge plate

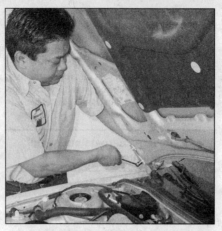

9.4 Support the hood with your shoulder while removing the hood nuts

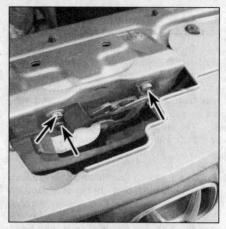

9.11a To adjust the hood latch, loosen the retaining bolts, move the latch and retighten the bolts, then close the hood to check the fit

9.11b Adjust the hood closing height by turning the hood bumpers in or out

3   Most interiors have cloth or vinyl uphol- stery, either of which can be cleaned and maintained with a number of material-specific cleaners or shampoos available in auto supply stores. Follow the directions on the product for usage, and always spot-test any upholstery cleaner on an inconspicuous area (bottom edge of a backseat cushion) to ensure that it doesn't cause a color shift in the material.
4   After cleaning, vinyl upholstery should be treated with a protectant.
Note: *Make sure the protectant container indi- cates the product can be used on seats - some products may make a seat too slippery.*
Caution: *Do not use protectant on vinyl-cov- ered steering wheels.*
5   Leather upholstery requires special care. It should be cleaned regularly with saddle- soap or leather cleaner. Never use alcohol, gasoline, nail polish remover or thinner to clean leather upholstery.
6   After cleaning, regularly treat leather upholstery with a leather conditioner, rubbed in with a soft cotton cloth. Never use car wax

on leather upholstery.
7   In areas where the interior of the vehi- cle is subject to bright sunlight, cover leather seating areas of the seats with a sheet if the vehicle is to be left out for any length of time.

Vinyl trim
8   Don't clean vinyl trim with detergents, caustic soap or petroleum-based cleaners. Plain soap and water works just fine, with a soft brush to clean dirt that may be ingrained. Wash the vinyl as frequently as the rest of the vehicle.
9   After cleaning, application of a high-qual- ity rubber and vinyl protectant will help prevent oxidation and cracks. The protectant can also be applied to weather-stripping, vacuum lines and rubber hoses, which often fail as a result of chemical degradation, and to the tires.

7   Hinges and locks - maintenance

1   Once every 3000 miles, or every three months, the hinges and latch assemblies on the doors, hood and trunk should be given a few drops of light oil or lock lubricant. The door latch strikers should also be lubricated with a thin coat of grease to reduce wear and ensure free movement. Lubricate the door and trunk locks with spray-on graphite lubricant.

8   Windshield and fixed glass - replacement

1   Replacement of the windshield and fixed glass requires the use of special fast-setting adhesive/caulk materials and some special- ized tools. It is recommended that these oper- ations be left to a dealer or a shop specializ- ing in glass work.

9   Hood - removal, installation and adjustment

Note: *The hood is heavy and somewhat awk- ward to remove and install - at least two peo- ple should perform this procedure.*

Removal and installation
1   Use blankets or pads to cover the cowl area of the body and fenders. This will protect the body and paint as the hood is lifted off.
2   Make marks or scribe a line around the hood hinge to ensure proper alignment during installation (see illustration).
3   Disconnect any cables or wires that will interfere with removal.
4   Have an assistant support one side of the hood while you support the other. Remove the hinge-to-hood nuts (see illustration).
5   Lift off the hood.
6   Installation is the reverse of removal.

Adjustment
7   Fore-and-aft and side-to-side adjust- ment of the hood is done by moving the hinge plate slot after loosening the mounting bolts or nuts.
8   Scribe a line around the entire hinge plate so you can determine the amount of movement (see illustration 9.2).
9   Remove the cowl cover (see Section 25).
10   Loosen the bolts or nuts and move the hood into correct alignment. Move it only a lit- tle at a time. Tighten the hinge bolts and care- fully lower the hood to check the position.
11   If necessary after installation, the entire hood latch assembly can be adjusted up-and- down by turning the hood edge cushions so the hood closes securely and is flush with the fenders (see illustrations).
Note: *Adjust the hood latch to obtain the prop- er height at the forward edge, and move the hood latch right or left until the striker is cen- tered in the hood latch.*

12   Scribe a line or mark around the hood latch mounting bolts to provide a reference point for adjustment.
13   Loosen the mounting bolts and reposition the latch assembly as necessary.
14   Retighten the latch mounting bolts.

10   Hood release latch and cable - removal and installation

Latch

1   Scribe a line around the latch to aid alignment when installing.
2   Remove the latch mounting bolts, then remove the hood latch from the body and disconnect the hood opener cable from the hood latch (see illustration).
3   Installation is the reverse of removal. Adjust the latch so the hood engages securely when closed and the hood bumpers are slightly compressed.

Cable

4   On 2008 and earlier models, remove the front bumper cover (see Section 19).
5   On 2009 and later models, remove the grill cover (see Section 11).
6   Disconnect the hood opener cable from the hood latch (see Steps 1 and 2).
7   Remove the right front inner fender splash shield (see Section 18).
8   Remove the lower part of the air intake silencer by pulling it down.
9   Using a clip remover, detach the clip, peel off the vinyl tape wrapped around the engine compartment wire harness and the opener cable.
10   Remove the cable from the harness clips and remove the grommet from the body.
11   Attach a piece of wire or string to the end of the cable.
12   Working in the passenger's compart

ment, remove the driver's side kick panel (see Section 24).
13   Remove the fastener securing the hood release handle (see illustration), then disconnect the cable from the handle.
14   Push the grommet through the body and into the passenger compartment. Ensure that the new cable has a grommet attached, then remove the old cable from the wire and replace it with the new cable.
15   Pull the wire back through the body.
16   Installation is the reverse of removal.
Note: *Push on the grommet with your fingers from the passenger compartment to seat the grommet in the firewall completely.*

11   Radiator grille - removal and installation

Warning: *The models covered by this manual are equipped with a Supplemental Restraint System (SRS), more commonly known as airbags. Always disarm the airbag system before working in the vicinity of any airbag system component to avoid the possibility of accidental deployment of the airbag, which could cause personal injury (see Chapter 12). Do not use a memory saving device to preserve the PCM's memory when working on or near airbag system components.*

2008 and earlier models

1   Remove the front bumper cover (see Section 19).
2   Remove the screws, and release the hooks, then remove the front grille from the front bumper.
3   Installation is the reversal of removal.

2009 and later models

4   Remove fasteners from front grille cover (see illustration).
5   While pulling the rear edge of the cover

up, slide the entire cover rearward to release it from the groove in the front grille.
6   Remove push pin fasteners and screws from the grille, then pull the grille out to release it from the bumper cover.
7   Installation is the reverse of removal.

12   Liftgate - removal, installation and adjustment

Note: *The liftgate is heavy and somewhat awkward to remove and install - at least two people should perform this procedure.*

Removal and installation

1   Open the liftgate. Cover the surrounding body with pads or cloths to protect the painted surfaces when the liftgate is removed.
2   Peel off the liftgate inner door seal.
3   Remove the cargo floor and box.
4   Remove the left side rear seat belt lower anchor bolt.

10.2 Detach the cable (A) then unhook the end from the latch (B)

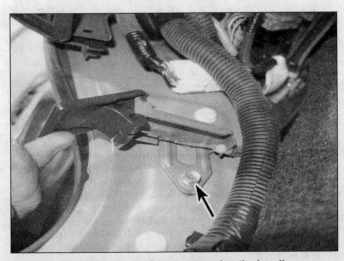

10.13 Remove the fastener securing the handle

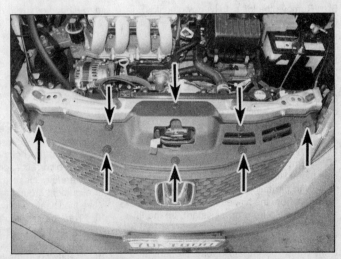

11.4 Fasteners securing the grille cover

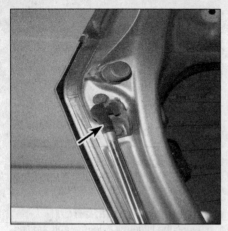

12.10 Release the the strut support clip and detach it from the ballstud

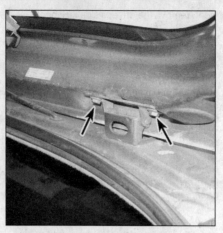

12.11 Remove the fasteners from the hinges (right side shown, left side similar)

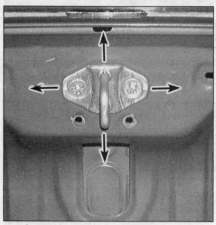

12.20 To adjust the liftgate striker, loosen the screws and move the striker as necessary

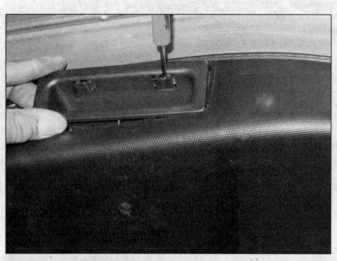

13.1a Carefully pry off the inside pull handle. . .

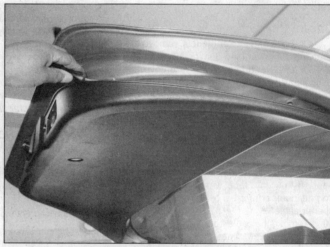

13.1b. . . then using a trim removal tool, carefully pry around the edges of the panel to release the clips

5   Remove the left side tie down hook(s).
6   Remove the screws securing the left side cargo area trim panel.
7   Starting at the front of the cargo area trim panel, carefully pry loose the clips securing the trim panel then remove it from the vehicle.
8   Working in the left side of the cargo area, disconnect the electrical connector for the liftgate wiring harness.
0   Make alignment marks around the hinge mounting bolts with a marking pen.
10   Remove the support struts from each side of the liftgate (see illustration).
11   With the tailgate supported, remove the fasteners from the hinges (see illustration).
12   With help from an assistant, lift the liftgate from the vehicle.
13   Installation is the reverse of removal. Check that the liftgate opens properly and locks securely.
Note: *When reinstalling the liftgate, align the*

lid-to-hinge bolts with the marks made during removal.

Adjustment
14   Fore-and-aft and side-to-side adjustments of the liftgate are accomplished by moving the lid in relation to the hinge after loosening the bolts or nuts.
15   Scribe a line around the entire hinge plate so you can determine the amount of movement.
16   Loosen the bolts or nuts and move the liftgate into correct alignment.
17   Carefully close the trunk lid and check for alignment around the edges of the liftgate. Move the liftgate gently into alignment.
18   Turn the liftgate edge cushions in or out as necessary to make the liftgate fit flush with the body at the side edges.
19   Gently open the liftgate and tighten the bolts at the hinge plate.
20   Adjust the fit between the liftgate and

tailgate opening by moving the striker and adjust the striker right or left until it is centered in the liftgate latch (see illustrations).
21   The liftgate latch assembly, as well as the hinges, should be periodically lubricated with white lithium-base grease to prevent sticking and wear.

13   Liftgate latch and striker - removal and installation

Note: *If the liftgate latch can't be unlocked using the power door lock system, it can be unlocked manually. Remove the maintenance cap from the liftgate lower trim panel, then unlock the liftgate latch by turning the pivot of the lever clockwise with a flat-tip screwdriver.*
1   Remove the liftgate lower trim panel (see illustrations).
2   Scribe a line around the liftgate lid latch

13.3 Electrical connector (A), lock cylinder rod (B) and release cable (C) (2008 and earlier model shown, 2009 and later models similar)

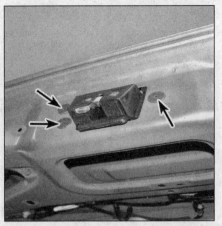

13.5 Liftgate latch mounting fasteners

14.2a Remove the screw from the door handle. . .

14.2b. . . then remove the cover

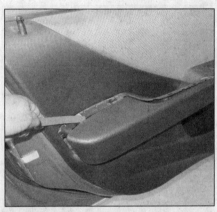

14.3 Carefully pry off the door pull cover

14.4 Carefully pry off the door pull cover

14.5 Carefully pry the clips free of the door

14.7 Peel back the plastic watershield for inner door procedures

for a reference point to aid the installation procedure.

3 Disconnect the liftgate opener cable from the liftgate latch (see illustration). Take care not to kink the cable.

4 Disconnect the liftgate latch actuator connector and the liftgate lock switch connector and detach the clip, then remove the liftgate latch.

5 Remove the bolts, then pull out the latch from the liftgate (see illustration).

6 Installation is the reverse of removal.

14 Door trim panel - removal and installation

Caution: *Plastic trim tools must be used on all operations in this Section to avoid damage to the soft plastic interior parts (see Section 6).*
Note: *This procedure is the same for the front or rear doors.*

1 Open the door and lower the window.

2 Remove the screw securing the inner door handle and remove the cover (see illustrations).

3 Remove the door pull cover by prying out the front bottom edge of the cover, while pushing up the hooks (see illustration).

4 Carefully pry up the power window switch, then disconnect the power window switch connector (see illustration).

5 Remove the door trim panel using a door panel removal tool. Start at the bottom edge of the panel and work around the perimeter until all the fasteners have been released from the door (see illustration).

6 Remove the door panel by pulling the panel upward.

7 For access to the door outside handle or the door window regulator inside the door, raise the window fully, then carefully peel back the plastic watershield (see illustration).

8 Installation is the reverse of removal.

15.4 Door stop strut bolt (A) and the lower hinge-to-door mounting fasteners (B)

15.11 Adjust the door lock striker by loosening the mounting screws and gently tapping the striker in the desired direction

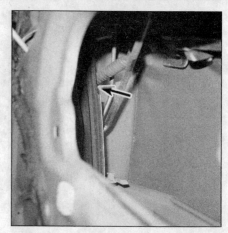

16.3a Pull the channel out of the way. . .

16.3b. . . then remove the fastener securing the center lower glass run channel

16.4 The door latch rod (A) and lock rod (B)

15   Door - removal, installation and adjustment

Note: *The door is heavy and somewhat awkward to remove and install - at least two people should perform this procedure.*

Removal and installation

1   Lower the window completely in the door.

2   Open the door all the way and support it on jacks or blocks covered with rags to prevent damaging the paint.

3   Remove the kick panel underneath the instrument panel (if removing a front door) or the center pillar trim panel (if removing a rear door), then unplug the door wiring harness electrical connectors. Push the rubber conduit out of the door pillar and pull the wiring harness through.

4   Unbolt the door stop strut (see illustration).

5   Mark around the door hinges with a pen

or a scribe to facilitate realignment during reassembly.

6   With an assistant holding the door, remove the upper and lower hinge-to-door mounting fasteners (see illustration 15.4) and lift the door off.

7   Installation is the reverse of removal.

Adjustment

Note: *When adjusting front doors remove the front inner fender panel. On rear door remove the B pillar lower trim.*

8   Having proper door-to-body alignment is a critical part of a well-functioning door assembly. First check the door hinge pins for excessive play. Fully open the door and lift up and down on the door without lifting the body. If a door has 1/16-inch or more excessive play, the hinges should be replaced.

9   Door-to-body alignment adjustments are made by loosening the hinge-to-body bolts or hinge-to-door bolts and moving the door. Proper body alignment is achieved when the top of the doors are parallel with the roof section, the front door is flush with the fender, the rear door is flush with the rear quarter panel

and the bottom of the doors are aligned with the lower rocker panel. If these goals can't be reached by adjusting the hinge-to-body or hinge-to-door fasteners, body alignment shims may have to be purchased and inserted behind the hinges to achieve correct alignment.

10   To adjust the door closed position, scribe a line or mark around the striker plate to provide a reference point, then check that the door latch is contacting the center of the latch striker. If not, adjust the up and down position first.

Note: *Check that the door and body edges are parallel. If necessary, adjust the door cushions to make the front and rear of the doors flush with the body.*

11   Finally, adjust the latch striker sideways position, so that the door panel is flush with the center pillar or rear quarter panel and provides positive engagement with the latch mechanism (see illustration).

16   Door latch, lock cylinder and outside handle - removal and installation

Caution: *Wear gloves when working inside the door openings to protect against cuts from sharp metal edges.*

Door latch

1   Raise the window all the way up.

2   Remove the door trim panel and watershield (see Section 14).

3   If necessary, pull the glass run channel out of the way, then remove the fastener securing the center lower glass run channel (see illustrations). Remove the center lower glass run channel.

2008 and earlier models

4   Remove the clips, and release the latch and lock rod from the door handle assembly (see illustration).

16.5 Disconnect the electrical connectors from the door latch

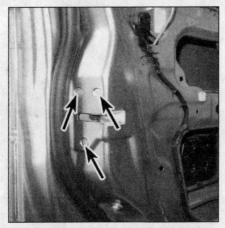

16.6 Door latch mounting fasteners

16.14 Remove the mounting fastener (Door handle removed for clarity)

16.15a Unclip the wiring harness. . .

16.15b. . . then disconnect the lock switch

16.16a Remove the fasteners. . .

5   Disconnect the actuator electrical connectors (see illustration).
6   Remove the fasteners securing the latch, then remove the latch (see illustration).
7   Installation is the reverse of removal.

2009 and later models
8   If equipped with power door locks, disconnect the door lock actuator electrical connector and detach the harness clip.
9   Detach the rod fastener then disconnect the outer handle rod from the handle.
10   Disconnect the lock cylinder cable from the latch.
11   Remove the door latch mounting fasteners, then remove the latch.
12   Installation is the reverse of removal.

Door handle and lock cylinder
13   Raise window all the way up and remove door trim panel Section 14
14   Remove the cylinder switch mounting fastener (see illustration).
15   Unclip the wiring harness, then discon-

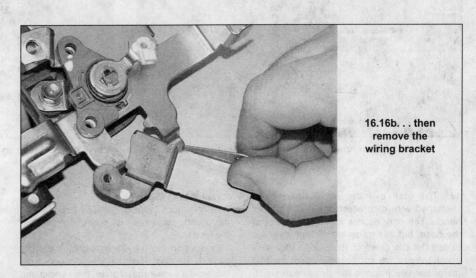

16.16b. . . then remove the wiring bracket

nect the cylinder switch electrical connector, and pull the switch and harness from inside the door(see illustrations).

16   Remove the wiring bracket mounting fastener, then remove the bracket (see illustrations).

16.17a At first, there was no room to pry down the clip. . .

16.17b. . . but when the thin metal bar broke, the clip could be pried down. . .

16.17c. . . and removed, which allows the lock cylinder. . .

16.17d. . . to be removed from the handle

16.19a Remove the two handle-to-plat mounting fasteners. . .

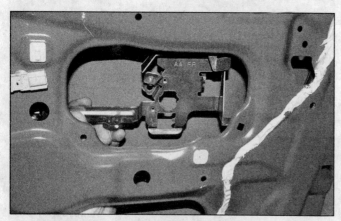

16.19b. . . then remove the metal plate inside the door

16.19c Unclip and remove the handle from the outside

17   The lock cylinder is retained by a U-shaped wire clip, which fits into the door handle. The only access is via a thin slot at the base, but this gives insufficient leverage to pull the clip down to release it. After several attempts, we accidentally broke the thin metal bar which forms the base of this slot, and found that this gave the leverage needed (the slot appears to serve no useful purpose). Once the cylinder is released, withdraw it into the door, and disconnect the lock cylinder lever rod (see illustrations).

18   If the lock cylinder cannot be remove as described, disconnect its operating rod from the handle.

19   Support the handle by taping it temporarily to the door. Remove the fasteners from the handle's inner metal plate, then unclip and remove the plate inside the door. Take off the handle from outside of the door (see illustrations).

20   Installation is the reverse of removal.

17   Door window glass and regulator - removal and installation

Caution: *Wear gloves when working inside the door openings to protect against cuts from sharp metal edges.*

Window glass

1   Remove the door trim panel and the

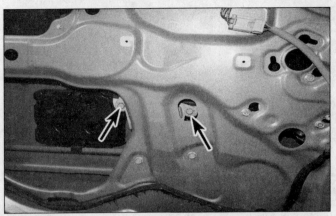

17.3 Remove the mounting fasteners securing the window glass

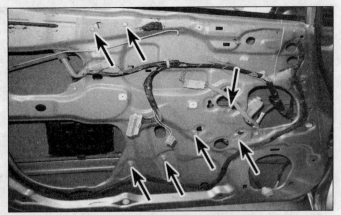

17.8 Window regulator mounting fasteners

18.2a Carefully pry out the clips. . .

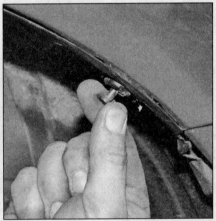

18.2b. . . then remove the clips around the arch. . .

18.2c. . . and remove the splash shield

plastic watershield (see Section 14).

2   On 2009 and later models, remove the door speaker (Chapter 12).

3   Move the window glass until the mounting fasteners are accessible, then remove them (see illustration).

4   Carefully pull the glass out through the window slot.

5   Installation is the reverse of removal.

Window regulator

6   Remove the window glass see Steps 1 thru 4.

7   Disconnect the electrical connector for the window regulator motor.

8   Remove the window regulator mounting fasteners (see illustration).

9   Carefully guide the regulator out of the door.

10   Installation is the reverse of removal.

18 Fenders - removal and installation

1   On 2009 and earlier models, remove the headlight housings (see Chapter 12).

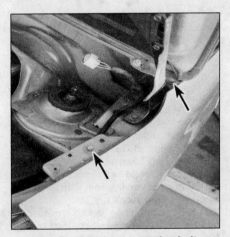

18.3a Fender upper mounting bolts

2   Remove the inner fender splash shield (see illustrations).

3   Remove the fender mounting bolts (see illustrations).

4   Carefully remove the front fender.

5   Installation is the reverse of removal.

18.3b Open the door and remove this fender bolt

19 Bumper covers - removal and installation

Warning: *The models covered by this manual are equipped with a Supplemental Restraint System (SRS), more commonly known as air-*

18.3c Fender rear lower mounting bolt

18.3d Fender front lower mounting bolt

19.3 Bumper cover upper mounting
fasteners (2008 and earlier models)

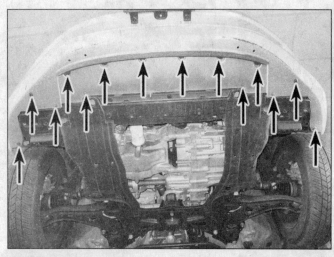

19.4 Bumper cover lower mounting fasteners (2009 alter models
shown, 2008 and earlier models similar

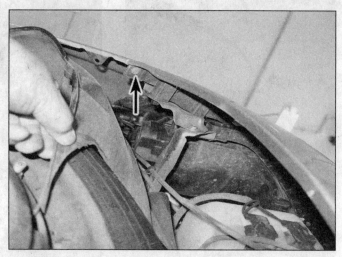

19.6 Remove the remaining fastener from both sides of the
bumper cover

bags. *Always disarm the airbag system before working in the vicinity of any airbag system component to avoid the possibility of accidental deployment of the airbag, which could cause personal injury (see Chapter 12). Do not use a memory saving device to preserve the PCM's memory when working on or near airbag system components.*
Note: *The bumper covers should be removed with the help of an assistant to prevent damage during removal.*

Front bumper cover

1   Apply protective tape to the front bumper edges where it contacts the headlights.
2   On 2009 and later models, remove the upper grille cover (see illustration 11.4).
3   On 2008 and earlier models, remove the bumper cover upper mounting fasteners (see illustration).
4   Remove the fasteners securing the bot-

tom of the bumper cover (see illustration).
5   Remove the fasteners securing the front of the inner fender splash shield (see illustrations 18.2a and 18.2b).
6   Gently pull down on the front of the inner fender splash shield and remove the remaining bumper cover fastener (left and right sides) (see illustration).
7   With the help of an assistant, release the attachment hooks and pull the front bumper forward and remove the cover.
8   Hold the bumper, and disconnect the front fog light connectors (if equipped).
9   Installation is the reverse of removal.

Rear bumper cover

10   Open the liftgate lid.
11   Remove the fasteners securing the upper part of the bumper cover (see illustration).
12   Remove the fasteners securing the bottom of the bumper cover (see illustration).

13   Working inside the rear fender well, remove the fastener securing the bumper cover (see illustration).
14   With the help of an assistant, hold the wheel arch portions away from the side spacer and pull the rear bumper to release the bumper from the hooks on the body.
15   Installation is the reverse of removal.

20   Mirrors - removal and installation

1   Raise the window all the way up.
2   Remove the inner door panel and plastic cover (Section 14).
3   If equipped with a power mirror, disconnect the electrical connector from the mirror (see illustration).
4   Remove the mounting fasteners securing the mirror (see illustration 20.3).

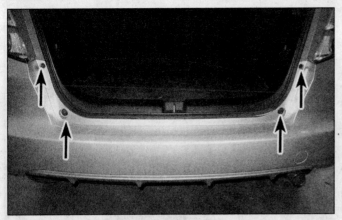

19.11 Remove the upper fasteners

19.12 Remove the bottom fasteners

19.13 Remove the fastener in the wheel well (right shown, left side similar

20.3 Power mirror electrical connector (A) and mounting fasteners (B)

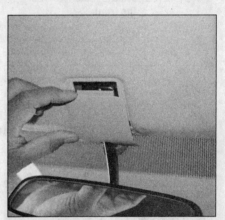

20.7 Pry off the cover

20.8 Remove the mounting fasteners

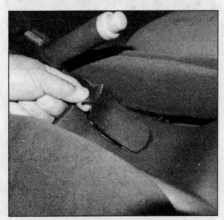

21.1 Carefully pry off the cover

21.2 Twist the shift knob counterclockwise to remove it

5   Remove the mirror.
6   Installation is the reverse of removal.

Inside mirror

7   Carefully pry off the mirror cover (see illustration).
8   Remove the fasteners securing the mirror (see illustration).
9   Installation is the reverse of removal.

21   Center console - removal and installation

Warning: *The models covered by this manual are equipped with a Supplemental Restraint System (SRS), more commonly known as airbags. Always disarm the airbag system before working in the vicinity of any airbag system component to avoid the possibility of accidental deployment of the airbag, which could*

cause personal injury (see Chapter 12). Do not use a memory saving device to preserve the PCM's memory when working on or near airbag system components.

1   On 2008 and earlier models, remove the parking brake cover lid (see illustration).
2   On manual transaxle models, remove the shift knob (see illustration).
3   On 2009 and later models, remove the console lid (cup holders) by prying up on the rear hook using a plastic tool. Continue to pry

21.4a Remove the fasteners from the front. . .

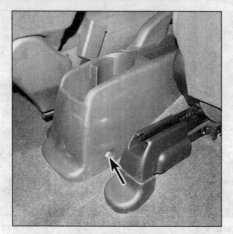

21.4b. . . and at the rear of the console (2008 and earlier model shown, 2009 and later models similar)

22.3a Remove the mounting fastener. . .

22.3b. . . then carefully pry around the edges of the panel to remove it

22.4a Disconnect the air mix cable. . .

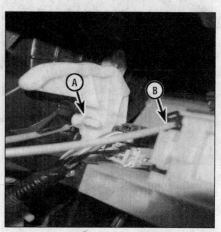

22.4b. . . mode control cable (A) and the recirculation control cable (B). . .

the lid up until it comes free.

4   Remove the fasteners securing the center console (see illustrations).

5   On 2008 and earlier models, lift up on the rear of the center console and pull the console rearward to release the front hook from the heater unit.

6   On 2009 and later models lift the rear of the console up to detach the clip, and pull the front pin from the heater unit.

7   Disconnect the accessory socket connector, and if equipped, auxiliary jack connector

8   Installation is the reverse of removal.

22 Dashboard trim panels - removal and installation

Warning: *The models covered by this manual are equipped with a Supplemental Restraint System (SRS), more commonly known as airbags. Always disarm the airbag system before*

working in the vicinity of any airbag system component to avoid the possibility of accidental deployment of the airbag, which could cause personal injury (see Chapter 12). Do not use a memory saving device to preserve the PCM's memory when working on or near airbag system components.

Caution: *Plastic trim tools must be used on all operations in this Section to avoid damage to the soft plastic interior parts (see Section 6).*

1   Disconnect the cable from the negative terminal of the battery (see Chapter 5)

Center panel

2008 and earlier models

2   Remove the glove box (see Steps 32 through 34).

3   Remove the lower vent cover by removing the mounting fastener, then carefully pry the panel loose to release the clips (see illustrations).

4   Working inside the glove box opening, disconnect the air mix control, mode control

and recirculation control cables (see illustrations).

5   Remove the fasteners securing the center panel (see illustration).

6   Carefully pry around the center panel to release the clips, then disconnect the electrical connectors (see illustration).

7   Remove the center panel.

8   Installation is the reverse of removal.

2009 and later models

Note: *The audio unit (radio) is part of the center panel. Be sure the record the 4-digit anti-theft code for the audio system before removing the center panel.*

9   Carefully pry out the lower center cover and remove it (see illustration). Disconnect any electric connectors from the panel.

10   Place the recirculation control lever on Fresh air position (see illustration) for access to the audio unit mounting fastener, then remove the fastener.

11   Open the dashboard upper try (see illustration), then working in the left corner of the

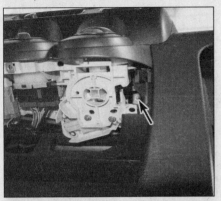

22.5 Center panel mounting fastener (right side fastener shown, left side similar)

22.6 Pry around the outside of the panel to release the clips

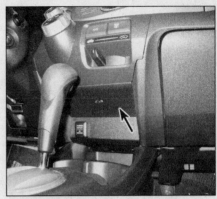

22.9 Remove the lower center cover

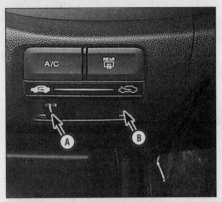

22.10 Move the control lever (A) to the Fresh air position (B)

22.11 Dashboard upper tray

22.16 Pry the cluster bezel rearward to release its clips (2008 and earlier model shown, 2009 and later models similar)

22.19 Lower visor mounting fasteners

22.20 Pull the visor rearward to remove it

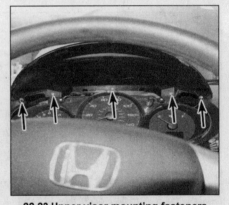

22.23 Upper visor mounting fasteners

tray, find the small groove on the edge of the center panel. Insert a flat-tip screwdriver into the groove and pry upward on the edge of the center panel.

12   Pull the center panel outward to release the clips, then disconnect the electrical connectors and remove the center panel.

13   Installation is the reverse of removal.

Instrument cluster bezel

14   Pull the steering wheel out, and tilt it all the way down.

15   On 2009 and later models, pull out the select/reset knob to disconnect it from the cluster.

16   Pull or pry the bezel rearward to unclip the it (see illustration), then remove it from the instrument panel. On 2009 and later models, disconnect the power mirror electrical connector.

17   Installation is the reverse of removal.

Instrument cluster visor (2008 and earlier models)

Lower visor

18   Remove the instrument cluster bezel

(see Steps 14 thru 16).

19   Remove the fasteners securing the lower visor (see illustration).

20   Pull the visor rearward to release any clips, then remove the visor (see illustration).

21   Installation is the reverse of removal.

Upper visor

22   Remove the lower visor (see Steps 18 thru 20).

23   Remove the fasteners securing the upper visor (see illustration).

22.24 Pull the visor rearward to remove it

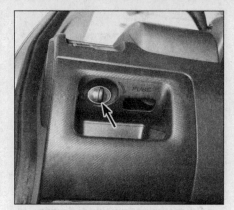

22.26 Turn the knob 90-degrees counterclockwise

22.27 Pull the access door rearward and remove it

22.29a Place your hand in the slot. . .

22.29b. . . and pull downward and away to release the clips

22.32 Remove the glove box mounting fasteners

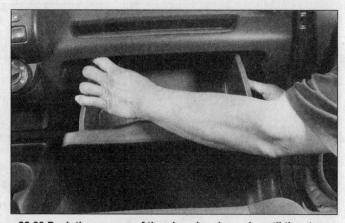

22.33 Push the corners of the glove box inwards until the stops clear, then pull out the box

24   Pull the visor rearward and remove the visor (see illustration).
25   Installation is the reverse of removal.

Under-dash fuse/relay box access door

2008 and earlier models

26   Turn the access knob 90-degrees counterclockwise to release the latch (see illustration).

27   Pull the access door rearward to release the clips, then remove the door (see illustration).
28   Installation is the reverse of removal.

2009 and later models

29   Pull the access panel downward to release the clips, then pull the panel rearward to release the hinges (see illustrations).
30   If equipped, disconnect the electrical connector, then remove the panel.

31   Installation is the reverse of removal.

Glove box

32   Remove the two glove box mounting fasteners (see illustration).
33   While holding the glove box, disengage the stops from the sides of the glove box (see illustration).
34   Remove the glove box.
35   Installation is the reverse of removal.

22.36 Turn the release knob 90-degrees

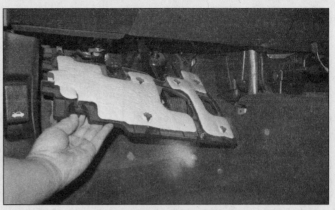

22.37 Pull the panel down and away

22.39a Pull down on the nearest edge

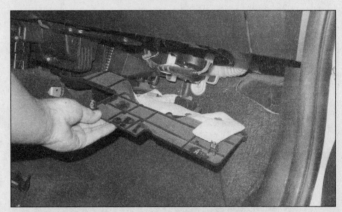

22.39b Remove the panel from the dashboard

23.2 Steering column cover fasteners

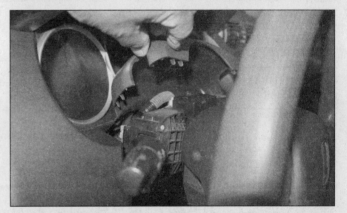

23.3 Separate the steering column covers

Dashboard underpanel

Left side underpanel

36   Turn the release knob 90-degrees to release the panel (see illustration).

37   Pull the panel down and away from the dashboard to remove the panel (see illustration).

38   Installation is the revers of removal.

Right side underpanel

39   Carefully pull down on the nearest edge to release the clips, then pull the panel away from the dashboard to remove it (see illustrations).

40   Installation is the reverse of removal.

23   Steering column covers - removal and installation

Warning: *The models covered by this manual are equipped with a Supplemental Restraint System (SRS), more commonly known as airbags. Always disarm the airbag system before working in the vicinity of any airbag system component to avoid the possibility of accidental deployment of the airbag, which could cause personal injury (see Chapter 12). Do not use a memory saving device to preserve the PCM's memory when working on or near airbag system components.*

Note: *Release the tilt/telescope steering wheel lever (if equipped), tilt the steering column fully down, and pull the steering wheel all the way out to make cover removal easier.*

1   Disconnect the cable from the negative terminal of the battery (see Chapter 5).

2   Remove the fasteners securing the steering column cover (see illustration),

3   Pry the upper cover until it unclips from the lower cover (see illustration).

4   Installation is the reverse of removal.

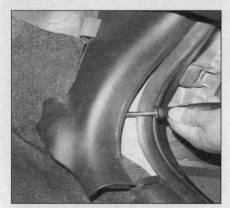

24.10 Carefully pry off the kick panels from both sides of the passenger compartment

24.11 Unplug the fusebox electrical connectors

24.12 Disconnect the electrical connectors

24.17 Disconnect the electrical connectors at the blower motor

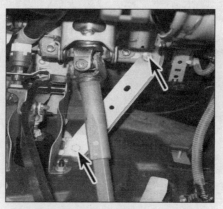

24.18 Remove the fasteners securing the brace

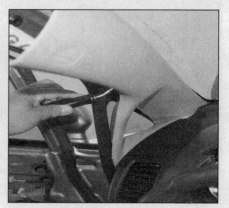

24.20 Carefully pry off the A-pillar trim panels

24   Instrument panel - removal and installation

Warning: *The models covered by this manual are equipped with a Supplemental Restraint System (SRS), more commonly known as airbags. Always disarm the airbag system before working in the vicinity of any airbag system component to avoid the possibility of accidental deployment of the airbag, which could cause personal injury (see Chapter 12). Do not use a memory saving device to preserve the PCM's memory when working on or near airbag system components.*

Note: *This is a difficult procedure for the home mechanic. There are many hidden fasteners, difficult angles to work in and many electrical connectors to tag and disconnect/connect. We recommend that this procedure be done only by an experienced do-it-yourselfer.*

Note: *During removal of the instrument panel, make careful notes of how each piece comes off, where it fits in relation to the other pieces and what holds it in place. If you note note how each part is installed before removing it, getting the instrument panel back together again will be much easier.*

1   Disconnect the cable from the negative

terminal of the battery (see Chapter 5).
2   Remove the center console (see Section 21).
3   Remove the steering wheel (see Chapter 10).
4   Remove the dashboard trim panels (see Section 22).
5   Remove the steering column covers (see Section 23).
6   Remove the glove box (see Section 22).
7   Remove the front seats (see Section 26), (though not absolutely necessary, removing both front seats allows more room to work and eliminates the possibility of damage to the seats during the procedure)
8   Remove the bolt securing the under-dash fuse/relay box on the driver's side.
9   Remove the heater upper duct by taking out the insulation, detaching the clips and lifting the rear of the duct upward.
10   Remove the right and left side kick panels (see illustration).
11   Disconnect all the connectors from the under-dash fuse/relay box (see illustration).
12   From under the dash, disconnect the driver's door wire harness connectors, brake switch connector, accelerator pedal position sensor connector, and on M/T models, clutch switch connector(s) (see illustration).

13   Remove the radio (see Chapter 12).
14   From under the dash, disconnect the ECM/PCM connectors, engine wire harness connector, passenger door wire harness connector (front SRS sensor), subwire harness connector and antenna connector.
15   On 2009 and later models, from under dash disconnect SRS control unit connector, and if equipped, the yaw rate-lateral acceleration sensor connector and detach the harness clips.
16   On 2009 and later models, disconnect the antenna lead connector on the passenger side.
17   On 2009 and later models, disconnect all the electrical connectors at the heater blower motor (see illustration).
18   Remove the bolts, then remove the brake pedal support brace (see illustration).
19   Mark the relationship of the upper steering column shaft to the lower shaft, remove the steering column pinch-bolt and separate the upper column shaft from the lower shaft. Discard the old pinch bolt and install a new one when you reassemble the steering column.
20   Remove the A-pillar trim panels (see illustration).
21   Remove the heater floor duct (see illustrations).

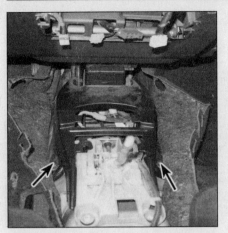

24.21a Remove the push pin fasteners. . .

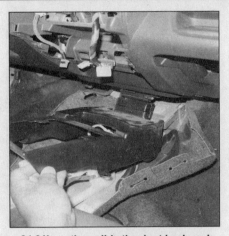

24.21b. . . then slide the duct back and lift it out

24.22 Floor support mounting fasteners (left side shown, right side similar)

24.23 Pry the caps off

24.24 Unscrew the bolt, pull it out, then unscrew it until it can be removed

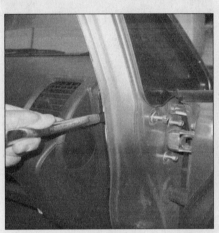

24.25 Gently turn the three nuts fully counterclockwise

22   Remove the fasteners for the brace-to-floor support bracket (see illustration).

Note: *The instrument panel is attached with 6 special bolts (3 per side at each end). These are difficult to access and the door may interfere with their removal. To prevent damaging the door and/or the bolts, do not move the door past the second detent position while the forward bolt is loosened.*

23   Remove the plastic caps from the instrument panel mounting bolts on the passenger side (see illustration).

24   Unscrew the first bolt until it is felt to be free of the threads, then continue turning in a loosening direction. Keep turning the bolt until it can be removed completely (see illustration). Repeat this process for the other two bolts.

Note: *The bolt which is furthest to the front cannot be removed completely as it hits the door - remove as far as possible for now.*

25   The three large nuts now visible at the end of the instrument panel have a left-hand thread, meaning they tighten by turning in the unscrewing direction (counterclockwise). Using a wrench, turn the three nuts gently counterclockwise - do not use any force, just ensure they are turned fully counterclockwise (see illustration).

26   Open the driver's door, and pry off the caps from the three bolts on the end of the instrument panel. Unscrew and remove the bolts.

27   The instrument panel now rests on five locating pins - one on each side, and three along the windshield. With the help of an assistant, lift the instrument panel evenly both sides to clear the pins. Check that nothing is still attached to the instrument panel to prevent its removal, then take the instrument panel out through one of the doors (see illustration).

28   Installation is the reverse of removal. When installing the A-pillar trim panels, attach the tethers.

24.27 With the help of an assistant, remove the instrument panel through the door

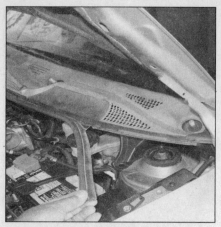

25.2 Carefully remove the hood seal

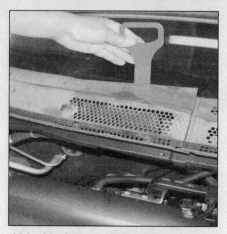

25.3a Carefully pry off the right side cowl from the rear of the cowl. . .

25.3b. . . then remove the cowl cover from the left side

25.7 Carefully pry up the hinge covers

25.9 Carefully pry off the fasteners from both ends of the cowl

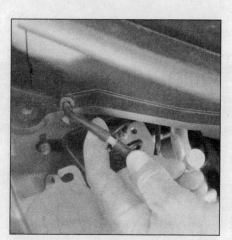

25.10 Disconnect the washer tube

25 Cowl cover and lower cowl - removal and installation

Cowl cover

2008 and earlier models

1   Remove the windshield wiper arms (see Chapter 12).
2   Remove the seal for the hood (see illustration).
3   Carefully pry the right side cowl cover, then the left side cover (see illustrations).
4   Pull the cowl cover forward to release the hooks, then remove the cover.
5   Disconnect the tubes for the windshield washer fluid.
6   Installation is the reverse of removal.

2009 and later models

7   Remove the left and right hood hinge covers (see illustration).
8   Open the hood and remove the windshield wiper arms.
9   Remove the fasteners securing the ends of the cowl cover (see illustration).
10   Disconnect the windshield washer tube (see illustration).

11   Detach the clips by carefully prying the windshield side edge of the cowl cover upward (see illustration).
12   Pull the cowl cover forward to release the front hooks from the under-cowl panel.
13   Remove the cowl cover.
14   Installation is the reverse of removal.

Lower cowl (2009 and later models)

15   Remove the cowl cover (see Steps 8 through 13).
16   Disconnct the wiper motor electrical connector, then remove the cowl mounting fasteners (see illustrations).
17   Remove the cowl and wiper motor assembly from the vehicle.
Note: *It isn't necessary to remove the wiper motor assembly from the lower cowl.*
18   Installation is the reverse of removal.

26 Seats - removal and installation

Warning: *The models covered by this manual are equipped with a Supplemental Restraint System (SRS), more commonly known as air-*

25.11 Only use a plastic pry tool when prying the cover up from the windshield

bags. Always disarm the airbag system before working in the vicinity of any airbag system component to avoid the possibility of accidental deployment of the airbag, which could cause personal injury (see Chapter 12). Do not use a memory saving device to preserve the PCM's memory when working on or near airbag system components.

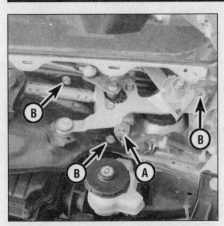

25.16a Disconnect the electrical connector
(A) , then remove the mounting fasteners
(B) from the left. . .

25.16b. . . middle. . .

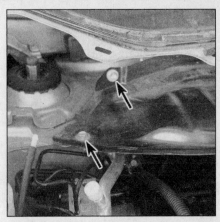

25.16c. . . and right side of the lower cowl

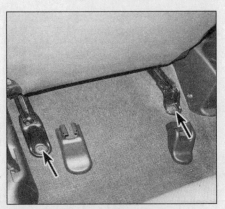

26.2 Remove the seat rear
mounting fasteners

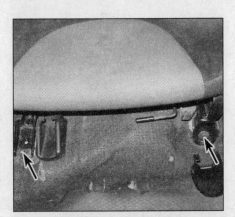

26.3 Remove the seat front
mounting fasteners

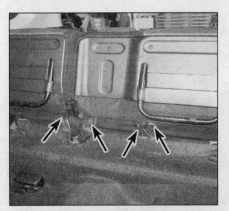

26.8 Pull the seat belt buckles through the
slots in the seat cushions

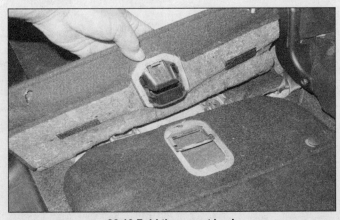

26.10 Fold the carpet back

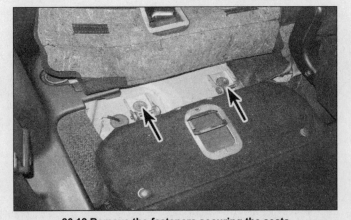

26.12 Remove the fasteners securing the seats

Front seat

1   Disconnect the cable from the negative terminal of the battery (see Chapter 5).
2   Move the seat to the fully forward position, remove the two seat track covers, then remove the front seat rear mounting fasteners (see illustration).
3   Move the seat to the rearward position, remove the track covers, then remove the front mounting fasteners (see illustration).
4   Lift up the front seat and detach the har-
ness clips then disconnect the electrical connectors.
5   Remove the seat head restraint.
6   With the help of an assistant, carefully remove the front seat.
7   Installation is the reverse of removal.

Rear seat

8   Pull the rear seat belt buckles and the center seat belt detachable anchor out through each elastic band on both seat cushions with
the seat cushions lifted up (see illustration).
9   Fold both rear seats forward.
10   From bottom of both rear seat-backs, release the fasteners at the rear of the carpet and fold the carpet back (see illustration).
11   On 2009 and later models, lift up the cargo floor lids.
12   Remover the seat mounting fasteners (see illustration).
13   Remove the rear seats through the rear of the liftgate.
14   Installation is the reverse of removal.

Notes

Chapter 12
Chassis electrical system

Contents

1   General information

1   The electrical system is a 12-volt, negative ground type. Power for the lights and all electrical accessories is supplied by a lead/acid-type battery that is charged by the alternator.

2   This Chapter covers repair and service procedures for the various electrical components not associated with the engine. Information on the battery, alternator, ignition system and starter motor can be found in Chapter 5.

3   It should be noted that when portions of the electrical system are serviced, the negative cable should be disconnected from the battery to prevent electrical shorts and/or fires.

2   Electrical troubleshooting - general information

1   A typical electrical circuit consists of an electrical component, any switches, relays, motors, fuses, fusible links or circuit breakers related to that component and the wiring and connectors that link the component to both the battery and the chassis. To help you pinpoint an electrical circuit problem, wiring diagrams are included in Chapter 13.

2   Before tackling any troublesome electrical circuit, first study the appropriate wiring diagrams to get a complete understanding of what makes up that individual circuit. Trouble spots, for instance, can often be narrowed down by noting if other components related to the circuit are operating properly.

If several components or circuits fail at one time, chances are the problem is in a fuse or ground connection, because several circuits are often routed through the same fuse and ground connections.

3   Electrical problems usually stem from simple causes, such as loose or corroded connections, a blown fuse, a melted fusible link or a failed relay. Visually inspect the condition of all fuses, wires and connections in a problem circuit before troubleshooting the circuit.

4   If test equipment and instruments are going to be utilized, use the diagrams to plan ahead of time where you will make the necessary connections in order to accurately pinpoint the trouble spot.

5   The basic tools needed for electrical troubleshooting include a circuit tester or

voltmeter (a 12-volt bulb with a set of test leads can also be used), a continuity tester, which includes a bulb, battery and set of test leads, and a jumper wire, preferably with a circuit breaker incorporated, which can be used to bypass electrical components (see illustrations). Before attempting to locate a problem with test instruments, use the wiring diagram(s) to decide where to make the connections.

Voltage checks

6   Voltage checks should be performed if a circuit is not functioning properly. Connect one lead of a circuit tester to either the negative battery terminal or a known good ground. Connect the other lead to a connector in the circuit being tested, preferably nearest to the battery or fuse (see illustration). If the bulb of the tester lights, voltage is present, which means that the part of the circuit between the connector and the battery is problem free. Continue checking the rest of the circuit in the same fashion. When you reach a point at which no voltage is present, the problem lies between that point and the last test point with voltage. Most of the time the problem can be traced to a loose connection.

Note: *Keep in mind that some circuits receive voltage only when the ignition key is in the Accessory or Run position.*

Finding a short

7   One method of finding shorts in a circuit is to remove the fuse and connect a test light or voltmeter in place of the fuse terminals. There should be no voltage present in the circuit. Move the wiring harness from side-to-side while watching the test light. If the bulb goes on, there is a short to ground somewhere in that area, probably where the insulation has rubbed through. The same test can be performed on each component in the

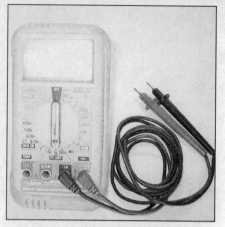

2.5a The most useful tool for electrical troubleshooting is a digital multimeter that can check volts, amps, and test continuity

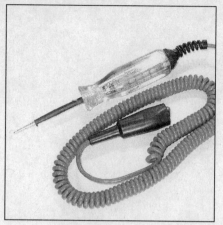

2.5b A test light is a very handy tool for checking voltage

circuit, even a switch.

8   If the short isn't obvious or you're having trouble locating it, seek professional help from an electrical repair shop or dealership.

Ground check

9   Perform a ground test to check whether a component is properly grounded. Disconnect the battery and connect one lead of a continuity tester or multimeter (set to the ohms scale), to a known good ground. Connect the other lead to the wire or ground connection being tested. If the resistance is low (less than 5 ohms), the ground is good. If the bulb on a self-powered test light does not go on, the ground is not good.

Continuity check

10   A continuity check is done to determine if there are any breaks in a circuit - if it is passing electricity properly. With the circuit off (no

power in the circuit), a self-powered continuity tester or multimeter can be used to check the circuit. Connect the test leads to both ends of the circuit (or to the power end and a good ground), and if the test light comes on the circuit is passing current properly (see illustration). If the resistance is low (less than 5 ohms), there is continuity; if the reading is 10,000 ohms or higher, there is a break somewhere in the circuit. The same procedure can be used to test a switch, by connecting the continuity tester to the switch terminals. With the switch turned On, the test light should come on (or low resistance should be indicated on a meter).

Finding an open circuit

11   When diagnosing for possible open circuits, it is often difficult to locate them by sight because the connectors hide oxidation or terminal misalignment. Merely wiggling a

2.6 In use, a basic test light's lead is clipped to a known good ground, then the pointed probe can test connectors, wires or electrical sockets - if the bulb lights, the part being tested has battery voltage

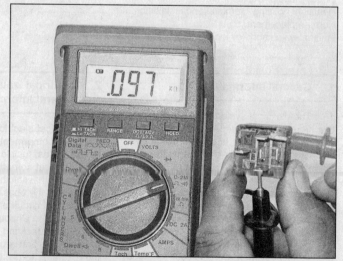

2.10 With a multimeter set to the ohms scale, resistance can be checked across two terminals - when checking for continuity, a low reading indicates continuity, a high reading indicates lack of continuity

4.1a The interior fuse box is located under the left side of the dash. This is a earlier model . . .

4.1b . . . and this is a 2009 and later model

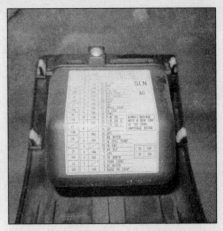

4.1c The fuse box chart is on the cover

connector on a sensor or in the wiring harness may correct the open circuit condition. Remember this when an open circuit is indicated when troubleshooting a circuit. Intermittent problems may also be caused by oxidized or loose connections.

12 Electrical troubleshooting is simple if you keep in mind that all electrical circuits are basically electricity running from the battery, through the wires, switches, relays, fuses and fusible links to each electrical component (light bulb, motor, etc.) and to ground, from which it is passed back to the battery. Any electrical problem is an interruption in the flow of electricity to and from the battery.

13 Start by reading the wiring diagram. Knowing where the lead starts and ends will be important in tracing out an open circuit. Always check either side of any connector (when possible) to make sure the open isn't in the connection. Pick a point in the circuit that you can easily access and test backward in both directions. Once you have found which half the open is in, do the same thing to that half, soon and so on, until you've found it.

---

3 Parasitic battery drain

1 Parasitic drain (sometimes referred to as a parasitic load) is the tendency of the electrical system to drain down the battery's usable energy over a certain amount of time when the ignition is turned off. The small amount of current draw is described in milliamps (mA). 30 milliamps (0.030 amps) is the allowable amount of current draw. An amp meter placed between the post and the battery clamp is used to obtain the readings. Each model, and each model type (depending on which accessories have been added, or were factory equipped) will have a slightly different acceptable parasitic drain.

2 Parasitic battery drain is different from an open or a short in the system; this parasitic load is supposed to be there to allow certain modules, computers, and other devices to

4.1d The engine compartment fuse/relay box is located along the left side of the engine compartment. To release the cover, depress the tabs and lift upwards

gain the necessary voltage to maintain internal requirements. Some modules will power down after a few minutes, some can take up to 45 minutes or more to completely power down (commonly called "going to sleep" or "sleep mode"). Checking for a battery drain on these models takes a highly skilled technician with the proper equipment. It is not advisable to attempt this without proper training.

---

4 Fuses, fusible links and circuit breakers - general information

Fuses

1 The electrical circuits of the vehicle are protected by a combination of fuses, circuit breakers and fusible links. The main fuse/relay panel is in the engine compartment on the driver's (left) side, next to the battery. The interior fuse/relay panel is located inside the passenger compartment under the driver's (left) side of the dash (see illustrations). Each of the fuses is designed to protect a specific

4.3 When a fuse blows, the element between the terminals melts

circuit, and the various circuits are identified on the fuse panel itself.

2 Several sizes of fuses are employed in the fuse blocks. There are small, medium and large sizes of the same design, all with the same blade terminal design. The medium and large fuses can be removed with your fingers, but the small fuses require the use of pliers or the small plastic fuse-puller tool found in most fuse boxes.

3 If an electrical component fails, always check the fuse first. The best way to check the fuses is with a test light. Check for power at the exposed terminal tips of each fuse. If power is present at one side of the fuse but not the other, the fuse is blown. A blown fuse can also be identified by visually inspecting it (see illustration).

4 Be sure to replace blown fuses with the correct type. Fuses (of the same physical size) of different ratings may be physically interchangeable, but only fuses of the proper rating should be used. Replacing a fuse with one of a higher or lower value than specified is not recommended. Each electrical circuit needs a specific amount of protection. The

amperage value of each fuse is molded into the top of the fuse body.

5   If the replacement fuse immediately fails, don't replace it again until the cause of the problem is isolated and corrected. In most cases, this will be a short circuit in the wiring caused by a broken or deteriorated wire.

Fusible links

6   Some circuits are protected by fusible links. The links are used in circuits which are not ordinarily fused, or which carry high current, such as the circuit between the alternator and the starter motor. Cartridge-type fusible links are located in the engine compartment fuse/relay box and are similar to a large fuse. After disconnecting the negative battery cable, simply unplug the fusible link and replace it with a fusible link of the same amperage. If you have to replace a blown fusible link, make sure that you replace it with one of the same rating. If the replacement fusible link blows in the same circuit, make sure that you troubleshoot the circuit in which the fusible link melted BEFORE installing another fusible link.

Circuit breakers

7   Circuit breakers protect certain circuits, such as the power windows or heated seats. Depending on the vehicle's accessories, there may be one or two circuit breakers, located in the fuse/relay box in the engine compartment.

8   Because the circuit breakers reset automatically, an electrical overload in a circuit breaker-protected system will cause the circuit to fail momentarily, then come back on. If the circuit does not come back on, check it immediately.

9   For a basic check, pull the circuit breaker up out of its socket on the fuse panel, but just far enough to probe with a voltmeter. The breaker should still contact the sockets. With the voltmeter negative lead on a good chassis ground, touch each end prong of the circuit breaker with the positive meter probe. There should be battery voltage at each end. If there is battery voltage only at one end, the circuit

breaker must be replaced.

10   Some circuit breakers must be reset manually.

5   Relays - general information and testing

General information

1   Several electrical accessories in the vehicle, such as the fuel injection system, horns, starter, and fog lamps use relays to transmit the electrical signal to the component. Relays use a low-current circuit (the control circuit) to open and close a high-current circuit (the power circuit). If the relay is defective, that component will not operate properly. Most relays are mounted in the engine compartment and interior fuse/relay boxes. If a faulty relay is suspected, it can be removed and tested using the procedure below or by a dealer service department or a repair shop. Defective relays must be replaced as a unit.

Testing

2   Most of the relays used in these vehicles are of a type often called ISO relays, which refers to the International Standards Organization. The terminals of ISO relays are numbered to indicate their usual circuit connections and functions. There are two basic layouts of terminals on the relays used in these vehicles (see illustrations).

3   Refer to the wiring diagram for the circuit to determine the proper connections for the relay you're testing. If you can't determine the correct connection from the wiring diagrams, however, you may be able to determine the test connections from the information that follows.

4   Two of the terminals are the relay control circuit and connect to the relay coil. The other relay terminals are the power circuit. When the relay is energized, the coil creates a magnetic field that closes the larger contacts of the power circuit to provide power to the cir-

cuit loads.

5   Terminals 85 and 86 are normally the control circuit. If the relay contains a diode, terminal 86 must be connected to battery positive (B+) voltage and terminal 85 to ground. If the relay contains a resistor, terminals 85 and 86 can be connected in either direction with respect to B+ and ground.

6   Terminal 30 is normally connected to the battery voltage (B+) source for the circuit loads. Terminal 87 is connected to the ground side of the circuit, either directly or through a load. If the relay has several alternate terminals for load or ground connections, they usually are numbered 87A, 87B, 87C, and so on.

7   Use an ohmmeter to check continuity through the relay control coil.

Connect the meter according to the polarity shown in the illustration for one check; then reverse the ohmmeter leads and check continuity in the other direction.

If the relay contains a resistor, resistance should be indicated on the meter, and should be the same value with the ohmmeter in either direction.

If the relay contains a diode, resistance should be higher with the ohmmeter in the forward polarity direction than with the meter leads reversed.

If the ohmmeter shows infinite resistance in both directions, replace the relay.

8   Remove the relay from the vehicle and use the ohmmeter to check for continuity between the relay power circuit terminals. There should be no continuity between terminal 30 and 87 with the relay de-energized.

9   Connect a fused jumper wire to terminal 86 and the positive battery terminal. Connect another jumper wire between terminal 85 and ground. When the connections are made, the relay should click.

10   With the jumper wires connected, check for continuity between the power circuit terminals. Now, there should be continuity between terminals 30 and 87.

11   If the relay fails any of the above tests, replace it.

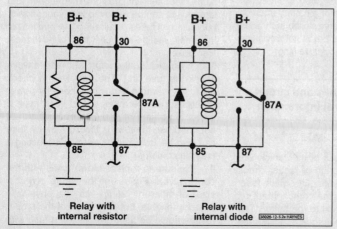

5.2a Typical ISO relay designs, terminal numbering and circuit connections

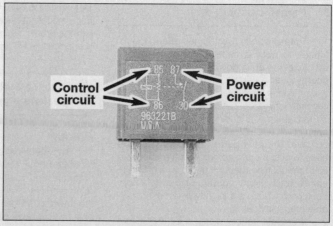

5.2b Most relays are marked on the outside to easily identify the control circuit and power circuit - this one is of the four-terminal type

6   Electrical connectors - general information

1   Most electrical connections on these vehicles are made with multiwire plastic connectors. The mating halves of many connectors are secured with locking clips molded into the plastic connector shells. The mating halves of some large connectors, such as some of those under the instrument panel, are held together by a bolt through the center of the connector.

2   To separate a connector with locking clips, use a small screwdriver to pry the clips apart carefully, then separate the connec-tor halves. Pull only on the shell, never pull on the wiring harness as you may damage the individual wires and terminals inside the connectors. Look at the connector closely before trying to separate the halves. Often the locking clips are engaged in a way that is not immediately clear. Additionally, many connectors have more than one set of clips.

3   Each pair of connector terminals has a male half and a female half. When you look at the end view of a connector in a diagram, be sure to understand whether the view shows the harness side or the component side of the connector. Connector halves are mirror images of each other, and a terminal shown on the right side end-view of one half will be on the left side end-view of the other half.

4   It is often necessary to take circuit voltage measurements with a connector connected. Whenever possible, carefully insert a small straight pin (not your meter probe) into the rear of the connector shell to contact the terminal inside, then clip your meter lead to the pin. This kind of connection is called "backprobing." When inserting a test probe into a terminal, be careful not to distort the terminal opening. Doing so can lead to a poor connection and corrosion at that terminal later. Using the small straight pin instead of a meter probe results in less chance of deforming the terminal connector.

Electrical connectors

Most electrical connectors have a single release tab that you depress to release the connector

Some electrical connectors have a retaining tab which must be pried up to free the connector

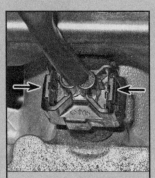

Some connectors have two release tabs that you must squeeze to release the connector

Some connectors use wire retainers that you squeeze to release the connector

Critical connectors often employ a sliding lock (1) that you must pull out before you can depress the release tab (2)

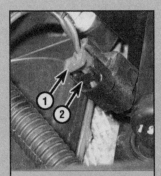

Here's another sliding-lock style connector, with the lock (1) and the release tab (2) on the side of the connector

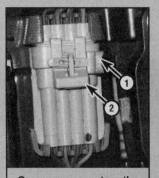

On some connectors the lock (1) must be pulled out to the side and removed before you can lift the release tab (2)

Some critical connectors, like the multi-pin connectors at the Powertrain Control Module employ pivoting locks that must be flipped open

7.1 Remove the screw

7.2a Separate the two halves of the transmitter housing

7.2b Remove the transmitter from the transmitter housing. . .

7.2c. . . then pry open the retainers on both ends of the transmitter. . .

7.2d. . . and carefully remove the battery

7.2e When installing the new battery, make sure that the positive side faces down (toward the transmitter)

7   Remote keyless entry fob - battery replacement

Note: *The ignition key and the key fob are built together as one assembly.*
1   Remove the single screw from the key assembly (see illustration).

2   Carefully separate the key fob housing (see illustrations).
Caution: *Handle the battery by its edges only; holding it like a coin (touching the top and bottom flat surfaces) can reduce the battery's life by partially discharging it.*
3   Installation is the reverse of removal.
Note: *For key fob programming see they keyless entry system Section 23.*

8   Steering column switches - replacement

Warning: *The models covered by this manual are equipped with Supplemental Restraint Systems (SRS), more commonly known as airbags. Always disable the airbag system before working in the vicinity of any airbag system components to avoid the possibility of accidental deployment of the airbags, which could cause personal injury (see Section 24).*
1   Disconnect the cable from the negative terminal of the battery (see Chapter 5).
2   Remove the steering column covers (see Chapter 11).

Wiper/washer switch

3   Turn the steering wheel 90 degrees from the straight ahead position to gain access to the screws.
4   Disconnect the wiper/washer switch electrical connector (see illustration).
5   Remove the two screws securing the switch to the steering column (see illustration).
6   Pull the switch away from the column to remove it.
7   Installation is the reverse of removal.

8.4 Disconnect the electrical connector

8.5 Remove the mounting fasteners

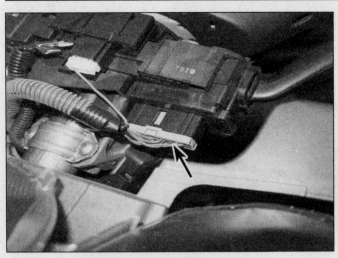
8.8 Disconnect the electrical connector

8.9 Remove the two screws securing the switch to the
steering column.

9.4 Instrument cluster mounting fasteners (2008 and earlier
models shown, 2009 and later models similar)

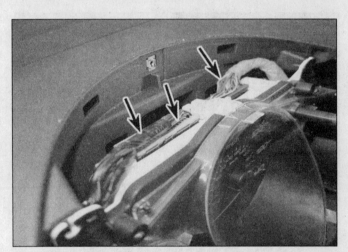
9.5 Disconnect the electrical connectors

Turn signal/headlight switch

Note: *The lighting and turn signal switch is also know as the combination switch.*

8   Disconnect the electrical connector from the switch (see illustration).
9   Turn the steering wheel 90 degrees from the straight ahead position and remove the fasteners securing the combination switch (see illustration).
10   Pull the switch away from the steering column to remove it.
11   Installation is the reverse of removal.

Hazard switch- replacement

Note: *The hazard switch is part of the turn signal system. The right or left turn signal can fail due to a faulty hazard switch as well as a faulty turn signal switch. Before replacing either switch try clicking the hazard switch on and off several times to check whether or not the switch is stuck between positions.*

2008 and earlier models models

12   Remove the Instrument cluster (see Section 9).
13   Reach behind the hazard switch and press in on the tabs securing the switch to the dash.
14   While pressing in on the tabs push the switch out of the dash.
15   Disconnect the electrical connector.
16   Installation is the reverse of removal.

2009 and later models

17   Remove the radio assembly (see Section 10).
18   Remove the two screws securing the hazard switch to the trim panel.
19   Disconnect the electrical connector.
20   Installation is the reverse of removal.

9   Instrument cluster - removal and installation

Warning: *The models covered by this manual are equipped with Supplemental Restraint Systems (SRS), more commonly known as airbags. Always disable the airbag system before working in the vicinity of any airbag system components to avoid the possibility of accidental deployment of the airbags, which could cause personal injury (see Section 24).*

1   Disconnect the cable from the negative terminal of the battery (see Chapter 5).
2   Tilt steering wheel to its lowest position.
3   Remove the instrument cluster bezel (see Chapter 11).
4   Remove the fasteners securing the instrument cluster (see illustration).
5   Pull the cluster outward, then disconnect the instrument cluster electrical connectors (see illustration).
6   Remove the instrument cluster.
7   Installation is the reverse of removal.

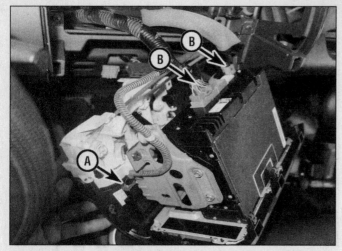

10.2 Disconnect the antenna (A) and the electrical connectors (B)

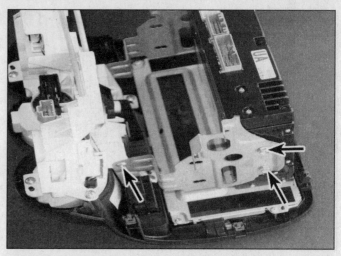

10.3 Remove the fasteners securing the brackets (left side shown)

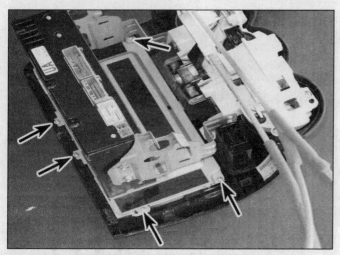

10.4 Remove the fasteners securing the radio to the center panel (not all fasteners shown in picture)

10.12 Carefully pry at the top of the speaker to release the clip

10   Radio, speakers - removal and installation

Warning: *The models covered by this manual are equipped with Supplemental Restraint Systems (SRS), more commonly known as airbags. Always disable the airbag system before working in the vicinity of any airbag system components to avoid the possibility of accidental deployment of the airbags, which could cause personal injury (see Section 24).*

Radio

Note: *Make sure to have the radio security codes and the relearn procedure before attempting any repairs.*
Note: *Anytime the battery is disconnected the audio system will need to be reset. You should have your 5 digit code already but if you don't there is a procedure to find out what the code is. With the ignition ON and radio OFF depress the 1 and 6 preset buttons then turn on the radio. The display should show "S/N 12345678"*

for example. The eight numbers are the audio units serial number. Call your local dealership parts department to obtain the 5 digit code for reprogramming your audio system.
1   Disconnect the cable from the negative terminal of the battery (see Chapter 5).

2008 and earlier models

2   Remove the center panel (see Chapter 11). Once the panel is free and far enough out to reach behind it disconnect the antenna and the radio electrical connectors (see illustration).
3   Remove the mounting fasteners that secure the mounting brackets (see illustration).
4   Remove the fasteners securing the audio unit to the center panel (see illustration).
5   Installation is the reverse of removal. Reconnect the battery and perform the necessary re-learn procedures (see Chapter 5).

2009 and later models

6   Remove the center dash lower cover

and center panel (see Chapter 11)
7   Remove the USB adapter which is secured by two screws on the bottom side of the radio/audio unit mounting bracket.
8   Remove the bracket that secures the center panel and the radio/audio unit to each other.
9   Now remove the screws securing the audio unit to the center panel.
10   Installation is the reverse of removal.

Speakers

2008 and earlier models door speaker

Note: *Rear door speaker removal is the same as the front speaker procedures.*
11   Remove the door trim panel (see Chapter 11).
12   Pry the top of the speaker straight out away from the door. This will release the top clip (see illustration).
13   The lower part of the speaker is attached by two hook shaped loops. Lift the speaker up

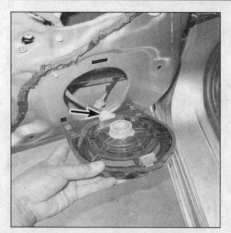

10.14 Disconnect the electrical connector

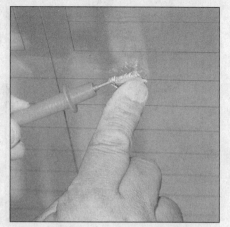

12.4 When measuring the voltage at the rear window defogger grid, wrap a piece of aluminum foil around the negative probe of the voltmeter and press the foil against the wire with your finger

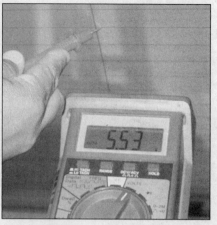

12.5 To determine if a heating element has broken, check the voltage at the center of each element - if the voltage is approximately 6-volts, the element is unbroken; if the voltage is 10 or 12-volts, the element is broken between the center and the ground side; if there is no voltage, the element is broken between the center and the positive side

to release the hooks.

14   Disconnect the electrical connector (see illustration).

15   Installation is the reverse of removal.

2009 and later models door speaker removal

Note: *Rear door speaker removal is the same as the front speaker procedures.*

16   Remove door trim panel (see Chapter 11)

17   Remove the single screw at the 12:00 o'clock position of the speaker.

18   Pull up to disengage the lower clips.

19   Disconnect the electrical connector and remove the speaker.

20   Installation is the reverse of removal.

Door tweeter speakers

21   Remove door trim panel (see Chapter 11)

22   Disconnect the electrical connector.

23   Remove the screws from the tweeter grill and speaker.

24   Installation is the reverse of removal.

---

11   Antenna - removal and installation

Radio antenna

1   On these models the antenna is mounted on the roof. To replace it you must remove the headliner. We therefore recommend that you have this type of antenna replaced by a dealer service department or other qualified repair shop.

---

12   Rear window defogger - check and repair

---

1   The rear window defogger consists of a number of horizontal heating elements baked

onto the inside surface of the glass. Power is supplied through two fuses and a relay in the IPDM relay box in the engine compartment. A defogger switch on the instrument panel controls the defogger grid.

2   Small breaks in the element can be repaired without removing the rear window.

Check

3   Turn the ignition switch and defogger system switches to the ON position. Using a voltmeter, place the positive probe against the defogger grid positive side and the negative probe against the ground side. If battery voltage is not indicated, check that the ignition switch is On and that the feed and ground wires are properly connected. Check the two fuses, defogger switch, defogger relay and related wiring. A dealer can scan the body control module if necessary. If voltage is indicated, but all or part of the defogger doesn't heat, proceed with the following tests.

4   When measuring voltage during the next two tests, wrap a piece of aluminum foil around the tip of the voltmeter positive probe and press the foil against the heating element with your finger (see illustration). Place the negative probe on the defogger grid ground terminal.

5   Check the voltage at the center of each heating element (see illustration). If the voltage is 5 to 6 volts, the element is okay (there is no break). If the voltage is 0 volts, the element is broken between the center of the element and the positive end. If the voltage is 10 to 12 volts, the element is broken between the center of the element and the ground side. Check each heating element.

6   If none of the elements are broken, connect the negative probe to a good chassis ground. The voltage reading should stay the same; if it doesn't, the ground connection is bad.

7   To find the break, place the voltmeter negative probe against the defogger ground

12.7 To find the break, place the voltmeter negative lead against the defogger ground terminal, place the voltmeter positive lead with the foil strip against the heat wire at the positive terminal end and slide it toward the negative terminal end. The point at which the voltmeter deflects from several volts to zero volts is the point at which the wire is broken12.13 To use a defogger repair kit, apply masking tape to the inside of the window at the damaged area, then brush on the special conductive coating

terminal. Place the voltmeter positive probe with the foil strip against the heating element at the positive side and slide it toward the negative side. The point at which the voltmeter deflects from several volts to zero is the point where the heating element is broken (see illustration).

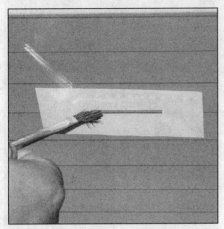

12.13 To use a defogger repair kit, apply masking tape to the inside of the window at the damaged area, then brush on the special conductive coating

13.3a Remove the upper cover mounting fastener

13.3b Then remove the cover

13.4a Headlight housing upper mounting fastener

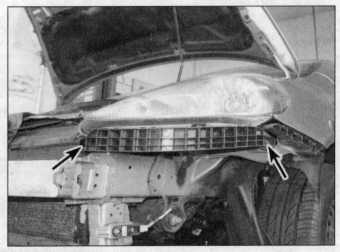

13.4b Headlight housing lower mounting fasteners

Repair

8   Repair the break in the element using a repair kit specifically recommended for this purpose, available at most auto parts stores. Included in this kit is a plastic conductive epoxy.

9   Before repairing a break, turn off the system and allow it to cool for a few minutes.

10   Lightly buff the element area with fine steel wool, then clean it thoroughly with rubbing alcohol.

11   Use masking tape to mask off the area being repaired.

12   Thoroughly mix the epoxy, following the kit instructions.

13   Apply the epoxy material to the slit in the masking tape, overlapping the undamaged area about 3/4-inch on either end (see illustration).

14   Allow the repair to cure for 24 hours before removing the tape and using the system.

13   Headlight housing - removal and installation

Warning: *The models covered by this manual are equipped with Supplemental Restraint Systems (SRS), more commonly known as airbags. Always disable the airbag system before working in the vicinity of any airbag system components to avoid the possibility of accidental deployment of the airbags, which could cause personal injury (see Section 24).*

1   Disconnect the cable from the negative terminal of the battery (see Chapter 5).

2   Remove the front bumper cover (see Chapter 11).

3   Remove the upper cover (see illustrations).

4   Remove the headlight housing mounting fasteners (see illustrations).

5   Pull out the headlight housing, disconnect the electrical connector and remove the housing.

6   Installation is the reverse of removal.

14   Headlight bulb - replacement

Halogen bulbs

Warning: *Halogen gas-filled bulbs, which are under pressure, may shatter if the surface is scratched or the bulb is dropped. Wear eye protection and handle the bulbs carefully, grasping only the base whenever possible. Do not touch the surface of the bulb with your fingers because the oil from your skin could cause it to overheat and fail prematurely. If you do touch the bulb surface, clean it with rubbing alcohol.*

Note: *It is not necessary to remove the headlight housing to replace the bulbs.*

2008 and earlier models

1   Remove the inner fender splash shield from the side of the car that you are changing the bulb on (see Chapter 11).

2   Disconnect the electrical connector and

14.2 Disconnect the electrical connector

14.3a Release the retaining spring. . .

14.3b. . . then remove the bulb

15.1 Headlight housing adjustment screw

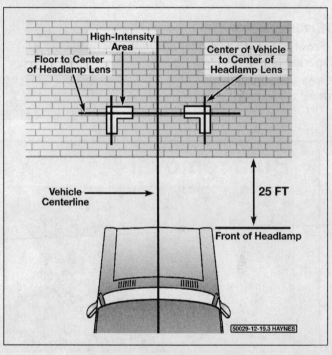

15.5 Headlight adjustment details

remove the rubber dust cap (see illustration).
Note: *The retaining spring is made with a small handle that you push down and inward (toward the bulb) to release the spring from the notch it rests in. Be sure to clip the retaining spring back under this notch when reinstalling the new bulb.*
3   Pull the retaining spring out of the way and remove the bulb (see illustrations).
Caution: *Don't touch the bulb surface with your fingers, because the oil from your skin could cause it to overhead and fail prematurely. If you accidentally touch the bulb surface, clean it with rubbing alcohol.*
4   Installation is the reverse of removal.

2009 and later models
5   Raise the hood and reach in to the back of the headlight housing and disconnect the electrical connector.
6   Remove the rubber dust cover.

7   Pull the retaining spring out of the way and remove the bulb.
Note: *When replacing the bulb be sure to have the notch in the bulb base aligned before re-installing the retaining spring.*
8   Installation is the reverse of removal.

15 Headlights - adjustment

Note: *It is important that the headlights are aimed correctly. If adjusted incorrectly they could blind the driver of an oncoming vehicle and cause a serious accident or seriously reduce your ability to see the road. The headlights should be checked for proper aim every 12 months and any time a new headlight is installed or front end body work is performed. It should be emphasized that the following procedure is only an interim step that will provide temporary adjustment until the headlights can*

be adjusted by a properly equipped shop.
1   All models are equipped with one adjustment screw in each headlight housing (see illustration). The headlights are only adjustable vertically.
2   There are several methods of adjusting the headlights. The simplest method requires a blank wall 25 feet in front of the vehicle and a level floor.
3   Position masking tape vertically on the wall in reference to the vehicle centerline and the centerlines of both headlights.
4   Position a horizontal tape line in reference to the centerline of all the headlights.
Note: *It may be easier to position the tape on the wall with the vehicle parked only a few inches away.*
5   Adjustment should be made with the vehicle sitting level, the tires properly inflated, the gas tank half-full and no unusually heavy load in the vehicle (see illustration).

6   Starting with the low beam adjustment, position the high intensity zone so it is two inches below the horizontal line.

7   With the high beams on, the high intensity zone should be vertically centered with the exact center just below the horizontal line. **Note:** *It may not be possible to position the headlight aim exactly for both high and low beams. If a compromise must be made, keep in mind that the low beams are the most used and have the greatest effect on safety.*

8   Have the headlights adjusted by a dealer service department or service station at the earliest opportunity.

16   Bulb replacement

Exterior lights

Front parking/turn signal and side marker lights

2008 and earlier models
Note: *It is not necessary to remove the headlight housing to access these bulbs*

1   Remove the front inner fender on the side you are working on (see Chapter 11).
2   Disconnect the electrical connector.
3   Twist the bulb socket 45 degrees counterclockwise and remove the socket (see illustration).
4   Pull the bulb from the socket and replace it.
5   Installation is the reverse of removal.

2009 and later models
6   Open the hood and locate the bulb connection.
7   Disconnect the electrical connection.
8   Turn the bulb socket 45 degrees counterclockwise and remove it.
9   Pull the bulb from the socket and replace it.

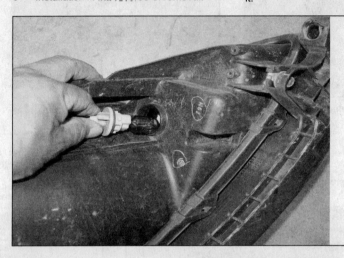

16.3 Remove the socket (headlight housing removed for clarity)

Bulb removal

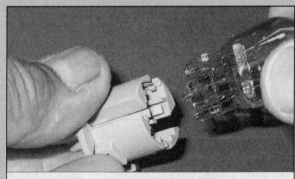

To remove many modern exterior bulbs from their holders, simply pull them out

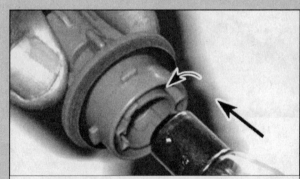

On bulbs with a cylindrical base ("bayonet" bulbs), the socket is spring-loaded; a pair of small posts on the side of the base hold the bulb in place against spring pressure. To remove this type of bulb, push it into the holder, rotate it 1/4-turn counterclockwise, then pull it out

If a bayonet bulb has dual filaments, the posts are staggered, so the bulb can only be installed one way

To remove most overhead interior light bulbs, simply unclip them

10   Installation is the reverse of removal.

Rear turn signal/brake/tail/side marker/back-up lights

11   Open the tailgate and remove the access panel from the side you are changing the bulb on (see illustration).
12   Turn the bulb socket 45 degrees counterclockwise and remove it (see illustration).
13   Pull the bulb from the socket and replace the bulb.
14   Installation is the reverse of removal.

Fog lights

Warning: *Wear eye protection and handle the bulbs carefully, grasping only the base whenever possible. Do not touch the surface of the bulb with your fingers because the oil from your skin could cause it to overheat and fail prematurely. If you do touch the bulb surface, clean it with rubbing alcohol.*

2008 and earlier models

15   Remove the single screw hidden inside the lower grill and pull the housing out of the front bumper.
16   Disconnect the fog light electrical connector.
17   Turn the bulb holder counterclockwise and pull it out of the housing.
18   Installation is the reverse of removal.

2009 through 2011 models

19   Remove the mounting screw in the upper outside corner of the fog light assembly and pull the assembly out of the front bumper.
20   Disconnect the electrical connector.
21   Twist the bulb socket counterclockwise and remove it.
22   Pull the bulb from socket and replace it.
23   Installation is the reverse of removal.

2012 and later models

24   Use a flat tipped small screwdriver to carefully pry out the cap cover located on the upper inside corner in the front section of the front bumper.
25   Pull the assembly out of the front bumper.

26   Disconnect the electrical connector.
27   Twist the bulb socket counterclockwise and remove it.
28   Pull the bulb from socket and replace it.
29   Installation is the reverse of removal.

Fog light aiming

30   Ensure all tires are inflated to the correct pressure. Set the vehicle on a level surface, with no load in vehicle other than the driver (or equivalent weight placed in driver's position), and with a full fuel tank.
31   Adjust aiming in the vertical direction by turning the adjusting screw, which is accessed from a small hole on the lower corner of the bumper.
32   Follow the aiming procedure in Section 15, but use these measurements:

   a) *Position a horizontal tape line level with the top of the fog lights.*
   b) *The highest intensity of the beam should fall 4 inches below the horizontal tape line.*

License plate light

2008 and earlier models

33   Open the tailgate and remove the tail-

gate lower trim (see Chapter 11).
34   Disconnect the electrical connector to the license plate light.
35   Grasp the light socket and depress the clips on either side while pulling outwards.
36   Remove the bulb.
37   Installation is the reverse of removal.

2009 and later models

38   Open tailgate and press in on the two clips securing the tag light housing while pulling outwards.
39   Separate the bulb lens cover from the tag light housing by pushing in on the clips.
40   Remove the bulb.
41   Installation is the reverse of removal.

High-mounted brake light

42   Locate the high mounted brake light unit and remove the cover by pressing in on the tabs that are on either end of the housing (see illustration).
43   Disconnect the electrical connector (see illustration).
44   Twist out the bulb holder (see illustration).
45   Replace the bulbs as needed.
46   Installation is the reverse of removal.

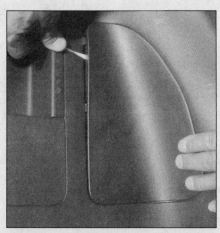

16.11 Use a screwdriver and carefully pry open the access panel

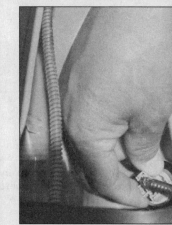

16.12 Remove the bulb socket

16.42 Detach the cover

16.43 Disconnect the electrical connector

16.44 Remove the bulb holder

Interior lights

47   All interior light bulbs are replaced in the same general way. Use a small screwdriver or trim tool to carefully pry off the lens (see illustration).
48   Installation is the reverse of removal.

Instrument cluster illumination

49   Instrument cluster illumination is contained within the cluster. Replace the cluster (see Section 9) as a complete unit if there is a problem with any of its individual components.

Interior Lighting and illumination

Note: *The interior lighting system is controlled by the Gauge Control Module (Instrument cluster). No diagnostics beyond bulb replacement and the associated wiring schematics are offered in this manual. Proper diagnostics of the interior lighting system is accomplished by a qualified technician at your local dealership or independent repair facility.*

17   Horn - replacement

1   On 2008 and earlier models, remove the front bumper cover (see Chapter 11).
2   On 2009 and later models, remove the front grill (see Chapter 11).
3   Disconnect the horn electrical connector and remove the horn mounting fastener (see illustration). Remove the horn.
4   Installation is the reverse of removal.

18   Wiper motor - replacement

Front wiper motor

1   Mark the positions of the blades on the windshield with tape so they can be installed in the same alignment.
2   Disconnect the cable from the negative terminal of the battery (see Chapter 5).
3   Pry off the wiper arm pivot caps (see illustration),then remove the retaining nuts.
4   Mark the position of each wiper arm in relation to its splined shaft (see illustration).
5   Remove the wiper arms from the drive studs and disconnect the washer hose.
6   Secure the wiper arm from moving and wiggle the arm off of the stud.

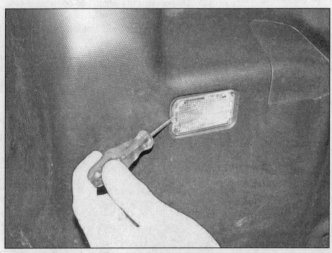

16.47 Using a small screwdriver carefully pry off the lens16.50a To remove many modern exterior bulbs from their holders, simply pull them out

17.3 Unscrew the horn mounting fastener

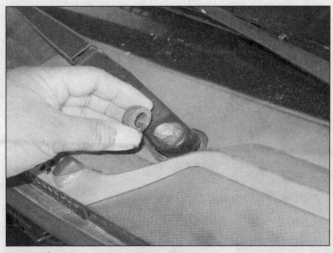

18.3 Remove the caps from the wiper arms

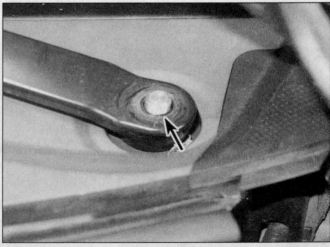

18.4 Mark the relationship of each wiper arm to its splined shaft before removing the arm

7   Remove the cowl cover (see Chapter 11).
8   Disconnect the electrical connector from the wiper motor, then remove the mounting fasteners and remove the wiper motor and drive assembly as a single unit (see illustrations).
9   Separate the windshield wiper linkage from the crank arm (see illustration).
Note: *Before removing the crank arm scribe a match mark to the arm and the motor so you an re-install the crank arm back onto the motor in the exact same position.*
10 Remove the crank arm nut and separate the crank from the shaft.
11 Remove the screws and detach the motor from the drive assembly.
12 Installation is the reverse of removal.

Rear wiper motor

13 Remove the wiper arm pivot cap and the nut securing the wiper arm to the shaft.
14 While holding the wiper arm to prevent

it from moving around too much and keeping the shaft and wiper arm aligned (to prevent binding) wiggle the arm off of the shaft.
15 Open the tailgate and remove the lower trim.
16 Remove the bolts securing the motor assembly and bracket to the tailgate.
17 Remove the bolts securing the motor to the bracket.
18 Installation is the reverse of removal.

19   Ignition switch and key lock cylinder

Warning: *The models covered by this manual are equipped with Supplemental Restraint Systems (SRS), more commonly known as airbags. Always disable the airbag system before working in the vicinity of any airbag system components to avoid the possibility of accidental deployment of the airbags, which*

could cause personal injury (see Section 24).
Note: *Make sure to have the audio security codes handy for reprogramming the audio system (see Section 10).*
1   Disconnect the cable from the negative terminal of the battery (see Chapter 5).

Ignition switch

2   Remove the steering column covers (see Chapter 11).
3   Disconnect the electrical connector from the ignition switch (see illustration).
4   Remove the mounting fasteners and pull the switch from the lock cylinder housing (see illustration).
5   Before installing the new switch, make sure hub of the switch is aligned with the blade on the ignition lock cylinder.
6   The remainder of installation is the reverse of removal. Reconnect the battery and perform the necessary re-learn procedures (see Chapter 5).

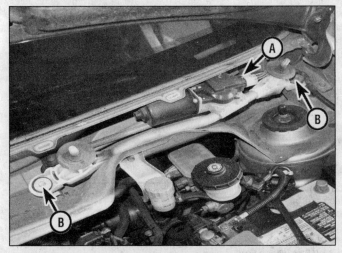

18.8a Disconnect the electrical connector (A), then remove the mounting fasteners (B) (2008 and earlier models)

18.8b Disconnect the electrical connector (A), then remove the mounting fasteners (B) (2009 and later models)

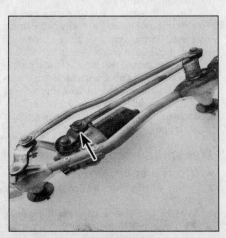

18.9 Pry the two halves of the spherical bearing apart

19.3 Disconnect the electrical connectors

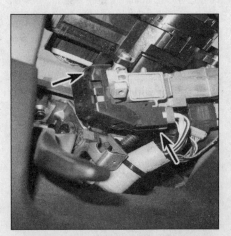

19.4 Remove the mounting fasteners

Ignition lock cylinder housing

7   Remove steering column from the car (see Chapter 10).

8   With steering column on a flat surface center punch the break off bolts that secure the housing to the steering column shaft.

9   Drill out the break off bolts with a 5mm (3/16 in.) bit and discard them.

10   Remove the remaining section of the break off bolts from the steering column housing.

11   Remove the lock housing from the steering column housing.

12   Install the replacement housing loosely with the new break off bolts provided.

13   Insert the key and turn the key several times to make sure it works freely. This will also help align the steering wheel lock in the correct spot. Now tighten down the break off bolts until they shear off completely.

14   The remaining installation is the reverse of removal.

15   Reconnect the battery and perform the necessary re-learn procedures (see Chapter 5).

20   Cruise control system - description and check

1   All models have an electronically-controlled throttle body - there is no accelerator cable (or cruise control cable). When you select the speed that you want to maintain, the PCM controls vehicle speed by opening and closing the throttle plate by means of a computer-controlled solenoid (motor) inside the throttle body.

2   The diagnostic procedures for troubleshooting the cruise control system are beyond the scope of this manual, but if the system can't be set, or the set speed doesn't cancel when the brake pedal is depressed, check the fuses. Start with the fuses in the engine compartment fuse and relay box, then check the fuses in the under-dash fuse and relay box. If the set speed doesn't cancel when the CANCEL button is depressed, check the fuse for that circuit. Also check the operation and adjustment of the brake light switch (see Chapter 9) and, on manual transaxle models, the ASCD switch.

21   Power window system - general information

1   The power window system operates electric motors, mounted on the doors, which lower and raise the windows. The system consists of the control switches, the motors, regulators, glass mechanisms, and associated wiring.

2   The power windows can be lowered and raised from the master control switch by the driver or by the switch located at the passenger window. Each window has a separate motor that is reversible. The position of

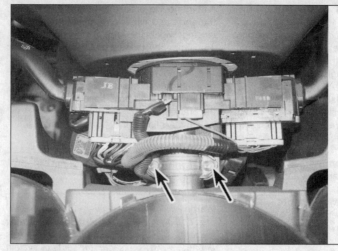

19.13 To detach the key lock cylinder housing from the steering column, drill out the bolts with a drill bit and remove the bolts with a screw extractor

the control switch determines the polarity and therefore the direction of operation.

3   The circuit is protected by fuses and a circuit breaker. Check the fuses in the fuse panel. There is a motor for each window in each door. Each motor is equipped with an internal circuit breaker; this prevents one stuck window from disabling the whole system. Refer to the wiring diagrams at the end of this Chapter. If you have eliminated any obvious causes of a problem, have the vehicle checked at a dealership service department or other properly equipped repair shop.

22   Power door lock system - general information

1   The power door lock system operates the power door motors, which are integral components of the door latch units in each door. The system consists of a fuse (in the engine compartment fuse and relay box), the Gauge Control Module, control switches (in each of the front doors), the power door motors and the electrical wiring harnesses connecting all of these components.

2   The lock mechanisms in the door latch units are actuated by a reversible electric motor in each door. When you push the door lock switch to LOCK, the motor operates one way and locks the latch mechanism. When you push the door lock switch the other way, to the UNLOCK position, the motor operates in the other direction, unlocking the latch mechanism. Because the motors and lock mechanisms are an integral part of the door latch units, they cannot be repaired. If a door lock motor or lock mechanism fails, replace the door latch unit (see Chapter 11).

3   Some vehicles have an optional Keyless entry system that allows you to lock and unlock the doors from outside the vehicle. The Keyless entry system consists of the transmitter (the electronic push-button "key") and a remote keyless entry receiver. The keyless entry receiver is part of the Gauge Control Module.

4   Some features of the door lock system

on these vehicles rely on resources that they share with other electronic modules through the data bus network. Professional diagnosis of these modules and the data bus network requires the use of a scan tool and factory diagnostic information. At-home repairs are therefore limited to inspecting the wiring for bad connections and for minor faults that can be easily repaired. If you are unable to locate the trouble using the following general steps, consult your dealer service department or a qualified independent repair facility.

Note: *It is not uncommon for wires to break in the harness between the body and the door because repeatedly opening and closing the door fatigues and eventually breaks the wires.*

23   Remote keyless entry system

Description

1   Remote keyless entry is a radio frequency signal sent from a matching key fob to the Gauge Control Module. The keyless entry system allows the driver to control interior lights illumination, the horn and the trunk release with the key fob.

2   Up to three key fob ID codes can be stored in one vehicle. Each key fob can be registered to the vehicle with a scanner or without. (Follow the procedures in this section for programming the key fob transmitters without a scanner.) If you are uncomfortable with the non-scanner procedure take your vehicle and the transmitters to a dealer repair center, locksmith, or qualified independent repair facility for programming with a scanner.

Transmitter programming without a scanner

3   Turn the ignition switch to ON with engine OFF.

4   Within 1 to 4 seconds press the unlock or lock button on the transmitter while aiming it at the left side of the dash.

5   Within 1 to 4 seconds turn the ignition switch OFF.

24.3a The airbag diagnosis/sensor unit is mounted under the center console

24.3b The front crash zone sensor is mounted to the rear of the radiator support panel

6   Within 1 to 4 seconds turn the ignition switch back ON with engine OFF.
7   Within 1 to 4 seconds press either the unlock or lock button while aiming it at the left side of the dash.
8   Within 1 to 4 seconds turn the ignition OFF.
9   Within 1 to 4 seconds turn the ignition switch back ON with engine OFF.
10   Within 1 to 4 seconds press the unlock or lock button on the transmitter while aiming it at the left side of the dash.
11   Within 1 to 4 seconds turn the ignition switch OFF.
12   WIthin 1 to 4 seconds turn the ignition switch back ON with engine OFF.
13   The door locks should actuate one time.
14   Within 1 to 4 seconds after hearing the door locks actuate press the unlock or lock button on the transmitter while aiming it at the left side of the dash.
15   Within 10 seconds press the unlock or lock button on the transmitter or transmitters you'd like to program to the car.
16   Make sure you hear the door locks actuate after each transmitter lock or unlock button is pressed.
17   Turn key OFF and remove the key.
18   Check each of the transmitters for proper operation.
19   Each step must be followed exactly. If any step is missed or too much time is taken between each step you will have to start all over again.
Note: *As each transmitter button is pressed a signal is sent to the Gauge Control Module (Instrument Cluster) and the appropriate lock or unlock response is sent to the door lock actuators. Basic repairs such as blown fuses or faulty components can be accomplished without the use of expensive diagnostic equipment. Repair procedures require the use of a scanner and schematics. No coverage is of-*

fered in this manual for any of the diagnostic procedures.

24   Airbag system - general information

1   These models are equipped with a Supplemental Restraint System (SRS), more commonly known as airbags, designed to protect the driver and the passenger from serious injury in the event of a head-on collision. Some models are also equipped with side impact airbags in the front seats and along the roof rail. All models have a diagnostic control unit, located on the floor under the center console.
Warning: *If your vehicle is ever involved in a flood, or the interior carpeting is soaked for any reason, disconnect the battery and do not start the vehicle until the airbag system can be checked by a dealer service department or other repair facility equipped with the proper tool. If the SRS system is subjected to flooding, the airbags could go off upon starting the vehicle, even without an accident taking place.*

Airbag modules
2   The airbag modules consist of a housing incorporating the cushion (airbag) and inflator unit. The inflator assembly is mounted on the back of the housing over a hole through which gas is expelled, inflating the bag almost instantaneously when an electrical signal is sent from the system. The specially wound wire on the driver's side that carries this signal to the module is called a spiral cable. The spiral cable is a flat, ribbon-like electrically conductive tape that is wound many times so that it can transmit an electrical signal regardless of steering wheel position. Airbag mod-

ules are located in the steering wheel, on the passenger's side above the glove box and, on some models, in the seat backs and along the roof rails (side curtain airbags).

Control unit and sensors
3   The diagnosis/sensor unit contains an on-board microprocessor which monitors the operation of the system, and also contains a crash sensor. It checks this system every time the vehicle is started, causing the "AIRBAG" light to go on then off, if the system is operating properly. If there is a fault in the system, the light will go on and stay on and the unit will store fault codes indicating the nature of the fault. If the AIRBAG light goes on and stays on, the vehicle should be taken to your dealer immediately for service. The diagnosis/sensor unit is located under the center console (see illustration). The crash zone sensor is located on the radiator support (see illustration), and the side airbag sensors (satellite crash sensor) are in each door "B" pillar.

Operation
4   For the airbag(s) to deploy, the impact sensor(s) must be activated. When this condition occurs, the circuit to the airbag inflator is closed and the airbag inflates.

Self-diagnosis system
5   A self-diagnosis circuit in the SRS unit displays a light on the instrument panel when the ignition switch is turned to the On position. If the system is operating normally, the light should go out after about five seconds. If the light doesn't come on, or doesn't go out after a short time, or if it comes on while you're driving the vehicle, or if it blinks at any time, there's a malfunction in the SRS system. Have it inspected and repaired as soon as possible. Do not attempt to troubleshoot or service the SRS system yourself. Even a small mistake

could cause the SRS system to malfunction when you need it.

Servicing components near the SRS system

6   If you will be working around components and wire harnesses for the SRS system, you must disable the system before beginning any work.

Warning: *Do not use electrical test equipment on airbag system wires; it could cause the airbag(s) to deploy. ALWAYS DISABLE THE SRS SYSTEM BEFORE WORKING NEAR THE SRS SYSTEM COMPONENTS OR RELATED WIRING.*

Disabling the SRS system

Warning: *Any time you are working in the vicinity of airbag wiring or components, DISABLE THE SRS SYSTEM.*

Warning: *An auxiliary voltage input device (memory saver) must not be used when working near airbag system components.*

7   To disable the airbag system, perform the following steps:

Turn the steering wheel to the straight-ahead position and turn the ignition switch to the Lock position, then remove the key.

Disconnect the battery negative and positive cables, then wait ten minutes before proceeding with any work.

Before touching any airbag system component, ground yourself to a metal part of the vehicle to discharge any static electricity built up in your body.

Enabling the system

8   After you've disabled the airbag and performed the necessary service, reconnect the two-pin airbag connector into the two-pin spiral cable connector (driver's side), the SRS main harness (passenger's side) or the side-impact airbag. Reinstall the lid to the underside of the steering wheel or reinstall the

glove box/trim panel or upper trim panels.

9   To enable the airbag system, perform the following steps:

a) Turn the ignition switch to the On position.

b) Make sure nobody is inside the vehicle.

c) Make sure the ignition is in the Off position, then connect the battery cables (positive first, negative last).

d) With your body out of the path of the airbag(s), turn the ignition switch to the On position. Confirm that the airbag warning light is functioning properly.

e) Perform the necessary re-learn procedures (see Chapter 5).

f) Take the vehicle to a dealer service department or other qualified repair facility and have the airbag system checked and the warning light canceled if it remains lit.

Removal and installation

Warning: *The bolts used throughout the airbag system to mount the airbag modules, diagnosis sensor unit, crash zone sensor and satellite sensors have a special coating. These bolts are designed to be used once. Replace them with new factory bolts, and never use a substitute fastener.*

Driver's side airbag and spiral cable

10   Refer to , Section for removal and installation of the driver's side airbag and steering wheel (which will give you access to the spiral cable).

Warning: *When installing the spiral cable, be sure to follow the centering instructions carefully.*

Passenger's side airbag and other airbag modules

11   Even if you remove the instrument panel, it's not necessary to remove the passenger's

airbag module to do so; it can simply remain installed in the instrument panel. We don't recommend removing any of the other airbag modules either. These jobs are best left to a professional.

Impact seat belt retractors

12   All models are equipped with pyrotechnic (explosive) units in the front seat belt retracting mechanisms for both the lap and shoulder belts. During an impact that would trigger the airbag system, the airbag control unit also triggers the seat belt retractors. When the pyrotechnic charges go off, they accelerate the retractors to instantly take up any slack in the seat belt system to more fully prepare the driver and front seat passenger for impact. The airbag system should be disabled any time work is done to or around the seats.

Warning: *Never strike the pillars or floor pan with a hammer or use an impact-driver tool in these areas unless the system is disabled.*

25   Wiring diagrams - general information

1   Since it isn't possible to include all wiring diagrams for every year and model covered by this manual, the following diagrams are those that are typical and most commonly needed.

2   Prior to troubleshooting any circuits, check the fuses and circuit breakers (if equipped) to make sure they are in good condition. Make sure the battery is properly charged and has clean, tight cable connections (see Chapter 1).

3   When checking the wiring system, make sure that all electrical connectors are clean, with no broken or loose pins. When unplugging an electrical connector, do not pull on the wires, only on the connector housings themselves.

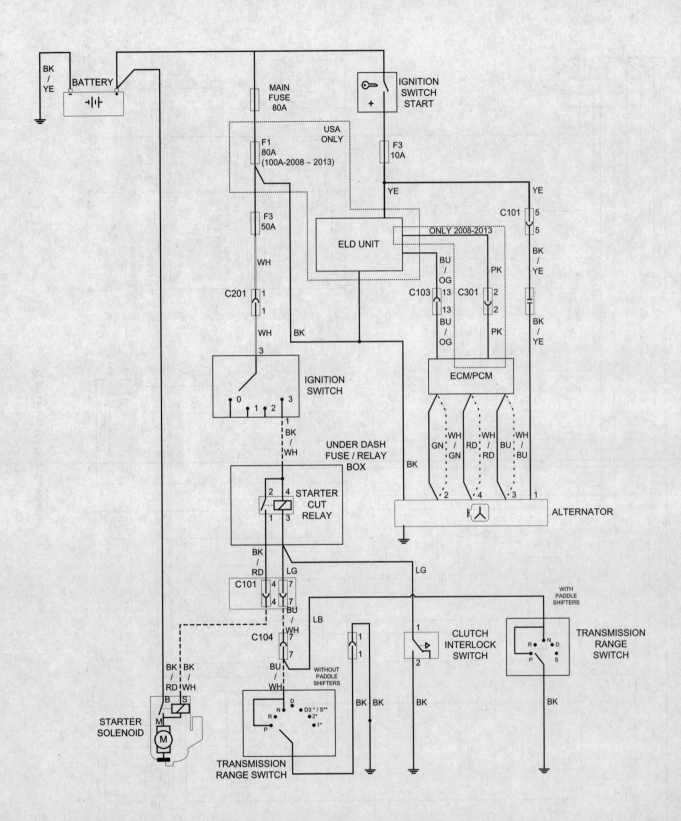

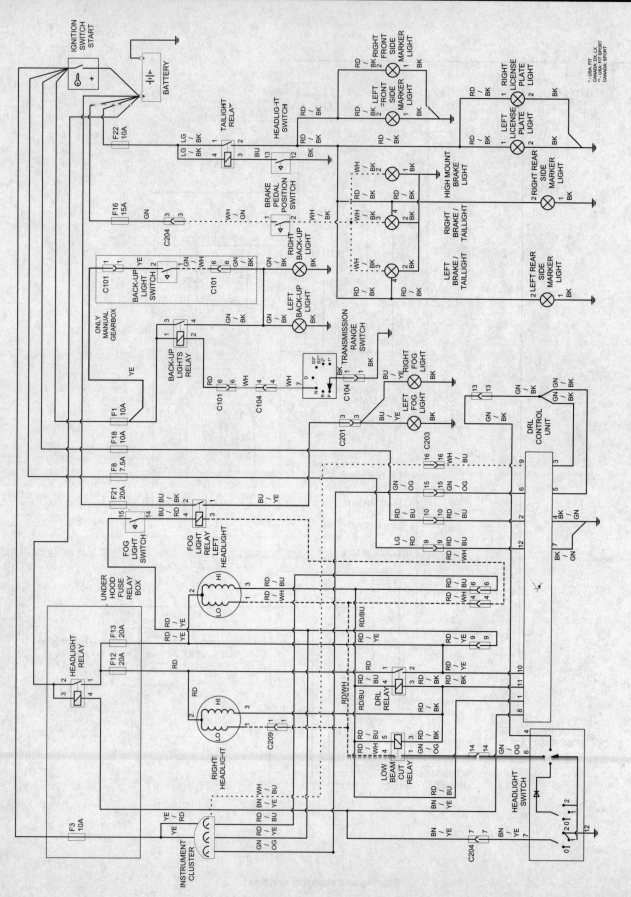

Exterior lighting system (1 of 2)

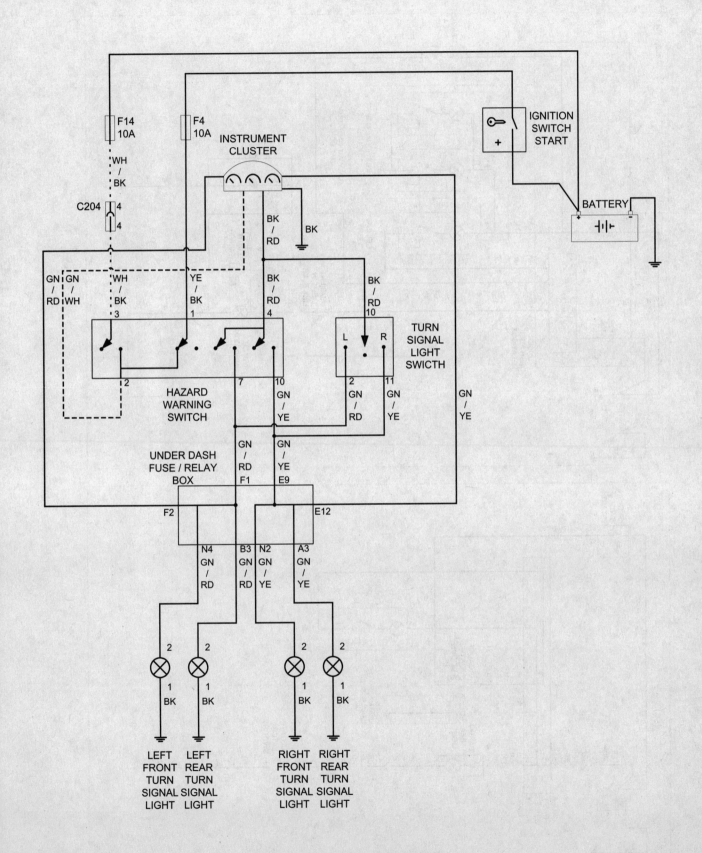

Exterior lighting system (2 of 2)

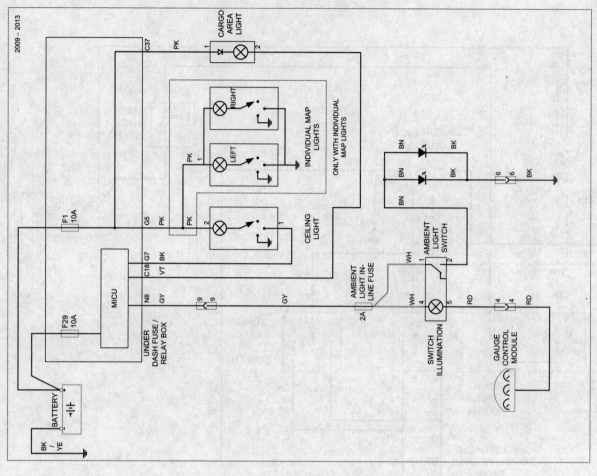

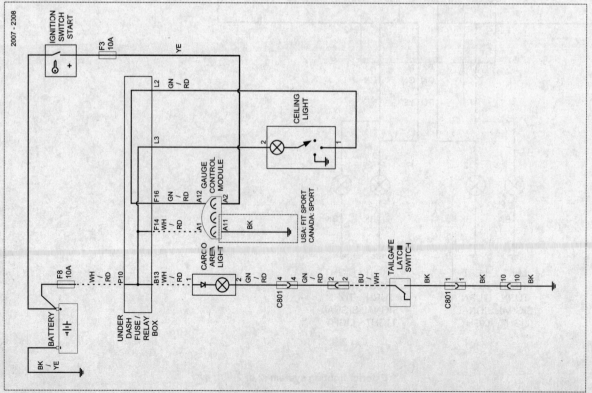

Interior lighting system

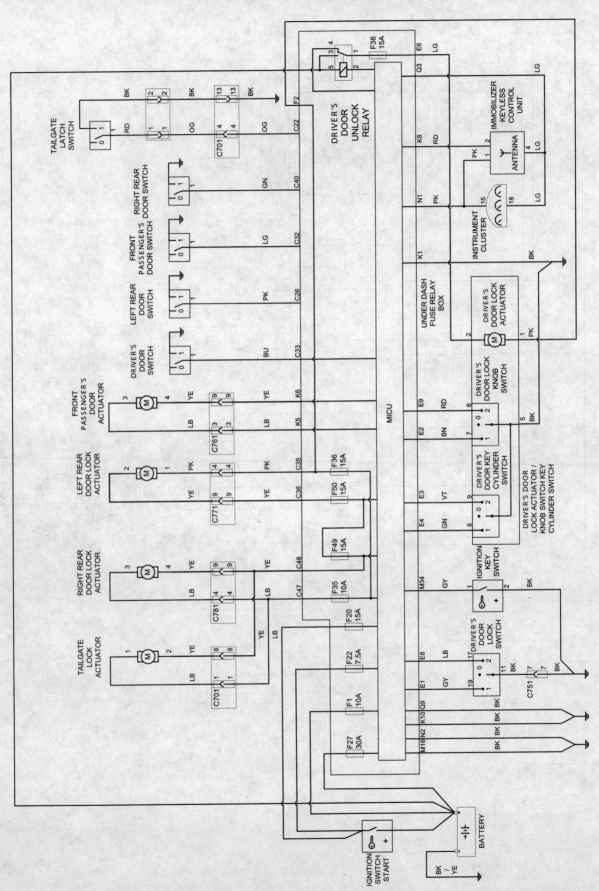

Power door lock system

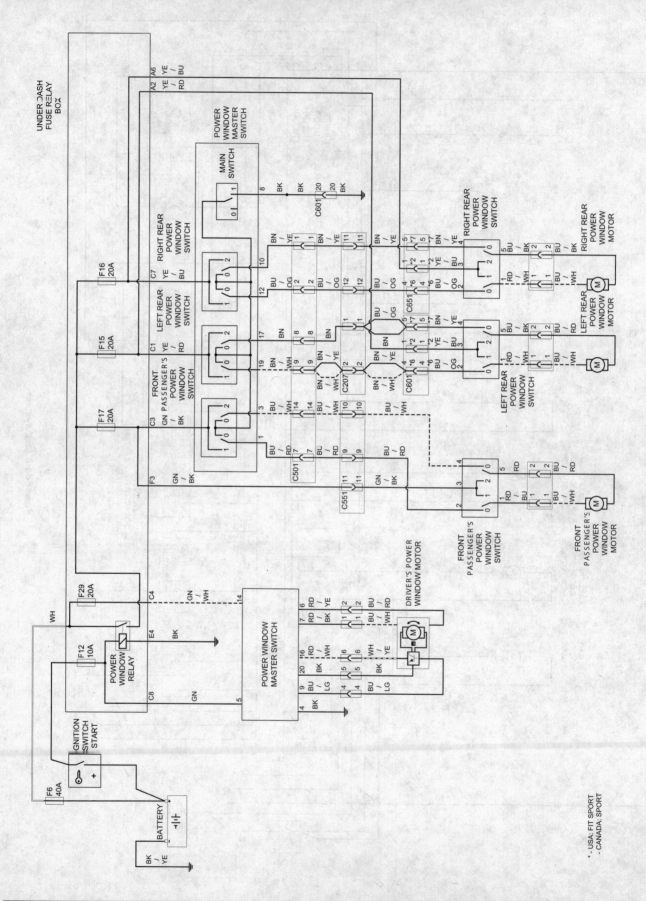

Power window system

*- USA: FIT SPORT
- CANADA: SPORT

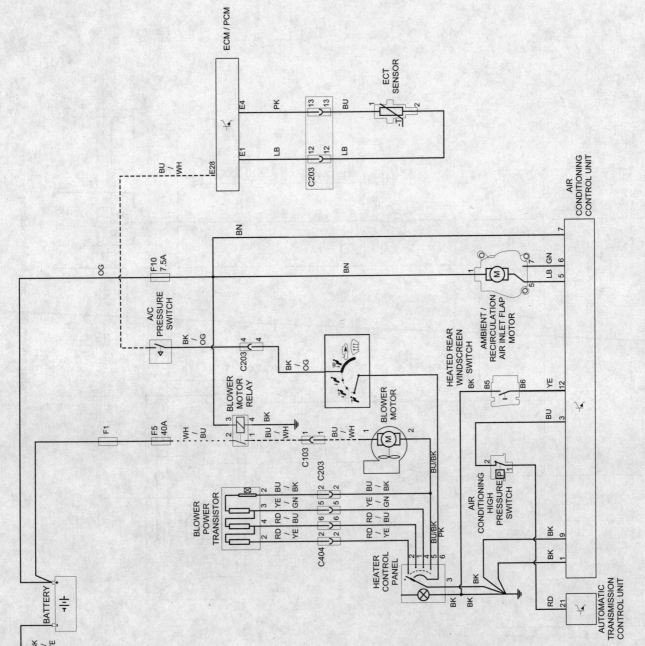

Heating and air conditioning system

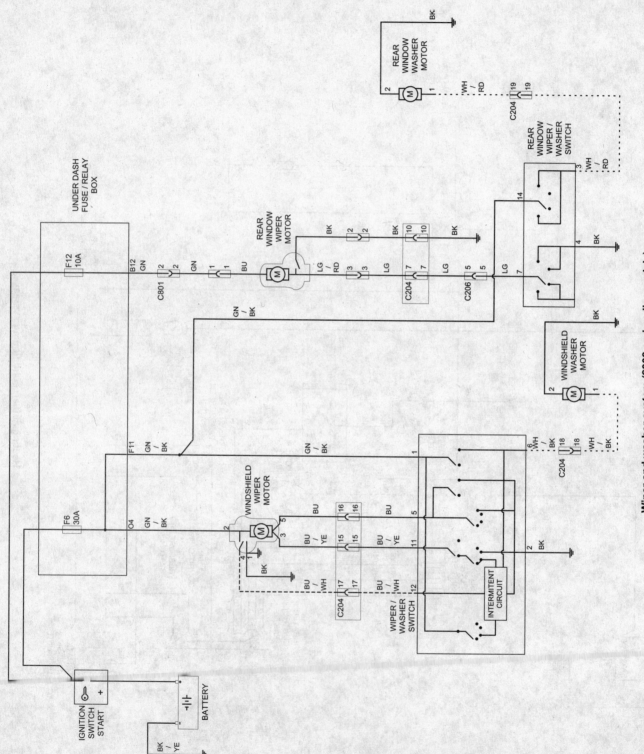

Wiper and washer system (2008 and earlier models)

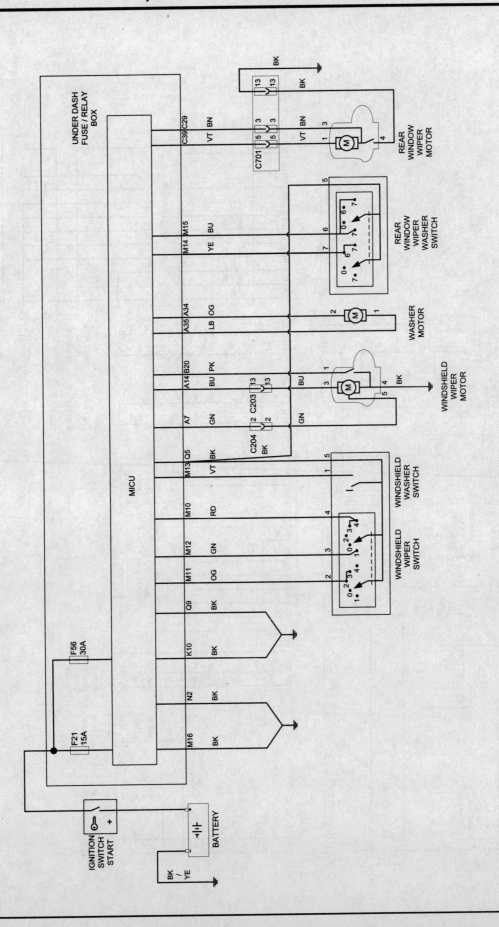

Wiper and washer system (2009 and later models)

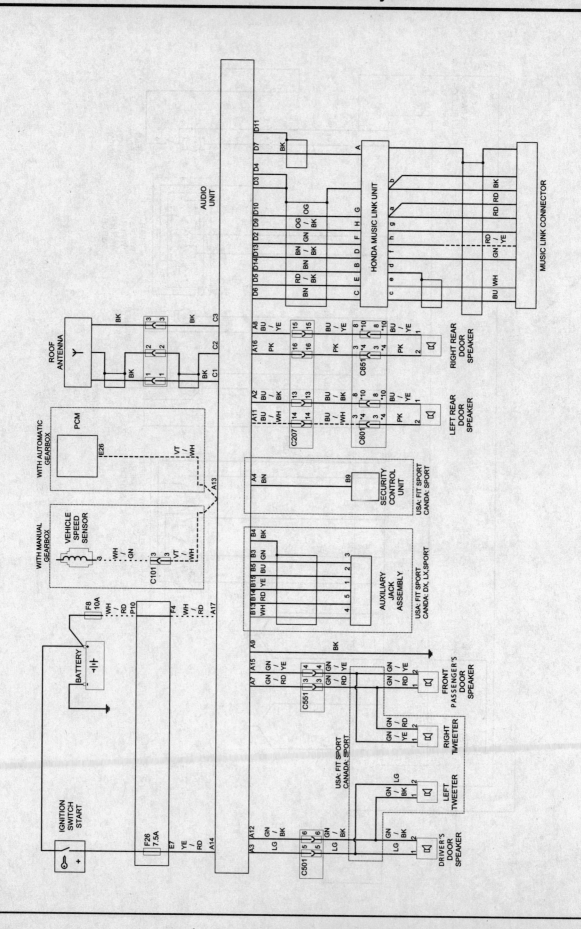

Audio system (2008 and earlier models)

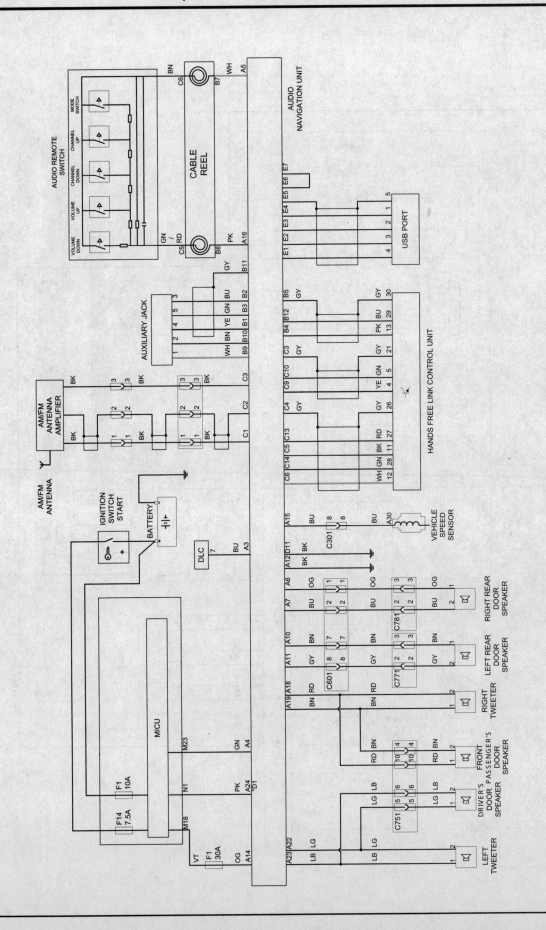

Audio system (2009 and later models)

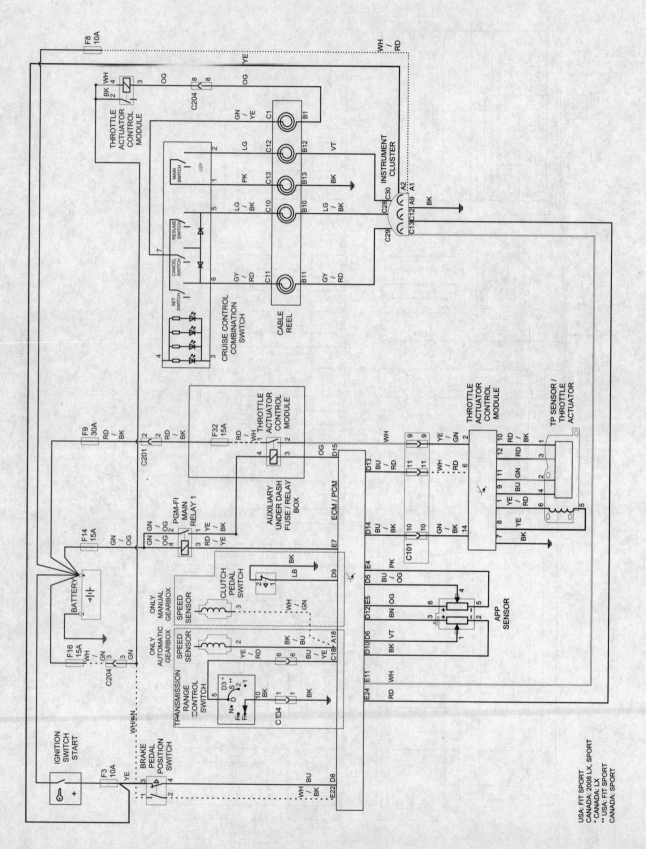

Cruise control system

Index

Notes

Haynes Automotive Manuals

NOTE: If you do not see a listing for your vehicle, consult your local Haynes dealer for the latest product information.

ACURA
- **12020 Integra** '86 thru '89 **& Legend** '86 thru '90
- **12021 Integra** '90 thru '93 **& Legend** '91 thru '95
  Integra '94 thru '00 - see HONDA Civic (42025)
  MDX '01 thru '07 - see HONDA Pilot (42037)
- **12050 Acura TL** all models '99 thru '08

AMC
- **Jeep CJ** - see JEEP (50020)
- **14020 Mid-size models** '70 thru '83
- **14025 (Renault) Alliance & Encore** '83 thru '87

AUDI
- **15020 4000** all models '80 thru '87
- **15025 5000** all models '77 thru '83
- **15026 5000** all models '84 thru '88
  Audi A4 '96 thru '01 - see VW Passat (96023)
- **15030 Audi A4** '02 thru '08

AUSTIN-HEALEY
- **Sprite** - see MG Midget (66015)

BMW
- **18020 3/5 Series** '82 thru '92
- **18021 3-Series** incl. Z3 models '92 thru '98
- **18022 3-Series** incl. Z4 models '99 thru '05
- **18023 3-Series** '06 thru '10
- **18025 320i** all 4 cyl models '75 thru '83
- **18050 1500 thru 2002** except Turbo '59 thru '77

BUICK
- **19010 Buick Century** '97 thru '05
  Century (front-wheel drive) - see GM (38005)
- **19020 Buick, Oldsmobile & Pontiac Full-size**
  (Front-wheel drive) '85 thru '05
  Buick Electra, LeSabre and Park Avenue;
  Oldsmobile Delta 88 Royale, Ninety Eight
  and Regency; **Pontiac** Bonneville
- **19025 Buick, Oldsmobile & Pontiac Full-size**
  (Rear wheel drive) '70 thru '90
  Buick Estate, Electra, LeSabre, Limited,
  Oldsmobile Custom Cruiser, Delta 88,
  Ninety-eight, **Pontiac** Bonneville,
  Catalina, Grandville, Parisienne
- **19030 Mid-size Regal & Century** all rear-drive
  models with V6, V8 and Turbo '74 thru '87
  Regal - see GENERAL MOTORS (38010)
  Riviera - see GENERAL MOTORS (38030)
  Roadmaster - see CHEVROLET (24046)
  Skyhawk - see GENERAL MOTORS (38015)
  Skylark - see GM (38020, 38025)
  Somerset - see GENERAL MOTORS (38025)

CADILLAC
- **21015 CTS & CTS-V** '03 thru '12
- **21030 Cadillac Rear Wheel Drive** '70 thru '93
  Cimarron - see GENERAL MOTORS (38015)
  DeVille - see GM (38031 & 38032)
  Eldorado - see GM (38030 & 38031)
  Fleetwood - see GM (38031)
  Seville - see GM (38030, 38031 & 38032)

CHEVROLET
- **10305 Chevrolet Engine Overhaul Manual**
- **24010 Astro & GMC Safari Mini-vans** '85 thru '05
- **24015 Camaro V8** all models '70 thru '81
- **24016 Camaro** all models '82 thru '92
- **24017 Camaro & Firebird** '93 thru '02
  Cavalier - see GENERAL MOTORS (38016)
  Celebrity - see GENERAL MOTORS (38005)
- **24020 Chevelle, Malibu & El Camino** '69 thru '87
- **24024 Chevette & Pontiac T1000** '76 thru '87
  Citation - see GENERAL MOTORS (38020)
- **24027 Colorado & GMC Canyon** '04 thru '10
- **24032 Corsica/Beretta** all models '87 thru '96
- **24040 Corvette** all V8 models '68 thru '82
- **24041 Corvette** all models '84 thru '96
- **24045 Full-size Sedans** Caprice, Impala, Biscayne,
  Bel Air & Wagons '69 thru '90
- **24046 Impala SS & Caprice and Buick Roadmaster**
  '91 thru '96
  Impala '00 thru '05 - see LUMINA (24048)
- **24047 Impala & Monte Carlo** all models '06 thru '11
  Lumina '90 thru '94 - see GM (38010)
- **24048 Lumina & Monte Carlo** '95 thru '05
  Lumina APV - see GM (38035)
- **24050 Luv Pick-up** all 2WD & 4WD '72 thru '82
  Malibu '97 thru '00 - see GM (38026)
- **24055 Monte Carlo** all models '70 thru '88
  Monte Carlo '95 thru '01 - see LUMINA (24048)
- **24059 Nova** all V8 models '69 thru '79
- **24060 Nova and Geo Prizm** '85 thru '92
- **24064 Pick-ups** '67 thru '87 - Chevrolet & GMC
- **24065 Pick-ups** '88 thru '98 - Chevrolet & GMC

- **24066 Pick-ups** '99 thru '06 - Chevrolet & GMC
- **24067 Chevrolet Silverado & GMC Sierra** '07 thru '12
- **24070 S-10 & S-15 Pick-ups** '82 thru '93,
  Blazer & Jimmy '83 thru '94,
- **24071 S-10 & Sonoma Pick-ups** '94 thru '04, including **Blazer, Jimmy & Hombre**
- **24072 Chevrolet TrailBlazer, GMC Envoy &**
  Oldsmobile Bravada '02 thru '09
- **24075 Sprint** '85 thru '88 **& Geo Metro** '89 thru '01
- **24080 Vans - Chevrolet & GMC** '68 thru '96
- **24081 Chevrolet Express & GMC Savana**
  Full-size Vans '96 thru '10

CHRYSLER
- **10310 Chrysler Engine Overhaul Manual**
- **25015 Chrysler Cirrus, Dodge Stratus,**
  Plymouth Breeze '95 thru '00
- **25020 Full-size Front-Wheel Drive** '88 thru '93
  K-Cars - see DODGE Aries (30008)
  Laser - see DODGE Daytona (30030)
- **25025 Chrysler LHS, Concorde, New Yorker,**
  Dodge Intrepid, Eagle Vision, '93 thru '97
- **25026 Chrysler LHS, Concorde, 300M,**
  Dodge Intrepid, '98 thru '04
- **25027 Chrysler 300, Dodge Charger &**
  Magnum '05 thru '09
- **25030 Chrysler & Plymouth Mid-size**
  front wheel drive '82 thru '95
  Rear-wheel Drive - see Dodge (30050)
- **25035 PT Cruiser** all models '01 thru '10
- **25040 Chrysler Sebring** '95 thru '06, **Dodge Stratus**
  '01 thru '06, **Dodge Avenger** '95 thru '00

DATSUN
- **28005 200SX** all models '80 thru '83
- **28007 B-210** all models '73 thru '78
- **28009 210** all models '79 thru '82
- **28012 240Z, 260Z & 280Z** Coupe '70 thru '78
- **28014 280ZX** Coupe & 2+2 '79 thru '83
  300ZX - see NISSAN (72010)
- **28018 510 & PL521 Pick-up** '68 thru '73
- **28020 510** all models '78 thru '81
- **28022 620 Series Pick-up** all models '73 thru '79
  720 Series Pick-up - see NISSAN (72030)
- **28025 810/Maxima** all gasoline models '77 thru '84

DODGE
- **400 & 600** - see CHRYSLER (25030)
- **30008 Aries & Plymouth Reliant** '81 thru '89
- **30010 Caravan & Plymouth Voyager** '84 thru '95
- **30011 Caravan & Plymouth Voyager** '96 thru '02
- **30012 Challenger/Plymouth Saporro** '78 thru '83
- **30013 Caravan, Chrysler Voyager, Town &**
  Country '03 thru '07
- **30016 Colt & Plymouth Champ** '78 thru '87
- **30020 Dakota Pick-ups** all models '87 thru '96
- **30021 Durango** '98 & '99, **Dakota** '97 thru '99
- **30022 Durango** '00 thru '03 **Dakota** '00 thru '04
- **30023 Durango** '04 thru '09, **Dakota** '05 thru '11
- **30025 Dart, Demon, Plymouth Barracuda,**
  Duster & Valiant 6 cyl models '67 thru '76
- **30030 Daytona & Chrysler Laser** '84 thru '89
  Intrepid - see CHRYSLER (25025, 25026)
- **30034 Neon** all models '95 thru '99
- **30035 Omni & Plymouth Horizon** '78 thru '90
- **30036 Dodge and Plymouth Neon** '00 thru '05
- **30040 Pick-ups** all full-size models '74 thru '93
- **30041 Pick-ups** all full-size models '94 thru '01
- **30042 Pick-ups** full-size models '02 thru '08
- **30045 Ram 50/D50 Pick-ups & Raider and**
  Plymouth Arrow Pick-ups '79 thru '93
- **30050 Dodge/Plymouth/Chrysler RWD** '71 thru '89
- **30055 Shadow & Plymouth Sundance** '87 thru '94
- **30060 Spirit & Plymouth Acclaim** '89 thru '95
- **30065 Vans - Dodge & Plymouth** '71 thru '03

EAGLE
- **Talon** - see MITSUBISHI (68030, 68031)
- **Vision** - see CHRYSLER (25025)

FIAT
- **34010 124 Sport Coupe & Spider** '68 thru '78
- **34025 X1/9** all models '74 thru '80

FORD
- **10320 Ford Engine Overhaul Manual**
- **10355 Ford Automatic Transmission Overhaul**
- **11500 Mustang** '64-1/2 thru '70 Restoration Guide
- **36004 Aerostar Mini-vans** all models '86 thru '97
- **36006 Contour & Mercury Mystique** '95 thru '00
- **36008 Courier Pick-up** all models '72 thru '82
- **36012 Crown Victoria & Mercury Grand**
  Marquis '88 thru '10
- **36016 Escort/Mercury Lynx** all models '81 thru '90
- **36020 Escort/Mercury Tracer** '91 thru '02

- **36022 Escape & Mazda Tribute** '01 thru '11
- **36024 Explorer & Mazda Navajo** '91 thru '01
- **36025 Explorer/Mercury Mountaineer** '02 thru '10
- **36028 Fairmont & Mercury Zephyr** '78 thru '83
- **36030 Festiva & Aspire** '88 thru '97
- **36032 Fiesta** all models '77 thru '80
- **36034 Focus** all models '00 thru '11
- **36036 Ford & Mercury Full-size** '75 thru '87
- **36044 Ford & Mercury Mid-size** '75 thru '86
- **36045 Fusion & Mercury Milan** '06 thru '10
- **36048 Mustang V8** all models '64-1/2 thru '73
- **36049 Mustang II** 4 cyl, V6 & V8 models '74 thru '78
- **36050 Mustang & Mercury Capri** '79 thru '93
- **36051 Mustang** all models '94 thru '04
- **36052 Mustang** '05 thru '10
- **36054 Pick-ups & Bronco** '73 thru '79
- **36058 Pick-ups & Bronco** '80 thru '96
- **36059 F-150 & Expedition** '97 thru '09, **F-250** '97
  thru '99 **& Lincoln Navigator** '98 thru '09
- **36060 Super Duty Pick-ups, Excursion** '99 thru '10
- **36061 F-150** full-size '04 thru '10
- **36062 Pinto & Mercury Bobcat** '75 thru '80
- **36066 Probe** all models '89 thru '92
  Probe '93 thru '97 - see MAZDA 626 (61042)
- **36070 Ranger/Bronco II** gasoline models '83 thru '92
- **36071 Ranger** '93 thru '10 **& Mazda Pick-ups** '94 thru '09
- **36074 Taurus & Mercury Sable** '86 thru '95
- **36075 Taurus & Mercury Sable** '96 thru '05
- **36078 Tempo & Mercury Topaz** '84 thru '94
- **36082 Thunderbird/Mercury Cougar** '83 thru '88
- **36086 Thunderbird/Mercury Cougar** '89 thru '97
- **36090 Vans** all V8 Econoline models '69 thru '91
- **36094 Vans** full size '92 thru '10
- **36097 Windstar Mini-van** '95 thru '07

GENERAL MOTORS
- **10360 GM Automatic Transmission Overhaul**
- **38005 Buick Century, Chevrolet Celebrity,**
  Oldsmobile Cutlass Ciera & Pontiac 6000
  all models '82 thru '96
- **38010 Buick Regal, Chevrolet Lumina,**
  Oldsmobile Cutlass Supreme &
  Pontiac Grand Prix (FWD) '88 thru '07
- **38015 Buick Skyhawk, Cadillac Cimarron,**
  Chevrolet Cavalier, Oldsmobile Firenza &
  Pontiac J-2000 & Sunbird '82 thru '94
- **38016 Chevrolet Cavalier &**
  Pontiac Sunfire '95 thru '05
- **38017 Chevrolet Cobalt & Pontiac G5** '05 thru '11
- **38020 Buick Skylark, Chevrolet Citation,**
  Olds Omega, Pontiac Phoenix '80 thru '85
- **38025 Buick Skylark & Somerset,**
  Oldsmobile Achieva & Calais and
  Pontiac Grand Am all models '85 thru '98
- **38026 Chevrolet Malibu, Olds Alero & Cutlass,**
  Pontiac Grand Am '97 thru '03
- **38027 Chevrolet Malibu** '04 thru '10
- **38030 Cadillac Eldorado, Seville, Oldsmobile**
  Toronado, Buick Riviera '71 thru '85
- **38031 Cadillac Eldorado & Seville, DeVille, Fleetwood**
  & Olds Toronado, Buick Riviera '86 thru '93
- **38032 Cadillac DeVille** '94 thru '05 **& Seville** '92 thru '04
  Cadillac DTS '06 thru '10
- **38035 Chevrolet Lumina APV, Olds Silhouette**
  & Pontiac Trans Sport all models '90 thru '96
- **38036 Chevrolet Venture, Olds Silhouette,**
  Pontiac Trans Sport & Montana '97 thru '05
  General Motors Full-size
  Rear-wheel Drive - see BUICK (19025)
- **38040 Chevrolet Equinox** '05 thru '09 **Pontiac**
  Torrent '06 thru '09
- **38070 Chevrolet HHR** '06 thru '11

GEO
- **Metro** - see CHEVROLET Sprint (24075)
  Prizm - '85 thru '92 see CHEVY (24060),
  '93 thru '02 see TOYOTA Corolla (92036)
- **40030 Storm** all models '90 thru '93
  Tracker - see SUZUKI Samurai (90010)

GMC
- **Vans & Pick-ups** - see CHEVROLET

HONDA
- **42010 Accord CVCC** all models '76 thru '83
- **42011 Accord** all models '84 thru '89
- **42012 Accord** all models '90 thru '93
- **42013 Accord** all models '94 thru '97
- **42014 Accord** all models '98 thru '02
- **42015 Accord** '03 thru '07
- **42020 Civic 1200** all models '73 thru '79
- **42021 Civic 1300 & 1500 CVCC** '80 thru '83
- **42022 Civic 1500 CVCC** all models '75 thru '79

(Continued on other side)

Haynes North America, Inc., 861 Lawrence Drive, Newbury Park, CA 91320-1514 • (805) 498-6703 • http://www.haynes.com

Haynes Automotive Manuals (continued)

NOTE: If you do not see a listing for your vehicle, consult your local Haynes dealer for the latest product information.

42023 Civic all models '84 thru '91
42024 Civic & del Sol '92 thru '95
42025 Civic '96 thru '00, CR-V '97 thru '01, Acura Integra '94 thru '00
42026 Civic '01 thru '10, CR-V '02 thru '09
42035 Odyssey all models '99 thru '10
Passport - *see ISUZU Rodeo (47017)*
42037 Honda Pilot '03 thru '07, Acura MDX '01 thru '07
42040 Prelude CVCC all models '79 thru '89

HYUNDAI
43010 Elantra all models '96 thru '10
43015 Excel & Accent all models '86 thru '09
43050 Santa Fe all models '01 thru '06
43055 Sonata all models '99 thru '08

INFINITI
G35 '03 thru '08 - *see NISSAN 350Z (72011)*

ISUZU
Hombre - *see CHEVROLET S-10 (24071)*
47017 Rodeo, Amigo & Honda Passport '89 thru '02
47020 Trooper & Pick-up '81 thru '93

JAGUAR
49010 XJ6 all 6 cyl models '68 thru '86
49011 XJ6 all models '88 thru '94
49015 XJ12 & XJS all 12 cyl models '72 thru '85

JEEP
50010 Cherokee, Comanche & Wagoneer Limited all models '84 thru '01
50020 CJ all models '49 thru '86
50025 Grand Cherokee all models '93 thru '04
50026 Grand Cherokee '05 thru '09
50029 Grand Wagoneer & Pick-up '72 thru '91 Grand Wagoneer '84 thru '91, Cherokee & Wagoneer '72 thru '83, Pick-up '72 thru '88
50030 Wrangler all models '87 thru '11
50035 Liberty '02 thru '07

KIA
54050 Optima '01 thru '10
54070 Sephia '94 thru '01, Spectra '00 thru '09, Sportage '05 thru '10

LEXUS
ES 300/330 - *see TOYOTA Camry (92007) (92008)*
RX 330 - *see TOYOTA Highlander (92095)*

LINCOLN
Navigator - *see FORD Pick-up (36059)*
59010 Rear-Wheel Drive all models '70 thru '10

MAZDA
61010 GLC Hatchback (rear-wheel drive) '77 thru '83
61011 GLC (front-wheel drive) '81 thru '85
61012 Mazda3 '04 thru '11
61015 323 & Protegé '90 thru '03
61016 MX-5 Miata '90 thru '09
61020 MPV all models '89 thru '98
Navajo - *see Ford Explorer (36024)*
61030 Pick-ups '72 thru '93
Pick-ups '94 thru '00 - *see Ford Ranger (36071)*
61035 RX-7 all models '79 thru '85
61036 RX-7 all models '86 thru '91
61040 626 (rear-wheel drive) all models '79 thru '82
61041 626/MX-6 (front-wheel drive) '83 thru '92
61042 626, MX-6/Ford Probe '93 thru '02
61043 Mazda6 '03 thru '11

MERCEDES-BENZ
63012 123 Series Diesel '76 thru '85
63015 190 Series four-cyl gas models, '84 thru '88
63020 230/250/280 6 cyl sohc models '68 thru '72
63025 280 123 Series gasoline models '77 thru '81
63030 350 & 450 all models '71 thru '80
63040 C-Class: C230/C240/C280/C320/C350 '01 thru '07

MERCURY
64200 Villager & Nissan Quest '93 thru '01
All other titles, see FORD Listing.

MG
66010 MGB Roadster & GT Coupe '62 thru '80
66015 MG Midget, Austin Healey Sprite '58 thru '80

MINI
67020 Mini '02 thru '11

MITSUBISHI
68020 Cordia, Tredia, Galant, Precis & Mirage '83 thru '93
68030 Eclipse, Eagle Talon & Ply. Laser '90 thru '94
68031 Eclipse '95 thru '05, Eagle Talon '95 thru '98
68035 Galant '94 thru '10
68040 Pick-up '83 thru '96 & Montero '83 thru '93

NISSAN
72010 300ZX all models including Turbo '84 thru '89
72011 350Z & Infiniti G35 all models '03 thru '08
72015 Altima all models '93 thru '06
72016 Altima '07 thru '10
72020 Maxima all models '85 thru '92
72021 Maxima all models '93 thru '04
72025 Murano '03 thru '10
72030 Pick-ups '80 thru '97 Pathfinder '87 thru '95
72031 Frontier Pick-up, Xterra, Pathfinder '96 thru '04
72032 Frontier & Xterra '05 thru '11
72040 Pulsar all models '83 thru '86
Quest - *see MERCURY Villager (64200)*
72050 Sentra all models '82 thru '94
72051 Sentra & 200SX all models '95 thru '06
72060 Stanza all models '82 thru '90
72070 Titan pick-ups '04 thru '10 Armada '05 thru '10

OLDSMOBILE
73015 Cutlass V6 & V8 gas models '74 thru '88
For other OLDSMOBILE titles, see BUICK, CHEVROLET or GENERAL MOTORS listing.

PLYMOUTH
For PLYMOUTH titles, see DODGE listing.

PONTIAC
79008 Fiero all models '84 thru '88
79018 Firebird V8 models except Turbo '70 thru '81
79019 Firebird all models '82 thru '92
79025 G6 all models '05 thru '09
79040 Mid-size Rear-wheel Drive '70 thru '87
Vibe '03 thru '11 - *see TOYOTA Matrix (92060)*
For other PONTIAC titles, see BUICK, CHEVROLET or GENERAL MOTORS listing.

PORSCHE
80020 911 except Turbo & Carrera 4 '65 thru '89
80025 914 all 4 cyl models '69 thru '76
80030 924 all models including Turbo '76 thru '82
80035 944 all models including Turbo '83 thru '89

RENAULT
Alliance & Encore - *see AMC (14020)*

SAAB
84010 900 all models including Turbo '79 thru '88

SATURN
87010 Saturn all S-series models '91 thru '02
87011 Saturn Ion '03 thru '07
87020 Saturn all L-series models '00 thru '04
87040 Saturn VUE '02 thru '07

SUBARU
89002 1100, 1300, 1400 & 1600 '71 thru '79
89003 1600 & 1800 2WD & 4WD '80 thru '94
89100 Legacy all models '90 thru '99
89101 Legacy & Forester '00 thru '06

SUZUKI
90010 Samurai/Sidekick & Geo Tracker '86 thru '01

TOYOTA
92005 Camry all models '83 thru '91
92006 Camry all models '92 thru '96
92007 Camry, Avalon, Solara, Lexus ES 300 '97 thru '01
92008 Toyota Camry, Avalon and Solara and Lexus ES 300/330 all models '02 thru '06
92009 Camry '07 thru '11
92015 Celica Rear Wheel Drive '71 thru '85
92020 Celica Front Wheel Drive '86 thru '99
92025 Celica Supra all models '79 thru '92
92030 Corolla all models '75 thru '79
92032 Corolla all rear wheel drive models '80 thru '87
92035 Corolla all front wheel drive models '84 thru '92
92036 Corolla & Geo Prizm '93 thru '02
92037 Corolla models '03 thru '11
92040 Corolla Tercel all models '80 thru '82
92045 Corona all models '74 thru '82
92050 Cressida all models '78 thru '82
92055 Land Cruiser FJ40, 43, 45, 55 '68 thru '82
92056 Land Cruiser FJ60, 62, 80, FZJ80 '80 thru '96
92060 Matrix & Pontiac Vibe '03 thru '11
92065 MR2 all models '85 thru '87
92070 Pick-up all models '69 thru '78
92075 Pick-up all models '79 thru '95
92076 Tacoma, 4Runner & T100 '93 thru '04
92077 Tacoma all models '05 thru '09
92078 Tundra '00 thru '06 & Sequoia '01 thru '07
92079 4Runner all models '03 thru '09
92080 Previa all models '91 thru '95
92081 Prius all models '01 thru '08
92082 RAV4 all models '96 thru '10
92085 Tercel all models '87 thru '94
92090 Sienna all models '98 thru '09
92095 Highlander & Lexus RX-330 '99 thru '07

TRIUMPH
94007 Spitfire all models '62 thru '81
94010 TR7 all models '75 thru '81

VW
96008 Beetle & Karmann Ghia '54 thru '79
96009 New Beetle '98 thru '11
96016 Rabbit, Jetta, Scirocco & Pick-up gas models '75 thru '92 & Convertible '80 thru '92
96017 Golf, GTI & Jetta '93 thru '98, Cabrio '95 thru '02
96018 Golf, GTI, Jetta '99 thru '05
96019 Jetta, Rabbit, GTI & Golf '05 thru '11
96020 Rabbit, Jetta & Pick-up diesel '77 thru '84
96023 Passat '98 thru '05, Audi A4 '96 thru '01
96030 Transporter 1600 all models '68 thru '79
96035 Transporter 1700, 1800 & 2000 '72 thru '79
96040 Type 3 1500 & 1600 all models '63 thru '73
96045 Vanagon all air-cooled models '80 thru '83

VOLVO
97010 120, 130 Series & 1800 Sports '61 thru '73
97015 140 Series all models '66 thru '74
97020 240 Series all models '76 thru '93
97040 740 & 760 Series all models '82 thru '88
97050 850 Series all models '93 thru '97

TECHBOOK MANUALS
10205 Automotive Computer Codes
10206 OBD-II & Electronic Engine Management
10210 Automotive Emissions Control Manual
10215 Fuel Injection Manual '78 thru '85
10220 Fuel Injection Manual '86 thru '99
10225 Holley Carburetor Manual
10230 Rochester Carburetor Manual
10240 Weber/Zenith/Stromberg/SU Carburetors
10305 Chevrolet Engine Overhaul Manual
10310 Chrysler Engine Overhaul Manual
10320 Ford Engine Overhaul Manual
10330 GM and Ford Diesel Engine Repair Manual
10333 Engine Performance Manual
10340 Small Engine Repair Manual, 5 HP & Less
10341 Small Engine Repair Manual, 5.5 - 20 HP
10345 Suspension, Steering & Driveline Manual
10355 Ford Automatic Transmission Overhaul
10360 GM Automatic Transmission Overhaul
10405 Automotive Body Repair & Painting
10410 Automotive Brake Manual
10411 Automotive Anti-lock Brake (ABS) Systems
10415 Automotive Detailing Manual
10420 Automotive Electrical Manual
10425 Automotive Heating & Air Conditioning
10430 Automotive Reference Manual & Dictionary
10435 Automotive Tools Manual
10440 Used Car Buying Guide
10445 Welding Manual
10450 ATV Basics
10452 Scooters 50cc to 250cc

SPANISH MANUALS
98903 Reparación de Carrocería & Pintura
98904 Manual de Carburador Modelos Holley & Rochester
98905 Códigos Automotrices de la Computadora
98906 OBD-II & Sistemas de Control Electrónico del Motor
98910 Frenos Automotriz
98913 Electricidad Automotriz
98915 Inyección de Combustible '86 al '99
99040 Chevrolet & GMC Camionetas '67 al '87
99041 Chevrolet & GMC Camionetas '88 al '98
99042 Chevrolet & GMC Camionetas Cerradas '68 al '95
99043 Chevrolet/GMC Camionetas '94 al '04
99048 Chevrolet/GMC Camionetas '99 al '06
99055 Dodge Caravan & Plymouth Voyager '84 al '95
99075 Ford Camionetas y Bronco '80 al '94
99076 Ford F-150 '97 al '09
99077 Ford Camionetas Cerradas '69 al '91
99088 Ford Modelos de Tamaño Mediano '75 al '86
99089 Ford Camionetas Ranger '93 al '10
99091 Ford Taurus & Mercury Sable '86 al '95
99095 GM Modelos de Tamaño Grande '70 al '88
99100 GM Modelos de Tamaño Mediano '70 al '88
99106 Jeep Cherokee, Wagoneer & Comanche '84 al '00
99110 Nissan Camioneta '80 al '96, Pathfinder '87 al '95
99118 Nissan Sentra '82 al '94
99125 Toyota Camionetas y 4Runner '79 al '95

Over 100 Haynes motorcycle manuals also available

7-12